Official Guide
to the
Rules of Golf

Effective January 2019

R&A   USGA®

Official Guide
to the
Rules of Golf

Effective January 2019

For more information on the USGA®, contact:
United States Golf Association®
Golf House
77 Liberty Corner Rd.
Liberty Corner, NJ 07938
T 908.234.2300

Printed in the United States of America

General Contents

Explanation of the Official Guide to the Rules of Golf

The R&A and the USGA have produced the Official Guide to the Rules of Golf as a reference book designed for those involved in the administration of golf at all levels of the game. The latest edition of the Rules is a result of the Rules Modernization initiative, which has been fundamental and far-reaching, bringing the Rules up to date to fit the needs of the game today, while preserving golf's essential principles and character.

The Rules of Golf with Interpretations

The first section of the Official Guide focuses on the Rules of Golf effective from January 2019. The Rules of Golf are reproduced in full in the Official Guide, and presented on a shaded background for ease of reference.

The Rules are supplemented by Interpretations, which are located directly under the sub-Rule they relate to, and appear on a white background so that they are easily distinguished from the Rules.

The vast majority of questions that arise on the course will be answerable solely by reference to the Rules of Golf. It is strongly recommended that a thorough review of the relevant Rule is undertaken before referring to the Interpretations for guidance on a specific point. Interpretations are provided only for aspects of the Rules that are considered to require additional clarification, which is then provided by way of explanation and, in many cases, using examples.

For users of the Official Guide who have been familiar with the former "Decisions on the Rules of Golf", you will find that a large number of the Decisions from that publication, particularly those that contained important points of principle, now form part of the Rules of Golf. This has been one of the key features of the modernization of the Rules.

Committee Procedures

The second section, entitled "Committee Procedures", contains practical guidance for those involved in running day to day play at golf courses or running competitions at all levels of the game. It is divided into guidance for "general play" (when the Committee is not running a competition) and guidance for "competitions", while recognizing that the two often overlap.

The Committee Procedures is a compendium of information that was previously contained in a variety of different publications, but which has now been brought together to provide a much more accessible, user-friendly guide to all aspects of Rules-related golf administration.

The role of the Committee, how to mark and set up the course, establishing the Terms of the Competition and Local Rules, starting and scoring, pace of play policies and establishing a code of conduct are just some of the subjects that are covered in the Committee Procedures. Section 8 in the Committee Procedures provides Model Local Rules that Committees can adopt to meet local needs, and also provides important guidance relating to the introduction of Local Rules that differ from the Model Local Rules.

There is a very detailed Contents page for the Committee Precedures (see page 369), which should enable the reader to locate specific items.

The Modified Rules of Golf for Players with Disabilities

The Modified Rules of Golf for Players with Disabilities are reproduced in the final section of the Official Guide. The goal of The R&A and the USGA in producing these Modified Rules is to allow a player with a disability to play fairly with players who have no disabilities, the same disability or different types of disabilities. The R&A and the USGA have received valuable input from the community of players with disabilities, disability organizations and other sources to identify modifications that are fair and appropriate from all perspectives.

The Rules of Golf
with Interpretations

Contents

Contents

II   Playing the Round and a Hole (Rules 5–6)

Contents

III Playing the Ball (Rules 7–11)

Contents

2/6/19

2/7/19

Contents

Contents

VI Free Relief (Rules 15–16)

Contents

VII Penalty Relief (Rules 17–19)

Contents

Contents

VIII Procedures for Players and Committee When Issues Arise in Applying the Rules (Rule 20)

IX Other Forms of Play (Rules 21–24)

Contents

Contents

Definitions 327

Contents

Fundamentals of the Game

Rules 1–4

RULE

1

The Game, Player Conduct and the Rules

Purpose of Rule:

Rule 1 introduces these central principles of the game for the player:

- Play the course as you find it and play the ball as it lies.

- Play by the Rules and in the spirit of the game.

- You are responsible for applying your own penalties if you breach a Rule, so that you cannot gain any potential advantage over your opponent in match play or other players in stroke play.

1.1   The Game of Golf

Golf is played in a *round* of 18 (or fewer) holes on a *course* by striking a ball with a club.

Each hole starts with a *stroke* from the *teeing area* and ends when the ball is *holed* on the *putting green* (or when the Rules otherwise say the hole is completed).

For each *stroke*, the player:

- Plays the *course* as he or she finds it, and

- Plays the ball as it lies.

But there are exceptions where the Rules allow the player to alter conditions on the *course* and require or allow the player to play the ball from a different place than where it lies.

1.2   Standards of Player Conduct

1.2a   Conduct Expected of All Players

All players are expected to play in the spirit of the game by:

- Acting with integrity – for example, by following the Rules, applying all penalties, and being honest in all aspects of play.

- Showing consideration to others – for example, by playing at a prompt pace, looking out for the safety of others, and not distracting the play of another player.

- Taking good care of the *course* – for example, by replacing divots, smoothing *bunkers*, repairing ball-marks, and not causing unnecessary damage to the *course*.

There is no penalty under the Rules for failing to act in this way, **except** that the *Committee* may disqualify a player for acting contrary to the spirit of the game if it finds that the player has committed serious misconduct.

Penalties other than disqualification may be imposed for player misconduct only if those penalties are adopted as part of a Code of Conduct under Rule 1.2b.

Rule 1.2a Interpretations:
1.2a/1 – Meaning of Serious Misconduct

The phrase "serious misconduct" in Rule 1.2a is intended to cover player misconduct that is so far removed from the expected norm in golf that the most severe sanction of removing a player from the competition is justified. This includes dishonesty, deliberately interfering with another player's rights, or endangering the safety of others.

The *Committee* must determine if the misconduct is serious considering all the circumstances. Even if the *Committee* determines that the misconduct is serious, it may take the view that it is more appropriate to warn the player that a repeat of the misconduct or similar misconduct will result in disqualification, instead of disqualifying him or her in the first instance.

Examples of actions by a player that are likely to be considered serious misconduct include:

- Deliberately causing serious damage to a *putting green*.

- Disagreeing with the course setup and taking it on himself or herself to move tee-markers or boundary stakes.

- Throwing a club towards another player or spectator.

- Deliberately distracting other players while they are making *strokes*.

- Removing *loose impediments* or *movable obstructions* to disadvantage another player after that other player has asked him or her to leave them in place.

- Repeatedly refusing to lift a ball at rest when it interferes with another player in stroke play.

- Deliberately playing away from the *hole* and then towards the *hole* to assist the player's *partner* (such as helping the player's *partner* learn the break on the *putting green*).

- Deliberately not playing in accordance with the Rules and potentially gaining a significant advantage by doing so, despite incurring a penalty for a breach of the relevant Rule.

- Repeatedly using vulgar or offensive language.

- Using a handicap that has been established for the purpose of providing an unfair advantage or using the *round* being played to establish such a handicap.

Examples of actions by a player that, although involving misconduct, are unlikely to be considered serious misconduct include:

- Slamming a club to the ground, damaging the club and causing minor damage to the turf.

- Throwing a club towards a golf bag that unintentionally hits another person.

- Carelessly distracting another player making a *stroke*.

1.2b   Code of Conduct

The *Committee* may set its own standards of player conduct in a Code of Conduct adopted as a Local Rule.

- The Code may include penalties for breach of its standards, such as a one-stroke penalty or the *general penalty*.

- The *Committee* may also disqualify a player for serious misconduct in failing to meet the Code's standards.

See Committee Procedures, Section 5H (explaining the standards of player conduct that may be adopted).

1.3   Playing by the Rules

1.3a   Meaning of "Rules"; Terms of the Competition

The "Rules" means:

- Rules 1–24 and the Definitions in these Rules of Golf, and

- Any "Local Rules" the *Committee* adopts for the competition or the *course*.

Players are also responsible for complying with all "Terms of the Competition" adopted by the *Committee* (such as entry requirements, the form and dates of play, the number of *rounds* and the number and order of holes in a *round*).

See Committee Procedures, Section 5C and Section 8 (Local Rules and full set of authorized Model Local Rules); **Section 5A** (Terms of the Competition).

1.3b   Applying the Rules

(1) **Player Responsibility for Applying the Rules**. Players are responsible for applying the Rules to themselves:

- Players are expected to recognize when they have breached a Rule and to be honest in applying their own penalties.

  » If a player knows that he or she has breached a Rule that involves a penalty and deliberately fails to apply the penalty, the player is **disqualified**.

  » If two or more players deliberately agree to ignore any Rule or penalty they know applies and any of those players have started the *round*, they are **disqualified** (even if they have not yet acted on the agreement).

- When it is necessary to decide questions of fact, a player is responsible for considering not only his or her own knowledge of the facts but also all other information that is reasonably available.

- A player may ask for help with the Rules from a *referee* or the *Committee*, **but** if help is not available in a reasonable time the player must play on and raise the issue with a *referee* or the *Committee* when they become available (see Rule 20.1).

Rule 1.3b(1) Interpretations:

1.3b(1)/1 – Disqualifying Players Who Know a Rule but Deliberately Agree to Ignore It

If two or more players deliberately agree to ignore any Rule or penalty they know applies, they will be disqualified unless the agreement is made before the *round* and is cancelled before any player involved in the agreement begins his or her *round*.

For example, in *stroke play*, two players agree to consider putts within a club-length of the *hole holed*, when they know that they must *hole out* on each *hole*.

While on the first *putting green*, another player in the group learns of this agreement. That player insists the two players who made the agreement *hole out*, and they do so.

Even though neither player who made the agreement acted on it by failing to *hole out*, they are still disqualified because they deliberately agreed to ignore Rule 3.3c (Failure to Hole Out).

1.3b(1)/2 – In Order to Agree to Ignore a Rule or Penalty, Players Must Be Aware the Rule Exists

Rule 1.3b(1) does not apply and there is no penalty if players agree to waive a Rule that they are not aware of or fail to apply a penalty that they do not know exists.

Examples where two players are unaware of a Rule, or where they have failed to apply a penalty, and therefore are not disqualified under Rule 1.3b(1), include:

- In a match, two players agree in advance to concede all putts within a specific length but are unaware that the Rules prohibit them from agreeing to concede putts in this way.

- Before a 36-hole match, two players agree that they will play only 18 holes and whoever is behind at that point will concede the match, not knowing that this agreement does not comply with the Terms of the Competition.

  The match goes forward on that basis and the player behind after 18 holes concedes the match. Since the players do not know such an agreement is not allowed, the concession stands.

- In a *stroke-play* competition, a player and his or her *marker*, who is also a player, are unsure if the *relief area* for *ground under repair* is one *club-length* or two. Unaware of the Rule, they agree that it is two *club-lengths* and the player takes relief by *dropping* a ball almost two *club-lengths* from the *nearest point of complete relief*. Later in the round the *Committee* becomes aware of this.

  Although neither player is disqualified under Rule 1.3b(1) because they were unaware of the Rule, the player has played from a *wrong place* and gets the penalty under Rule 14.7 (Playing from Wrong Place). There is no penalty for accidentally giving incorrect information on the Rules of Golf.

(2) **Accepting Player's "Reasonable Judgment" in Determining a Location When Applying the Rules.**

- Many Rules require a player to determine a spot, point, line, area or other location under the Rules, such as:

  » Estimating where a ball last crossed the edge of a *penalty area*,

  » Estimating or measuring when *dropping* or placing a ball in taking relief, or

  » *Replacing* a ball on its original spot (whether the spot is known or estimated).

- Such determinations about location need to be made promptly and with care but often cannot be precise.

- So long as the player does what can be reasonably expected under the circumstances to make an accurate determination, the player's reasonable judgment will be accepted even if, after the *stroke* is made, the determination is shown to be wrong by video evidence or other information.

- If a player becomes aware of a wrong determination before the *stroke* is made, it must be corrected (see Rule 14.5).

Interpretations Related to Rule 1.3b(2):

- 6.1/1 – What to Do When One or More Tee-Markers Are Missing
- 9.6/2 – Where to Replace Ball When It Was Moved from Unknown Location
- 17.1a/2 – Ball Lost in Either Penalty Area or Abnormal Course Condition Adjacent to Penalty Area
- 17.1d(3)/2 – Player Drops Ball Based on Estimate of Where the Ball Last Crossed Edge of Penalty Area That Turns Out to Be the Wrong Point

1.3c   Penalties

(1) **Actions Giving Rise to Penalties**. A penalty applies when a breach of a Rule results from a player's own actions or the actions of his or her *caddie* (see Rule 10.3c).

A penalty also applies when:

- Another person takes an action that would breach the Rules if taken by the player or *caddie* and that person does so at the player's request or while acting with the player's authority, or

• The player sees another person about to take an action concerning the player's ball or *equipment* that he or she knows would breach the Rules if taken by the player or *caddie* and does not take reasonable steps to object or stop it from happening.

Rule 1.3c(1) Interpretations:

1.3c(1)/1 – Action of Another Person Breaches a Rule For Player

A player is responsible when another person's action breaches a Rule with respect to the player if it is done at the player's request or if the player sees the action and allows it.

Examples of when a player gets the penalty because he or she requested or allowed the action include:

• A player asks a spectator to move a *loose impediment* near his or her ball. If the ball *moves* the player gets one penalty stroke under Rule 9.4b (Penalty for Lifting or Deliberately Touching Ball or Causing It to Move) and the ball must be *replaced*.

• A player's ball is being searched for in tall grass. A spectator finds the ball and presses the grass down around the ball, *improving* the *conditions affecting the stroke*. If the player, seeing that this is about to happen, does not take reasonable steps to try to stop the spectator, he or she gets the *general penalty* for a breach of Rule 8.1a (Player's Actions That Improve Conditions Affecting the Stroke).

(2) **Levels of Penalties**. Penalties are meant to cancel out any potential advantage to the player. There are three main penalty levels:

• One-Stroke Penalty. This penalty applies in both *match play* and *stroke play* under certain Rules where either (a) the potential advantage from a breach is minor or (b) a player takes penalty relief by playing a ball from a different place than where the original ball lies.

• General Penalty (Loss of Hole in Match Play, Two-Stroke Penalty in Stroke Play). This penalty applies for a breach of most Rules, where the potential advantage is more significant than where only one penalty stroke applies.

• Disqualification. In both *match play* and *stroke play*, a player may be disqualified from the competition for certain actions or Rule breaches involving serious misconduct (see Rule 1.2) or where the potential advantage is too significant for the player's score to be considered valid.

(3) **No Discretion to Vary Penalties**. Penalties need to be applied only as provided in the Rules:

- Neither a player nor the *Committee* has authority to apply penalties in a different way, and

- A wrong application of a penalty or a failure to apply a penalty may stand only if it is too late to correct it (see Rules 20.1b(2)-(4), 20.2d and 20.2e).

In *match play*, the player and *opponent* may agree how to decide a Rules issue so long as they do not deliberately agree to apply the Rules in the wrong way (see Rule 20.1b(1)).

(4) **Applying Penalties to Multiple Breaches of the Rules**. If a player breaches multiple Rules or the same Rule multiple times before an intervening event happens (such as making a *stroke* or becoming aware of the breach), the penalty that applies depends on what the player did:

- When Breaches Resulted from Unrelated Acts. The player gets a separate penalty for each breach.

- When Breaches Resulted from a Single Act or Related Acts. The player gets only one penalty; **but** if the act or acts breached multiple Rules involving different penalties, the higher-level penalty applies. For example:

  » Multiple Procedural Breaches. If a player's single act or related acts breach more than one of the procedural requirements for *marking*, lifting, cleaning, *dropping*, *replacing* or placing a ball where the penalty is one stroke, such as both lifting a ball without *marking* its spot and cleaning the lifted ball when not allowed, the player gets **one penalty stroke in total**.

  » Playing Incorrectly Substituted Ball from a Wrong Place. In *stroke play*, if a player plays a *substituted* ball when not allowed in breach of Rule 6.3b and also plays that ball from a *wrong place* in breach of Rule 14.7a, the player gets **two penalty strokes in total**.

  » Combined Procedural and Substitution/Wrong Place Breaches: In *stroke play*, if a player's single act or related acts breach one or more procedural requirements where the penalty is one stroke and also breach one or both of the Rules against playing an incorrectly *substituted* ball and playing from a *wrong place*, the player gets **two penalty strokes in total**.

But any penalty strokes a player gets for taking penalty relief (such as a one-stroke penalty under Rules 17.1, 18.1 and 19.2) are always applied in addition to any other penalties.

Rule 1.3c(4) Interpretations:

1.3c(4)/1 – Intervening Event Between Breaches Results in Multiple Penalties

When a player breaches multiple Rules or the same Rule multiple times, any relationship between the breaches is broken by an intervening event and the player will get multiple penalties.

The three types of intervening events where the player will get multiple penalties are:

- Making a *stroke*. Example: In *stroke play*, a player's ball is near a bush. The player breaks branches and this *improves* the area of intended swing (a breach of Rule 8.1a). The player makes a *stroke*, misses the ball, and then breaks more branches (a breach of Rule 8.1a). In this case, the *stroke* that missed the ball is an intervening event between the two breaches. Therefore, the player gets two separate two-stroke penalties under Rule 8.1a, for four penalty strokes in total.

- Putting a ball *in play*. Examples:

  » In *stroke play*, a player's ball is under a tree. The player breaks tree branches, *improving* the *conditions affecting the stroke*, but then decides the ball is unplayable. The player *drops* a ball within two *club-lengths* under Rule 19.2c (Unplayable Ball Relief) and then breaks more tree branches. In addition to the one penalty stroke under Rule 19.2, the player gets two separate two-stroke penalties under Rule 8.1a for *improving conditions affecting the stroke*, for five penalty strokes in total.

  » A player's ball lies in the fairway and he or she accidentally *moves* the ball at rest. As required by Rule 9.4 (Ball Lifted or Moved by Player), the player *replaces* the ball and adds one penalty stroke. Before making a *stroke*, the player accidentally *moves* the ball again. The player gets an additional penalty stroke and must again *replace* the ball, for two penalty strokes in total.

- Becoming aware of the breach. Example: In *stroke play*, a player's ball lies in a *bunker* where the player takes several practice swings each time touching the sand. Another player advises the player that this is a breach of the Rules. The player disagrees and takes several more practice swings, again touching the sand before making a *stroke*. Correctly informing the player of the breach of the Rules is an intervening event and, therefore, the player gets two separate two-stroke penalties under Rule 12.2b (Restrictions on Touching Sand in Bunker), for four penalty strokes in total.

1.3c(4)/2 – Multiple Breaches From a Single Act Result in a Single Penalty

A single act may breach two different Rules. In this situation, one penalty is applied. In the case of two Rules with different penalties, the higher-level penalty will apply.

For example, a player presses down the grass behind his or her ball *in play* and *improves* the *lie* in the rough, accidentally *moving* the ball as well. This single act (that is, pressing down the grass) breached two Rules, Rule 8.1a (Actions That Improve Conditions Affecting the Stroke) and Rule 9.4b (Lifting or Deliberately Touching Ball or Causing It to Move) and only one penalty applies.

In this case, the penalty under Rule 8.1a is the *general penalty* and the penalty under Rule 9.4b is one penalty stroke. Therefore, the higher-level penalty applies and the player loses the hole in *match play* or must add a total penalty of two strokes in *stroke play* under Rule 8.1a and the ball must be *replaced*.

1.3c(4)/3 – Meaning of Unrelated Acts

Unrelated acts in the context of Rule 1.3c(4) are acts of a player that are of a different type or associated with a different process.

Examples of unrelated acts where multiple penalties apply include:

• Making a practice swing that touches sand in a *bunker* and bending an overhanging tree branch that interferes with the player's swing.

• Moving an *immovable obstruction* that *improves* the area of the player's swing and pressing down grass behind the ball.

Examples of related acts where only one penalty applies include:

• Making several practice swings that touch sand in a *bunker*.

• Asking for two different pieces of *advice*, such as what club the player used and what the wind direction is, both related to the process of selecting what club to use for the next *stroke*.

1.3c(4)/4 – Not Replacing the Ball May Be Considered a Separate and Unrelated Act

In the example given in 1.3c(4)/2, a single act of pressing down grass and *moving* the ball breached two Rules (Rule 8.1a and Rule 9.4b) and resulted in a single penalty being applied under Rule 8.1a (Actions That Improve Conditions Affecting the Stroke).

However, Rule 9.4b (Lifting or Deliberately Touching Ball or Causing It to Move) requires that the *moved* ball be *replaced* and, if it is not *replaced* before the *stroke*, the player will get an additional penalty of two strokes under Rule 9.4b. The failure to *replace* the ball is considered a separate and unrelated act.

Rule 1.3c General Interpretations:

1.3c/1 – Player Is Not Disqualified from a Competition When That Round Does Not Count

In competitions where not all *rounds* count, a player is not disqualified from the competition for being disqualified from a single *round*.

Examples of when a player is not disqualified from the competition:

- In a handicap competition where the two best of four *rounds* count, a player mistakenly returns his or her *scorecard* with a higher handicap that affects how many strokes are received in the first *round*.

  Since the higher handicap affected the number of handicap strokes received, the player is disqualified from the first *round* of the competition and now has three rounds in which to determine his or her two best net scores.

- In a team competition with four-player teams, where the three best scores for each *round* are added up to make the team's score for each *round*, a player is disqualified from the second *round* for not correcting the play of a *wrong ball*. That player's score does not count for the team score in the second *round* but the player's score would count for any other *round* of the competition.

1.3c/2 – Applying Disqualification Penalties, Concessions and Wrong Number of Strokes in a Stroke-Play Play-Off

During a play-off in a *stroke-play* competition the Rules are applied as follows:

- If a player is disqualified (such as for making a *stroke* with a non-conforming club), the player is disqualified from the play-off only and the player is entitled to any prize that may have been won in the competition itself.

- If two players are in the play-off, one player is allowed to concede the play-off to the other player.

- If Player A mistakenly gives the wrong number of strokes to Player B and that mistake results in Player B lifting his or her ball (such as when Player B thinks he or she has lost the play-off to Player A), Player B is allowed to *replace* the ball without penalty and complete the hole. There is no penalty to Player A.

RULE 2

The Course

Purpose of Rule:

Rule 2 introduces the basic things every player should know about the course:

• There are five defined areas of the course, and

• There are several types of defined objects and conditions that can interfere with play.

It is important to know the area of the course where the ball lies and the status of any interfering objects and conditions, because they often affect the player's options for playing the ball or taking relief.

2.1 Course Boundaries and Out of Bounds

Golf is played on a *course* whose boundaries are set by the *Committee*. Areas not on the *course* are *out of bounds*.

2.2 Defined Areas of the Course

There are five *areas of the course*.

2.2a The General Area

The *general area* covers the entire *course* **except** for the four specific *areas of the course* described in Rule 2.2b.

It is called the "general area" because:

• It covers most of the *course* and is where a player's ball will most often be played until the ball reaches the *putting green*.

• It includes every type of ground and growing or attached objects found in that area, such as fairway, rough and trees.

2.2b The Four Specific Areas

Certain Rules apply specifically to the four *areas of the course* that are not in the *general area*:

- The *teeing area* the player must use in starting the hole he or she is playing (Rule 6.2),
- All *penalty areas* (Rule 17),
- All *bunkers* (Rule 12), and
- The *putting green* of the hole the player is playing (Rule 13).

DIAGRAM 2.2:   DEFINED AREAS OF THE COURSE

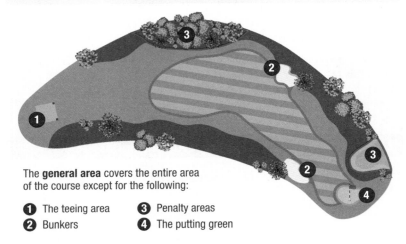

The **general area** covers the entire area
of the course except for the following:

1 The teeing area   **3** Penalty areas
2 Bunkers   **4** The putting green

2.2c   Determining Area of Course Where Ball Lies

The *area of the course* where a player's ball lies affects the Rules that apply in playing the ball or taking relief.

A ball is always treated as lying in only one *area of the course*:

- If part of the ball is in both the *general area* and one of the four specific *areas of the course*, it is treated as lying in that specific *area of the course*.
- If part of the ball is in two specific *areas of the course*, it is treated as lying in the specific area that comes first in this order: *penalty area, bunker, putting green.*

2.3 Objects or Conditions That Can Interfere with Play

Certain Rules may give free relief (relief with no penalty) from interference by certain defined objects or conditions, such as:

- *Loose impediments* (Rule 15.1),

- *Movable obstructions* (Rule 15.2), and

- *Abnormal course conditions*, which are *animal holes*, *ground under repair*, *immovable obstructions* and *temporary water* (Rule 16.1).

But there is no free relief from *boundary objects* or *integral objects* that interfere with play.

2.4 No Play Zones

A *no play zone* is a defined part of an *abnormal course condition* (see Rule 16.1f) or a *penalty area* (see Rule 17.1e) where play is not allowed.

A player must take relief when:

- His or her ball is in a *no play zone*, or

- A *no play zone* interferes with his or her area of intended *stance* or area of intended swing in playing a ball outside the *no play zone* (see Rules 16.1f and 17.1e).

See Committee Procedures, Section 5H(1) (a Code of Conduct may tell players to stay out of a *no play zone* entirely).

RULE 3

The Competition

Purpose of Rule:

Rule 3 covers the three central elements of all golf competitions:

- Playing either match play or stroke play,

- Playing either as an individual or with a partner as part of a side, and

- Scoring either by gross scores (no handicap strokes applied) or net scores (handicap strokes applied).

3.1 Central Elements of Every Competition

3.1a Form of Play: Match Play or Stroke Play

(1) **Match Play or Regular Stroke Play**. These are very different forms of play:

- In *match play* (see Rule 3.2), a player and an *opponent* compete against each other based on holes won, lost or tied.

- In the regular form of *stroke play* (see Rule 3.3), all players compete with one another based on the total score – that is, adding up each player's total number of strokes (including *strokes* made and penalty strokes) on each hole in all *rounds*.

Most of the Rules apply in both forms of play, but certain Rules apply in only one or the other.

See Committee Procedures, Section 6C (considerations for the *Committee* if it runs a competition that combines the two forms of play in a single *round*).

(2) **Other Forms of Stroke Play**. Rule 21 covers other forms of *stroke play* (*Stableford*, *Maximum Score* and *Par/Bogey*) that use a different scoring method. Rules 1–20 apply in these forms of play, as modified by Rule 21.

3.1b   How Players Compete: Playing as an Individual or as Partners

Golf is played either by individual players competing on their own or by *partners* competing together as a *side*.

Although Rules 1–20 focus on individual play, they also apply:

- In competitions involving *partners* (*Foursomes* and *Four-Ball*), as modified by Rules 22 and 23, and

- In team competitions, as modified by Rule 24.

3.1c   How Players Score: Gross Scores or Net Scores

(1) **Scratch Competitions**. In a scratch competition:

- The player's "gross score" for a hole or the *round* is his or her total number of strokes (including *strokes* made and penalty strokes).

- The player's handicap is not applied.

(2) **Handicap Competitions**. In a handicap competition:

- The player's "net score" for a hole or the *round* is the gross score adjusted for the player's handicap strokes.

- This is done so that players of differing abilities can compete in a fair way.

3.2   Match Play

Purpose of Rule:

Match play has specific Rules (particularly about concessions and giving information about the number of strokes taken) because the player and opponent:

- Compete solely against each other on every hole,

- Can see each other's play, and

- Can protect their own interests.

3.2a   Result of Hole and Match

(1) **Winning a Hole**. A player wins a hole when:

- The player completes the hole in fewer strokes (including *strokes* made and penalty strokes) than the *opponent*,

- The *opponent* concedes the hole, or

- The *opponent* gets the *general penalty* (loss of hole).

If the *opponent's* ball in motion needs to be *holed* to tie the hole and the ball is deliberately deflected or stopped by any person at a time when there is no reasonable chance it can be *holed* (such as when the ball has rolled past the *hole* and will not roll back there), the result of the hole has been decided and the player wins the hole (see Rule 11.2a, Exception).

(2) **Tying a Hole**. A hole is tied (also known as "halved") when:

- The player and *opponent* complete the hole in the same number of strokes (including *strokes* made and penalty strokes), or

- The player and *opponent* agree to treat the hole as tied (**but** this is allowed only after at least one of the players has made a *stroke* to begin the hole).

(3) **Winning a Match**. A player wins a match when:

- The player leads the *opponent* by more holes than remain to be played,

- The *opponent* concedes the match, or

- The *opponent* is disqualified.

(4) **Extending a Tied Match**. If a match is tied after the final hole:

- The match is extended one hole at a time until there is a winner. See Rule 5.1 (an extended match is a continuation of the same *round*, not a new *round*).

- The holes are played in the same order as in the *round*, unless the *Committee* sets a different order.

But the Terms of the Competition may say that the match will end in a tie rather than be extended.

(5) **When Result is Final**. The result of a match becomes final in the way stated by the *Committee* (which should be set out in the Terms of the Competition), such as:

- When the result is recorded on an official scoreboard or other identified place, or

- When the result is reported to a person identified by the *Committee*.

See Committee Procedures, Section 5A(7) (recommendations on how the result of a match becomes final).

3.2b   Concessions

(1) **Player May Concede Stroke, Hole or Match**. A player may concede the *opponent's* next *stroke*, a hole or the match:

- <u>Conceding Next Stroke</u>. This is allowed any time before the *opponent's* next *stroke* is made.

  » The *opponent* has then completed the hole with a score that includes that conceded *stroke*, and the ball may be removed by anyone.

  » A concession made while the *opponent's* ball is still in motion after the previous *stroke* applies to the *opponent's* next *stroke*, unless the ball is *holed* (in which case the concession does not matter).

  » The player may concede the *opponent's* next *stroke* by deflecting or stopping the *opponent's* ball in motion only if that is done specifically to concede the next *stroke* and only when there is no reasonable chance the ball can be *holed*.

- <u>Conceding a Hole</u>. This is allowed any time before the hole is completed (see Rule 6.5), including before the players start the hole.

- <u>Conceding the Match</u>. This is allowed any time before the result of the match is decided (see Rules 3.2a(3) and (4)), including before the players start the match.

Rule 3.2b(1) Interpretations:
3.2b(1)/1 – Players Must Not Concede Holes to Deliberately Shorten a Match

Although a player is allowed to concede a hole to his or her *opponent* at any time before that hole is completed, a player and *opponent* are not allowed to agree to concede holes to each other to deliberately shorten the match.

For example, before starting a match, a player and his or her *opponent* agree to alternate the concession of holes 6, 7, 8 and 9 to one another.

If they know that the Rules do not allow them to make concessions in this way and start the match without cancelling the agreement, both players are disqualified under Rule 1.3b(1) (Player Responsibility for Applying the Rules).

If the players are unaware that this is not allowed, the match stands as played.

(2) **How Concessions Are Made**. A concession is made only when clearly communicated:

- This can be done either verbally or by an action that clearly shows the player's intent to concede the *stroke*, the hole or the match (such as making a gesture).

- If the *opponent* lifts his or her ball in breach of a Rule because of a reasonable misunderstanding that the player's statement or action was a concession of the next *stroke* or a hole or the match, there is no penalty and the ball must be *replaced* on its original spot (which if not known must be estimated) (see Rule 14.2).

A concession is final and cannot be declined or withdrawn.

Rule 3.2b(2) Interpretations:

3.2b(2)/1 – Concession Is Not Valid When Caddie Attempts to Make Concession

One of the actions a *caddie* is not allowed to take is to concede the next *stroke*, a hole or the match to the *opponent*. If a *caddie* attempts to concede, that concession is not valid. There is no penalty to the player for this action of the *caddie* since Rule 10.3b(3) (Actions Not Allowed By Caddie) does not specify a penalty.

If the *opponent* takes an action based on the *caddie's* attempt to concede, such as lifting a ball *in play* or a *ball-marker*, this would be a reasonable misunderstanding under Rule 3.2b(2). There is no penalty and the ball or *ball-marker* must be *replaced* unless the player then makes a concession.

However, if the *caddie* who made the invalid concession lifted the *opponent's* ball or *ball-marker* or the ball or *ball-marker* of his or her player, that *caddie's* player would get a penalty if that act was a breach of Rule 9.4 or Rule 9.5.

3.2c Applying Handicaps in Handicap Match

(1) **Declaring Handicaps**. The player and *opponent* should tell each other their handicaps before the match.

If a player declares a wrong handicap either before or during the match and does not correct the mistake before the *opponent* makes his or her next *stroke*:

- Declared Handicap Too High. The player is **disqualified** if this affects the number of strokes the player gives or gets. If it does not, there is no penalty.

- Declared Handicap Too Low. There is no penalty and the player must play off the declared lower handicap.

Rule 3.2c(1) Interpretations:

3.2c(1)/1 – Declaring Higher Handicap Is a Breach Even If Affected Hole Has Not Been Played

If a player declares a higher handicap to his or her *opponent* before playing the hole that would be affected, the player is still disqualified since this could have affected the *opponent's* strategy.

For example, while waiting on the first tee to start the match, Player A declares that his or her handicap is 12, when it is really 11. Player B declares that his or her handicap is 10, and Player B makes a *stroke* to start play of the 1st hole.

Player A is disqualified under Rule 3.2c(1) because Player B made a *stroke* in the match with the understanding that Player A gets two handicap strokes.

(2) **Holes Where Handicap Strokes Applied**.

- Handicap strokes are given by hole, and the lower net score wins the hole.

- If a tied match is extended, handicap strokes are given by hole in the same way as in the *round* (unless the *Committee* sets a different way of doing so).

Each player is responsible for knowing the holes where he or she gives or gets handicap strokes, based on the stroke index allocation set by the *Committee* (which is usually found on the scorecard).

If the players mistakenly apply handicap strokes on a hole, the agreed result of the hole stands, unless the players correct that mistake in time (see Rule 3.2d(3)).

Rule 3.2c(2) Interpretations:

3.2c(2)/1 – Handicap Stroke Not Applied During a Match Is Discovered Later in Match

Handicap strokes that a player fails to apply are treated in the same way as those that are mistakenly applied.

3.2d Responsibilities of Player and Opponent

(1) **Telling Opponent about Number of Strokes Taken**. At any time during play of a hole or after the hole is completed, the *opponent* may ask the player for the number of strokes (including *strokes* made and penalty strokes) the player has taken on the hole.

This is to allow the *opponent* to decide how to play the next *stroke* and the rest of the hole, or to confirm the result of the hole just completed.

When asked for the number of strokes taken, or when giving that information without being asked:

- The player must give the right number of strokes taken.

- A player who fails to respond to the *opponent's* request is treated as giving the wrong number of strokes taken.

The player gets the **general penalty (loss of hole)** if he or she gives the *opponent* the wrong number of strokes taken, unless the player corrects that mistake in time:

- Wrong Number of Strokes Given While Playing Hole. The player must give the right number of strokes taken before the *opponent* makes another *stroke* or takes a similar action (such as conceding the player's next *stroke* or the hole).

- Wrong Number of Strokes Given After Hole Completed. The player must give the right number of strokes taken:

  » Before either player makes a *stroke* to begin another hole or takes a similar action (such as conceding the next hole or the match) or,

  » For the final hole of the match, before the result of the match is final (see Rule 3.2a(5)).

Exception – No Penalty If No Effect on Result of Hole: If the player gives the wrong number of strokes taken after a hole is completed but this does not affect the *opponent's* understanding of whether the hole was won, lost or tied, there is no penalty.

Rule 3.2d(1) Interpretations:

3.2d(1)/1 – Number of Strokes Taken During Play of a Hole Does Not Need to Be Given by Player If It Is the Player's Turn to Play

If the *opponent* asks the player for the number of strokes taken when it is the player's turn to play, the player is not required to give this information right away.

The player is required to provide the number of strokes taken only before the *opponent* makes his or her next *stroke* or takes a similar action. The player may play his or her shot before giving such information.

3.2d(1)/2 – Meaning of the "No Penalty If No Effect on Result of Hole" Exception

During play of a hole, a player must give the right number of strokes taken so his or her *opponent* can decide how to play the hole. However, after a hole is completed, if a player gives the wrong number of strokes taken, there is no penalty under the Exception to Rule 3.2d(1) if doing so did not affect the *opponent's* understanding of whether the hole was won, lost or tied.

For example, after completing a hole at which the *opponent* scored a 7, the player mistakenly states that he or she scored a 5, when the player actually scored a 6. After starting the next hole, the player realizes that he or she scored a 6. Since the wrong number of strokes taken did not change the fact that the player had won the hole, there is no penalty.

3.2d(1)/3 – Wrong Number of Strokes Given by Player After Hole Completed and the Mistake Is Discovered Several Holes Later

If a player gives the wrong number of strokes taken after a hole is completed, the player gets the *general penalty* if the mistake affects the result of the hole and is not corrected in time. In such a case, the match score must be corrected.

For example, after completing the 1st hole the player tells the *opponent* that he or she scored a 4 but actually scored a 5. The *opponent* scored a 5 on the hole. After playing several more holes, the player realizes that he or she gave the *opponent* the wrong number of strokes taken on the 1st hole.

Even though the hole would have been a tie if the right number of strokes taken had been given, the player gets a loss-of-hole penalty on the first hole because the mistake affected the understanding of the result of the hole. The match score must be corrected.

3.2d(1)/4 – Wrong Number of Strokes Given by Player After Hole Completed and the Mistake Is Discovered After Result of the Match Is Final

If a player unknowingly gives the wrong number of strokes taken after a hole is completed but the mistake is not realized until after the result of the match is final (Rule 3.2a(5) – When Result Is Final), the result of the match stands as played.

For example, after completing the 17th hole, the player tells the *opponent* that he or she scored a 3, but actually scored a 4. The *opponent* scored a 4 on the hole. The players play the 18th hole, and the result of the player winning the match 1 up is made final. The player then realizes that he or she gave the *opponent* the wrong number of strokes taken on the 17th hole.

Because the player unknowingly gave the wrong number of strokes and the result of the match is final, there is no penalty and the match result stands, with the player as the winner (Rule 20.1b(3) – Ruling Request Made After Result of Match Is Final).

3.2d(1)/5 – Changing Mind About Taking Penalty Relief Is Not Giving Wrong Number of Strokes Taken

The right number of strokes taken means only the *strokes* a player has already made and any penalty strokes already received.

For example, the player's ball lies in a *penalty area* and the *opponent* asks how the player intends to proceed. Although not required to answer the question, the player advises that he or she will take penalty relief. After the *opponent* plays, the player decides to play the ball as it lies in the *penalty area*.

The player was entitled to change his or her mind and there was no penalty for doing so since stating future intentions is not the same as giving the number of strokes taken.

(2) **Telling Opponent about Penalty.** When a player gets a penalty:

- The player must tell the *opponent* about that penalty as soon as reasonably possible, taking into account how near the player is to the *opponent* and other practical factors.

- This requirement applies even if the player does not know about the penalty (because players are expected to recognize when they have breached a Rule).

If the player fails to do so and does not correct that mistake before the *opponent* makes another *stroke* or takes a similar action (such as conceding the player's next *stroke* or the hole), the player gets the *general penalty* (**loss of hole**).

Exception – No Penalty When Opponent Knew of Player's Penalty: If the *opponent* knew that the player had a penalty, such as when seeing the player obviously take penalty relief, the player gets no penalty for failing to tell the *opponent* about it.

Rule 3.2d(2) Interpretations:

3.2d(2)/1 – "As Soon as Reasonably Possible" Is Not Always Before the Opponent's Next Stroke

The broad phrase of "as soon as reasonably possible" allows for consideration of all relevant circumstances, especially how near the player is to the *opponent*.

For example, if the player takes unplayable ball relief when the *opponent* is on the opposite side of the fairway and the *opponent* plays before the player can walk over to tell the *opponent* about the penalty, "as soon as reasonably possible" may be while they are walking up to the *hole* to make their next *strokes*.

There is no set procedure for determining what is "as soon as reasonably possible", but it does not always mean before the *opponent* makes the next *stroke*.

(3) **Knowing Match Score**. The players are expected to know the match score – that is, whether one of them leads by a certain number of holes ("holes up" in the match) or the match is tied (also known as "all square").

If the players mistakenly agree on a wrong match score:

- They may correct the match score before either player makes a *stroke* to begin another hole or, for the final hole, before the result of the match is final (see Rule 3.2a(5)).

- If not corrected in that time, that wrong match score becomes the actual match score.

Exception – When Player Requests Ruling in Time: If the player makes a timely request for a ruling (see Rule 20.1b), and it is found that the *opponent* either (1) gave the wrong number of strokes taken or (2) failed to tell the player about a penalty, the wrong match score must be corrected.

Rule 3.2d(3) Interpretations:

3.2d(3)/1 – Deliberately Giving Incorrect Match Score or Failing to Correct Opponent's Misunderstanding of Match Score May Result in Disqualification

Rule 3.2d(3) expects players to know the match score, but does not require a player to give the match score to the *opponent*.

If a player deliberately gives an incorrect match score or deliberately fails to correct the *opponent's* misunderstanding of the match score, he or she has not given the wrong number of strokes taken. But the *Committee* should disqualify the player under Rule 1.2a (Serious Misconduct).

3.2d(3)/2 – Agreement to Wrong Match Score at a Prior Hole Discovered Later in Match

If a player and his or her *opponent* agree to a wrong match score, the match score stands. This is not the same as giving an incorrect number of strokes taken.

For example, after the 10th hole, a player mistakenly says to his or her *opponent* that the match score is tied and his or her *opponent* agrees to this score. Before starting the 12th hole, the *opponent* realizes that he or she was actually 1 up after the 10th hole and requests a ruling on the basis that the player gave the wrong match score.

Players are expected to know the match score and, because the players agreed to the wrong match score and this was not corrected before starting the 11th hole, the wrong match score stands. There is no penalty to the player who mistakenly gave the wrong match score.

(4) **Protecting Own Rights and Interests**. The players in a match should protect their own rights and interests under the Rules:

- If the player knows or believes that the *opponent* has breached a Rule that has a penalty, the player may act on the breach or choose to ignore it.

- **But** if the player and *opponent* deliberately agree to ignore a breach or penalty they know applies, both players are **disqualified** under Rule 1.3b.

- If the player and *opponent* disagree whether one of them has breached a Rule, either player may protect his or her rights by asking for a ruling under Rule 20.1b.

3.3   Stroke Play

Purpose of Rule:

Stroke play has specific Rules (particularly for scorecards and holing out) because:

- Each player competes against all the other players in the competition, and

- All players need to be treated equally under the Rules.

- After the round, the player and the marker (who keeps the player's score) must certify that the player's score for each hole is right and the player must return the scorecard to the Committee.

3.3a Winner in Stroke Play

The player who completes all *rounds* in the fewest total strokes (including *strokes* made and penalty strokes) is the winner.

In a handicap competition, this means the fewest total net strokes.

See Committee Procedures, Section 5A(6) (the Terms of the Competition should say how ties will be decided).

3.3b Scoring in Stroke Play

The player's score is kept on his or her *scorecard* by the *marker*, who is either identified by the *Committee* or chosen by the player in a way approved by the *Committee*.

The player must use the same *marker* for the entire *round*, unless the *Committee* approves a change either before or after it happens.

(1) **Marker's Responsibility: Entering and Certifying Hole Scores on Scorecard**. After each hole during the *round*, the *marker* should confirm with the player the number of strokes on that hole (including *strokes* made and penalty strokes) and enter that gross score on the *scorecard*.

When the *round* has ended:

- The *marker* must certify the hole scores on the *scorecard*.

- If the player had more than one *marker*, each *marker* must certify the scores for those holes where he or she was the *marker*.

Rule 3.3b(1) Interpretations:

3.3b(1)/1 – Marker Should Be Disqualified if He or She Knowingly Certifies a Wrong Score For Another Player

If a *marker*, who is a player, knowingly certifies a wrong score for a hole (including a hole score that does not include a penalty that the *marker* knew the player received on that hole), the *marker* should be disqualified under Rule 1.2a (Serious Misconduct).

For example, a player returns a *scorecard* with a hole score that is lower than actually taken because he or she was unaware of a penalty that should have been included. However, the player's *marker* was aware of the penalty before the *scorecard* was returned, but knowingly failed to notify the player and certified the *scorecard* anyway.

Although Rule 3.3b(1) does not apply a penalty for knowingly certifying a wrong score for another player, it is not in the spirit of the game. Therefore, the *Committee* should disqualify the *marker* under Rule 1.2a (Serious Misconduct).

The player's score is then revised as provided in Rule 3.3b(3) (Wrong Score for a Hole).

3.3b(1)/2 – Marker May Refuse to Certify Player's Score Based on a Disagreement

A *marker* is not required to certify a hole score that he or she believes is wrong.

For example, if there is a dispute between a player and his or her *marker* about whether there was a breach of the Rules or the player's score for a hole and the *marker* reports the facts of the disagreement to the *Committee*, the *marker* is not required to certify the hole score for the hole that he or she believes is incorrect.

The *Committee* will need to consider the available facts and make a decision as to the player's score on the hole in question. If the *marker* refuses to certify that hole score, the *Committee* should accept certification from someone else who saw the player's actions on the hole in question (such as another player) or the *Committee* itself can certify the player's score on that hole.

(2) **Player's Responsibility: Certifying Hole Scores and Returning Scorecard**. During the *round*, the player should keep track of his or her scores for each hole.

When the *round* has ended, the player:

- Should carefully check the hole scores entered by the *marker* and raise any issues with the *Committee*,

- Must make sure that the *marker* certifies the hole scores on the *scorecard*,

- Must not change a hole score entered by the *marker* **except** with the *marker's* agreement or the *Committee's* approval, and

- Must certify the hole scores on the *scorecard* and promptly return it to the *Committee*, after which the player must not change the *scorecard*.

If the player breaches any of these requirements in Rule 3.3b, the player is **disqualified**.

Exception – No Penalty When Breach Due to Marker Failing to Carry Out Responsibilities: There is no penalty if the *Committee* finds that the player's breach of Rule 3.3b(2) was caused by the *marker's* failure to carry out his or her responsibilities (such as the *marker* leaving with the player's *scorecard* or without certifying the *scorecard*), so long as this was beyond the player's control.

See Committee Procedures, Section 5A(5) (recommendations on how to define when a *scorecard* has been returned); **Section 5F(3)** (what the *Committee* should do if the *marker* does not carry out his or her responsibilities).

DIAGRAM 3.3b: SCORECARD RESPONSIBILITIES IN HANDICAP STROKE PLAY

Name: John Smith   Handicap: 5   Date: 09/07/19

Responsibilities

○ Committee
○ Player
○ Player and marker

HOLE	1	2	3	4	5	6	7	8	9	Out
PAR	5	4	4	4	4	5	3	4	4	37
SCORE	5	5	5	4	3	5	4	3	4	38

HOLE	10	11	12	13	14	15	16	17	18	In	Total
PAR	3	4	5	3	4	5	3	4	4	35	72
SCORE	3	4	4	4	5	5	4	3	4	36	74

NET: 69

Marker's Signature: Player's Signature:

49

Rule 3.3b(2) Interpretations:

3.3b(2)/1 – Players Are Required to Enter Only Scores on a Scorecard

There is a difference between requiring players to enter a score for a *round* into a computer (such as for handicapping purposes) and being required to enter hole scores using an electronic form of *scorecard* approved by the *Committee* (such as a mobile scoring application).

The *Committee* may require players to use a *scorecard* other than a paper *scorecard* (such as an electronic form of *scorecard*), but the *Committee* has no authority to impose a penalty under Rule 3.3b(2) for failing to enter scores elsewhere.

However, to help in administrative matters (such as the efficient production and communication of competition results), a *Committee* may apply a penalty under a Code of Conduct (Rule 1.2b) or provide disciplinary sanctions (such as revoking entry into the next competition) for failing to enter scores elsewhere.

3.3b(2)/2 – No Extra Certification Is Required When Changes on Scorecard Are Made

When the *marker* or the *Committee* approves a change in a hole score on the *scorecard*, neither the player nor the *marker* is required to initial or make any extra certification of the changed score.

The player's certification applies to all hole scores, including those that were changed.

3.3b(2)/3 – Application of the Exception for Marker Failing to Carry Out His or Her Responsibilities

Under the Exception to Rule 3.3b(2), a player gets no penalty if there is a breach of the *scorecard* requirements because of a failure of the *marker* that is beyond the player's control.

Examples of how the Exception operates include:

- If a *marker* leaves the *course* with a player's *scorecard* after a *round*, the *Committee* should try to contact the *marker*. However, if unable to do so, the *Committee* should accept certification of the player's scores by someone who saw the *round*. If no one else is available, the *Committee* itself can certify the player's scores.

- If a player needs to correct a hole score after the *scorecard* has been certified by the *marker*, but the *marker* is not available or has already left, the *Committee* should try to contact the *marker*. If unable to do so, the *Committee* should accept certification of the alteration by someone else who saw the player play that hole or, if no such person is available, the *Committee* itself can certify that score.

(3) **Wrong Score for a Hole**. If the player returns a *scorecard* with a wrong score for any hole:

- <u>Returned Score Higher Than Actual Score</u>. The higher returned score for the hole stands.

- <u>Returned Score Lower Than Actual Score or No Score Returned</u>. The player is **disqualified**.

Exception – Failure to Include Unknown Penalty: If one or more of the player's hole scores are lower than the actual scores because he or she excluded one or more penalty strokes that the player did not know about before returning the *scorecard*:

- The player is not disqualified.

- Instead, if the mistake is found before the close of the competition, the *Committee* will revise the player's score for that hole or holes by adding **the penalty stroke(s) that should have been included** in the score for that hole or holes under the Rules.

This exception does not apply:

- When the excluded penalty is disqualification, or

- When the player was told that a penalty might apply or was uncertain whether a penalty applied and did not raise this with the *Committee* before returning the *scorecard*.

Rule 3.3b(3) Interpretations:

3.3b(3)/I – Scores on Scorecard Must Be Identifiable to Correct Hole

Under Rule 3.3b, each hole score on the *scorecard* must be identifiable to the correct hole.

For example, if a *marker* enters the player's front-nine scores in the back-nine boxes and the back-nine scores in the front-nine boxes, the *scorecard* will still be acceptable if the mistake is corrected by altering the hole numbers so that they go with the right score for each hole.

However, if this mistake is not corrected and, as a result, a hole score is lower than actually taken on that hole, the player is disqualified under Rule 3.3b(3).

(4) **Scoring in Handicap Competition.** The player is responsible for making sure that his or her handicap is shown on the *scorecard*. If the player returns a *scorecard* without the right handicap:

- Handicap on Scorecard Too High or No Handicap Shown. If this affects the number of strokes the player gets, the player is **disqualified** from the handicap competition. If it does not, there is no penalty.

- Handicap on Scorecard Too Low. There is no penalty and the player's net score stands using the lower handicap as shown.

Rule 3.3b(4) Interpretations:

3.3b(4)/1 – Meaning of "Handicap" Player Must Show on Scorecard

In net-score *stroke-play* competitions, it is the player's responsibility to ensure that his or her handicap is shown on the *scorecard*. "Handicap" means the handicap for the *course* and tees being played, excluding any handicap allowances as set out within the Terms of the Competition. The *Committee* is responsible for applying any handicap allowances and adjustments.

3.3b(4)/2 – Player Not Exempt From Penalty When Committee Provides a Scorecard With an Incorrect Handicap

If the *Committee* provides players with *scorecards* containing their handicaps, each player must make sure that the right handicap is shown on his or her *scorecard* before returning it.

For example, as a courtesy, the *Committee* chooses to issue pre-printed *scorecards* containing the date and each player's name and handicap.

If such a *scorecard* mistakenly has a player's handicap being higher than it actually is, and this affects the number of strokes he or she gets, the player is disqualified under Rule 3.3b(4) if he or she does not correct this mistake before returning the *scorecard*.

3.3b(4)/3 – No Penalty When a Higher Handicap Has No Effect

If a player returns his or her *scorecard* with a higher handicap than he or she is entitled to, but that higher handicap does not affect how many handicap strokes he or she gets, there is no penalty since it does not affect the competition.

For example, a Term of the Competition is to use 90% of each player's handicap. A player is a 5 handicap, but the player returns his or her *scorecard* showing a handicap of 6. Since 90% of 5 or 6 equals 5 when rounded to the nearest whole number, using the handicap of 6 does not affect how many handicap strokes the player gets, so there is no penalty.

(5) **Player Not Responsible for Adding Up Scores or Applying Handicap.** The *Committee* is responsible for adding up the player's hole scores and, in a handicap competition, applying the player's handicap strokes.

If the player returns a *scorecard* on which he or she has made a mistake in adding up the scores or applying handicap strokes, there is no penalty for doing so.

Rule 3.3b General Interpretations:

3.3b/1 – Players Must Be Accompanied by a Marker for the Entire Round

The purpose of a *marker* is to certify that a player's score for each hole is correctly shown on the player's *scorecard*. If a *marker* is not with the player for the entire *round*, the *scorecard* cannot be properly certified.

For example, if a player plays several holes without his or her *marker* and the *marker* enters the player's scores for the holes the player played alone, the *scorecard* cannot be properly certified under Rule 3.3b.

The player should have insisted that the *marker* accompany the player for all of the holes. If the *marker* was unable to do so, the player should have asked another person to serve as his or her *marker*. If that was not possible, the player was required to stop play and report to the *Committee* so that another *marker* could be assigned.

3.3b/2 – Information Put in Wrong Location on Scorecard May Still Be Acceptable

Although all requirements of Rule 3.3b must be met before a *scorecard* is returned, there is no penalty if the correct information is mistakenly entered on the *scorecard* in a place other than where it was expected to be, except that each hole score on the *scorecard* must be identifiable to the correct hole (see 3.3b(3)/1).

For example:

- If the player and *marker* certify the hole scores in the location where the other was meant to certify, the player's scores have been certified as required under Rule 3.3b. The same would be true if initials were used to certify, rather than the full name.

- If the player's scores are recorded on the *marker's scorecard* and the *marker's* on the player's, but the scores are correct and both *scorecards* are certified, the *scorecards* are acceptable so long as the players tell the *Committee* which *scorecard* belongs to which player. As the nature of this mistake is administrative, there is no time limit on making such a correction (see 20.2d/1).

3.3b/3 – Another Scorecard May Be Used if Official Scorecard Is Misplaced

Although a player should return the *scorecard* that he or she was given by the *Committee*, Rule 3.3b does not require the same *scorecard* to be returned if it was damaged or misplaced.

For example, if the *marker* misplaces a paper *scorecard* that had been handed out by the *Committee*, it would be acceptable to use another *scorecard* (such as a club *scorecard*) so long as that *scorecard* has the player's name and hole scores, and is certified by the player and *marker*.

When an electronic scoring system is used and the player or *marker* loses internet connectivity or there is a technical issue, the players should raise the matter with the *Committee* as soon as possible and no later than immediately after the *round* is completed.

3.3c Failure to Hole Out

A player must *hole out* at each hole in a *round*. If the player fails to *hole out* at any hole:

- The player must correct that mistake before making a *stroke* to begin another hole or, for the final hole of the *round*, before returning the *scorecard*.

- If the mistake is not corrected in that time, the player is **disqualified**.

See Rules 21.1, 21.2 and 21.3 (Rules for other forms of *stroke play* (*Stableford*, *Maximum Score* and *Par/Bogey*) where scoring is different and a player is not disqualified if he or she does not *hole out*).

RULE 4

The Player's Equipment

Purpose of Rule:

Rule 4 covers the equipment that players may use during a round. Based on the principle that golf is a challenging game in which success should depend on the player's judgment, skills and abilities, the player:

- Must use conforming clubs and balls,

- Is limited to no more than 14 clubs and normally must not replace damaged or lost clubs, and

- Is restricted in the use of other equipment that gives artificial help to his or her play.

4.1 Clubs

For detailed requirements for clubs, balls and other *equipment* and the process for consultation and submission of *equipment* for conformity review, see the *Equipment Rules*.

4.1a Clubs Allowed in Making a Stroke

(1) **Conforming Clubs**. In making a *stroke*, a player must use a club that conforms to the requirements in the *Equipment Rules*:

- A club used to make a *stroke* must conform not only when the club is new, but also when it has been deliberately or accidentally changed in any way.

- **But** if the performance characteristics of a conforming club change because of wear through normal use, it is still a conforming club.

"Performance characteristics" means any part of the club that affects how it performs in making a *stroke*, such as its grip, shaft, clubhead or lie or loft (including lie or loft of an adjustable club).

Rule 4.1a(1) Interpretations:

4.1a(1)/1 – Wear Through Normal Use Does Not Change Conformity

Normal use includes *strokes*, practice *strokes* and practice swings, as well as acts such as removing a club from and replacing a club into the golf bag. If wear through normal use occurs, the player's club is treated as conforming, and he or she may continue to use it.

Examples of wear through normal use include when:

- Material inside a clubhead has broken loose and may rattle during the *stroke* or when the head is shaken.

- A wear mark has formed on the club's grip where the thumbs are placed.

- A depression is formed on the club face through repeated use.

- The grooves on the club's face are worn.

4.1a(1)/2 – No Penalty for Stroke with Non-Conforming Club When Stroke Disregarded

If a player makes a *stroke* with a non-conforming club, the player is not disqualified if the *stroke* does not count in the player's score.

Examples of when the player gets no penalty for making a *stroke* with a non-conforming club include when:

- The player used the club to make a *stroke* at a *provisional ball*, but it never became the ball *in play*.

- The player used the club to make a *stroke*, but the *stroke* was cancelled.

- The player used the club to make a *stroke* at a second ball under Rule 20.1c(3), but that ball was not the ball that counted for his or her score.

(2) **Use or Repair of Club Damaged During Round**. If a conforming club is damaged during a *round* or while play is stopped under Rule 5.7a, the player normally must not replace it with another club. (For a limited **exception** when the player did not cause the damage, see Rule 4.1b(3)).

But no matter what the nature or cause of the damage, the damaged club is treated as conforming for the rest of the *round* (**but** not during a play-off in *stroke play*, which is a new *round*).

For the rest of the *round*, the player may:

- Continue to make *strokes* with the damaged club, or

- Have the club repaired by restoring it as nearly as possible to its condition before the damage happened during the *round* or while play was stopped, while still using the original grip, shaft and clubhead. **But** in doing so:

  » The player must not unreasonably delay play (see Rule 5.6a), and

  » Any damage that existed before the *round* must not be repaired.

"Damaged during a *round*" means when the club's performance characteristics are changed because of any act during the *round* (including while play is stopped under Rule 5.7a), whether:

- By the player (such as making a *stroke* or practice swing with the club, putting it in or taking it out of a golf bag, dropping or leaning on it, or throwing or abusing it), or

- By any other person, *outside influence* or *natural forces*.

But a club is not "damaged during a *round*" if its performance characteristics are deliberately changed by the player during the *round*, as covered by Rule 4.1a(3).

Rule 4.1a(2) Interpretations:
4.1a(2)/1 – Meaning of "Repair"

Examples of repair include:

- Replacing lead tape that fell off during a *stroke*. Given the nature of lead tape, if the lead tape will not remain on the club in the same location, new tape may be used.

- Tightening clubs with adjustable mechanisms that come loose during the *round*, but not adjusting the club to a different setting.

(3) **Deliberately Changing Club's Performance Characteristics During Round**. A player must not make a *stroke* with a club whose performance characteristics he or she deliberately changed during the *round* (including while play is stopped under Rule 5.7a):

- By using an adjustable feature or physically changing the club (**except** when allowed to repair damage under Rule 4.1a(2)), or

- By applying any substance to the clubhead (other than in cleaning it) to affect how it performs in making a *stroke*.

Exception – Adjustable Club Restored to Original Position:

If a club's performance characteristics were changed by using an adjustable feature and, before the club is used to make a *stroke*, the club is restored as nearly as possible to its original position by adjusting the feature back to where it was, there is no penalty and the club may be used to make a *stroke*.

Penalty for Making *Stroke* in Breach of Rule 4.1a: Disqualification.

- There is no penalty under this Rule for merely having (but not making a *stroke* with) a non-conforming club or a club whose performance characteristics were deliberately changed during the *round*.

- **But** such a club still counts towards the 14-club limit in Rule 4.1b(1).

4.1b   Limit of 14 Clubs; Sharing, Adding or Replacing Clubs During Round

(1) **Limit of 14 Clubs**. A player must not:

- Start a *round* with more than 14 clubs, or

- Have more than 14 clubs during the *round*.

If the player starts a *round* with fewer than 14 clubs, he or she may add clubs during the *round* up to the 14-club limit (see Rule 4.1b(4) for restrictions in doing this).

When the player becomes aware that he or she is in breach of this Rule by having more than 14 clubs, the player must immediately take the excess club or clubs out of play, using the procedure in Rule 4.1c(1):

- If the player started with more than 14 clubs, he or she may choose which club or clubs will be taken out of play.

- If the player added excess clubs during the *round*, those added clubs are the ones that must be taken out of play.

After a player's *round* has started, if the player picks up another player's club that was left behind, or a club is mistakenly put in the player's bag without his or her knowledge, the club is not treated as one of the player's clubs for purposes of the 14-club limit (**but** it must not be used).

Rule 4.1b(1) Interpretations:
4.1b(1)/1 – Separate Clubhead and Shaft Are Not a Club

With respect to Rule 4.1b(1), separated parts of a club are not a club and do not count towards a player's 14-club limit.

For example, if a player starts his or her *round* with 14 clubs and is also carrying separated club components, the player is considered to be carrying only 14 clubs and there is no breach of Rule 4.1b(1).

4.1b(1)/2 – Club Broken into Pieces Does Not Count Towards the 14-Club Limit

A club that has broken into pieces does not count towards the player's 14-club limit even when the player begins a *round* with that broken club.

For example, while warming up on the practice range, a player's club breaks just below the grip and the player starts the round with that broken club in his or her bag. That club does not count as one of the 14 clubs the player is allowed to carry.

4.1b(1)/3 – Clubs Carried for Player Count Towards the 14-Club Limit

The 14-club limit applies to any clubs being carried by the player, his or her *caddie*, or any other person he or she asks to carry clubs.

For example, if a player begins the *round* with 10 clubs and asks another person to walk along with the group and carry 8 additional clubs from which the player intends to add to his or her bag during the *round*, the player is considered to have started the *round* with more than 14 clubs.

4.1b(1)/4 – Club Is Considered Added When Next Stroke Made

A club is considered added when the player makes his or her next *stroke* with any club while the added club is in the player's possession. This applies whether or not the player is allowed to add or replace a club.

For example, if a player who starts the *round* with 14 clubs decides to replace his or her putter with another putter between the play of two holes and does so without unreasonably delaying play, the player is not penalized if he or she realizes the mistake and corrects it prior to making the next *stroke* with any club.

(2) **No Sharing of Clubs**. A player is limited to those clubs he or she started with or added as allowed in (1):

- The player must not make a *stroke* with a club being used by anyone else who is playing on the *course* (even if the other player is playing in a different group or competition).

- When the player becomes aware that he or she has breached this Rule by making a *stroke* with another player's club, the player must immediately take that club out of play, using the procedure in Rule 4.1c(1).

See Rules 22.5 and 23.7 (limited exception in *partner* forms of play allowing *partners* to share clubs if they have no more than 14 clubs between them).

Rule 4.1b(2) Interpretations:

4.1b(2)/1 – Multiple Players May Carry Clubs in One Bag

The Rules do not restrict multiple players (such as *partners*) from carrying their clubs in one bag. However, to reduce the risk of penalty under Rule 4.1b, they should make sure the clubs are clearly identifiable to each player.

4.1b(2)/2 – Sharing Clubs Is Not Allowed for Strokes That Count in a Player's Score

The prohibition against sharing clubs applies only to *strokes* that count in a player's score. It does not apply to practice swings, practice *strokes* or *strokes* made after the result of a hole is decided.

For example, there is no penalty under Rule 4.1b if, between the play of two holes, a player borrows another player's putter and makes several practice putts on the *putting green* of the hole just completed.

(3) **No Replacing Lost or Damaged Clubs**. If a player started with 14 clubs or added clubs up to the limit of 14 and then loses or damages a club during the *round* or while play is stopped under Rule 5.7a, the player must not replace it with another club.

Exception – Replacing Damaged Club When Player Did Not Cause Damage: If a player's club is damaged during the *round* (including while play is stopped) (see Rule 4.1a(2)) by an *outside influence* or *natural forces* or by any person other than the player or his or her *caddie*:

- The player may replace the damaged club with any club under Rule 4.1b(4).

- **But** when the player does so, the player must immediately take the damaged club out of play, using the procedure in Rule 4.1c(1).

(4) **Restrictions When Adding or Replacing Clubs.** When adding or replacing a club under (1) or (3), a player must not:

- Unreasonably delay play (see Rule 5.6a),

- Add or borrow any club from anyone else who is playing on the *course* (even if the other player is playing in a different group or competition), or

- Build a club from parts carried by anyone for the player during the *round*.

Rule 4.1b(4) Interpretations:

4.1b(4)/1 – Club Components May Be Assembled When Not Carried By or For Player

Rule 4.1b(4) restricts a player from building a club from parts that he or she is carrying or parts that any other person is carrying for him or her. It does not restrict the player from retrieving parts to build a club or having parts brought to him or her.

For example, if a player is permitted to add a club (see Rule 4.1b(1)) or replace a damaged club (see Rule 4.1b(3)), club components brought from the clubhouse (such as the player's locker), the golf shop, or a manufacturer's truck, or other similar locations, are not considered to be "carried by anyone for the player during the *round*" and are allowed to be assembled by the player or anyone else.

Penalty for Breach of Rule 4.1b: The penalty applies based on when the player becomes aware of the breach:

- Player Becomes Aware of Breach While Playing the Hole. The penalty is applied at the end of the hole being played. In *match play*, the player must complete the hole, apply the result of that hole to the match score and then apply the penalty to adjust the match score.

- Player Becomes Aware of Breach Between Two Holes. The penalty is applied as of the end of the hole just completed, not the next hole.

Penalty in Match Play – Match Score Revised by Deducting Hole, Maximum of Two Holes:

- This is a match adjustment penalty – it is not the same as a loss of hole penalty.

- At the end of the hole being played or just completed, the match score is revised by deducting **one hole** for each hole where a breach happened, with a **maximum deduction of two holes** in the *round*.

- For example, if a player who started with 15 clubs becomes aware of the breach while playing the 3rd hole and then wins that hole to go three up in the match, the maximum adjustment of two holes applies and the player would now be one up in the match.

Penalty in Stroke Play – Two Penalty Strokes, Maximum of Four Strokes: The player gets the *general penalty* (**two penalty strokes**) for each hole where a breach happened, with a **maximum of four penalty strokes** in the *round* (adding two penalty strokes at each of the first two holes where a breach happened).

Rule 4.1b Interpretations:

4.1b/1 – How to Apply Adjustment Penalty Once Any Player Starts Hole During Match

If any player in a match has started play of a hole when a breach of Rule 4.1b is discovered, the match-adjustment penalty is applied at the end of that hole. If the player in breach has not started that hole, he or she is between holes and is not in breach on the next hole.

For example, after completing the first hole, the player tees off on the second hole. Before the *opponent* tees off, the *opponent* becomes aware that he or she is carrying 15 clubs in breach of Rule 4.1b(1). Since the *opponent* has not started the second hole, the match score is only adjusted by one hole in the player's favour, but the match score is not revised until the second hole is completed since the second hole started when the player teed off.

4.1c   Procedure for Taking Clubs Out of Play

(1) **During Round.** When a player becomes aware during a *round* that he or she is in breach of Rule 4.1b(1), (2) or (3) for having more than 14 clubs or for making a *stroke* with another player's club, the player must immediately take an action that clearly indicates each club that is being taken out of play.

This may be done either by:

- Declaring this to the *opponent* in *match play* or the *marker* or another player in the group in *stroke play*, or

- Taking some other clear action (such as turning the club upside down in the bag, placing it on the floor of the golf cart or giving the club to another person).

The player must not make a *stroke* for the rest of the *round* with any club taken out of play.

If a club taken out of play is another player's club, that other player may continue to use the club.

Penalty for Breach of Rule 4.1c(1): Disqualification.

(2) **Before Round**. If a player becomes aware shortly before starting a *round* that he or she accidentally has more than 14 clubs, the player should try to leave the excess club or clubs behind.

But as an option without penalty:

- The player may take any such excess clubs out of play before the start of the *round*, using the procedure in (1), and

- The excess clubs may be kept by the player (**but** must not be used) during the *round*, and they do not count towards the 14-club limit.

If a player deliberately brings more than 14 clubs to his or her first *teeing area* and starts the *round* without leaving the excess clubs behind, this option is not allowed and Rule 4.1b(1) applies.

4.2 Balls

4.2a Balls Allowed in Play of Round

(1) **Conforming Ball Must Be Played**. In making each *stroke*, a player must use a ball that conforms to the requirements in the *Equipment Rules*.

A player may get a conforming ball to play from anyone else, including another player on the *course*.

Rule 4.2a(1) Interpretations:

4.2a(1)/1 – Status of Ball Not on List of Conforming Golf Balls

In a competition in which the *Committee* has not adopted the Local Rule requiring players to use a brand and model of ball on the current List of Conforming Golf Balls, a player may use the following golf balls:

- Brands and models that have never been tested – these are presumed to conform and the onus of proof is on the person alleging that the ball does not conform.

- Brands and models that appeared on a previous List but have not been re-submitted for inclusion on the current List – these are presumed to continue to conform.

However, brands and models that have been tested and found not to conform to the *Equipment Rules* must not be played, whether or not the Local Rule has been adopted.

4.2a(1)/2 – Status of "X-Out", "Refurbished" and "Practice" Balls

If a player chooses to play a ball that is marked as "X-Out" or "Practice" by the manufacturer, or a ball that has been refurbished, these balls are treated as follows under the *Equipment Rules*:

- "X-Out" is the common name used for a golf ball that a manufacturer considers to be imperfect (often for aesthetic reasons only, such as paint or printing errors) and, therefore, has crossed out the brand name. "Refurbished" refers to a second-hand golf ball that has been cleaned and stamped as "refurbished" or a similar stamping.

  In the absence of strong evidence to suggest that an "X-Out" or "refurbished" ball does not conform to the *Equipment Rules*, a player is allowed to use it.

  However, if the *Committee* has adopted the List of Conforming Golf Balls as a Local Rule, such a ball must not be used even if the identification markings on the ball in question appear on the List.

- "Practice" balls are typically listed, conforming golf balls that have been stamped "Practice" or with a similar stamping. "Practice" balls are treated in the same way as golf balls that feature a golf club or course, company, school or other logo.

  Such balls may be used even where the *Committee* has adopted the List of Conforming Golf Balls as a Local Rule.

4.2a(1)/3 – No Penalty for Playing Non-Conforming Ball When Stroke Is Disregarded

If a player makes a *stroke* at a non-conforming ball or a ball not on the List of Conforming Golf Balls when the Local Rule is in effect, the player is not disqualified if the *stroke* does not count in the player's score.

Examples of when a player gets no penalty include when the player plays a ball that is not allowed:

- As a *provisional ball*, but the *provisional ball* never becomes the ball *in play*.

- When the *stroke* with that ball is cancelled.

- As a second ball under Rule 20.1c(3), but that ball is not the ball that counts for his or her score.

(2) **Deliberately Altered Ball Must Not Be Played**. A player must not make a *stroke* at a ball whose performance characteristics have been deliberately altered, such as by scuffing or heating the ball or by applying any substance (other than in cleaning it).

Penalty for Making Stroke in Breach of Rule 4.2a: Disqualification.

4.2b   Ball Breaks into Pieces While Playing Hole

If a player's ball breaks into pieces after a *stroke*, there is no penalty and the *stroke* does not count.

The player must play another ball from where that *stroke* was made (see Rule 14.6).

Penalty for Playing Ball from a *Wrong Place* in Breach of Rule 4.2b: *General Penalty* Under Rule 14.7a.

4.2c   Ball Becomes Cut or Cracked While Playing Hole

(1) **Lifting Ball to See If Cut or Cracked**. If a player reasonably believes that his or her ball has been cut or cracked while playing a hole:

- The player may lift the ball to look at it, **but**:

- The spot of the ball must first be *marked*, and the ball must not be cleaned (**except** on the *putting green*) (see Rule 14.1).

If the player lifts the ball without having this reasonable belief (**except** on the *putting green* where the player may lift under Rule 13.1b), fails to *mark* the spot of the ball before lifting it or cleans it when not allowed, the player gets **one penalty stroke**.

If multiple Rule breaches with a one-stroke penalty result from a single act or related acts, see Rule 1.3c(4).

(2) **When Another Ball May Be Substituted**. The player may only *substitute* another ball if it can be clearly seen that the original ball is cut or cracked and this damage happened during the hole being played – **but** not if it is only scratched or scraped or its paint is only damaged or discoloured.

- If the original ball is cut or cracked, the player must *replace* either another ball or the original ball on the original spot (see Rule 14.2).

- If the original ball is not cut or cracked, the player must *replace* it on its original spot (see Rule 14.2).

Nothing in this Rule prohibits a player from *substituting* another ball under any other Rule or changing balls between two holes.

Penalty for Playing Incorrectly *Substituted* Ball or Playing Ball from a *Wrong Place* in Breach of Rule 4.2c: *General Penalty* Under Rule 6.3b or 14.7a.

If multiple Rule breaches result from a single act or related acts, see Rule 1.3c(4).

4.3   Use of Equipment

Rule 4.3 applies to all types of *equipment* that a player might use during a *round*, **except** that the requirement to play with conforming clubs and balls is covered by Rules 4.1 and 4.2, not by this Rule.

This Rule only concerns how *equipment* is used. It does not limit the *equipment* that a player may have with him or her during a *round*.

4.3a   Allowed and Prohibited Uses of Equipment

A player may use *equipment* to help his or her play during a *round*, **except** that a player must not create a potential advantage by:

- Using *equipment* (other than a club or a ball) that artificially eliminates or reduces the need for a skill or judgment that is essential to the challenge of the game, or

- Using *equipment* (including a club or a ball) in an abnormal way in making a *stroke*. "Abnormal way" means a way that is fundamentally different than its intended use and is not normally recognized as part of playing the game.

This Rule does not affect the application of any other Rule that limits actions a player is allowed to take with a club, ball or other *equipment* (such as setting down a club or other object to help the player in lining up, see Rule 10.2b(3)).

Common examples of uses of *equipment* that are allowed and not allowed during a player's *round* under this Rule are:

(1) **Distance and Directional Information**.

- Allowed. Getting information on distance or direction (such as from a distance-measuring device or compass).

- Not Allowed.

  » Measuring elevation changes, or

  » Interpreting distance or directional information (such as using a device to get a recommended *line of play* or club selection based on the location of the player's ball).

See Committee Procedures, Section 8; Model Local Rule G-5 (the *Committee* may adopt a Local Rule prohibiting the use of distance-measuring devices).

Rule 4.3a(1) Interpretations:

4.3a(1)/1 – Restrictions on Using Equipment to Gauge Slope

Although a player may use his or her club as a plumb line to assist in judging or gauging slope and contours, there is other *equipment* that a player may not use in judging a slope or contour.

For example, a player is not allowed to gauge slope by:

- Placing a bottled drink to act as a level.

- Holding or placing a bubble level.

- Using a weight suspended on a string as a plumb line.

(2) **Information on Wind and Other Weather Conditions**.

- Allowed.

  » Getting any type of weather information (including wind speed) that is available from weather forecasts, or

  » Measuring temperature and humidity at the *course*.

- Not Allowed.

  » Measuring wind speed at the *course*, or

  » Using an artificial object to get other wind-related information (such as using powder to assess wind direction).

Rule 4.3a(2) Interpretations:

4.3a(2)/1 – Using Artificial Objects to Get Wind-Related Information Is Not Allowed

Rule 4.3a(2) gives a single example of an artificial object not allowed to get wind-related information (powder to assess wind direction). However, other artificial objects must not be used for the sole purpose of getting wind-related information.

For example, if a player takes a handkerchief out for the sole purpose of holding it in the air to see which direction the wind is blowing, the player's action is a breach of Rule 4.3.

(3) **Information Gathered Before or During Round**.

- Allowed.

  » Using information that was gathered before the *round* (such as playing information from previous *rounds*, swing tips or club recommendations), or

  » Recording (for use after the *round*) playing or physiological information from the *round* (such as club distance, playing statistics or heart rate).

- Not Allowed.

  » Processing or interpreting playing information from the *round* (such as club recommendations based on current *round* distances), or

  » Using any physiological information recorded during the *round*.

(4) **Audio and Video**.

- Allowed.

  » Listening to audio or watching video on matters unrelated to the competition being played (such as a news report or background music).

  » **But** in doing so, consideration should be shown to others (see Rule 1.2).

- Not Allowed.

  » Listening to music or other audio to eliminate distractions or to help with swing tempo, or

  » Viewing video showing play of the player or other players during the competition that helps the player in choosing a club, making a *stroke*, or deciding how to play during the *round*.

See Committee Procedures, Section 8; Model Local Rule G-8 (the *Committee* may adopt a Local Rule prohibiting or restricting the use of audio and video devices during a *round*).

Rule 4.3a(4) Interpretations:

4.3a(4)/1 – Viewing Video That Is Being Shown at the Course

There is no breach of Rule 4.3a(4) if a player views video that is being shown for the benefit of spectators at a golf competition.

For example, if a player is standing on a tee waiting to play, and he or she is able to see a public screen showing live coverage of the competition, statistical information, wind speed or other similar things, there is no breach of the Rule 4.3 if the player watches the coverage or views the information, even if it could help the player in choosing a club, making a *stroke*, or deciding how to play.

(5) **Gloves and Gripping Agents**.

- Allowed.

  » Using a plain glove that meets the requirements in the *Equipment Rules*,

  » Using resin, powders and other moisturizing or drying agents, or

  » Wrapping a towel or handkerchief around the grip.

- Not Allowed.

  >> Using a glove that does not meet the requirements in the *Equipment Rules*, or

  >> Using other *equipment* that gives an unfair advantage with hand position or grip pressure.

(6) **Stretching Devices and Training or Swing Aids**.

- Allowed.

  >> Using any *equipment* for general stretching (other than in making a practice swing), whether the *equipment* is designed for stretching, for use in golf (such as an alignment rod placed across the shoulders) or for any purpose unrelated to golf (such as rubber tubing or a section of pipe).

- Not Allowed.

  >> Using any type of golf training or swing aid (such as an alignment rod or a weighted headcover or "donut") or a non-conforming club to make a practice swing or in any other way that creates a potential advantage by helping the player in preparing for or making a *stroke* (such as help with swing plane, grip, alignment, ball position or posture).

Further guidance on the use of *equipment* described above and other types of *equipment* (such as clothing and shoes) is found in the *Equipment Rules*.

A player who is uncertain whether he or she may use a piece of *equipment* in a particular way should ask the *Committee* for a ruling (see Rule 20.2b).

See Committee Procedures, Section 8; Model Local Rule G-6 (the *Committee* may adopt a Local Rule prohibiting the use of motorized transportation during a *round*).

4.3b   Equipment Used for Medical Reasons

(1) **Medical Exception**. A player is not in breach of Rule 4.3 if he or she uses *equipment* to help with a medical condition, so long as:

- The player has a medical reason to use the *equipment*, and

- The *Committee* decides that its use does not give the player any unfair advantage over other players.

(2) **Tape or Similar Coverings**. A player may use adhesive tape or a similar covering for any medical reason (such as to prevent an injury or help with an existing injury), **but** the tape or covering must not:

- Be applied excessively, or

- Help the player more than is necessary for the medical reason (for example, it must not immobilize a joint to help the player swing the club).

A player who is uncertain about where or how tape or similar coverings may be applied should ask the *Committee* for a ruling.

Penalty for Breach of Rule 4.3:

- **Penalty for first breach from single act or related acts:** *General Penalty*.

- **Penalty for second breach unrelated to first breach: Disqualification.** This penalty applies even if the nature of the breach was entirely different than the breach resulting in the first penalty.

Rule 4.3 General Interpretation:

Rule 4.3/1 – Player Breaches Rule 4.3 Between Holes; How to Apply the Penalty

For the first breach of Rule 4.3, the player gets the *general penalty* on the hole where the breach occurs. However, if the player breaches Rule 4.3 between the play of two holes, the penalty is applied to the next hole to be played.

For example, a player uses an alignment rod to check his or her swing plane between the play of two holes.

In *match play*, the player loses the next hole or, in *stroke play*, he or she gets two penalty strokes and will start the next hole making his or her third *stroke*.

Playing the Round
and a Hole

Rules 5–6

RULE 5

Playing the Round

Purpose of Rule:

Rule 5 covers how to play a round – such as where and when a player may practise on the course before or during a round, when a round starts and ends and what happens when play has to stop or resume. Players are expected to:

- Start each round on time, and

- Play continuously and at a prompt pace during each hole until the round is completed.

When it is a player's turn to play, it is recommended that he or she make the stroke in no more than 40 seconds, and usually more quickly than that.

5.1 Meaning of Round

A "*round*" is 18 or fewer holes played in the order set by the *Committee*.

When a *round* ends in a tie and play will go on until there is a winner:

- Tied Match Extended One Hole at a Time. This is the continuation of the same *round*, not a new *round*.

- Play-off in Stroke Play. This is a new *round*.

A player is playing his or her *round* from when it starts until it ends (see Rule 5.3), **except** while play is stopped under Rule 5.7a.

When a Rule refers to actions taken "during a *round*", that does not include while play is stopped under Rule 5.7a unless the Rule says otherwise.

5.2 Practising on Course Before or Between Rounds

For purposes of this Rule:

- "Practising on the *course*" means playing a ball, or testing the surface of the *putting green* of any hole by rolling a ball or rubbing the surface, and

- The limitations on practice on the *course* before or between *rounds* apply only to the player, not to the player's *caddie*.

5.2a   Match Play

A player may practise on the *course* before a *round* or between *rounds* of a match-play competition.

5.2b   Stroke Play

On the day of a *stroke-play* competition:

- A player must not practise on the *course* before a *round*, **except** that the player may practise putting or chipping on or near his or her first *teeing area* and practise on any practice area.

- A player may practise on the *course* after completing play of his or her final *round* for that day.

See Committee Procedures, Section 8; Model Local Rule I-1 (in either form of play, the *Committee* may adopt a Local Rule prohibiting, restricting or allowing practice on the *course* before or between *rounds*).

Rule 5.2b Interpretations:

5.2b/1 – Meaning of "Completing Play of His or Her Final Round for That Day" in Stroke Play

In *stroke play*, a player has completed his or her final *round* for that day when he or she will not play any more holes that day on the *course* as part of the competition.

For example, having completed play in the first *round* on the first day of a two-day 36-hole *stroke-play* competition, a player is permitted by Rule 5.2b to practise on the competition *course* later that day as long as his or her next *round* will not start until the next day.

However, if the player finishes one *round* but will play another *round* or part of a *round* on the *course* on that same day, practising on the *course* would breach Rule 5.2b.

For example, having completed play in a *stroke-play* qualifying *round* for a *match-play* competition, a player practises on the *course*. After the conclusion of play, the player is tied for the last qualifying place for the *match-play* competition. The tie is to be decided by a hole-by-hole *stroke-play* play-off that is scheduled to be played immediately after play the same day on that *course*.

If the player's practice on the *course* was his or her first breach of Rule 5.2b, the player gets the *general penalty* applied to the first hole of the play-off. Otherwise, the player is disqualified from the play-off under Rule 5.2b for practising on the *course* before the play-off.

5.2b/2 – Practice Stroke After Hole but Between Rounds Allowed

The permissions for practising in Rule 5.5b (Restriction on Practice Strokes Between Two Holes) override the prohibitions in Rule 5.2b in that a player is allowed to practise on or near the *putting green* of the hole just completed even if he or she will play that hole again on the same day.

Examples of when practising putting or chipping on or near the *putting green* of the hole just completed is allowed even though play for the day is not over include when:

- A player is playing an 18-hole *stroke-play* competition on a 9-hole *course* in one day and practises putting on the 3rd *green* after completing the 3rd hole during the first *round*.

- A player is playing a 36-hole *stroke-play* competition on the same *course* in one day and practises chipping near the 18th *green* after completing the 18th hole during the first *round*.

5.2b/3 – Practising May Be Allowed on Course Before a Round in a Competition that Covers Consecutive Days

When a competition is scheduled on a *course* over consecutive days and the *Committee* schedules some players to play on the first day and others to play on a later day, a player is allowed to practise on the *course* on any day that he or she is not scheduled to play his or her *round*.

For example, if a competition is scheduled for Saturday and Sunday and a player is only scheduled to play on Sunday, that player is allowed to practise on the *course* on Saturday.

Penalty for Breach of Rule 5.2:

- **Penalty for first breach: *General Penalty*** (applied to the player's first hole).

- **Penalty for second breach: Disqualification.**

5.3 Starting and Ending Round

5.3a When to Start Round

A player's *round* starts when the player makes a *stroke* to start his or her first hole (see Rule 6.1a).

The player must start at (and not before) his or her starting time:

- This means that the player must be ready to play at the starting time and starting point set by the *Committee*.

- A starting time set by the *Committee* is treated as an exact time (for example, 9 am means 9:00:00 am, not any time until 9:01 am).

If the starting time is delayed for any reason (such as weather, slow play of other groups or the need for a ruling by a *referee*), there is no breach of this Rule if the player is present and ready to play when the player's group is able to start.

Penalty for Breach of Rule 5.3a: Disqualification, except in these three cases:

- **Exception 1 – Player Arrives at Starting Point, Ready to Play, No More Than Five Minutes Late:** The player gets the *general penalty* applied to his or her first hole.

- **Exception 2 – Player Starts No More Than Five Minutes Early:** The player gets the *general penalty* applied to his or her first hole.

- **Exception 3 – Committee Decides that Exceptional Circumstances Prevented Player from Starting on Time:** There is no breach of this Rule and no penalty.

Rule 5.3a Interpretations:

5.3a/1 – Exceptional Circumstances That Warrant Waiving Starting Time Penalty

The term "exceptional circumstances" in Exception 3 under Rule 5.3a does not mean unfortunate or unexpected events outside a player's control. It is a player's responsibility to allow enough time to reach the *course* and he or she must make allowances for possible delays.

There is no specific guidance in the Rules for deciding what is exceptional, as it depends on the circumstances in each case and must be left to the determination of the *Committee*.

One important factor not included in the examples below is that consideration should be given to a situation where multiple players are involved to the extent that the *Committee* should consider the situation to be exceptional.

Examples of circumstances that should be considered as exceptional include:

* The player was present at the scene of an accident and provided medical assistance or was required to give a statement as a witness and otherwise would have started on time.

* There is a fire alarm at the player's hotel and he or she must evacuate. By the time the player can return to the room to dress or retrieve his or her *equipment*, the player is unable to make his or her starting time.

Examples of circumstances that would not generally be considered exceptional include:

* The player gets lost or his or her car breaks down on the way to the *course*.

* Heavy traffic or an accident results in the journey to the *course* taking longer than expected.

5.3a/2 – Meaning of "Starting Point"

In Rule 5.3a, the "starting point" is the *teeing area* of the hole where the player will start his or her *round* as set by the *Committee*.

For example, the *Committee* may start some groups on the 1st tee and some groups on the 10th tee. In a "shotgun start", the *Committee* may assign each group a different hole to start on.

The *Committee* may set a standard for what it means for the player to be at the starting point. For example, the *Committee* may state that, to be at the starting point, the player must be within the gallery ropes of the *teeing area* of the hole to be played.

5.3a/3 – Meaning of "Ready to Play"

The term "ready to play" means that the player has at least one club and ball ready for immediate use.

For example, if a player arrives at his or her starting point by the starting time with a ball and a club (even if just the player's putter), the player is considered ready to play. Should the player decide to wait for a different club when it is his or her turn to play, he or she may get a penalty for unreasonably delaying play (Rule 5.6a).

5.3a/4 – Player at Starting Point but Then Leaves Starting Point

When a player is ready to play at the starting point, but then leaves the starting point for some reason, the Rule that applies depends if he or she is ready to play at the starting point at the starting time.

For example, a player's starting time is 9:00 am and he or she is ready to play at the starting point at 8:57 am. The player realizes that he or she left something in a locker and leaves the starting point to get it. If the player does not arrive back at the starting point at 9:00:00 am, the player is late to his or her starting time, and Rule 5.3a applies.

However, if the player was ready to play at the starting point at 9:00 am and then went to his or her locker, the player may get the penalty under Rule 5.6a (Unreasonable Delay) since he or she satisfied the requirement of Rule 5.3a by being ready to play at the starting point by the starting time.

5.3a/5 – Match Starts on Second Hole When Both Players Late

When both players in a match arrive at the starting point ready to play no more than five minutes after their starting time and neither has experienced exceptional circumstances (Exception 3), they both get a loss-of-hole penalty and the result of the first hole is a tie.

For example, if the starting time is 9:00 am and the player arrives at the starting point ready to play at 9:02 am and the *opponent* arrives ready to play at 9:04 am, they both get a loss-of-hole penalty even though the player arrived before the *opponent* (Exception 1). Therefore, the first hole is tied and the match starts on the second hole all square. There is no penalty if they play the first hole to get to the *teeing area* of the second hole.

5.3b   When Round Ends

A player's *round* ends:

- In *match play*, when the result of the match is decided under Rule 3.2a(3) or (4).

- In *stroke play*, when the player *holes out* at the final hole (including correction of a mistake, such as under Rule 6.1 or 14.7b).

See Rules 21.1d, 21.2d, 21.3d and 23.3b (when a *round* starts and ends in other forms of *stroke play* and in *Four-Ball*).

Rule 5

5.4 Playing in Groups

5.4a Match Play

During a *round*, the player and *opponent* must play each hole in the same group.

5.4b Stroke Play

During a *round*, the player must remain in the group set by the *Committee*, unless the *Committee* approves a change either before or after it happens.

Penalty for Breach of Rule 5.4: Disqualification.

5.5 Practising During Round or While Play Is Stopped

5.5a No Practice Strokes While Playing Hole

While playing a hole, a player must not make a practice *stroke* at any ball on or off the *course*.

These are not practice *strokes*:

- A practice swing made with no intent to strike a ball.
- Hitting a ball back to a practice area or to another player, when done solely as a courtesy.
- *Strokes* made by a player in playing out a hole whose result has been decided.

Rule 5.5a Interpretations:

5.5a/1 – Practice Stroke with Ball of Similar Size to Conforming Ball is Breach

A "practice *stroke*" under Rule 5.5a covers not only hitting a conforming ball with a club but hitting any other type of ball that is similar in size to a golf ball, such as a plastic practice ball.

Striking a *tee* or natural object with a club (such as a stone or a pine cone) is not a practice *stroke*.

5.5b Restriction on Practice Strokes Between Two Holes

Between two holes, a player must not make a practice *stroke*.

80

Exception – Where Player Allowed to Practise Putting or Chipping: The player may practise putting or chipping on or near:

- The putting green of the hole just completed and any practice green (see Rule 13.1e), and
- The *teeing area* of the next hole.

But such practice *strokes* must not be made from a *bunker* and must not unreasonably delay play (see Rule 5.6a).

See Committee Procedures, Section 8; Model Local Rule I-2 (the *Committee* may adopt a Local Rule prohibiting practice putting or chipping on or near the *putting green* of the hole just completed).

Rule 5.5b Interpretations:

5.5b/1 – When Practising Between Holes Is Allowed

A player is allowed to practise putting and chipping when he or she is between the play of two holes. This is when the player has completed play of the previous hole, or in a form of play involving a *partner*, when the side has completed play of the previous hole.

Examples of when a player is between the play of two holes:

Match Play:

Single	When the player has *holed out*, his or her next *stroke* has been conceded, or the outcome of the hole has been determined.
Foursome	When the *side* has *holed out*, its next *stroke* has been conceded, or the outcome of the hole has been determined.
Four-Ball	When both *partners* have *holed out*, their next *strokes* have been conceded, or the outcome of the hole has been determined.

Stroke Play:

Individual	When the player has *holed out*.
Foursome	When the *side* has *holed out*.
Four-Ball	When both *partners* have *holed out*, or one partner has *holed out* and the other cannot better the *side's* score.
Stableford, Par/Bogey, and Maximum Score	When the player has *holed out*, or has picked up after scoring zero points, losing the hole or reaching the maximum score.

5.5c Practice While Play Is Suspended or Otherwise Stopped

While play is suspended or otherwise stopped under Rule 5.7a, a player must not make a practice *stroke* **except**:

- As allowed in Rule 5.5b,
- Anywhere outside the *course*, and
- Anywhere on the *course* the *Committee* allows.

If a match is stopped by agreement of the players and will not be resumed on the same day, the players may practise on the *course* without restriction before the match is resumed.

Rule 5.5c Interpretations:

5.5c/1 – Extra Practice Permissions No Longer Apply When Stroke-Play Round Resumed

In *stroke play,* when play is resumed by the *Committee* after it had been suspended, all players who had started their *rounds* prior to the suspension have resumed the play of their *round*. Consequently, those players are no longer allowed to practise other than as allowed by Rule 5.5b (Restriction on Practice Strokes Between Two Holes).

For example, if the *Committee* suspends play for the day and play will resume at 8:00 am on the following day, a player whose group will be the third group to play from a particular *teeing area* is not allowed to continue practising on the designated practice area after play has resumed at 8:00 am.

The player's *round* has resumed, even though players in his or her group will not be able to make their next *strokes* right away. The only practice that is allowed is putting or chipping on or near the *putting green* of the hole last competed, any practice *putting green*, or the *teeing area* of the next hole.

Penalty for Breach of Rule 5.5: *General Penalty.*

If the breach happens between two holes, the penalty applies to the next hole.

5.6   Unreasonable Delay; Prompt Pace of Play

5.6a   Unreasonable Delay of Play

A player must not unreasonably delay play, either when playing a hole or between two holes.

A player may be allowed a short delay for certain reasons, such as:

- When the player seeks help from a *referee* or the *Committee*,

- When the player becomes injured or ill, or

- When there is another good reason.

Penalty for Breach of Rule 5.6a:

- **Penalty for first breach: One penalty stroke**.

- **Penalty for second breach: *General Penalty***.

- **Penalty for third breach: Disqualification**.

If the player unreasonably delays play between two holes, the penalty applies to the next hole.

Rule 5.6a Interpretations:

5.6a/1 – Examples of Delays That Are Considered Reasonable or Unreasonable

Unreasonable delays in the context of Rule 5.6a are delays caused by a player's actions that are within the player's control and affect other players or delay the competition. Brief delays that are a result of normal events that happen during a *round* or are outside the player's control are generally treated as "reasonable".

Determining which actions are reasonable or unreasonable depends on all the circumstances, including whether the player is waiting for other players in the group or the group ahead.

Examples of actions that are likely to be treated as reasonable are:

- Briefly stopping by the clubhouse or half-way house to get food or drink.

- Taking time to consult with others in the playing group to decide whether to play out the hole when there is a normal suspension by the *Committee* (Rule 5.7b(2)).

Examples of actions that, if causing more than a brief delay in play, are likely to be treated as unreasonable delay are:

- Returning to the *teeing area* from the *putting green* to retrieve a lost club.

- Continuing to search for a *lost* ball for several minutes after the allowed three-minute search time has expired.

- Stopping by the clubhouse or half-way house to get food or drink for more than a few minutes if the *Committee* has not allowed for it.

5.6a/2 – Player Who Gets Sudden Illness or Injury Is Normally Allowed 15 Minutes to Recover

If a player gets a sudden illness or injury (such as from heat exhaustion, a bee sting or being struck by a golf ball), the *Committee* should normally allow that player up to 15 minutes to recover before the player's failure to continue play would be unreasonably delaying play.

The *Committee* should also normally apply this same time limit to the total time a player uses when he or she receives repeated treatments during a *round* to alleviate an injury.

5.6b   Prompt Pace of Play

A *round* of golf is meant to be played at a prompt pace.

Each player should recognize that his or her pace of play is likely to affect how long it will take other players to play their *rounds*, including both those in the player's own group and those in following groups.

Players are encouraged to allow faster groups to play through.

(1) **Pace of Play Recommendations**. The player should play at a prompt pace throughout the *round*, including the time taken to:

- Prepare for and make each *stroke*,

- Move from one place to another between *strokes*, and

- Move to the next *teeing area* after completing a hole.

A player should prepare in advance for the next *stroke* and be ready to play when it is his or her turn.

When it is the player's turn to play:

- It is recommended that the player make the *stroke* in no more than 40 seconds after he or she is (or should be) able to play without interference or distraction, and

- The player should usually be able to play more quickly than that and is encouraged to do so.

(2) **Playing Out of Turn to Help Pace of Play**. Depending on the form of play, there are times when players may play out of turn to help the pace of play:

- In *match play*, the players may agree that one of them will play out of turn to save time (see Rule 6.4a).

- In *stroke play*, players may play "ready golf" in a safe and responsible way (see Rule 6.4b Exception).

(3) **Committee Pace of Play Policy**. To encourage and enforce prompt play, the *Committee* should adopt a Local Rule setting a Pace of Play Policy.

This Policy may set a maximum time to complete a *round*, a hole or series of holes and a *stroke*, and it may set penalties for not following the Policy.

See Committee Procedures, Section 5G (recommendations on contents of Pace of Play Policy).

5.7   Stopping Play; Resuming Play

5.7a   When Players May or Must Stop Play

During a *round*, a player must not stop play **except** in these cases:

- Suspension by Committee. All players must stop play if the *Committee* suspends play (see Rule 5.7b).

- Stopping Play by Agreement in Match Play. Players in a match may agree to stop play for any reason, **except** if doing so delays the competition. If they agree to stop play and then one player wants to resume play, the agreement has ended and the other player must resume play.

- Individual Player Stopping Play Because of Lightning. A player may stop play if he or she reasonably believes there is danger from lightning, **but** must report to the *Committee* as soon as possible.

Leaving the *course* is not, by itself, stopping play. A player's delay of play is covered by Rule 5.6a, not by this Rule.

If a player stops play for any reason not allowed under this Rules or fails to report to the *Committee* when required to do so, the player is disqualified.

Rule 5.7a Interpretations:

5.7a/1 – When a Player Has Stopped Play

Stopping play in the context of Rule 5.7a can either be an intentional act by the player or it can be a delay long enough to constitute stopping. Temporary delays, whether reasonable or unreasonable, are covered by Rule 5.6a (Unreasonable Delay).

Examples where the *Committee* is likely to disqualify a player under Rule 5.7a for stopping play include when:

- The player walks off the *course* in frustration with no intent to return.

- The player stops in the clubhouse after nine holes for an extended time to watch television or to have lunch when the *Committee* has not allowed for this.

- The player takes shelter from rain for a significant amount of time.

5.7b. What Players Must Do When Committee Suspends Play

There are two types of *Committee* suspensions of play, each with different requirements for when players must stop play.

(1) Immediate Suspension (Such as When There Is Imminent Danger). If the *Committee* declares an immediate suspension of play, all players must stop play at once and must not make another *stroke* until the *Committee* resumes play.

The *Committee* should use a distinct method of telling players about an immediate suspension.

Rule 5.7b(1) Interpretations:

5.7b(1)/1 – Circumstances That Justify a Player's Failure to Stop Play

Under Rule 5.7b(1), if the *Committee* declares an immediate suspension of play, all players must stop play at once. The intent of this suspension is to enable the *course* to be cleared as quickly as possible when a potentially dangerous situation, such as lightning, exists.

However, there can be confusion or uncertainty when a suspension is declared and there can be circumstances that explain or justify why the player didn't stop at once. In these cases, the Exception to Rule 5.7b allows the *Committee* to decide that there is no breach of the Rule.

If a player makes a *stroke* after play has been suspended, the *Committee* must consider all relevant facts in determining if the player should be disqualified.

Examples where the *Committee* is likely to determine that continuing play after suspension is justified include when a player:

- Is in a remote part of the *course* and does not hear the signal for suspension of play, or confuses the signal for something else, such as a vehicle horn.

- Has already taken a *stance* with a club behind the ball or has begun the backswing for a *stroke* and completes the *stroke* without hesitation.

An example where the *Committee* is likely to determine that continuing play after suspension is not justified is when a player hears the signal to suspend play but wants to make a *stroke* quickly prior to stopping, such as to complete a hole with a short putt or to take advantage of a favourable wind.

(2) **Normal Suspension (Such as for Darkness or Unplayable Course)**. If the *Committee* suspends play for normal reasons, what happens next depends on where each playing group is:

- **Between Two Holes**. If all players in the group are between two holes, they must stop play and must not make a *stroke* to begin another hole until the *Committee* resumes play.

- **While Playing Hole**. If any player in the group has started a hole, the players may choose either to stop play or to play out the hole.

  » The players are allowed a brief amount of time (which normally should be no more than two minutes) to decide whether to stop play or play out the hole.

  » If the players continue play of the hole, they may go on to complete the hole or may stop before completing the hole.

  » Once the players complete the hole or stop before completing the hole, they must not make another *stroke* until the *Committee* resumes play under Rule 5.7c.

If the players do not agree on what to do:

  » **Match Play**. If the *opponent* stops play, the player must also stop play and both players must not play again until the *Committee* resumes play. If the player does not stop play, the player gets the *general penalty* (**loss of hole**).

  » **Stroke Play**. Any player in the group may choose to stop play or go on to continue the hole, no matter what the others in the group decide to do, **except** that the player may continue play only if the player's *marker* stays to keep the player's score.

Penalty for Breach of Rule 5.7b: Disqualification.

Exception – No Penalty If Committee Decides That Failure to Stop Was Justified: There is no breach of this Rule and no penalty if the *Committee* decides that circumstances justified the player's failure to stop play when required to do so.

See Committee Procedures, Section 8; Model Local Rule J-1 (recommended ways for *Committee* to indicate immediate and normal suspensions to players).

Rule 5.7b General Interpretations:

5.7b/1 – Dropping a Ball After Play Has Been Suspended Is Not Failing to Stop Play

Stopping play in the context of Rule 5.7b means making no further *strokes*. Therefore, if, after a suspension of play, a player proceeds under a Rule, such as by *dropping* a ball, determining the *nearest point of complete relief* or continuing a search, there is no penalty.

However, if the *Committee* has signalled an immediate suspension, in view of the purpose of Rule 5.7b(1), it is recommended that all players take shelter immediately without taking further actions.

5.7c. What Players Must Do When Play Resumes

(1) **Where to Resume Play**. A player must resume play from where he or she stopped play on a hole or, if between two holes, at the next *teeing area*, even if play is resumed on a later day.

(2) **When to Resume Play**. The player must be present at the location identified in (1) and ready to play:

   • At the time set by the *Committee* for play to resume, and

   • The player must resume play at (and not before) that time.

If the ability to resume play is delayed for any reason (such as when players in the group ahead need to play first and move out of the way), there is no breach of this Rule if the player is present and ready to play when the player's group is able to resume play.

Penalty for Breach of Rule 5.7c: Disqualification.

Exceptions to Disqualification for Failure to Resume on Time: Exceptions 1, 2 and 3 in Rule 5.3a and the Exception to Rule 5.7b apply here as well.

Rule 5.7c General Interpretations:

5.7c/1 – Players Must Resume When Committee Concludes There Is No Danger from Lightning

The safety of players is paramount and *Committees* should not risk exposing players to danger. Rule 5.7a (When Players May or Must Stop Play) allows a player to stop play if he or she reasonably believes that there is danger from lightning. In this situation, if the player's belief is reasonable, the player is the final judge.

However, if the *Committee* has ordered a resumption of play after using all reasonable means to conclude that danger from lightning no longer exists, all players must resume play. If a player refuses because he or she believes there is still danger, the *Committee* may conclude that the player's belief is unreasonable and he or she may be disqualified under Rule 5.7c.

5.7d. Lifting Ball When Play Stops; Replacing and Substituting Ball When Play Resumes

(1) **Lifting Ball When Play Stops or Before Play Resumes.** When stopping play of a hole under this Rule, the player may *mark* the spot of his or her ball and lift the ball (see Rule 14.1).

Either before or when play is resumed:

- **When Player's Ball Was Lifted When Play Stopped.** The player must *replace* the original ball or another ball on the original spot (which if not known must be estimated) (see Rule 14.2).

- **When Player's Ball Was Not Lifted When Play Stopped.** The player may play the ball as it lies, or may *mark* the spot of the ball, lift the ball (see Rule 14.1) and *replace* that ball or another ball on the original spot (see Rule 14.2).

In either case:

- If the *lie* of the ball is altered as a result of lifting the ball, the player must *replace* that ball or another ball as required under Rule 14.2d.

- If the *lie* of the ball is altered after the ball was lifted and before a ball is *replaced*, Rule 14.2d does not apply.

  » The original ball or another ball must be *replaced* on the original spot (which if not known must be estimated) (see Rule 14.2).

  » If the *lie* or other *conditions affecting the stroke* were worsened during this time, Rule 8.1d applies.

Rule 5.7d(1) Interpretations:

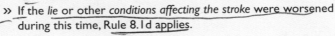

5.7d(1)/1 – Whether Player Must Accept Improved or Worsened Lie in Bunker During a Suspension

When *replacing* a ball in resuming play, Rule 14.2d (Where to Replace Ball When Original Lie Altered) does not apply and the player is not required to re-create the original lie.

For example, a player's ball is embedded in a *bunker* when play is suspended. During the suspension of play the *bunker* is prepared by the maintenance staff and the surface of the sand is now smooth. The player must resume play by placing a ball on the estimated spot from which the ball was lifted, even though this will be on the surface of the sand and not embedded.

However, if the *bunker* has not been prepared by the maintenance staff, the player is not necessarily entitled to the *conditions affecting the stroke* he or she had before play was stopped. If the *conditions affecting the stroke* are worsened by *natural forces* (such as wind or water), the player must not *improve* those worsened conditions (Rule 8.1d).

5.7d(1)/2 – Removal of Loose Impediments Before Replacing Ball When Play Is Resumed

The player must not remove a *loose impediment* before *replacing* a ball that, if removed when the ball was at rest, would have been likely to cause the ball to *move* (Exception 1 to Rule 15.1a). However, when resuming play, if a *loose impediment* is now present that was not there when the ball was lifted, that *loose impediment* may be removed before the ball is *replaced*.

(2) What to Do If Ball or Ball-Marker Is Moved While Play Stopped. If the player's ball or *ball-marker* is moved in any way before play resumes (including by *natural forces*), the player must either:

- *Replace* the original ball or another ball on the original spot (which if not known must be estimated) (see Rule 14.2), or

- Place a *ball-marker* to *mark* that original spot, and then *replace* the original ball or another ball on that spot (see Rules 14.1 and 14.2).

If the player's *conditions affecting the stroke* were worsened while play was stopped, see Rule 8.1d.

Penalty for Playing Ball from a *Wrong Place* in Breach of Rule 5.7d: *General Penalty* Under Rule 14.7a.

If multiple Rule breaches result from a single act or related acts, see Rule 1.3c(4).

RULE 6

Playing a Hole

Purpose of Rule:

Rule 6 covers how to play a hole – such as the specific Rules for teeing off to start a hole, the requirement to use the same ball for an entire hole except when substitution is allowed, the order of play (which matters more in match play than stroke play) and completing a hole.

6.1 Starting Play of a Hole

6.1a When Hole Starts

A player has started a hole when he or she makes a *stroke* to begin the hole.

The hole has started even if the *stroke* was made from outside the *teeing area* (see Rule 6.1b) or the *stroke* was cancelled under a Rule.

6.1b Ball Must Be Played from Inside Teeing Area

A player must start each hole by playing a ball from anywhere inside the *teeing area* under Rule 6.2b.

If a player who is starting a hole plays a ball from outside the *teeing area* (including from a wrong set of tee markers for a different teeing location on the same hole or a different hole):

(1) **Match Play**. There is no penalty, **but** the *opponent* may cancel the *stroke*:

- This must be done promptly and before either player makes another *stroke*. When the *opponent* cancels the *stroke*, he or she cannot withdraw the cancellation.

- If the *opponent* cancels the *stroke*, the player must play a ball from inside the *teeing area* and it is still his or her turn to play.

- If the *opponent* does not cancel the *stroke*, the *stroke* counts and the ball is *in play* and must be played as it lies.

Rule 6.1b(1) Interpretations:

6.1b(1)/1 – Ball Played from Outside Teeing Area in Match Play and Stroke Not Cancelled by Opponent

If, in starting the play of the hole in *match play*, a *stroke* made from outside the *teeing area* is not cancelled, Rule 6.1b(1) provides that the player plays the ball as it lies. However, the player may not always be permitted to play the ball as it lies.

For example, when starting play of a hole, a player hits a ball *out of bounds* from outside the *teeing area* (such as from a wrong set of tee-markers) and the *opponent* does not cancel the *stroke*.

Since, the player's *stroke* is not cancelled, and the ball is *out of bounds*, he or she must take *stroke-and-distance* relief by playing a ball from where the previous *stroke* was made. However, as the *stroke* was not made from inside the *teeing area*, the ball must be *dropped*, not teed (see Rule 14.6b – Previous Stroke from General Area, Penalty Area or Bunker).

(2) **Stroke Play**. The player gets the *general penalty* (two penalty strokes) and must correct the mistake by playing a ball from inside the *teeing area*:

- The ball played from outside the *teeing area* is not *in play*.

- That *stroke* and any more strokes before the mistake is corrected (including *strokes* made and any penalty strokes solely from playing that ball) do not count.

- If the player does not correct the mistake before making a *stroke* to begin another hole or, for the final hole of the *round*, before returning his or her *scorecard*, the player is **disqualified**.

Rule 6.1 General Interpretations:

6.1/1 – What to Do When One or Both Tee-Markers Are Missing

If a player finds one or both tee-markers missing, the player should seek help from the *Committee*.

However, if that help is not available in a reasonable time, the player should use his or her reasonable judgment (Rule 1.3b(2)) to estimate the location of the *teeing area*.

Recognizing that such an estimation must be made promptly and cannot be precise, the player's reasonable judgment of the location of the *teeing area* will be accepted even if later shown to be wrong (Rule 1.3b(2)).

6.2   Playing Ball from Teeing Area

6.2a   When Teeing Area Rules Apply

The *teeing area* Rules in Rule 6.2b apply whenever a player is required or
allowed to play a ball from the *teeing area*. This includes when:

- The player is starting play of the hole (see Rule 6.1),

- The player will play again from the *teeing area* under a Rule (see Rule
14.6), or

- The player's ball is *in play* in the *teeing area* after a *stroke* or after the
player has taken relief.

This Rule applies only to the *teeing area* the player must play from in
starting the hole he or she is playing, not to any other teeing locations on
the *course* (whether on the same hole or a different hole).

6.2b   Teeing Area Rules

(1) When Ball Is in Teeing Area.

- A ball is in the *teeing area* when any part of the ball touches or is
above any part of the *teeing area*.

- The player may stand outside the *teeing area* in making the *stroke* at
a ball in the *teeing area*.

DIAGRAM 6.2b: WHEN BALL IS IN TEEING AREA

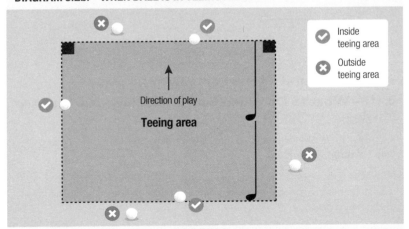

The dotted line defines the outside edges of the teeing area (see Definition of Teeing Area).
A ball is in the teeing area when any part of the ball touches or is above part of the teeing area.

(2) **Ball May Be Teed or Played from Ground**. The ball must be played from either:

- A *tee* placed in or on the ground, or

- The ground itself.

For purposes of this Rule, the "ground" includes sand or other natural materials put in place to set the *tee* or ball on.

The player must not make a *stroke* at a ball on a non-conforming *tee* or a ball teed in a way not allowed by this Rule.

Penalty for Breach of Rule 6.2b(2):

- **Penalty for first breach from single act or related acts:** *General Penalty*.

- **Penalty for second breach unrelated to first breach: Disqualification**.

(3) **Certain Conditions in Teeing Area May Be Improved**. Before making a *stroke*, the player may take these actions in the *teeing area* to *improve* the *conditions affecting the stroke* (see Rule 8.1b(8)):

- Alter the surface of the ground in the *teeing area* (such as by making an indentation with a club or foot),

- Move, bend or break grass, weeds and other natural objects that are attached or growing in the ground in the *teeing area*,

- Remove or press down sand and soil in the *teeing area*, and

- Remove dew, frost and water in the *teeing area*.

But the player gets the **general penalty** if he or she takes any other action to *improve* the *conditions affecting the stroke* in breach of Rule 8.1a.

(4) **Restriction on Moving Tee-Markers When Playing from Teeing Area**.

- The location of the tee-markers is set by the *Committee* to define each *teeing area* and should remain in that same location for all players who will play from that *teeing area*.

- If the player *improves* the *conditions affecting the stroke* by moving any such tee-marker before playing from the *teeing area*, he or she gets the **general penalty** for breach of Rule 8.1a(1).

In all other situations, the tee-markers are treated as regular *movable obstructions* that may be removed as allowed in Rule 15.2.

95

Rule 6.2b(4) Interpretations:

6.2b(4)/1 – Tee-Marker Moved by Player Should Be Replaced

Before making a stroke when playing from a *teeing area,* a player must not move a tee-marker in the *teeing area* to *improve* the *conditions affecting the stroke* (Rule 6.2b(4)).

However, there would be no penalty if a player moves a tee-marker by:

- Tripping over it,

- Hitting it in anger (though a *Committee* could consider this serious misconduct), or

- Lifting it for no apparent reason.

Because moving tee-markers can have a significant effect on the competition, they should not be moved and, if they are moved, they should be replaced.

However, if a player moves a tee-marker because he or she thinks it should be in a different position, or deliberately destroys the tee-marker, the *Committee* may choose to disqualify the player for serious misconduct contrary to the spirit of the game (Rule 1.2a).

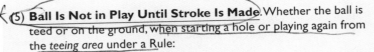

(5) **Ball Is Not in Play Until Stroke Is Made**. Whether the ball is teed or on the ground, when starting a hole or playing again from the *teeing area* under a Rule:

- The ball is not *in play* until the player makes a *stroke* at it, and

- The ball may be lifted or *moved* without penalty before the *stroke* is made.

If a teed ball falls off the *tee* or is knocked off the *tee* by the player before the player has made a *stroke* at it, it may be re-teed anywhere in the *teeing area* without penalty.

But if the player makes a *stroke* at that ball while it is falling or after it has fallen off, there is no penalty, the *stroke* counts and the ball is *in play*.

(6) **When Ball in Play Lies in Teeing Area**. If the player's ball *in play* is in the *teeing area* after a *stroke* (such as a teed ball after a *stroke* that missed the ball) or after taking relief, the player may:

- Lift or *move* the ball without penalty (see Rule 9.4b, Exception 1), and

- Play that ball or another ball from anywhere in the *teeing area* from a *tee* or the ground under (2), including playing the ball as it lies.

Penalty for Playing Ball from a *Wrong Place* in Breach of Rule 6.2b(6): *General Penalty* Under Rule 14.7a.

If multiple Rule breaches result from a single act or related acts, see Rule 1.3c(4).

Rule 6.2b(6) Interpretations:

6.2b(6)/1 – Ball That Comes to Rest in Teeing Area Does Not Have to Be Played as It Lies

Any time a player's ball is inside the *teeing area*, the player may move the ball to another spot within the *teeing area*, and may play it from a *tee* without penalty.

For example, a player makes his or her first *stroke* from the *teeing area*, barely making contact with the ball, and the ball either comes to rest on the ground within the *teeing area* or remains on the *tee*.

Since the ball is in the *teeing area*, the player may play the ball as it lies or, even though the ball is *in play*, may move the ball to any other spot within the *teeing area* and play from there without penalty. The player may also place the ball on a *tee* or adjust the height of the *tee* the ball is resting on.

6.3 Ball Used in Play of Hole

Purpose of Rule:

A hole is played as a progression of strokes made from the teeing area to the putting green and into the hole. After teeing off, the player is normally required to play the same ball until the hole is completed. The player gets a penalty for making a stroke at a wrong ball or a substituted ball when substitution is not allowed by the Rules.

6.3a Holing Out with Same Ball Played from Teeing Area

A player may play any conforming ball when starting a hole from the *teeing area* and may change balls between two holes.

The player must *hole out* with the same ball played from the *teeing area*, **except** when:

- That ball is *lost* or comes to rest *out of bounds*, or

- The player *substitutes* another ball (whether or not allowed to do so).

The player should put an identifying mark on the ball to be played (see Rule 7.2).

Rule 6.3a Interpretations:

6.3a/1 – What to Do When Balls Exchanged at Unknown Place

If, after *holing out*, two players discover that they finished a hole with the other player's ball but cannot establish whether the balls were exchanged during play of the hole, there is no penalty.

For example, after play of a hole, it was discovered that Player A *holed out* with Player B's ball and Player B *holed out* with Player A's ball. Both players are certain they *holed out* with the ball they played from the *teeing area*.

In this situation, and because a player is allowed to start each hole with any conforming ball (Rule 6.3a), it should be determined that the balls were exchanged before play on that hole began, unless there is evidence to the contrary.

6.3b   Substitution of Another Ball While Playing Hole

(1) **When Player Is Allowed and Not Allowed to Substitute Another Ball**. Certain Rules allow a player to change the ball he or she is using to play a hole by *substituting* another ball as the ball *in play*, and others do not:

- When taking relief under a Rule, including when either *dropping* a ball or placing a ball (such as when a ball will not stay in the *relief area* or when taking relief on the *putting green*), the player may use either the original ball or another ball (Rule 14.3a),

- When playing again from where a *previous stroke* was made, the player may use either the original ball or another ball (Rule 14.6), and

- When *replacing* a ball on a spot, the player is not allowed to *substitute* a ball and must use the original ball, with certain exceptions (Rule 14.2a).

(2) **Substituted Ball Becomes Ball in Play**. When a player *substitutes* another ball as the ball *in play* (see Rule 14.4):

- The original ball is no longer *in play*, even if it is at rest on the *course*.

- This is true even if the player:

  » *Substituted* another ball for the original ball when not allowed by the Rules (whether or not the player realized that he or she was *substituting* another ball), or

  » *Replaced*, *dropped* or placed the *substituted* ball (1) in a *wrong place*, (2) in a wrong way or (3) by using a procedure that does not apply.

- For how to correct any error before playing the *substituted* ball, see Rule 14.5.

If the player's original ball has not been found and the player put another ball *in play* to take *stroke-and-distance* relief (see Rules 17.1d, 18.1, 18.2b and 19.2a) or as allowed under a Rule that applies when it is *known or virtually certain* what happened to the ball (see Rules 6.3c, 9.6, 11.2c, 15.2b, 16.1e and 17.1c):

- The player must continue playing with the *substituted* ball, and

- The player must not play the original ball even if it is found on the *course* before the end of the three-minute search time (see Rule 18.2a(1)).

(3) **Making Stroke at Incorrectly Substituted Ball**. If a player makes a *stroke* at an incorrectly *substituted* ball:

- The player gets the *general penalty*.

- In *stroke play*, the player must then play out the hole with the incorrectly *substituted* ball.

If multiple Rule breaches result from a single act or related acts, see Rule 1.3c(4).

6.3c Wrong Ball

(1) **Making Stroke at Wrong Ball**. A player must not make a *stroke* at a *wrong ball*.

Exception – Ball Moving in Water: There is no penalty if a player makes a *stroke* at a *wrong ball* that is moving in water in a *penalty area* or in *temporary water*:

- The *stroke* does not count, and

- The player must correct the mistake under the Rules by playing the right ball from its original spot or by taking relief under the Rules.

Rule 6

Penalty for Playing *Wrong Ball* in Breach of Rule 6.3c(1): *General Penalty*.

In *match play*:

- If the player and *opponent* play each other's ball during the play of a hole, the first to make a *stroke* at a *wrong ball* gets the *general penalty* (loss of hole).

- If it is not known which *wrong ball* was played first, there is no penalty and the hole must be played out with the balls exchanged.

In *stroke play*, the player must correct the mistake by continuing play with the original ball by playing it as it lies or taking relief under the Rules:

- The *stroke* made with the *wrong ball* and any more strokes before the mistake is corrected (including *strokes* made and any penalty strokes solely from playing that ball) do not count.

- If the player does not correct the mistake before making a *stroke* to begin another hole or, for the final hole of the *round*, before returning his or her *scorecard*, the player is **disqualified**.

Rule 6.3c(1) Interpretations:
6.3c(1)/1 – Meaning of "Penalty Strokes Solely From Playing That Ball"

When the *strokes* made at a particular ball do not count in the player's score, any penalty strokes that the player gets while playing that ball do not count unless the player gets a penalty that could also apply to his or her ball *in play*.

Examples of penalties that are disregarded because they could not also apply to the ball *in play* include:

- Deliberately touching or causing the ball to *move* (Rule 9.4).

- The player's *caddie* standing behind the player while taking a *stance* (Rule 10.2b(4)).

- Touching sand in the backswing for the *stroke* (Rule 12.2b(2)).

Examples of penalties that are not disregarded because they also apply to the ball *in play* include:

- Making a practice *stroke* during a hole (Rule 5.5a).

- Playing a *wrong ball* (Rule 6.3c(1)).

- Asking for or giving *advice* (Rule 10.2a).

(2) **What to Do When Player's Ball Was Played by Another Player as Wrong Ball**. If it is *known or virtually certain* that the player's ball was played by another player as a *wrong ball*, the player must *replace* the original ball or another ball on the original spot (which if not known must be estimated) (see Rule 14.2).

This applies whether or not the original ball has been found.

6.3d When Player May Play More Than One Ball at a Time

A player may play more than one ball at a time on a hole only when:

- Playing a *provisional ball* (which will either become the ball *in play* or be abandoned, as provided in Rule 18.3c) or

- Playing two balls in *stroke play* to correct a possible *serious breach* in playing from a *wrong place* (see Rule 14.7b) or when uncertain about the right procedure to use (see Rule 20.1c(3)).

6.4 Order of Play When Playing Hole

Purpose of Rule:

Rule 6.4 covers the order of play throughout a hole. The order of play from the teeing area depends on who has the honour, and after that is based on which ball is farthest from the hole.

- In match play, the order of play is fundamental; if a player plays out of turn, the opponent may cancel that stroke and make the player play again.

- In stroke play, there is no penalty for playing out of turn, and players are both allowed and encouraged to play "ready golf" – that is, to play out of turn in a safe and responsible way.

6.4a Match Play

(1) **Order of Play**. The player and *opponent* must play in this order:

- Starting First Hole. At the first hole, the *honour* is decided by the order of the draw set by the *Committee* or, if there is no draw, by agreement or by using a random method (such as tossing a coin).

- Starting All Other Holes.

>> The player who wins a hole has the *honour* at the next *teeing area*.

>> If the hole was tied, the player with the *honour* at the previous *teeing area* keeps it.

>> If a player makes a timely ruling request (see Rule 20.1b) that has not yet been decided by the *Committee* and could affect who has the *honour* on the next hole, the *honour* is decided by agreement or by using a random method.

• After Both Players Start a Hole.

>> The ball that is farther from the *hole* is to be played first.

>> If the balls are the same distance from the *hole* or their relative distances are not known, the ball to be played first is decided by agreement or by using a random method.

(2) **Opponent May Cancel Player's Stroke Made Out of Turn.** If the player plays when it was the *opponent's* turn to play, there is no penalty but the *opponent* may cancel the *stroke*:

• This must be done promptly and before either player makes another *stroke*. When the *opponent* cancels the *stroke*, he or she cannot withdraw the cancellation.

• If the *opponent* cancels the *stroke*, the player must, when it is his or her turn to play, play a ball from where that *stroke* was made (see Rule 14.6).

• If the *opponent* does not cancel the *stroke*, the *stroke* counts and the ball is *in play* and must be played as it lies.

Exception – Playing Out of Turn by Agreement to Save Time: To save time:

• The player may invite the *opponent* to play out of turn or may agree to the *opponent's* request to play out of turn.

• If the *opponent* then makes the *stroke* out of turn, the player has given up the right to cancel the *stroke*.

See Rule 23.6 (order of play in *Four-Ball*).

6.4b   Stroke Play

(1) **Normal Order of Play.**

• Starting First Hole. The *honour* at the first *teeing area* is decided by the order of the draw set by the *Committee* or, if there is no draw, by agreement or by using a random method (such as tossing a coin).

- Starting All Other Holes.

  » The player in the group with the lowest gross score at a hole has the *honour* at the next *teeing area*; the player with the second lowest gross score should play next; and so on.

  » If two or more players have the same score at a hole, they should play in the same order as at the previous *teeing area*.

  » The *honour* is based on gross scores, even in a handicap competition.

- After All Players Have Started a Hole.

  » The ball that is farthest from the *hole* should be played first.

  » If two or more balls are the same distance from the *hole* or their relative distances are not known, the ball to be played first should be decided by agreement or by using a random method.

There is no penalty if a player plays out of turn, **except** that if two or more players agree to play out of turn to give one of them an advantage, each of them gets the *general penalty* (two penalty strokes).

(2) **Playing Out of Turn in a Safe and Responsible Way ("Ready Golf")**. Players are both allowed and encouraged to play out of turn in a safe and responsible way, such as when:

- Two or more players agree to do so for convenience or to save time,

- A player's ball comes to rest a very short distance from the *hole* and the player wishes to *hole out*, or

- An individual player is ready and able to play before another player whose turn it is to play under the normal order of play in (1), so long as in playing out of turn the player does not endanger, distract or interfere with any other player.

But if the player whose turn it is to play under (1) is ready and able to play and indicates that he or she wants to play first, other players should generally wait until that player has played.

A player should not play out of turn to gain an advantage over other players.

6.4c When Player Will Play Provisional Ball or Another Ball from Teeing Area

The order of play in this case is for all other players in the group to make their first *stroke* on the hole before the player plays the *provisional ball* or another ball from the *teeing area*.

If more than one player will play a *provisional ball* or another ball from the *teeing area*, the order of play is the same order as before.

For a *provisional ball* or another ball played out of turn, see Rules 6.4a(2) and 6.4b.

Rule 6.4c Interpretations:

6.4c/1 – Stroke Cannot Be Cancelled When Provisional Ball Played Out of Turn from Teeing Area

If a player who has the *honour* decides to play a *provisional ball* after his or her *opponent* has played a *provisional ball*, the player may not cancel the *opponent's stroke* with the *provisional ball* under Rule 6.4a(2).

For example, Player A has the *honour* and plays first from the *teeing area*. Player B (the *opponent*) plays next and since his or her ball may be *out of bounds*, decides to play a *provisional ball* and does so. After Player B plays the *provisional ball*, Player A decides that he or she will also play a *provisional ball*.

Since Player A only made his or her intentions to play a *provisional ball* known after Player B had played, Player A has abandoned the right to cancel Player B's *stroke* with the *provisional ball*. However, Player A may still play a *provisional ball*.

6.4d When Player Takes Relief or Will Play Provisional Ball from Anywhere Except Teeing Area

The order of play under Rules 6.4a(1) and 6.4b(1) in these two cases is:

(1) Taking Relief to Play Ball from a Different Place Than Where It Lies.

- When Player Becomes Aware That He or She Is Required to Take Stroke-and-Distance Relief. The player's order of play is based on the spot where his or her previous *stroke* was made.

- **When Player Has Choice to Play Ball as It Lies or Take Relief**

  » The player's order of play is based on the spot where the original ball lies (which if not known must be estimated) (see Rule 14.2).

  » This applies even when the player has already decided to take *stroke-and-distance* relief or to take relief to play from a different place than where the original ball lies (such as when the original ball is in a *penalty area* or will be treated as unplayable).

(2) **Playing Provisional Ball.** The order of play is for the player to play the *provisional ball* right after making the previous *stroke* and before anyone else plays a ball, **except:**

- When starting a hole from the *teeing area* (see Rule 6.4c), or

- When the player waits before deciding to play a *provisional ball* (in which case the player's order of play, once he or she has decided to play a *provisional ball*, is based on the spot where the previous *stroke* was made).

6.5 Completing Play of a Hole

A player has completed a hole:

- In *match play*, when:

  » The player *holes out* or the player's next *stroke* is conceded, or

  » The result of the hole is decided (such as when the *opponent* concedes the hole, the *opponent*'s score for the hole is lower than the player possibly could make or the player or *opponent* gets the **general penalty** (loss of hole)).

- In *stroke play*, when the player *holes out* under Rule 3.3c.

See Rules 21.1b(1), 21.2b(1), 21.3b(1) and 23.3c (when a player has completed a hole in other forms of *stroke play* or in *Four-Ball*).

Rule 6.5 Interpretations:

6.5/1 – Another Ball Played After Hole Was Unknowingly Completed

When a player has *holed out*, the play of that hole is completed and the player gets no penalty for playing another ball.

For example:

- Being unable to find his or her ball, the player puts another ball *in play* or concedes the hole (the concession is not valid as the hole is completed).

- After searching for his or her ball for three minutes, the player cannot find it and continues play with a *provisional ball*.

- Believing it is the original ball, the player plays a *wrong ball*.

If the player did not know the hole was completed and attempts to complete play of the hole with another ball, the player's further play is not considered practice (Rule 5.5a).

Playing the Ball
Rules 7–11

RULE 7

Ball Search: Finding and Identifying Ball

Purpose of Rule:

Rule 7 allows the player to take reasonable actions to fairly search for his or her ball in play after each stroke.

- But the player still must be careful, as a penalty will apply if the player acts excessively and causes improvement to the conditions affecting his or her next stroke.

- The player gets no penalty if the ball is accidentally moved in trying to find or identify it, but must then replace the ball on its original spot.

7.1 How to Fairly Search for Ball

7.1a Player May Take Reasonable Actions to Find and Identify Ball

A player is responsible for finding his or her ball *in play* after each *stroke*.

The player may fairly search for the ball by taking reasonable actions to find and identify it, such as:

- Moving sand and water, and

- Moving or bending grass, bushes, tree branches and other growing or attached natural objects, and also breaking such objects, **but** only if such breaking is a result of other reasonable actions taken to find or identify the ball.

If taking such reasonable actions as part of a fair search *improves the conditions affecting the stroke*:

- There is no penalty under Rule 8.1a if the *improvement* results from a fair search.

- **But** if the *improvement* results from actions that exceeded what was reasonable for a fair search, the player gets the **general penalty** for breach of Rule 8.1a.

In trying to find and identify the ball, the player may remove *loose impediments* as allowed in Rule 15.1 and may remove *movable obstructions* as allowed in Rule 15.2.

Rule 7.1a Interpretations:

7.1a/1 – Examples of Actions Unlikely to Be Part of a Fair Search

Examples of actions that are unlikely to be considered reasonable as part of a fair search, and will result in the *general penalty* if there is an *improvement* to *conditions affecting the stroke*, include:

- Taking an action to flatten areas of grass beyond what is reasonably necessary to walk through or search for the ball in the area where the ball is thought to lie;

- Purposely removing any growing thing from the ground; or

- Breaking a tree branch to allow easier access to the ball when it could have been reached without doing so.

7.1b   What to Do If Sand Affecting Lie of Player's Ball Is Moved While Trying to Find or Identify It

- The player must re-create the original *lie* in the sand, **but** may leave a small part of the ball visible if the ball had been covered by sand.

- If the player plays the ball without having re-created the original *lie*, the player gets the *general penalty*.

7.2   How to Identify Ball

A player's ball at rest may be identified in any one of these ways:

- By the player or anyone else seeing a ball come to rest in circumstances where it is known to be the player's ball.

- By seeing the player's identifying mark on the ball (see Rule 6.3a).

- By finding a ball with the same brand, model, number and condition as the player's ball in an area where the player's ball is expected to be (**but** this does not apply if an identical ball is in the same area and there is no way to know which one is the player's ball).

If a player's *provisional ball* cannot be distinguished from his or her original ball, see Rule 18.3c(2).

Rule 7.2 Interpretations:
7.2/1 – Identifying Ball That Cannot Be Retrieved

If a player sees a ball in a tree or some other location where he or she is unable to retrieve the ball, the player may not assume that it is his or hers but rather must identify it in one of the ways provided in Rule 7.2.

This may be done even though the player is unable to retrieve the ball, such as by:

- Using binoculars or a distance-measuring device to see a mark that definitely identifies it as the player's ball, or

- Determining that another player or spectator saw the ball come to rest in that specific location after the player's *stroke*.

7.3   Lifting Ball to Identify It

If a ball might be a player's ball but cannot be identified as it lies:

- The player may lift the ball to identify it (including by rotating it), but:

- The spot of the ball must first be *marked*, and the ball must not be cleaned more than needed to identify it (**except** on the *putting green*) (see Rule 14.1).

If the lifted ball is the player's ball or another player's ball, it must be *replaced* on its original spot (see Rule 14.2).

If the player lifts his or her ball under this Rule when not reasonably necessary to identify it (**except** on the *putting green* where the player may lift under Rule 13.1b), fails to *mark* the spot of the ball before lifting it or cleans it when not allowed, the player gets **one penalty stroke**.

Penalty for Playing Incorrectly *Substituted* Ball or Playing Ball from a *Wrong Place* in Breach of Rule 7.3: *General Penalty* Under Rule 6.3b or 14.7a.

If multiple Rule breaches result from a single act or related acts, see Rule 1.3c(4).

7.4   Ball Accidentally Moved in Trying to Find or Identify It

There is no penalty if the player's ball is accidentally *moved* by the player, *opponent* or anyone else while trying to find or identify it.

If this happens, the ball must be _replaced_ on its original spot (which if not known must be estimated) (see Rule 14.2). In doing so:

* If the ball was on, under or against any _immovable obstruction, integral object, boundary object_ or growing or attached natural object, the ball must be _replaced_ on its original spot on, under or against such object (see Rule 14.2c).

* If the ball was covered by sand, the original _lie_ must be re-created and the ball must be _replaced_ in that _lie_ (see Rule 14.2d(1)). **But** the player may leave a small part of the ball visible when doing so.

See also Rule 15.1a (restriction on deliberately removing certain _loose impediments_ before _replacing_ ball).

Penalty for Breach of Rule 7.4: _General Penalty._

Rule 7.4 Interpretations:

7.4/1 – Estimating Original Spot on Which to Replace Ball Moved During Search

When a player's ball is accidentally _moved_ during a search and its original spot where it must be _replaced_ must be estimated, the player should consider all reasonably available evidence about where the ball was located before it was _moved_.

For example, when estimating a ball's original spot, the player should consider:

* How the ball was found (for example, whether it was stepped on, kicked or _moved_ with a probing club or hand),

* If it was visible or not, and

* Its location relative to the ground and any growing objects, such as whether it was lying against or under the grass and how deep in the grass it was located.

In _replacing_ the ball, the player is not required to replace _loose impediments_ (such as leaves) that may have been moved since _loose impediments_ are not part of the _lie_ and, in many cases, it would be nearly impossible to reconstruct the original situation if _loose impediments_ were required to be replaced.

For example, while searching for a ball that is covered by leaves in a _penalty area_, the player kicks the ball and moves the leaves that were close to the ball. Although the ball must be _replaced_ on its original or estimated spot, the leaves do not need to be put back in their original position even when the ball would certainly have been lying under the leaves.

7.4/2 – Player Attempts to Dislodge Ball in Tree or Step on Ball in Tall Grass During Search

If a ball is accidentally moved when a player is trying to find or identify it, Rule 7.4 applies, and the ball must be replaced on the estimated spot without penalty.

This Rule also applies in situations when the player is attempting to find the ball and takes reasonable actions that are likely to reveal the ball's location by moving it.

Example of these reasonable actions include when the player:

- Believes his or her ball has come to rest in a tree and shakes the tree hoping to dislodge and find the ball, or

- Is walking through long grass while sweeping his or feet back and forth hoping to step on or move the ball to find it.

RULE 8

Course Played as It Is Found

Purpose of Rule:

Rule 8 covers a central principle of the game: "play the course as you find it". When the player's ball comes to rest, he or she normally has to accept the conditions affecting the stroke and not improve them before playing the ball. However, a player may take certain reasonable actions even if they improve those conditions, and there are limited circumstances where conditions may be restored without penalty after they have been improved or worsened.

8.1 Player's Actions That Improve Conditions Affecting the Stroke

To support the principle of "play the *course* as you find it", this Rule restricts what a player may do to *improve* any of these protected "*conditions affecting the stroke*" (anywhere on or off the *course*) for the next *stroke* the player will make:

CATS
LSSLR

- The *lie* of the player's ball at rest,

- The *area* of the player's intended *stance*,

- The *area* of the player's intended swing,

- The player's *line of play*, and

- The *relief area* where the player will *drop* or place a ball.

This Rule applies to actions taken both during a *round* and while play is stopped under Rule 5.7a.

It does not apply to:

- The removal of *loose impediments* or *movable obstructions*, which is allowed to the extent provided in Rule 15, or

- An action taken while a player's ball is in motion, which is covered by Rule 11.

8.1a Actions That Are Not Allowed

Except in the limited ways allowed in Rules 8.1b, c and d, a player must not take any of these actions if they *improve* the *conditions affecting the stroke*:

(1) Move, bend or break any:

GONO IIBT

- Growing or attached natural object,

- *Immovable obstruction, integral object* or *boundary object*, or

- Tee-marker for the *teeing area* when playing a ball from that *teeing area*.

(2) Move a *loose impediment* or *movable obstruction* into position (such as to build a *stance* or to improve the *line of play*).

(3) Alter the surface of the ground, including by: RDX2, HINSUS

- Replacing divots in a divot hole,

- Removing or pressing down divots that have already been replaced or other cut turf that is already in place, or

- Creating or eliminating holes, indentations or uneven surfaces.

(4) Remove or press down sand or loose soil.

(5) Remove dew, frost or water.

Penalty for Breach of Rule 8.1a: *General Penalty*.

Rule 8.1a Interpretations:

8.1a/1 – Examples of Actions That Are Likely to Create Potential Advantage

Examples of actions that are likely to *improve conditions affecting the stroke* (that is, likely to give a player a potential advantage) include when:

- A player repairs a pitch-mark in the *general area* or replaces a divot in a divot hole a few yards in front of his or her ball on the *line of play* before making a *stroke* that might be affected by the pitch-mark or divot hole (for example, a putt or a low-running chip).

- A player's ball lies in a greenside *bunker*, and the player smooths footprints in front of the ball on his or her *line of play* before playing a short shot intended to be played over the smoothed area (see Rule 12.2b(2) – When Touching Sand Does Not Result in Penalty).

8.1a/2 – Examples of Actions Unlikely to Create Potential Advantage

Examples of actions that are unlikely to *improve conditions affecting the stroke* (that is, unlikely to give a player a potential advantage) include when:

- Before making a 150-yard approach shot from the *general area,* a player repairs a small pitch-mark, smooths a footprint in a *bunker* or replaces a divot in a divot hole on his or her *line of play* several yards in front of the ball.

- A player's ball lies in the middle of a long, shallow-faced fairway *bunker,* and the player smooths footprints several yards in front of the ball and on his or her *line of play* before playing a long shot over the smoothed area (see Rule 12.2b(2) – When Touching Sand Does Not Result in Penalty).

8.1a/3 – Player Who Improves Conditions for Intended Stroke in Breach Even if Different Stroke Is Made

If a player intends to play a ball in a certain way and *improves conditions affecting the stroke* for that particular *stroke,* and the penalty cannot be avoided by restoration, the player is in breach of Rule 8.1a whether he or she goes on to play the ball in that way or plays it in a different way that is unaffected by that improvement.

For example, if a player breaks a branch that interferes with his or her area of *stance* or swing for an intended *stroke* when a *stance* could have been taken without breaking the branch, a penalty cannot be avoided by playing the ball in a different direction or by taking relief to a different location where that branch would have had no effect on the *stroke.* This also applies if a player broke the branch when starting a *hole* and *moved* to a different location within the *teeing* area.

See Rule 8.1c for whether a penalty may be avoided by restoring *improved conditions.*

8.1a/4 – Example of Moving, Bending or Breaking an Immovable Obstruction

Part of a fence that is situated *out of bounds* (and so is not a *boundary object*) leans onto the *course* and the player pushes it back into an upright position. This action breaches Rule 8.1a, which prohibits a player from *improving conditions affecting the stroke* by moving *immovable obstructions.* The player gets the *general penalty* unless the player restores the *conditions* by returning the fence to its original position before his or her next *stroke* as permitted by Rule 8.1c (Avoiding Penalty by Restoring Improved Conditions).

In such a situation, although Rule 8.1a prohibits moving, bending or breaking the *immovable obstruction*, the player has the option to take free relief from interference by the part of the *immovable obstruction* that is leaning onto the *course* under Rule 16.1b. (Relief from Abnormal Course Conditions).

8.1a/5 – Building Stance by Positioning Object Such as Towel Is Not Permitted

The definition of "*stance*" includes not only where a player places his or her feet to stand, but also where the player's entire body is positioned in preparing for or making a *stroke*.

For example, a player is in breach of Rule 8.1a for *improving* the area of intended *stance* if he or she places a towel or other object on a bush to protect his or her body while making a *stroke*.

If a player needs to play from his or her knees because the ball is under a tree, and the player places a towel on the ground to avoid getting wet or dirty, the player is building his or her *stance*. But a player is allowed to wrap a towel around his or her waist or put on rain gear before kneeling to play the shot (see Rule 10.2b(5) – Physical Help and Protection From Elements).

If a player has positioned an object in a way that is not allowed but realizes the mistake before playing the ball, the penalty may be avoided by removing the object before making the *stroke*, so long as there has been no other improvement to *conditions affecting the stroke*.

8.1a/6 – Altering Surface of Ground to Build Stance Is Not Permitted

A player is allowed to place his or her feet firmly in taking a *stance*, but is in breach of Rule 8.1a if he or she alters the ground where the *stance* will be taken if altering the ground *improves* the area of intended *stance*.

Examples of altering the ground that are likely to *improve conditions affecting the stroke* include:

- Knocking down sand on the side of a *bunker* with a foot to create a level area to stand on.

- Excessively digging feet into soft ground to gain a firmer foundation for the *stance*.

A player is in breach of Rule 8.1a as soon as he or she has *improved conditions* by altering ground conditions to build a *stance* and cannot avoid a penalty by attempting to restore the ground conditions to their original state.

The restriction on altering the ground (Rule 8.1a(3)) does not include removing *loose impediments* or *movable obstructions* from the area of intended *stance*, such as removing large amounts of pine needles or leaves from where a player will stand to play the ball.

8.1a/7 – Player May Probe Near Ball to Determine if Tree Roots, Rocks or Obstructions Are Below Surface of Ground, but Only if This Does Not Improve Conditions

Rule 8.1a does not prohibit a player from touching the ground within an area covered by *conditions affecting the stroke*, so long as those *conditions* are not *improved*.

For example, without *improving* any of the *conditions affecting the stroke*, when the ball lies anywhere on the *course*, a player may probe the area around the ball with a tee or other object to see whether his or her club might strike a root, rock or *obstruction* below the surface of the ground when the *stroke* is made.

However, see 12.2b/2 if the player probes sand in a *bunker* to test the condition of the sand.

8.1a/8 – Altering Surface of Ground in Relief Area Is Not Allowed

Before *dropping* a ball to take relief, a player must not replace a divot in a divot hole in the *relief area* or take other actions to alter the ground surface in a way that *improves conditions affecting the stroke*.

However, this prohibition applies only after the player becomes aware that he or she is required or allowed to *drop* a ball in that *relief area*.

For example, if a player plays a ball, replaces the divot and only then realizes that he or she must or may play again from there under penalty of *stroke and distance* because the ball is *out of bounds*, is in a *penalty area*, is unplayable or that a *provisional ball* should be played, the player is not in breach of Rule 8.1a if that replaced divot is in the *relief area*.

8.1a/9 – When Divot Is Replaced and Must Not Be Removed or Pressed Down

Rule 8.1a(3) prohibits *improving conditions affecting the stroke* by pressing down, removing or repositioning a divot in a divot hole, which is treated as part of the ground (and not as a *loose impediment*), even if it is not yet attached or growing.

A divot has been replaced when most of it, with the roots down, is in a divot hole (whether or not the divot is in the same divot hole that it came from).

8.1b Actions That Are Allowed

In preparing for or making a *stroke*, a player may take any of these actions and there is no penalty even if doing so *improves* the *conditions affecting the stroke*:

(1) Fairly search for his or her ball by taking reasonable actions to find and identify it (see Rule 7.1a).

(2) Take reasonable actions to remove *loose impediments* (see Rule 15.1) and *movable obstructions* (see Rule 15.2).

(3) Take reasonable actions to *mark* the spot of a ball and to lift and *replace* the ball under Rules 14.1 and 14.2.

(4) Ground the club lightly right in front of or right behind the ball.

But this does not allow:

- Pressing the club on the ground, or

- When a ball is in a *bunker*, touching the sand right in front of or right behind the ball (see Rule 12.2b(1)).

(5) Firmly place the feet in taking a *stance*, including a reasonable amount of digging in with the feet in sand or loose soil.

(6) Fairly take a *stance* by taking reasonable actions to get to the ball and take a *stance*.

But when doing so the player:

- Is not entitled to a normal *stance* or swing, and

- Must use the least intrusive course of action to deal with the particular situation.

(7) Make a *stroke* or the backswing for a *stroke* which is then made.

But when the ball is in a *bunker*, touching the sand in the *bunker* in taking the backswing is not allowed under Rule 12.2b(1).

(8) In the *teeing area*:

- Place a *tee* in or on the ground (see Rule 6.2b(2)),

- Move, bend or break any growing or attached natural object (see Rule 6.2b(3)), and

- Alter the surface of the ground, remove or press down sand and soil, or remove dew, frost or water (see Rule 6.2b(3)).

(9) In a *bunker*, smooth sand to care for the *course* after a ball played from the *bunker* is outside the *bunker* (see Rule 12.2b(3)).

(10) On the *putting green*, remove sand and loose soil and repair damage (see Rule 13.1c).

(11) Move a natural object to see if it is loose.

But if the object is found to be growing or attached, it must stay attached and be returned as nearly as possible to its original position.

Rule 8.1b Interpretations:

8.1b/1 – Meaning of "Ground the Club Lightly"

Rule 8.1b allows a player to ground the club lightly directly in front of or behind the ball, even if that *improves* his or her *lie* or area of intended swing.

"Ground the club lightly" means allowing the weight of the club to be supported by the grass, soil, sand or other material on or above the ground surface.

But the player gets the penalty under Rule 8.1a if he or she *improves* the *lie* or area of intended swing by pressing the club down more than lightly.

See Rule 12.2b(1) (When Touching Sand Results in Penalty) for when a player gets a penalty for touching sand in a *bunker*.

8.1b/2 – Player Allowed to Dig in Firmly with Feet More Than Once in Taking Stance

Rule 8.1b allows a player to place his or her feet firmly in taking a *stance*, and this may be done more than once in preparing to make a *stroke*.

For example, a player may enter a *bunker* without a club, dig in with his or her feet in taking a *stance* to simulate playing the ball, leave to get a club, and then dig in again with his or her feet and make the *stroke*.

8.1b/3 – Examples of "Fairly Taking a Stance"

Although a player is allowed to play in any direction, he or she is not entitled to a normal *stance* or swing and must adapt to the situation and use the least intrusive course of action.

Examples of actions that are considered fairly taking a *stance* and are allowed under Rule 8.1b even if the action results in an *improvement* include:

- Backing into a branch or a *boundary object* when that is the only way to take a *stance* for the selected *stroke*, even if this moves the branch or *boundary object* out of the way or causes it to bend or break.

- Bending a branch with his or her hands to get under a tree to play a ball when that is the only way to get under the tree to take a *stance*.

See 8.1b/4 for when a player gets a penalty for doing more than is necessary to take a *stance*.

8.1b/4 – Examples of Not "Fairly Taking a Stance"

Examples of actions that are not considered fairly taking a *stance* and will result in a penalty under Rule 8.1a if they *improve conditions affecting the stroke* include:

- Deliberately moving, bending or breaking branches with a hand, a leg or the body to get them out of the way of the backswing or *stroke*.

- Standing on tall grass or weeds in a way that pushes them down and to the side so that they are out of the way of the area of intended *stance* or swing, when a *stance* could have been taken without doing so.

- Hooking one branch on another or braiding two weeds to keep them away from the *stance* or swing.

- Using a hand to bend a branch that obscures the view of the ball after taking the *stance*.

- Bending an interfering branch in taking a *stance* when a *stance* could have been taken without doing so.

8.1b/5 – Improving Conditions in Teeing Area Is Limited to Ground

Rule 8.1b(8) allows a player to take actions to *improve conditions affecting the stroke* in the *teeing area*. This limited exception to Rule 8.1a is intended to allow a player to only alter physical conditions on the surface of the ground inside the *teeing area* itself (including removing any natural objects that are growing from there) whether the ball is teed or played from the ground.

This exception does not allow a player to *improve conditions affecting the stroke* for his or her tee shot by taking actions outside the *teeing area*, such as breaking tree branches located either outside the *teeing area* or when they are rooted outside the *teeing area* but are hanging over the *teeing area* and may interfere with the area of intended swing.

8.1b/6 – Player Smooths Bunker to "Care for the Course" After Playing Out of Bunker

After a ball in a *bunker* is played and is outside the *bunker*, Rules 8.1b(9) and 12.2b(3) use care for the *course* to allow the player to restore the *bunker* to the condition that it should be in, even if the restoring *improves* the player's *conditions affecting the stroke*. This is true even if the player's action is deliberately taken both to care for the *course* and to *improve conditions affecting the stroke*.

For example, a player's ball comes to rest in a large *bunker* near a *putting green*. Not being able to play towards the *hole*, he or she plays out backwards towards the *teeing area* with the ball coming to rest outside the *bunker*.

In this case, the player may smooth the areas that he or she had altered as a result of playing the ball (including footprints getting to the ball) and may also smooth any other areas in the *bunker*, whether created by the player or those that were already present when the player arrived to play from the *bunker*.

8.1b/7 – When Damage That Is Partially On and Partially Off Putting Green May Be Repaired

If an individual area of damage is both on and off a *putting green*, the entire area of damage may be repaired.

For example, if a ball mark is partially on and partially off the edge of the *putting green*, it is unreasonable to allow a player to repair only the portion of damage on the *putting green*. Therefore, the entire ball mark (both on and off the *putting green*) may be repaired.

The same applies to other individual areas of damage, such as *animal* tracks or hoof marks, or club indentations.

However, if a portion of damage extends off the green and is not identifiable as part of the damage on the green, it may not be repaired if the repair *improves* the *conditions affecting the stroke*.

For example, an entire shoe print that starts on the *putting green* and extends off it may be repaired. However, if one shoe print is on the *putting green* and another shoe print is off the *putting green*, only the shoe print on the *putting green* may be repaired as they are two separate areas of damage.

8.1c Avoiding Penalty by Restoring Conditions Improved in Breach of Rule 8.1a(1) or 8.1a(2)

If a player has *improved* the *conditions affecting the stroke* by moving, bending or breaking an object in breach of Rule 8.1a(1) or moving an object into position in breach of Rule 8.1a(2):

- There is no penalty if, before making the next *stroke*, the player eliminates that *improvement* by restoring the original *conditions* in the ways allowed in (1) and (2) below.

- **But** if the player *improves* the *conditions affecting the stroke* by taking any of the other actions covered by Rules 8.1a(3)-(5), he or she cannot avoid penalty by restoring the original *conditions*.

(1) **How to Restore Conditions Improved by Moving, Bending or Breaking Object**. Before making the *stroke*, the player may avoid penalty for breach of Rule 8.1a(1) by restoring the original object as nearly as possible to its original position so that the *improvement* created by the breach is eliminated, such as by:

  - Replacing a *boundary object* (such as a boundary stake) that had been removed or moving the *boundary object* back into its original position after it had been pushed to a different angle, or

  - Returning a tree branch or grass, or an *immovable obstruction* to its original position after it had been moved.

  But the player cannot avoid penalty:

  - If the *improvement* is not eliminated (such as when a *boundary object* or branch has been bent or broken in a significant way so that it cannot be returned to the original position), or

  - By using anything other than the original object itself in trying to restore *conditions*, such as:

    » Using a different or additional object (for example, placing a different stake in a hole from which a boundary stake had been removed or tying a moved branch into place), or

    » Using other materials to repair the original object (for example, using tape to repair a broken *boundary object* or branch).

(2) **How to Restore Conditions Improved by Moving an Object into Position**. Before making the *stroke*, the player may avoid penalty for breach of Rule 8.1a(2) by removing the object that was moved into position.

8.1d   Restoring Conditions Worsened After Ball Came to Rest

If the *conditions affecting the stroke* are worsened after a player's ball came to rest:

(1) **When Restoration of Worsened Conditions Is Allowed**. If the *conditions affecting the stroke* are worsened by any person other than the player or by an *animal* or artificial object, without penalty under Rule 8.1a the player may:

- Restore the original *conditions* as nearly as possible.

- *Mark* the spot of the ball and lift, clean and *replace* the ball on its original spot (see Rules 14.1 and 14.2), if it is reasonable to do so to restore the original *conditions* or if material ended up on the ball when the *conditions* were worsened.

- If the worsened *conditions* cannot be easily restored, lift and *replace* the ball by placing it on the nearest spot (not nearer the *hole*) that (1) has the most similar *conditions affecting the stroke*, (2) is within one *club-length* of its original spot, and (3) is in the same *area of the course* as that spot.

  Exception – Lie of Ball Worsened When or After a Ball Is Lifted or Moved and Before It Is Replaced: This is covered by Rule 14.2d unless the *lie* was worsened when play was stopped and the ball was lifted in which case this Rule applies.

Rule 8.1d(1) Interpretations:

8.1d(1)/1 – Examples Where Player Is Allowed to Restore Conditions Altered by the Actions of Another Person or Outside Influence

Examples of when restoration is allowed include when:

- A player's *line of play* is worsened by a pitch-mark in the *general area* that was made by a ball played by someone else after the player's ball came to rest.

- A player's *lie* or area of intended *stance* or intended swing is worsened when another player's *stroke* creates a divot or deposits sand, soil, grass or other material on or around his or her ball.

- A player's ball in a *bunker* lies close to another player's ball in the *bunker*, and that other player's *stance* or swing in making the *stroke* worsens one or more of the player's *conditions affecting the stroke*.

In all such situations, the player is allowed to restore *conditions* without penalty, but is not required to do so.

8.1d(1)/2 – Player Is Entitled to Have Loose Impediments or Movable Obstructions Left Where They Were When Ball Came to Rest

Generally speaking, a player is entitled to the *conditions affecting the stroke* that he or she had when the ball came to rest. Any player may move *loose impediments* or *movable obstructions* (Rules 15.1 and 15.2), but if this worsened *conditions affecting the* stroke of another player, that player may restore the *conditions* by replacing the objects under Rule 8.1d.

For example, a player has a downhill putt and picks up *loose impediments* between his or her ball and the *hole* but deliberately leaves some behind the *hole*. Another player removes the *loose impediments* behind the *hole* that might have served as a backstop for the player's ball.

Since the player's *conditions affecting the stroke* have been worsened, he or she is allowed to replace the *loose impediments*.

(2) When Restoration of Worsened Conditions Is Not Allowed.

If the *conditions affecting the stroke* are worsened by the player, by a natural object or by *natural forces* such as wind or water, the player must not *improve* those worsened conditions in breach of Rule 8.1a (**except** as allowed in Rules 8.1c(1), 8.1c(2) and Rule 13.1c).

Rule 8.1d(2) Interpretations:

8.1d(2)/1 – Examples of Conditions Altered by a Natural Object or Natural Forces Where Player Is Not Allowed to Restore Worsened Conditions

Rule 8.1d does not allow a player to restore *conditions affecting* the *stroke* that were altered by a natural object or by *natural forces* (such as wind or water).

Examples of when restoration is not allowed include when:

- A branch falls from a tree and alters the *lie* of the player's ball or the area of his or her *stance* or swing, without causing the ball to *move*.

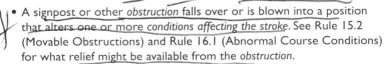

- A signpost or other *obstruction* falls over or is blown into a position that alters one or more *conditions affecting the stroke*. See Rule 15.2 (Movable Obstructions) and Rule 16.1 (Abnormal Course Conditions) for what relief might be available from the *obstruction*.

8.1d(2)/2 – Player Is Not Allowed to Restore Conditions Affecting the Stroke When Worsened by Caddie or Another Person at Player's Request

A player is not allowed to restore *conditions affecting the stroke* if the *conditions* are worsened by the player himself or herself.

This also includes when the *conditions* are worsened by the player's *caddie* or *partner* or another person taking an action that is authorized by the player.

Examples of situations where the *conditions* could not be restored include:

- The player's *caddie* or *partner* walks across a *bunker* to get a rake and leaves footprints in the sand that worsen the player's *line of play*, or
- The player asks another person to remove a gallery control rope and, in removing the rope, a branch that had been held back by the rope is freed and worsens the area of the player's intended swing.

8.1d(2)/3 – If Player Enters a Bunker on the Line of Play He or She Must Not Restore Worsened Conditions

Players should be careful when taking actions that might affect the *conditions affecting the stroke* because worsening these areas means that the player must accept the worsened *condition*.

For example, a player is taking relief from an *abnormal course condition* behind a *bunker* and the *dropped* ball rolls into the *bunker*. If the player creates footprints while walking into the *bunker* to retrieve the ball to *drop* it again, he or she is not allowed to restore the *bunker* to its previous *condition* under Rule 8 because the player was responsible for worsening its *condition*.

In such a case, the player could use another ball for the second *drop* (Rule 14.3a) or take additional care when retrieving the original ball to avoid worsening the *conditions affecting the stroke*.

Penalty for Playing Incorrectly *Substituted* Ball or Playing Ball from a *Wrong Place* in Breach of Rule 8.1d: General Penalty Under Rule 6.3b or 14.7a.

If multiple Rule breaches result from a single act or related acts, see Rule 1.3c(4).

See Rules 22.2 (in *Foursomes*, either *partner* may act for the *side* and action by the *partner* is treated as action of the player); **23.5** (in *Four-Ball*, either *partner* may act for the *side* and action by the *partner* concerning the player's ball or *equipment* is treated as action of the player).

8.2 Player's Deliberate Actions to Alter Other Physical Conditions to Affect the Player's Own Ball at Rest or Stroke to Be Made

8.2a When Rule 8.2 Applies

This Rule only covers a player's deliberate actions to alter other physical conditions to affect his or her ball at rest or *stroke* to be made.

This Rule does not apply to a player's actions to:

- Deliberately deflect or stop his or her own ball or to deliberately alter any physical conditions to affect where the ball might come to rest (which is covered by Rules 11.2 and 11.3), or

- Alter the player's *conditions affecting the stroke* (which is covered by Rule 8.1a).

8.2b Prohibited Actions to Alter Other Physical Conditions

A player must not deliberately take any actions listed in Rule 8.1a (**except** as allowed in Rule 8.1b, c or d) to alter any such other physical conditions to affect:

- Where the player's ball might go or come to rest after his or her next *stroke* or a later *stroke*, or

- Where the player's ball at rest might go or come to rest if it *moves* before the *stroke* is made (for example, when the ball is on a steep slope and the player is concerned that it might roll into a bush).

Exception – Actions to Care for the Course: There is no penalty under this Rule if the player alters any such other physical conditions to care for the *course* (such as smoothing footprints in a *bunker* or replacing a divot in a divot hole).

Rule 8.2b Interpretations:

8.2b/1 Examples of Player's Deliberate Actions to Improve Other Physical Conditions Affecting His or Her Own Play

Rule 8.2 applies only to altering physical conditions other than *conditions affecting the stroke* when the player's ball is at rest on the *course* or when he or she does not have a ball *in play*.

Examples of a player's actions listed in Rule 8.1a (Actions Not Allowed to Improve Conditions) that would be a breach of Rule 8.2 if taken to deliberately *improve* other physical conditions to affect his or her own play (except as expressly allowed in Rules 8.1b or c) include when:

- A player's ball is just short of the *putting green* and, although his or her *line of play* is straight at the *hole*, the player is concerned his or her ball might come to rest in a nearby *bunker*. Before making the *stroke*, the player smooths sand in the *bunker* to make sure of a good *lie* if the shot to be played goes into the *bunker*.

- A player's ball lies at the top of a steep hill and, because the player is concerned that the wind might blow the ball down the hill away from the *hole* before he or she is able to play it, the player deliberately presses down the grass at the bottom of the hill in case the ball might come to rest there.

- *Replacing* or placing a ball when returning it to play by firmly pressing it into the surface of the ground to help prevent it from being *moved* by wind or gravity and plays the ball. Since the spot of a ball includes vertical distance, the ball is in a *wrong place*. As these related acts breach multiple Rules, the player only gets the *general penalty*. See Rule 1.3c(4) (Applying Penalties to Multiple Breaches).

Penalty for Breach of Rule 8.2: *General Penalty*.

See Rules 22.2 (in *Foursomes*, either *partner* may act for the *side* and action by the *partner* is treated as action of the player); **23.5** (in *Four-Ball*, either *partner* may act for the *side* and action by the *partner* concerning the player's ball or *equipment* is treated as action of the player).

8.3 Player's Deliberate Actions to Alter Physical Conditions to Affect Another Player's Ball at Rest or Stroke to Be Made

8.3a When Rule 8.3 Applies

This Rule only covers a player's deliberate actions to alter physical conditions to affect another player's ball at rest or *stroke* to be made by that other player.

It does not apply to a player's actions to deliberately deflect or stop another player's ball in motion or to deliberately alter any physical conditions to affect where the ball might come to rest (which is covered by Rules 11.2 and 11.3).

8.3b Prohibited Actions to Alter Other Physical Conditions

A player must not deliberately take any of the actions listed in Rule 8.1a (**except** as allowed in Rule 8.1b, c or d) to:

- *Improve* or worsen the *conditions affecting the stroke* of another player, or

- Alter any other physical conditions to affect:

  » Where another player's ball might go or come to rest after that player's next *stroke* or a later *stroke*, or

  » Where another player's ball at rest might go or come to rest if it *moves* before the *stroke* is made.

Exception – Actions to Care for the Course: There is no penalty under this Rule if the player alters any such other physical conditions to care for the *course* (such as smoothing footprints in a *bunker* or replacing a divot in a divot hole).

Penalty for Breach of Rule 8.3: *General Penalty.*

See Rules 22.2 (in *Foursomes*, either *partner* may act for the *side* and action by the *partner* is treated as action of the player); **23.5** (in *Four-Ball*, either *partner* may act for the *side* and action by the *partner* concerning the player's ball or *equipment* is treated as action of the player).

Rule 8.3 Interpretations:

8.3/1 – Both Players Are Penalized if Physical Conditions Are Improved with Other Player's Knowledge

If a player asks, authorizes or allows another player to deliberately alter physical conditions to *improve* his or her play:

- The player acting on the request will get the *general penalty* under Rule 8.3, and

- The player who requests, authorizes or allows the improvement will also get the *general penalty* under either Rule 8.1 (Player's Actions That Improve Conditions Affecting the Stroke) or 8.2 (Player's Deliberate Actions to Alter Other Physical Conditions to Affect the Player's Own Ball at Rest or Stroke to Be Made), whichever applies.

For _example_, in _stroke play_, unaware of the Rules, Player A asks Player B to break a branch from a tree that is on Player A's _line of play_ and Player B complies; both players are penalized. Player A gets two penalty strokes for a breach of Rule 8.1 because Player B broke the branch at the request of Player A. Player B gets two penalty strokes for a breach of Rule 8.3.

RULE 9

Ball Played as It Lies; Ball at Rest Lifted or Moved

Purpose of Rule:

Rule 9 covers a central principle of the game: "play the ball as it lies".

- If the player's ball comes to rest and is then moved by natural forces such as wind or water, the player normally must play it from its new spot.

- If a ball at rest is lifted or moved by anyone or any outside influence before the stroke is made, the ball must be replaced on its original spot.

- Players should take care when near any ball at rest, and a player who causes his or her own ball or an opponent's ball to move will normally get a penalty (except on the putting green).

9.1 Ball Played as It Lies

Rule 9 applies to a ball *in play* at rest on the *course* and applies both during a *round* and while play is stopped under Rule 5.7a.

9.1a Playing Ball from Where It Came to Rest

A player's ball at rest on the *course* must be played as it lies, **except** when the Rules require or allow the player:

- To play a ball from another place on the *course*, or

- To lift a ball and then *replace* it on its original spot.

9.1b What to Do When Ball Moves During Backswing or Stroke

If a player's ball at rest begins moving after the player has begun the *stroke* or the backswing for a *stroke* and the player goes on to make the *stroke*:

- The ball must not be *replaced*, no matter what caused it to *move*.

- Instead, the player must play the ball from where it comes to rest after the *stroke*.

- If the player caused the ball to *move*, see Rule 9.4b to find out if there is a penalty.

Penalty for Playing Incorrectly *Substituted* Ball or Playing Ball from a *Wrong Place* in Breach of Rule 9.1: *General Penalty* Under Rule 6.3b or 14.7a.

If multiple Rule breaches result from a single act or related acts, see Rule 1.3c(4).

9.2 Deciding Whether Ball Moved and What Caused It to Move

9.2a Deciding Whether Ball Moved

A player's ball at rest is treated as having *moved* only if it is *known or virtually certain* that it did.

If the ball might have *moved* but this is not *known or virtually certain*, it is treated as not having *moved* and must be played as it lies.

Rule 9.2a Interpretations:

9.2a/1 – When a Ball Is Treated as Having Moved

As stated in the definitions, to "move", a ball at rest must leave its original spot and come to rest on any other spot and the movement must be enough that it can be seen by the naked eye. In order to treat the ball as *moved*, there must be *knowledge or virtual certainty* that the ball has *moved*.

An example of when it is *known or virtually certain* that a ball has *moved* is:

- A player marks, lifts and *replaces* his or her ball on the *putting green*. As the player walks away, the ball rolls a short distance and comes to rest. The player does not see this, but another player observes the ball *moving* and informs the player. Since it is *known* that the ball *moved*, the player must *replace* the ball on its original spot under Rule 13.1d(2) (Ball Moved by Natural Forces).

An example of when it is not *known or virtually certain* that a ball has *moved* is:

- Player A and Player B play their approach shots to the *putting green*, but because of the contours of the *putting green* they could not see where the two balls came to rest. Unknown to the players, Player B's ball struck Player A's ball at rest and it rolled some distance farther from the *hole*. As long as this information does not come to the attention of the players before Player A makes the next *stroke*, Player

A does not get a penalty for playing from where his or her ball came to rest after being struck by Player B's ball.

9.2a/2 – Player Responsible for Actions That Cause Ball to Move Even When Not Aware Ball Moved

In the second bullet point in 9.2a/1, the player did not make a *stroke* from a *wrong place* because it was not *known or virtually certain* that the ball had *moved* at the time the ball was played.

However, if it was the player's actions (or the actions of the player's *caddie* or *partner*) that caused the ball to *move*, the player is always responsible for the movement, even when the player is not aware that his or her actions caused the ball to *move*.

Examples of this include:

* A player's ball lies in the *general area* and he or she removes a *loose impediment* near the ball that causes the ball to *move*. Because the player is not looking at the ball, he or she was not aware that the ball *moved*. The player gets one penalty stroke under Rule 15.1b (Ball Moved When Removing Loose Impediment) and he or she must *replace* the ball.

* A player's *caddie* or his or her *partner* removed roping and staking, and this causes the player's ball to *move* while the player was watching another player make a *stroke*. There is no penalty for *moving* the ball under Rule 15.2a(1) (Removal of Movable Obstruction) but the player must *replace* the ball.

In both of these situations, even though the player was not aware that the ball *moved*, if the player makes a *stroke* without first replacing the ball, the player gets the *general penalty* for playing from a *wrong place* under Rule 14.7a (Place from Where Ball Must Be Played).

9.2b   Deciding What Caused Ball to Move

When a player's ball at rest has *moved*:

* It must be decided what caused it to *move*.

* This determines whether the player must *replace* the ball or play it as it lies and whether there is a penalty.

(1) **Four Possible Causes**. The Rules recognize only four possible causes for a ball at rest that *moves* before the player makes a *stroke*:

* *Natural forces*, such as wind or water (see Rule 9.3),

- The player, including the player's caddie (see Rule 9.4),

- The opponent in match play, including the opponent's caddie (see Rule 9.5), or

- An outside influence, including any other player in stroke play (see Rule 9.6).

See Rules 22.2 (in Foursomes, either partner may act for the side and action by the partner is treated as action of the player); 23.5 (in Four-Ball, either partner may act for the side and action by the partner concerning the player's ball or equipment is treated as action of the player).

(2) "Known or Virtually Certain" Standard for Deciding What Caused Ball to Move.

- The player, the opponent or an outside influence is treated as having caused the ball to move only if it is known or virtually certain to be the cause.

- If it is not known or virtually certain that at least one of these was the cause, the ball is treated as having been moved by natural forces.

In applying this standard, all reasonably available information must be considered, which means all information the player knows or can get with reasonable effort and without unreasonably delaying play.

See Interpretations for Definition of "Known or Virtually Certain" for guidance.

9.3 Ball Moved by Natural Forces

If natural forces (such as wind or water) cause a player's ball at rest to move:

- There is no penalty, and

- The ball must be played from its new spot.

Exception – Ball on Putting Green Must Be Replaced If It Moves After Having Already Been Lifted and Replaced (see Rule 13.1d): If the player's ball on the putting green moves after the player had already lifted and replaced the ball on the spot from which it moved:

- The ball must be replaced on its original spot (which if not known must be estimated) (see Rule 14.2).

- This is true no matter what caused it to move (including natural forces).

Penalty for Playing Incorrectly *Substituted* Ball or Playing Ball from a *Wrong Place* in Breach of Rule 9.3: *General Penalty* Under Rule 6.3b or 14.7a.

If multiple Rule breaches result from a single act or related acts, see Rule 1.3c(4).

9.4 Ball Lifted or Moved by Player

This Rule applies only when it is *known or virtually certain* that a player (including the player's *caddie*) lifted his or her ball at rest or caused it to *move*.

9.4a When Lifted or Moved Ball Must Be Replaced

If the player lifts his or her ball at rest or causes it to *move*, the ball must be *replaced* on its original spot (which if not known must be estimated) (see Rule 14.2), **except**:

- When the player lifts the ball under a Rule to take relief or to *replace* the ball on a different spot (see Rules 14.2d and 14.2e), or

- When the ball *moves* only after the player has begun the *stroke* or the backswing for a *stroke* and then goes on to make the *stroke* (see Rule 9.1b).

Rule 9.4a Interpretations:

9.4a/1 – Procedure When Player's Ball Is Dislodged From Tree

Rule 9.4 applies wherever a ball *in play* is on the *course*. This includes when a ball is in a tree. However, when the player does not intend to play the ball as it lies but is trying only to identify it, or intends to retrieve it to use another Rule, the Exceptions to Rule 9.4b apply and there is no penalty. For example:

- In searching for his or her ball, a player sees a ball lying in a tree but cannot identify it. The player climbs the tree in an attempt to identify the ball and in doing so accidentally dislodges the ball from the tree. The ball is identified as the player's ball.

  In this case, since the ball was accidentally *moved* in taking reasonable actions to identify it, there is no penalty for *moving* the ball (Rule 7.4).

  The player must *replace* the ball or may directly use a relief Rule (such as Rule 19 – Unplayable Ball).

In two situations, the player's only option is to take relief under a relief Rule:

» The player is unable to *replace* the ball because he or she cannot reach the spot where the ball was *moved* from when the player was identifying it, or

» The player can reach that spot but the ball will not come to rest on that spot and the player cannot reach the spot where it will come to rest under Rule 14.2e (Replaced Ball Does Not Stay on Spot)

• A player's ball has not yet been found but is believed to be lodged in a tree in the *general area*. The player makes it clear that if the ball is found he or she will take unplayable ball relief under Rule 19. The player shakes the tree; the ball falls down and is identified by the player within three minutes of starting search.

The player may now take relief under Rule 19 (Unplayable Ball) adding only the one penalty stroke prescribed by that Rule with no additional penalty for causing the ball to *move*. If not known, the player must estimate the spot where the ball lay in the tree when applying Rule 19.

However, if the player *moves* the ball when he or she is not intending to identify it or without intending to take relief under another Rule, the player does get a penalty for a breach of Rule 9.4. For example:

• A player's ball is in a tree and he or she intends to play it. In preparing for the *stroke*, the player accidentally dislodges the ball.

The player gets one penalty stroke under Rule 9.4 for causing the ball to *move*. The player must *replace* the ball or may take relief directly under a relief Rule. If the player takes relief under Rule 19, he or she gets a total of two penalty strokes, one under Rule 9.4 and one under Rule 19.

9.4b Penalty for Lifting or Deliberately Touching Ball or Causing It to Move

If the player lifts or deliberately touches his or her ball at rest or causes it to *move*, the player gets one penalty stroke.

But there are four exceptions:

Exception 1 – Player Allowed to Lift or Move Ball: There is no penalty when the player lifts the ball or causes it to *move* under a Rule that:

• Allows the ball to be lifted and then *replaced* on its original spot,

• Requires a *moved* ball to be *replaced* on its original spot, or

- Requires or allows the player to *drop* or place a ball again or to play a ball from a different place.

Exception 2 – Accidental Movement Before Ball Is Found: There is no penalty when the player accidentally causes the ball to *move* while trying to find or identify it (see Rule 7.4).

Exception 3 – Accidental Movement on Putting Green: There is no penalty when the player accidentally causes the ball to *move* on the *putting green* (see Rule 13.1d), no matter how that happens.

Exception 4 – Accidental Movement Anywhere Except on Putting Green While Applying Rule: There is no penalty when the player accidentally causes the ball to *move* anywhere except on the *putting green* while taking reasonable actions to:

- *Mark* the spot of the ball or lift or *replace* the ball, when allowed to do so (see Rules 14.1 and 14.2),

- Remove a *movable obstruction* (see Rule 15.2),

- Restore worsened conditions, when allowed to do so (see Rule 8.1d),

- Take relief under a Rule, including in determining whether relief is available under a Rule (such as swinging a club to see if there is interference from a condition), or where to take relief (such as determining the *nearest point of complete relief*), or

- Measure under a Rule (such as to decide the order of play under Rule 6.4).

Penalty for Playing Incorrectly *Substituted* Ball or Playing Ball from a *Wrong Place* in Breach of Rule 9.4: *General Penalty* Under Rule 6.3b or 14.7a.

If multiple Rule breaches result from a single act or related acts, see Rule 1.3c(4).

Rule 9.4b Interpretations:

9.4b/1 – Ball Deliberately Touched but Not Moved Results in Penalty to Player

When the ball *in play* is deliberately touched by the player, even if it does not *move*, the player gets one penalty stroke under Rule 9.4b.

For example, a player gets one penalty stroke if he or she:

- Without first *marking* the ball's spot, rotates the ball on the *putting green* to line up the trademark with the *hole*, even if the ball remains on the same spot. If the player had *marked* the ball before touching or rotating it, there would have been no penalty.

- Without first *marking* the ball's spot, rotates the ball anywhere on the course to identify it and the ball is the player's ball.

- Deliberately touches the ball with a club in preparing to make a *stroke*.

- Holds the ball steady with his or her hand or positions a pine cone or stick against the ball to prevent the ball from *moving* while he or she removes some *loose impediments* or brushes something off the ball.

9.4b/2 – Meaning of "Trying to Find"

In Rule 7.4 (Ball Accidentally Moved in Trying to Find or Identify It) and Exception 2 of Rule 9.4, there is no penalty if a ball is accidentally *moved* while "trying to find" it. "Trying to find" includes actions that can reasonably be considered part of searching for the ball, including the actions allowed by Rule 7.1 (How to Fairly Search for Ball). It does not include actions before a search begins such as walking to the area where the ball is expected to be.

For example, a player's ball is hit towards a wooded area. The player is not aware the ball has struck a tree and deflected back towards the *teeing area*. When the player is still some distance from the area where he or she believes the ball is likely to be and before starting to search, the player accidentally kicks his or her ball. Because this was not while trying to find the ball, the player gets one penalty stroke under Rule 9.4b for accidentally *moving* his or her ball and must *replace* the ball.

9.4b/3 – Ball Moved When Search Temporarily Stopped

In 9.4b/2 a player gets a penalty if the ball is *moved* when he or she is not trying to find it.

However, if a player accidentally *moves* his or her ball when search is temporarily stopped due to circumstances outside the player's control, the player gets no penalty for *moving* the ball.

For example:

- The player stops searching for his or her ball to get out of the way of another group who is going to play through. While getting out of the way, the player accidentally *moves* his or her ball.

- The *Committee* suspends play and the player begins to leave the area and accidentally steps on and *moves* his or her ball.

137

9.4b/4 – Meaning of "While" in Rule 9.4b Exception 4

Exception 4 uses "while" to govern the time period when the Exception will apply to a player who *moves* his or her ball *in play* as a result of "reasonable actions". For the meaning of "reasonable actions", see 9.4b/2.

The use of the word "while" indicates that every reasonable action in applying a Rule has a beginning and an end and, if the ball's movement occurs during the time that such action is taking place, the Exception applies.

Examples of situations covered by Exception 4, therefore resulting in no penalty for causing the ball to *move* include when:

- The player finds a ball that he or she believes to be his or her ball *in play*. In the process of identification, the player approaches the ball to *mark* and lift it and accidentally slips and *moves* the ball.

  Even though the player was not marking or lifting the ball when it was *moved*, it was still *moved* while the player was identifying the ball.

- The player has *dropped* a ball when taking relief and then reaches down to lift the *tee* that was marking the *relief area*. When standing up, he or she accidentally drops a club that he or she was holding and the club hits and *moves* the ball *in play*.

  Even though the player has already *dropped* the ball to take relief, the ball was moved while he or she was taking relief.

9.4b/5 – Meaning of "Reasonable Actions" in Rule 9.4b Exception 4

In many situations, the Rules require a player to perform actions near or next to the ball (such as lifting, *marking*, measuring, etc.). If the ball is accidentally *moved* while taking these "reasonable actions", Exception 4 to Rule 9.4 applies.

However, there are other situations when the player is taking actions farther from the ball where, even though the ball might be *moved* as a result of those actions, Exception 4 also applies because those actions are "reasonable".

These include when:

- The player approaches his or her ball for the purpose of taking relief and accidentally kicks a rock or accidentally drops his or her club that strikes and *moves* the ball.

- The player removes stakes and rope (*movable obstructions*) used for gallery control purposes some distance ahead of the ball and in removing one of the stakes, he or she causes the others to become loose and fall to the ground, *moving* his or her ball *in play*.

- The player restores the *line of play* by brushing sand away from the fringe with his or her hat under Rule 8.1d (Restoring Conditions Worsened After Ball Came to Rest), and the sand splashes onto the ball and causes it to *move*.

In other situations, Exception 4 to Rule 9.4 does not apply because the player's actions are not "reasonable".

These include when:

- The player approaches his or her ball to take relief and kicks a rock in frustration that accidentally strikes and *moves* the ball.

- The player throws a club down into the *relief area* in preparing to measure, and the club accidentally strikes and *moves* the ball.

- The player lifts a *bunker* rake or his or her club and throws it out of a *bunker*. The rake or club falls back into the *bunker*, striking and *moving* the ball.

9.4b/6 – Player Lifts Ball Under Rule 16.1b That Allows Free Relief but Then Decides Not to Take Free Relief

In the *general area*, if a player lifts his or her ball with the intention to take free relief under Rule 16.1b (Abnormal Course Conditions), but then decides not to proceed under that Rule despite relief being available, the player's right to lift the ball under Rule 16.1b is no longer valid.

After lifting the ball but before doing anything else, the player has the following options:

- *Replace* the ball in its original position with a penalty of one stroke (Rule 9.4b);

- *Replace* the ball in its original position with a penalty of one stroke (Rule 9.4b) and then take relief under Rule 19.2 (Unplayable Ball Relief), getting an additional penalty of one stroke for a total of two penalty strokes;

- Directly take relief under Rule 19.2b or c, without *replacing* the ball and using the spot where the original ball lay to determine the reference point for the relief procedure, getting a penalty of one stroke under Rule 19.2 and an additional penalty of one stroke under Rule 9.4b for a total of two penalty strokes;

- *Drop* the ball under Rule 16.1b and then either play the ball as it lies without penalty or using its new position to determine the reference point, take relief under any of the options of Rule 19.2, getting a penalty of only one stroke; or

- Directly take *stroke-and-distance* relief, without *dropping* the ball under Rule 16.1b, getting a penalty of one stroke under Rule 19.2a and no penalty under Rule 9.4b, as the player does not need to establish a new reference point before taking relief under Rule 19.2a.

9.5 Ball Lifted or Moved by Opponent in Match Play

This Rule applies only when it is *known or virtually certain* that the *opponent* (including the *opponent's caddie*) lifted a player's ball at rest or caused it to *move*.

If the *opponent* plays the player's ball as a *wrong ball*, that is covered by Rule 6.3c(1), not by this Rule.

9.5a When Lifted or Moved Ball Must Be Replaced

If the *opponent* lifts or *moves* the player's ball at rest, the ball must be *replaced* on its original spot (which if not known must be estimated) (see Rule 14.2), except:

- When the *opponent* is conceding the next *stroke*, a hole or the match (see Rule 3.2b), or

- When the *opponent* lifts or *moves* the ball at the player's request because the player intends to apply a Rule to take relief or to *replace* the ball on a different spot.

9.5b Penalty for Lifting or Deliberately Touching Ball or Causing It to Move

If the *opponent* lifts or deliberately touches the player's ball at rest or causes it to *move*, the *opponent* gets **one penalty stroke**.

But there are several **exceptions**:

Exception 1 – Opponent Allowed to Lift Player's Ball: There is no penalty when the *opponent* lifts the ball:

- When conceding the next *stroke*, a hole or the match to the player, or

- At the player's request.

Exception 2 – Marking and Lifting Player's Ball on Putting Green by Mistake: There is no penalty when the *opponent* marks the spot of the player's ball and lifts it on the *putting green* in the mistaken belief that it is the *opponent's* own ball.

~~Exception 3~~ **– Same Exceptions as for the Player:** There is no
penalty when the *opponent* accidentally causes the ball to *move* while
taking any of the actions covered by Exceptions 2, 3 or 4 in Rule 9.4b.

Penalty for Playing Incorrectly *Substituted* **Ball or Playing Ball
from a** *Wrong Place* **in Breach of Rule 9.5:** *General Penalty* **Under
Rule 6.3b or 14.7a.**

If multiple Rule breaches result from a single act or related acts, see Rule
1.3c(4).

Rule 9.5b Interpretations:

**9.5b/1 – Player Declares Found Ball as His or Hers and
This Causes Opponent to Lift Another Ball That Turns
Out to Be the Player's Ball** *no penalty; search*

Under Rule 9.5b, an *opponent* gets one penalty stroke for lifting the player's
ball unless one of the Exceptions applies.

For example, during a search Player A finds a ball and states that it is his
or hers. Player B (the *opponent*) finds another ball and lifts it. Player A then
realizes the found ball was not in fact his or her ball and the ball Player B
lifted was Player A's ball.

Since the ball was not in fact found when Player B lifted Player A's ball, it is
considered to have been accidentally *moved* during search and Exception 3
to Rule 9.5b applies. The player or *opponent* must *replace* the ball without
penalty to anyone.

9.6 Ball Lifted or Moved by Outside Influence

If it is *known or virtually certain* that an *outside influence* (including another
player in *stroke play* or another ball) lifted or *moved* a player's ball:

* There is no penalty, and
* The ball must be *replaced* on its original spot (which if not known
  must be estimated) (see Rule 14.2).

This applies whether or not the player's ball has been found.

But if it is not *known or virtually certain* that the ball was lifted or moved
by an *outside influence* and the ball is lost, the player must take *stroke-and-
distance* relief under Rule 18.2.

If the player's ball is played as a *wrong ball* by another player, that is
covered by Rule 6.3c(2), not by this Rule.

Penalty for Playing Incorrectly *Substituted* Ball or Playing Ball from a *Wrong Place* in Breach of Rule 9.6: *General Penalty* Under Rule 6.3b or 14.7a.

If multiple Rule breaches result from a single act or related acts, see Rule 1.3c(4).

Rule 9.6 Interpretations:

9.6/1 – Outside Influence Moved by Wind Causes Ball to Move

Wind is not itself an *outside influence*, but if wind causes an *outside influence* to *move* a player's ball, Rule 9.6 applies.

For example, if a player's ball comes to rest in a plastic bag (*movable obstruction*) that is lying on the ground, and a gust of wind blows the bag and *moves* the ball, the bag (*outside influence*) is considered to have *moved* the ball. The player may either:

- Directly take relief under Rule 15.2a by estimating the point right under where the ball was at rest in the plastic bag before the ball was *moved*, or

- *Replace* the ball *moved* by the bag by applying Rule 9.6 (by *replacing* the ball and the bag) and then decide to play the ball as it lies or take relief under Rule 15.2a (Relief From Movable Obstruction).

9.6/2 – Where to Replace Ball When It Was Moved from Unknown Location

If a ball has been *moved* by an *outside influence* and the original spot where the ball lay is not known, the player must use his or her reasonable judgment (Rule 1.3b(2)) to determine where the ball had come to rest before it was *moved*.

For example, on a particular hole, part of the *putting green* and adjoining area cannot be seen by the players playing towards it. Near the *putting green* there is a *bunker* and a *penalty area*. A player plays towards the *putting green* and cannot tell where the ball came to rest. The players see a person (*outside influence)* with a ball. The person drops the ball and runs away. The player identifies it as his or her ball. The player does not know whether the ball was on the *putting green*, in the *general area*, in the *bunker*, or in the *penalty area*.

As it is impossible to know where the ball should be *replaced*, the player must use reasonable judgment. If it is equally likely the ball came to rest on the *putting green*, in the *general area*, in the *bunker*, or in the *penalty area*, a reasonable judgment would be to estimate the ball came to rest in the *general area*.

9.6/3 – Player Learns That Ball Moved After Stroke Made

If it is not *known or virtually certain* that the player's ball has been *moved* by an *outside influence*, the player must play the ball as it lies. If information that the ball was in fact *moved* by an *outside influence* only becomes known to the player after the ball has been played, the player did not play from a *wrong place* because this knowledge did not exist when the player made the stroke.

9.6/4 – Ball at Rest Played and then Discovered to Have Been Moved by Outside Influence; Ball Turns Out to be Wrong Ball

If a player discovers, after playing his or her ball, that it had been *moved* onto the *course* by an *outside influence* after the ball had come to rest *out of bounds*, the player has played a *wrong ball* (see Definition). Because it was not *known or virtually certain* at the time the ball was played, the player does not get a penalty for playing a *wrong ball* under Rule 6.3c(1) but might need to correct the mistake by proceeding under Rule 18.2b (What to Do When Ball Is Lost or Out of Bounds) depending when that discovery is made:

- In *match play*, the player must correct the mistake if the discovery that the ball was *moved* onto the *course* by the *outside influence* is made before the *opponent* makes his or her next *stroke* or takes a similar action (such as conceding the hole).

  If that discovery occurs after the *opponent* makes his or her next *stroke* or takes a similar action, the player must continue to play out the hole with the *wrong ball*.

- In *stroke* play, the player must correct the mistake if the discovery that the ball was *moved* onto the *course* by an *outside influence* is made before making a *stroke* to begin another hole or, for the final hole of the *round*, before returning his or her *scorecard*.

  If that discovery occurs after the player has made a *stroke* on the next hole or, for the final hole of the *round*, after returning his or her *scorecard*, the player's score with the *wrong ball* counts.

9.7 Ball-Marker Lifted or Moved

This Rule covers what to do if a *ball-marker* that is *marking* the spot of a lifted ball is lifted or moved before the ball is *replaced*.

9.7a Ball or Ball-Marker Must Be Replaced

If a player's *ball-marker* is lifted or moved in any way (including by *natural forces*) before the ball is *replaced*, the player must either:

- *Replace* the ball on its original spot (which if not known must be estimated) (see Rule 14.2), or

- Place a *ball-marker* to *mark* that original spot.

9.7b Penalty for Lifting Ball-Marker or Causing It to Move

If the player, or his or her *opponent* in *match play*, lifts the player's *ball-marker* or causes it to move, the player or *opponent* gets **one penalty stroke**.

Exception – Rule 9.4b and 9.5b Exceptions Apply to Lifting Ball-Marker or Causing It to Move: In all cases where the player or *opponent* gets no penalty for lifting the player's ball or accidentally causing it to *move*, there is also no penalty for lifting or accidentally moving the player's *ball-marker*.

Penalty for Playing Incorrectly *Substituted* Ball or Playing Ball from a *Wrong Place* in Breach of Rule 9.7: *General Penalty* Under Rule 6.3b or 14.7a.

If multiple Rule breaches result from a single act or related acts, see Rule 1.3c(4).

RULE 10

Preparing for and Making a Stroke; Advice and Help; Caddies

Purpose of Rule:

Rule 10 covers how to prepare for and make a stroke, including advice and other help the player may get from others (including caddies). The underlying principle is that golf is a game of skill and personal challenge.

10.1 Making a Stroke

Purpose of Rule:

Rule 10.1 covers how to make a stroke and several acts that are prohibited in doing so. A stroke is made by fairly striking at a ball with the head of a club. The fundamental challenge is to direct and control the movement of the entire club by freely swinging the club without anchoring it.

10.1a Fairly Striking the Ball

In making a *stroke*:

- The player must fairly strike at the ball with the head of the club such that there is only momentary contact between the club and the ball and must not push, scrape or scoop the ball.

- If the player's club accidentally hits the ball more than once, there has been only one *stroke* and there is no penalty.

Rule 10.1a Interpretations:

10.1a/1 – Examples of Pushing, Scraping or Scooping

These terms have overlapping meanings but can be defined through these three examples of using the club in a manner not allowed by the Rule:

- A player *holes* a short putt by striking the ball with the bottom of the clubhead, using a motion similar to that used in making a shot in billiards or shuffleboard. *Moving the ball like this is a push.*

- A player moves the club along the surface of the ground pulling it towards him or her. *Moving* the ball like this is a scrape.

- A player slides a club beneath and very close to the ball. The player then lifts and *moves* the ball by use of a forward and upward motion. *Moving* the ball like this is a scoop.

10.1a/2 – Player May Use Any Part of Clubhead to Fairly Strike Ball

In fairly striking a ball, any part of the clubhead may be used, including the toe, heel and back of the clubhead.

10.1a/3 – Other Material May Intervene Between Ball and Clubhead During Stroke

In fairly striking a ball, it is not necessary for the clubhead to make contact with the ball. Sometimes other material may intervene.

An example of fairly striking a ball includes when a ball is lying against the base of a fence defining *out of bounds* and the player makes a *stroke* at the *out-of-bounds* side of the fence to make the ball *move*.

10.1b Anchoring the Club

In making a *stroke*, the player must not anchor the club, either:

- Directly, by holding the club or a gripping hand against any part of the body (**except** that the player may hold the club or a gripping hand against a hand or forearm), or

- Indirectly, through use of an "anchor point," by holding a forearm against any part of the body to use a gripping hand as a stable point around which the other hand may swing the club.

If the player's club, gripping hand or forearm merely touches his or her body or clothing during the *stroke*, without being held against the body, there is no breach of this Rule.

For the purposes of this Rule, "forearm" means the part of the arm below the elbow joint and includes the wrist.

DIAGRAM 10.1b: ANCHORING THE CLUB

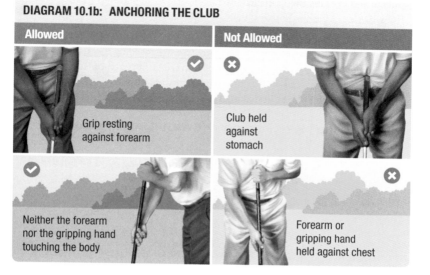

Allowed	Not Allowed
Grip resting against forearm	Club held against stomach
Neither the forearm nor the gripping hand touching the body	Forearm or gripping hand held against chest

Rule 10.1b Interpretations:

10.1b/1 – Player Must Not Anchor the Club with Forearm Against Body

Holding a forearm against the body during a *stroke* is an indirect means of anchoring the club.

For an "anchor point" to exist, two things must happen: (1) the player must hold a forearm against the body; and (2) the player must grip the club so that the hands are separated and work independently from each other.

For example, in making a *stroke* with a long putter, the player's forearm is held against his or her body to establish a stable point, while the bottom hand is held down the shaft to swing the lower portion of the club.

However, a player is allowed to hold one or both forearms against his or her body in making a *stroke*, so long as doing so does not create an anchor point.

10.1b/2 – Deliberate Contact with Clothing During Stroke Is a Breach

Clothing held against the body by a club or gripping hand is treated as if it is part of the player's body for the purpose of applying Rule 10.1b. The concept of a free-flowing swing may not be circumvented by having something intervene between the player's body and club or hand.

For example, if a player is wearing a rain jacket and is using a mid-length putter, and presses the club into his or her body, the player is in breach of Rule 10.1b.

Additionally, if the player deliberately uses a gripping hand to hold an article of clothing worn on any part of the body (such as holding the sleeve of a shirt with a hand) while making a *stroke*, there is a breach of Rule 4.3 (Prohibited Use of Equipment) since that is not its intended use and doing so might assist the player in making that *stroke*.

10.1b/3 – Inadvertent Contact with Clothing During Stroke Is Not a Breach

Touching an article of clothing with the club or gripping hand and making a *stroke* is allowed.

This might occur in various situations where a player:

- Wears loose fitting clothes or rain gear,
- Has a physical size or build that causes the arms naturally to rest close to the body,
- Holds the club extremely close to the body, or
- For some other reason touches his or her clothing in making a *stroke*.

10.1c Making Stroke While Standing Across or on Line of Play

The player must not make a *stroke* from a stance with a foot deliberately placed on each side of, or with either foot deliberately touching, the *line of play* or an extension of that line behind the ball.

For this Rule only, the *line of play* does not include a reasonable distance on either side.

Exception – There Is No Penalty If Stance Is Taken Accidentally or to Avoid Another Player's Line of Play.

10.1d Playing Moving Ball

A player must not make a *stroke* at a moving ball:

- A ball *in play* is "moving" when it is not at rest on a spot.
- If a ball that has come to rest is wobbling (sometimes referred to as oscillating) but stays on or returns to its original spot, it is treated as being at rest and is not a moving ball.

But there are three **exceptions** where there is no penalty:

Exception 1 – Ball Begins to Move Only after Player Begins Backswing for Stroke: Making a *stroke* at a moving ball in this situation is covered by Rule 9.1b, not by this Rule.

Exception 2 – Ball Falling Off Tee: Making a *stroke* at a ball falling off a *tee* is covered by Rule 6.2b(5), not by this Rule.

Exception 3 – Ball Moving in Water: When a ball is moving in *temporary water* or in water in a *penalty area*:

- The player may make a *stroke* at the moving ball without penalty, or
- The player may take relief under Rule 16.1 or 17, and may lift the moving ball.

In either case, the player must not unreasonably delay play (see Rule 5.6a) to allow the wind or water current to move the ball to a better place.

Penalty for Breach of Rule 10.1: General Penalty.

In *stroke play*, a *stroke* made in breach of this Rule counts and the player gets **two penalty strokes**.

10.2 Advice and Other Help

Purpose of Rule:

A fundamental challenge for the player is deciding the strategy and tactics for his or her play. So there are limits to the advice and other help the player may get during a round.

10.2a Advice

During a *round*, a player must not:

- Give *advice* to anyone in the competition who is playing on the *course*,
- Ask anyone for *advice*, other than the player's *caddie* or
- Touch another player's *equipment* to learn information that would be *advice* if given by or asked of the other player (such as touching the other player's clubs or bag to see what club is being used).

This does not apply before a *round*, while play is stopped under Rule 5.7a or between *rounds* in a competition.

See **Rules 22, 23 and 24** (in forms of play involving *partners*, a player may give *advice* to his or her *partner* or the *partner's caddie* and may ask the *partner* or *partner's caddie* for *advice*).

Rule 10.2a Interpretations:

10.2a/1 – Player May Get Information from Shared Caddie

If a *caddie* is being shared by more than one player, any of the players sharing that *caddie* may seek information from him or her.

For example, two players are sharing a *caddie* and both hit tee shots into a similar area. One of the players gets a club to make the *stroke*, while the other is undecided. The undecided player is allowed to ask the shared *caddie* what club the other player chose.

10.2a/2 – Player Must Try to Stop Ongoing Advice That Is Given Voluntarily

If a player gets *advice* from someone other than his or her *caddie* (such as a spectator) without asking for it, he or she gets no penalty. However, if the player continues to get *advice* from that same person, the player must try to stop that person from giving *advice*. If the player does not do so, he or she is treated as asking for that *advice* and gets the penalty under Rule 10.2a.

In a team competition (Rule 24), this also applies to a player who gets *advice* from a team captain who has not been named an advice giver.

10.2b Other Help

(1) **Pointing Out Line of Play for Ball Anywhere Except on Putting Green.** A player may have his or her *line of play* pointed out by:

- Having his or her *caddie* or any other person stand on or close to the player's *line of play* to show where it is, **but** that person must move away before the *stroke* is made.

- Having an object (such as a bag or towel) set down on the *course* to show the *line of play*, **but** the object must be removed before the *stroke* is made.

(2) **Pointing Out Line of Play for Ball on Putting Green.** Before the *stroke* is made, only the player and his or her *caddie* may point out the player's *line of play*, **but** with these limitations:

- The player or *caddie* may touch the *putting green* with a hand, foot or anything he or she is holding, **but** must not *improve* the *conditions affecting the stroke* in breach of Rule 8.1a, and

- The player or *caddie* must not set an object down anywhere on or off the *putting green* to show the *line of play*. This is not allowed even if that object is removed before the *stroke* is made.

While the *stroke* is being made, the caddie must not deliberately stand in a location on or close to the player's *line of play* or do anything else (such as pointing out a spot on the *putting green*) to point out the *line of play*.

Exception – Caddie Attending Flagstick: The *caddie* may stand in a location on or close to the player's line of play to attend the *flagstick*.

(3) **No Setting Down Object to Help in Taking Stance**. A player must not take a *stance* for the *stroke* using any object that was set down by or for the player to help in lining up his or her feet or body, such as a club set down on the ground to show the *line of play*.

If the player takes a *stance* in breach of this Rule, he or she cannot avoid penalty by backing away from the *stance* and removing the object.

Rule 10.2b(3) Interpretations:

10.2b(3)/1 – Setting Clubhead on Ground Behind Ball to Help the Player Take a Stance is Allowed

Rule 10.2b(3) does not allow a player to set down an object (such as an alignment rod or a golf club) to help the player take a *stance*.

However, this prohibition does not prevent a player from setting his or her clubhead behind the ball, such as when a player stands behind the ball and places the clubhead perpendicular to the *line of play* and then walks around from behind the ball to take his or her *stance*.

(4) **Restriction on Caddie Standing Behind Player.** When a player begins taking a *stance* for the *stroke* and until the *stroke* is made:

- The player's *caddie* must not deliberately stand in a location on or close to an extension of the *line of play* behind the ball for any reason.

- If the player takes a *stance* in breach of this Rule, he or she cannot avoid penalty by backing away.

Exception – Ball on Putting Green: When the player's ball is on the *putting green*, there is no penalty under this Rule if the player backs away from the *stance* and does not begin to take the *stance* again until after the *caddie* has moved out of that location.

See Rules 22, 23 and 24 (in forms of play involving *partners*, a player's *partner* and the *partner's caddie* may take the same actions (with the same limitations) as the player's *caddie* may take under Rules 10.2b(2) and (4)).

DIAGRAM 10.2b: CADDIE STANDING IN LOCATION ON OR CLOSE TO LINE OF PLAY BEHIND BALL

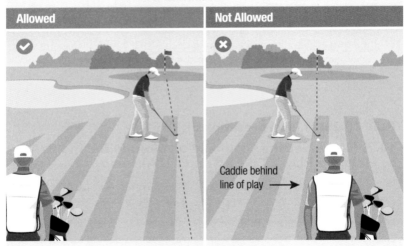

Allowed	Not Allowed

Caddie behind line of play →

The caddie is not standing in a location on or close to an extension of the line of play behind the ball when the player begins taking the stance for the stroke and, provided the caddie does not move into such a position prior to the stroke being made, there is no breach of Rule 10.2b(4).

The caddie is standing in a location on or close to an extension of the line of play behind the ball when the player begins taking the stance for the stroke, so there is a breach of Rule 10.2b(4).

Rule 10.2b(4) Interpretations:

10.2b(4)/1 – Examples of When Player Begins Taking His or Her Stance

Rule 10.2b(4) does not allow a player to have his or her *caddie* deliberately stand behind him or her when the player begins taking a *stance* because aiming at the intended target is one of the challenges the player must overcome alone.

There is no set procedure for determining when a player has begun to take a *stance* since each player has his or her own set-up routine. However, if a player has his or her feet or body close to a position where useful guidance on aiming at the intended target could be given, it should be decided that the player has begun to take his or her *stance*.

Examples of when a player has begun to take a *stance* include when:

- The player is standing beside the ball but facing the *hole* with his or her club behind the ball, and then starts to turn his or her body to face the ball.

- After standing behind the ball to determine the target line, the player takes a step forward and then starts to turn his or her body and puts a foot in place for the *stroke*.

(5) **Physical Help and Protection from Elements**. A player must not make a *stroke*:

- While getting physical help from his or her *caddie* or any other person, or

- With his or her *caddie* or any other person or object deliberately positioned to give protection from sunlight, rain, wind or other elements.

Before the *stroke* is made, such help or protection is allowed, **except as prohibited in Rules 10.2b(3) and (4)**.

This Rule does not prohibit the player from taking his or her own actions to protect against the elements while making a *stroke*, such as by wearing protective clothing or holding an umbrella over his or her own head.

Rule 10.2b(5) Interpretations:

10.2b(5)/1 – Player May Ask Another Person Who Was Not Deliberately Positioned to Move or Remain in Place

Although a player may not place an object or position a person for the purpose of blocking the sunlight from the ball, the player may ask a person (such as a spectator) not to move when that spectator is already in position, so that a shadow remains over the ball, or may ask that spectator to move, so that his or her shadow is no longer over the ball.

10.2b(5)/2 – Player May Wear Protective Clothing

Although a player must not *improve conditions affecting the stroke* to protect against the elements, he or she may wear protective clothing to protect against the elements.

For example, if a player's ball comes to rest right next to a cactus, it would breach Rule 8.1a (Actions That Improve Conditions Affecting the Stroke) if he or she placed a towel on the cactus to *improve* his or her area of intended *stance*. However, a towel may be wrapped around the player's body to protect him or her from the cactus.

Penalty for Breach of Rule 10.2: *General Penalty.*

10.3 Caddies

Purpose of Rule:

The player may have a caddie to carry the player's clubs and give advice and other help during the round, but there are limits to what the caddie is allowed to do. The player is responsible for the caddie's actions during the round and will get a penalty if the caddie breaches the Rules.

10.3a Caddie May Help Player During Round

(1) **Player Allowed Only One Caddie at a Time**.

A player may have a *caddie* to carry, transport and handle his or her clubs, give *advice* and help him or her in other ways allowed during a *round*, **but** with these limitations:

• The player must not have more than one *caddie* at any one time.

- The player may change *caddies* during a *round*, **but** must not do so temporarily for the sole purpose of getting *advice* from the new *caddie*.

  Whether or not the player has a *caddie*, any other person who walks or rides along with the player or who carries other things for the player (such as a rainsuit, umbrella or food and drink) is not the player's *caddie* unless he or she is named as such by the player or also carries, transports or handles the player's clubs.

(2) **Two or More Players May Share a Caddie.** When there is a Rules issue involving a specific action of a shared *caddie* and it needs to be decided which player the action was taken for:

- If the *caddie's* action was taken at the specific direction of one of the players sharing the *caddie*, the action was taken for that player.

- If none of those players specifically directed that action, the action is treated as taken for the player sharing the *caddie* whose ball was involved.

See Committee Procedures, Section 8; Model Local Rule H-1 (the *Committee* may adopt a Local Rule prohibiting or requiring the use of *caddies* or restricting a player's choice of *caddie*).

Penalty for Breach of Rule 10.3a:

- The player gets the *general penalty* for each hole during which he or she is helped by more than one *caddie* at any one time.

- If the breach happens or continues between two holes, the player gets the *general penalty* for the next hole.

Rule 10.3a Interpretations:

10.3a/1 – Player Transports Clubs on Motorized Golf Cart and Hires Individual to Perform All Other Functions of a Caddie

A player whose clubs are transported on a motorized golf cart that he or she is driving is allowed to hire an individual to perform all the other duties of a *caddie*, and this individual is considered to be a *caddie*.

This arrangement is allowed provided the player has not also hired someone else to drive the cart. In such a case, the cart driver is also a *caddie* since he is transporting the player's clubs, and the player gets a penalty under Rule 10.3a(1) for having more than one *caddie*.

10.3a/2 – Player May Caddie for Another Player When Not Playing a Round

A player in a competition may *caddie* for another player in the same competition, except when the player is playing his or her *round* or when a Local Rule restricts the player from being a *caddie*.

For example:

- If two players are playing in the same competition but at different times on the same day, they are allowed to *caddie* for each other.

- In *stroke play*, if one player in a group withdraws during a *round*, he or she may caddie for another player in the group.

10.3b What a Caddie May Do

These are examples of what a *caddie* is allowed and not allowed to do:

(1) **Actions Always Allowed**. A *caddie* may always take these actions when allowed under the Rules:

- Carry, transport and handle the player's clubs and other *equipment* (including driving a cart or pulling a trolley).

- Search for the player's ball (Rule 7.1).

- Give information, *advice* and other help before the *stroke* is made (Rules 10.2a and 10.2b).

- Smooth *bunkers* or take other actions to care for the *course* (Rules 8.2 Exception, 8.3 Exception and 12.2b(2) and (3)).

- Remove sand and loose soil and repair damage on the *putting green* (Rule 13.1c).

- Remove or attend the *flagstick* (Rule 13.2b).

- Mark the spot of the player's ball and lift and *replace* the ball on the *putting green* (Rules 14.1b Exception and 14.2b).

- Clean the player's ball (Rule 14.1c).

- Remove *loose impediments* and *movable obstructions* (Rules 15.1 and 15.2).

(2) **Actions Allowed Only With Player's Authorization**. A *caddie* may take these actions only when the Rules allow the player to take them and only with the player's authorization (which must be given specifically each time rather than given generally for a *round*):

156

- Restore conditions that were worsened after the player's ball came to rest (Rule 8.1d).

- When the player's ball is anywhere except on the *putting green*, lift the player's ball under a Rule requiring it to be *replaced* or after the player has decided to take relief under a Rule (Rule 14.1b).

(3) Actions Not Allowed. A caddie is not allowed to take these actions for the player:

- Concede the next *stroke*, a hole or the match to the *opponent* or agree with the *opponent* on the match score (Rule 3.2).

- Deliberately stand on or close to an extension of the *line of play* behind the player's ball when the player begins taking a *stance* for the *stroke* and until the *stroke* is made (Rule 10.2b(4)) or take other actions prohibited by Rule 10.2b.

- *Replace* a ball, unless the *caddie* had lifted or *moved* the ball (Rule 14.2b).

- *Drop* or place a ball in a *relief area* (Rule 14.3).

- Decide to take relief under a Rule (such as treating a ball as unplayable under Rule 19 or taking relief from an *abnormal course condition* or *penalty area* under Rule 16.1 or 17); the *caddie* may advise the player to do so, but the player must decide.

10.3c Player Responsible for Caddie's Actions and Breach of Rules

A player is responsible for his or her *caddie's* actions both during a *round* and while play is stopped under Rule 5.7a, but not before or after a *round*.

If the *caddie's* action breaches a Rule or would breach a Rule if the action was taken by the player, the player gets the penalty under that Rule.

When application of a Rule depends on whether the player is aware of certain facts, the player's knowledge is treated as including whatever is known by his or her *caddie*.

RULE 11

Ball in Motion Accidentally Hits Person, Animal or Object; Deliberate Actions to Affect Ball in Motion

Purpose of Rule:

Rule 11 covers what to do if the player's ball in motion hits a person, animal, equipment or anything else on the course. When this happens accidentally, there is no penalty and the player normally must accept the result, whether favourable or not, and play the ball from where it comes to rest. Rule 11 also restricts a player from deliberately taking actions to affect where any ball in motion might come to rest.

This Rule applies any time a ball *in play* is in motion (whether after a *stroke* or otherwise), **except** when a ball has been *dropped* in a *relief area* and has not yet come to rest. That situation is covered by Rule 14.3.

11.1 Ball in Motion Accidentally Hits Person or Outside Influence

11.1a No Penalty to Any Player

If a player's ball in motion accidentally hits any person or *outside influence*:

- There is no penalty to any player.

- This is true even if the ball hits the player, the *opponent* or any other player or any of their *caddies* or *equipment*.

Exception – Ball Played on Putting Green in Stroke Play: If the player's ball in motion hits another ball at rest on the *putting green* and both balls were on the *putting green* before the *stroke*, the player gets the *general penalty* (two penalty strokes).

11.1b Ball Must Be Played as It Lies

If a player's ball in motion accidentally hits any person or *outside influence*, the ball must be played as it lies, except in two situations:

Exception 1 – When Ball Played from Anywhere Except Putting Green Comes to Rest on Any Person, Animal or Moving Outside Influence: The player must not play the ball as it lies. Instead, the player must take relief:

- When Ball Is Anywhere Except on Putting Green. The player must *drop* the original ball or another ball in this *relief area* (see Rule 14.3):

» Reference Point: The estimated point right under where the ball first came to rest on the person, animal or moving outside influence.

» Size of Relief Area Measured from Reference Point: One club-length, **but** with these limits:

» Limits on Location of Relief Area:

  – Must be in the same *area of the course* as the reference point, and

  – Must not be nearer the *hole* than the reference point.

• When Ball Is on Putting Green. The player must place the original ball or another ball on the estimated spot right under where the ball first came to rest on the person, animal or moving *outside influence*, using the procedures for *replacing* a ball under Rules 14.2b(2) and 14.2e.

Exception 2 – When Ball Played from Putting Green Accidentally Hits Any Person, Animal or Movable Obstruction (Including Another Ball in Motion) on Putting Green: The *stroke* does not count and the original ball or another ball must be *replaced* on its original spot (which if not known must be estimated) (see Rule 14.2), **except** in these two cases:

• Ball in Motion Hits Another Ball at Rest or Ball-Marker on Putting Green. The *stroke* counts and the ball must be played as it lies. (See Rule 11.1a for whether a penalty applies in *stroke play*).

• Ball in Motion Accidentally Hits Flagstick or Person Attending Flagstick. This is covered by Rule 13.2b(2), not by this Rule.

Penalty for Playing Incorrectly *Substituted* **Ball or Playing Ball from a** *Wrong Place* **in Breach of Rule 11.1:** *General Penalty* **Under Rule 6.3b or 14.7a.**

If multiple Rule breaches result from a single act or related acts, see Rule 1.3c(4).

Rule 11.1b Interpretations:

11.1b/1 – Playing from Where Ball Came to Rest When Stroke Does Not Count Is Playing from Wrong Place

When a *stroke* is cancelled by an *opponent* (such as under Rule 6.4a(2) – Playing Out of Turn) or does not count under a Rule (such as under Exception 2 to Rule 11.1b – When Ball Played from Putting Green Accidentally Hits Any Person, Animal or Movable Obstruction (Including Another Ball in Motion) on Putting Green), it is disregarded from the player's score as if it never took place. If the player does not *replace* the ball, but instead plays from where the ball came to rest, he or she has played from a *wrong place* and Rule 14.7 (Playing from Wrong Place) applies since the player was required to replay the *stroke*.

For example, a player makes a *stroke* from the *putting green* that accidentally hits a hole-liner that came out of the *hole* when the *flagstick* was removed (Exception 2 to Rule 11.1b). Instead of *replacing* a ball and replaying the *stroke*, the player plays the ball from where it came to rest. The *stroke* with the ball that accidentally hit the hole-liner does not count in the player's score. However, by not *replacing* a ball as required, the player has played from a *wrong place* and Rule 14.7 applies.

This also applies if a player plays out of turn and the *stroke* is cancelled by an *opponent* under Rule 6.4a(2).

11.1b/2 – What to Do When Ball Moves After Being Accidentally Deflected or Stopped

If a ball comes to rest against a person or an *outside influence* after being accidentally deflected or stopped and the person or *outside influence* moves or is *moved*, Rule 9 applies, and the player must follow the Rule appropriately. However, there is no penalty under Rule 9 if the ball *moves* after coming to rest against a person or *equipment*.

Examples of where there is no penalty include when:

- The player's ball comes to rest against the *opponent's* foot after being accidentally stopped by him or her and the ball *moves* as a result of the *opponent* moving. The player must *replace* the ball as required by Rule 9.5 but neither the player nor the *opponent* gets a penalty.

- The player's ball in motion is accidentally stopped by his or her club after rolling back down a hill and the ball *moves* as a result of removing the club. The player must *replace* the ball as required by Rule 9.4 but gets no penalty.

For other situations when a ball is accidentally deflected or stopped by an *outside influence* (such as an *animal*), and that *outside influence* moves and causes the ball to *move*, see Rule 9.6 for what to do.

11.2 Ball in Motion Deliberately Deflected or Stopped by Person

11.2a When Rule 11.2 Applies

This Rule applies only when it is *known or virtually certain* that a player's ball in motion was deliberately deflected or stopped by a person, which is when:

- A person deliberately touches the ball in motion, or

- The ball in motion hits any *equipment* or other object (except a ball-marker or another ball at rest before the ball was played or otherwise went into motion) or any person (such as the player's *caddie*) that a player deliberately positioned or left in a particular location so that the *equipment*, object or person might deflect or stop the ball in motion.

Exception – Ball Deliberately Deflected or Stopped in Match Play When No Reasonable Chance It Can Be Holed: An *opponent's* ball in motion that is deliberately deflected or stopped at a time when there is no reasonable chance it can be *holed*, and when done either as a concession or when the ball needed to be *holed* to tie the hole, is covered by Rule 3.2a(1) or 3.2b(1), not by this Rule.

For a player's right to have a ball or *ball-marker* lifted before a *stroke* is made if he or she reasonably believes the ball or *ball-marker* might help or interfere with play, see Rule 15.3.

Rule 11.2a Interpretations:

11.2a/1 – Equipment Left in Position After Player Realizes It Could Be Helpful if the Ball Were to Hit It

Rule 11.2 applies to a situation where a player did not initially position the *equipment*, other object or person for the purpose of deflecting the ball in motion but once positioned by the player, he or she realizes it may deflect or stop the ball and deliberately leaves it there.

An example where the player gets a penalty is when:

- After raking a *bunker*, a player places the rake between the *putting green* and the *bunker*, without any thought of it influencing a ball. The player, who now has a downhill putt towards the *bunker*, realizes the rake might stop his or her ball and plays without first moving the rake. The player putts and the ball is stopped by that rake.

An example where the player does not get a penalty is when:

- A rake has been left by a preceding group between the *putting green* and a *bunker*. A player, who has a downhill putt towards the *bunker*, sees the rake and leaves it there because it might stop the ball if his or her putt is too strong. The player putts and the ball is stopped by that rake.

11.2b When Penalty Applies to a Player

- A player gets the *general penalty* if he or she deliberately deflects or stops any ball in motion.

- This is true whether it is the player's own ball or a ball played by an *opponent* or by another player in *stroke play*.

Exception – Ball Moving in Water: There is no penalty if a player lifts his or her ball moving in water in *temporary water* or in a *penalty area* when taking relief under Rule 16.1 or 17 (see Rule 10.1d Exception 3).

See Rules 22.2 (in *Foursomes*, either *partner* may act for the *side* and action by the *partner* is treated as action of the player); **23.5** (in *Four-Ball*, either *partner* may act for the *side* and action by the *partner* concerning the player's ball or *equipment* is treated as action of the player).

11.2c Place from Where Deliberately Deflected or Stopped Ball Must Be Played

If it is *known or virtually certain* that a player's ball in motion was deliberately deflected or stopped by a person (whether or not the ball has been found), it must not be played as it lies. Instead, the player must take relief:

(1) **Stroke Made from Anywhere Except Putting Green.** The player must take relief based on the estimated spot where the ball would have come to rest if not deflected or stopped:

- When Ball Would Have Come to Rest Anywhere on Course Except on Putting Green. The player must *drop* the original ball or another ball in this *relief area* (see Rule 14.3):

  » Reference Point: The estimated spot where the ball would have come to rest.

  » Size of Relief Area Measured from Reference Point: One *club-length*, **but** with these limits:

  » Limits on Location of Relief Area:

    — Must be in the same *area of the course* as the reference point, and

    — Must not be nearer the *hole* than the reference point.

- When Ball Would Have Come to Rest on Putting Green. The player must place the original ball or another ball on the estimated spot where the ball would have come to rest, using the procedures for *replacing* a ball under Rules 14.2b(2) and 14.2e.

- When Ball Would Have Come to Rest Out of Bounds. The player must take *stroke-and-distance* relief under Rule 18.2.

Rule 11.2c(1) Interpretations:

11.2c(1)/1 – Options When Ball Would Have Come to Rest in Penalty Area

When a ball in motion is deliberately deflected or stopped and it is estimated that it would have come to rest in a *penalty area*, the player has the choice to *drop* a ball in the *penalty area* (Rule 11.2c(1)) or take relief from the *penalty area* (Rule 17.1d).

If the player decides to take relief from the *penalty area* because he or she does not wish to *drop* a ball in the *relief area* in the *penalty area*, the player must estimate the point that the ball would have last crossed the edge of the *penalty area* when taking relief under Rule 17.1d.

(2) **Stroke Made from Putting Green.** The stroke does not count, and the original ball or another ball must be *replaced* on its original spot (which if not known must be estimated) (see Rule 14.2).

Penalty for Playing Incorrectly *Substituted* Ball or Playing Ball from a *Wrong Place* in Breach of Rule 11.2: *General Penalty* Under Rule 6.3b or 14.7a.

If multiple Rule breaches result from a single act or related acts, see Rule 1.3c(4).

11.3 Deliberately Moving Objects or Altering Conditions to Affect Ball in Motion

When a ball is in motion, a player must not deliberately take any of these actions to affect where that ball (whether the player's own ball or another player's ball) might come to rest:

- Alter physical conditions by taking any of the actions listed in Rule 8.1a (such as replacing a divot or pressing down a raised area of turf), or

- Lift or move:

  » A *loose impediment* (see Rule 15.1a, Exception 2), or

  » A *movable obstruction* (see Rule 15.2a, Exception 2).

Exception – Moving Flagstick, Ball at Rest on Putting Green and Other Player Equipment: This Rule does not prohibit a player from lifting or moving:

- A removed *flagstick,*

- A ball at rest on the *putting green,* or

- Any other player *equipment* (other than a ball at rest anywhere except the *putting green* or a *ball-marker* anywhere on the *course*).

Removing the *flagstick* from the *hole* (including by attending it) while a ball is in motion is covered by Rule 13.2, not by this Rule.

Penalty for Breach of Rule 11.3: *General Penalty.*

See Rules 22.2 (in *Foursomes,* either *partner* may act for the *side* and action by the *partner* is treated as action of the player); **23.5** (in *Four-Ball,* either *partner* may act for the *side* and action by the *partner* concerning the player's ball or *equipment* is treated as action of the player).

Rule 11.3 Interpretations:

11.3/1 – Outcome of Deliberate Actions to Affect Ball in Motion Is Irrelevant

Rule 11.3 applies when a player or *caddie* takes a deliberate action for the purpose of affecting a ball in motion, and the player is in breach of this Rule even if the deliberate action does not affect where the ball comes to rest.

Examples where the player gets the *general penalty* under Rule 11.3, and in *stroke play* must play the ball where it comes to rest, include when:

- The player's ball lies in the *general area* at the bottom of a slope. The player makes a *stroke* and, while the ball is rolling back down the slope, the player presses down a raised piece of turf for the purpose of preventing the ball from coming to rest in a bad lie.

- The player believes a rake lying on the ground may stop or deflect another player's ball in motion, so the player lifts the rake.

Examples where there is no penalty and in *stroke play* the ball must be played where it comes to rest, include when:

- A player's ball lies in the *general area* at the bottom of a slope. The player makes a *stroke* and the ball begins to roll back down the slope. Unaware that the ball was returning to the area from where it had been played, the player presses down a raised piece of turf without any intent to affect where the ball might come to rest.

There is no penalty even if the ball comes to rest in the pressed down area.

- After making a *stroke* and while the ball is in motion, a player lifts a nearby rake to give it to another player for an upcoming *bunker* shot. The player's ball rolls through the area that the rake was lifted from.

Specific Rules for Bunkers and Putting Greens

Rules 12–13

RULE 12 Bunkers

Purpose of Rule:

Rule 12 is a specific Rule for bunkers, which are specially prepared areas intended to test the player's ability to play a ball from the sand. To make sure the player confronts this challenge, there are some restrictions on touching the sand before the stroke is made and on where relief may be taken for a ball in a bunker.

DIAGRAM 12.1: WHEN BALL IS IN BUNKER

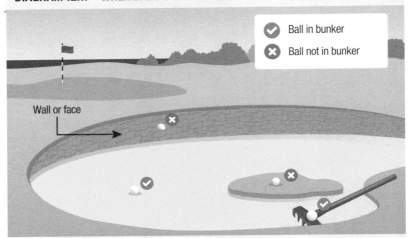

In line with the Definition of Bunker and Rule 12.1, the diagram provides examples of when a ball is in and not in a bunker.

12.1 When Ball Is in Bunker

A ball is in a *bunker* when any part of the ball:

- Touches sand on the ground inside the edge of the *bunker*, or

- Is inside the edge of the *bunker* and rests:

  » On ground where sand normally would be (such as where sand was blown or washed away by wind or water), or

» In or on a *loose impediment*, *movable obstruction*, *abnormal course condition* or *integral object* that touches sand in the *bunker* or is on ground where sand normally would be.

If a ball lies on soil or grass or other growing or attached natural objects inside the edge of the *bunker* without touching any sand, the ball is not in the *bunker*.

If part of the ball is both in a *bunker* and in another *area of the course*, see Rule 2.2c.

12.2 Playing Ball in Bunker

This Rule applies both during a *round* and while play is stopped under Rule 5.7a.

12.2a Removing Loose Impediments and Movable Obstructions

Before playing a ball in a *bunker*, a player may remove *loose impediments* under Rule 15.1 and *movable obstructions* under Rule 15.2.

This includes any reasonable touching or movement of the sand in the *bunker* that happens while doing so.

Rule 12.2a Interpretations:

12.2a/1 – Improvement Resulting from Removing Loose Impediment or Movable Obstruction from a Bunker

When removing a *loose impediment* or a *movable obstruction* from a *bunker*, sand is often moved as a result of removing the object, and there is no penalty if this *improves conditions affecting the stroke* if the actions taken to remove the *loose impediment* or *movable obstruction* were reasonable (Rule 8.1b(2)).

For example, a player removes a pine cone near his or her ball and improves the *conditions affecting the stroke* by dragging the pine cone away in a way that also removes a mound of sand from the area of his or her intended swing.

The player could have used a less intrusive way to remove the pine cone (such as lifting the pine cone straight up without dragging it behind the ball). Because his or her actions are not reasonable in this situation, the player gets a penalty for a breach of Rule 8.1a (Improving the Conditions Affecting the Stroke).

12.2b Restrictions on Touching Sand in Bunker

(1) When Touching Sand Results in Penalty. Before making a *stroke* at a ball in a *bunker*, a player must not:

- Deliberately touch sand in the *bunker* with a hand, club, rake or other object to test the condition of the sand to learn information for the next *stroke*, or

- Touch sand in the *bunker* with a club:

  » In the area right in front of or right behind the ball (**except** as allowed under Rule 7.1a in fairly searching for a ball or under Rule 12.2a in removing a *loose impediment* or *movable obstruction*),

  » In making a practice swing, or

  » In making the backswing for a *stroke*.

(2) When Touching Sand Does Not Result in Penalty. Except as covered by (1), this Rule does not prohibit the player from touching sand in the *bunker* in any other way, including:

- Digging in with the feet to take a *stance* for a practice swing or the *stroke*,

- Smoothing the *bunker* to care for the *course*,

- Placing clubs, *equipment* or other objects in the *bunker* (whether by throwing or setting them down),

- Measuring, *marking*, lifting, *replacing* or taking other actions under a Rule,

- Leaning on a club to rest, stay balanced or prevent a fall, or

- Striking the sand in frustration or anger.

But the player gets the *general penalty* if his or her actions in touching the sand *improve the conditions affecting the stroke* in breach of Rule 8.1a. (See also Rules 8.2 and 8.3 for limitations on *improving* or worsening other physical conditions to affect play.)

(3) No Restrictions After Ball Is Played Out of Bunker. After a ball in a *bunker* is played and it is outside the *bunker*, the player may:

- Touch sand in the *bunker* without penalty under Rule 12.2b(1), and

- Smooth sand in the *bunker* to care for the *course* without penalty under Rule 8.1a.

This is true even if the ball comes to rest outside the *bunker* and:

- The player is required or allowed by the Rules to take *stroke-and-distance* relief by *dropping* a ball in the *bunker*, or
- The sand in the *bunker* is on the player's *line of play* for the next stroke from outside the *bunker*.

But if the ball played from the *bunker* comes back into the *bunker*, or the player takes relief by *dropping* a ball in the *bunker*, the restrictions in Rules 12.2b(1) and 8.1a again apply to that ball *in play* in the *bunker*.

Penalty for Breach of Rule 12.2: General Penalty.

Rule 12.2b(3) Interpretations:

12.2b(3)/1 – Player Is Allowed to Smooth Sand in a Bunker to Care for the Course After Taking Relief Outside the Bunker

Under Rule 12.2b(3), a player may smooth sand in a *bunker* to care for the *course* without penalty under Rule 8.1a (Actions That Are Not Allowed) after a ball is played out of that *bunker*. The term "played out of the *bunker*" in Rule 12.2b(3) also includes taking relief outside the *bunker*.

For example, a player decides to take unplayable ball relief outside a *bunker* for a penalty of two strokes under Rule 19.3b (Back-On-the-Line Relief). Before *dropping* a ball using the back-on-the-line relief procedure outside the *bunker* or, after *dropping* a ball but before making his or her next *stroke*, the player smooths footprints in the *bunker* on the *line of play*. Rule 12.2b(3) applies and there is no penalty.

Provided that the player intended to take relief outside the *bunker*, there would be no penalty even if the player smoothed the *bunker* before *dropping* the ball outside the *bunker*.

Rule 12.2b Interpretations:

12.2b/1 – Rule 12.2b Applies to a Mound of Sand from an Animal Hole in a Bunker

If a player's ball lies in a *bunker* on or near a mound of sand that is part of an *animal hole*, the restrictions in Rule 12.2b(1) apply to touching that mound of sand.

However, the player may take relief from the *animal hole* (which is an *abnormal course condition*) under Rule 16.1c.

12.2b/2 – Whether Player May Probe in Bunker

8.1a/7 confirms that a player may probe anywhere on the *course* (including in a *bunker*) without penalty to determine if tree roots, rocks or *obstructions* might interfere with his or her *stroke*, as long as the player does not improve the *conditions affecting the stroke*.

For example, when a player's ball comes to rest near a drain in a *bunker*, the player may use a *tee* to probe the sand to determine the extent of the drain and whether it will interfere with his or her *stroke*.

However, if the purpose of the probing is to test the condition of the sand, the player is in breach of Rule 12.2b(1).

12.2b/3 – Rule 12.2 Continues to Apply When Player Has Lifted His or Her Ball from Bunker to Take Relief but Has Not Yet Decided Whether to Take Relief In or Out of Bunker

If a player has lifted the ball from a *bunker* to take relief under a Rule, but has not yet decided which relief option to use, the restrictions in Rule 12.2b(1) continue to apply.

For example, if a player's tee shot is unplayable in a *bunker* and he or she is deciding whether to go back to the *teeing area* to play again under penalty of *stroke and distance*, take relief in the *bunker* or take back-on-the-line relief outside the *bunker*, the player is in breach of Rule 12.2b if he or she deliberately tests the condition of the sand in the *bunker* or hits the sand with a practice swing.

However, just as Rule 12.2b(1) no longer applies after the player has played a ball and it is outside the *bunker*, Rule 12.2b(1) does not apply after the player decides to take relief outside the *bunker* so long as relief is actually taken outside the *bunker*.

12.3 Specific Rules for Relief for Ball in Bunker

When a ball is in a *bunker*, specific relief Rules may apply in these situations:

- Interference by an *abnormal course condition* (Rule 16.1c),
- Interference by a dangerous *animal* condition (Rule 16.2), and
- Unplayable ball (Rule 19.3).

RULE 13 Putting Greens

Purpose of Rule:

Rule 13 is a specific Rule for putting greens. Putting greens are specially prepared for playing the ball along the ground and there is a flagstick for the hole on each putting green, so certain different Rules apply than for other areas of the course.

13.1 Actions Allowed or Required on Putting Greens

Purpose of Rule:

This Rule allows the player to do things on the putting green that are normally not allowed off the putting green, such as being allowed to mark, lift, clean and replace a ball and to repair damage and remove sand and loose soil on the putting green. There is no penalty for accidentally causing a ball or ball-marker to move on the putting green.

13.1a When Ball Is on Putting Green

A ball is on the putting green when any part of the ball:

* Touches the putting green, or

* Lies on or in anything (such as a loose impediment or an obstruction) and is inside the edge of the putting green.

If part of the ball is both on the putting green and in another area of the course, see Rule 2.2c.

13.1b Marking, Lifting and Cleaning Ball on Putting Green

A ball on the putting green may be lifted and cleaned (see Rule 14.1).

The spot of the ball must be marked before it is lifted and the ball must be replaced on its original spot (see Rule 14.2).

13.1c Improvements Allowed on Putting Green

During a round and while play is stopped under Rule 5.7a, a player may take these two actions on the *putting green*, no matter whether the ball is on or off the *putting green*:

(1) **Removal of Sand and Loose Soil**. Sand and loose soil on the *putting green* (**but** not anywhere else on the *course*) may be removed without penalty.

(2) **Repair of Damage**. A player may repair damage on the *putting green* without penalty by taking reasonable actions to restore the *putting green* as nearly as possible to its original condition, **but** only:

- By using his or her hand, foot or other part of the body or a normal ball-mark repair tool, *tee*, club or similar item of normal *equipment*, and

- Without unreasonably delaying play (see Rule 5.6a).

But if the player *improves* the *putting green* by taking actions that exceed what is reasonable to restore the *putting green* to its original condition (such as by creating a pathway to the *hole* or by using an object that is not allowed), the player gets the **general penalty** for breach of Rule 8.1a.

"Damage on the *putting green*" means any damage caused by a person or *outside influence*, such as:

- Ball marks, shoe damage (such as spike marks) and scrapes or indentations caused by *equipment* or a *flagstick*,

- Old *hole* plugs, turf plugs, seams of cut turf and scrapes or indentations from maintenance tools or vehicles,

- *Animal* tracks or hoof indentations, and

- Embedded objects (such as a stone, acorn or *tee*).

But "damage on the *putting green*" does not include any damage or conditions that result from:

- Normal practices for maintaining the overall condition of the *putting green* (such as aeration holes and grooves from vertical mowing),

- Irrigation or rain or other *natural forces*,

- Natural surface imperfections (such as weeds or areas of bare, diseased or uneven growth), or

- Natural wear of the *hole*.

Rule 13.1c(2) Interpretations:

See 8.1b/7 for when damage partially on and partially off putting green may be repaired.

13.1c(2)/1 – Line of Play on Putting Green Accidentally Damaged May Be Repaired

A player is entitled to the *conditions affecting the stroke* that he or she had when his or her ball came to rest unless *natural forces* or the player caused the damage (Rule 8.1d). However, damage caused by the player to his or her own *line of play* on the *putting green* may be repaired under Rule 13.1c(2).

For example, if a player creates spike marks in assessing the *line of play*, he or she may take reasonable actions to repair the damage.

13.1c(2)/2 – Damaged Hole Is Part of Damage on the Putting Green

Damage to the *hole* is covered by Rule 13.1c as part of damage on a *putting green*. The player may repair a damaged *hole* unless the damage is natural wear that Rule 13.1c does not allow to be repaired.

For example, if the *hole* is damaged in removing the *flagstick*, it may be repaired by the player under Rule 13.1c, even if the damage has changed the dimensions of the *hole*.

However, if a *hole* has been damaged and the player cannot repair the damage (such as the *hole* cannot be made round again) or where natural wear that the player may not repair results in the *hole* not being round, the player should request that the *Committee* repair it.

13.1c(2)/3 – Player May Request Help from Committee When Unable to Repair Damage On Putting Green

If a player is unable to repair damage on the *putting green*, such as an indentation from a club or an old *hole* plug that has sunk below the surface, the player may request that the *Committee* repair the damage.

If the *Committee* is unable to repair the damage and the player's ball lies on the *putting green*, the *Committee* could consider providing relief to the player under Rule 16.1 by defining the damaged area as *ground under repair*.

13.1d When Ball or Ball-Marker Moves on Putting Green

There are two specific Rules for a ball or *ball-marker* that *moves* on the *putting green*.

(1) **No Penalty for Accidentally Causing Ball to Move**. There is no penalty if the player, *opponent* or another player in *stroke play* accidentally *moves* the player's ball or *ball-marker* on the *putting green*.

The player must:

• *Replace* the ball on its original spot (which if not known must be estimated) (see Rule 14.2), or

• Place a *ball-marker* to *mark* that original spot.

Exception – Ball Must Be Played as It Lies When Ball Begins to Move During Backswing or Stroke and Stroke Is Made (see Rule 9.1b).

If the player or *opponent* deliberately lifts the player's ball or *ball-marker* on the *putting green*, see Rule 9.4 or Rule 9.5 to find out if there is a penalty.

Rule 13.1d(1) Interpretations:

13.1d(1)/1 – No Penalty for Accidental Movement of Ball or Ball-Marker on Putting Green

Under Rule 13.1d(1) examples of actions that are accidental include when:

• The player takes normal actions near the ball before attempting a *stroke*, such as practice swings near the ball or addressing the ball by placing the putter on the ground near the ball.

• The player drops a coin or a club, hitting the ball and causing it to *move*.

• The *partner* or *opponent* of the player, or one of their *caddies*, unintentionally *moves* the ball or *ball-marker*, such as by kicking the ball, dropping something on the ball, or by pressing down the *ball-marker*.

• The player inadvertently steps on the *ball-marker* and it sticks to the bottom of his or her shoe.

In these examples of accidental *movement*, the ball or *ball-marker* must be *replaced* and there is no penalty to anyone. If the exact spot from where the ball or *ball-marker* was *moved* is not known, it must be estimated (Rule 14.2c).

(2) **When to Replace Ball Moved by Natural Forces**. If *natural forces* cause a player's ball on the *putting green* to move, where the player must play from next depends on whether the ball had already been lifted and *replaced* on its original spot:

- Ball Already Lifted and Replaced. The ball must be *replaced* on its original spot (which if not known must be estimated) (see Rule 14.2), even though it was *moved* by *natural forces* and not by the player, the *opponent* or an *outside influence* (see Rule 9.3, Exception).

- Ball Not Already Lifted and Replaced. The ball must be played from its new spot (see Rule 9.3).

Rule 13.1d(2) Interpretations:

13.1d(2)/1 – Ball Must Be Replaced if It Moves After Placing a Ball to Take Relief

A player's ball is on the *putting green* and he or she has interference from an *abnormal course condition*. The player decides to take free relief under Rule 16.1d. Once the ball is placed, it is treated as if it has been lifted and *replaced* under Rule 13.1d(2).

For example, a player's ball is in *temporary water* on the *putting green*. He or she decides to take relief and places a ball on the spot of the *nearest point of complete relief*. While the player is preparing to make the *stroke*, *natural forces* cause the ball to *move*. The player must *replace* the ball on the spot of the *nearest point of complete relief*.

13.1e No Deliberate Testing of Greens

During a *round* and while play is stopped under Rule 5.7a, a player must not deliberately take either of these actions to test the *putting green* or a *wrong green*:

- Rub the surface, or

- Roll a ball.

Exception – Testing Greens When Between Two Holes: Between two holes, a player may rub the surface or roll a ball on the *putting green* of the hole just completed and on any practice green (see Rule 5.5b).

Penalty for Testing the *Putting Green* or a *Wrong Green* in Breach of Rule 13.1e: *General Penalty*.

If multiple Rule breaches result from a single act or related acts, see Rule 1.3c(4).

See Committee Procedures, Section 8; Model Local Rule I-2 (the *Committee* may adopt a Local Rule prohibiting a player from rolling a ball on the *putting green* of the hole just completed.)

Rule 13.1e Interpretations:

13.1e/1 – Deliberately Testing Any Putting Green Is Not Allowed

Rule 13.1e prohibits a player from taking two specific actions on the *putting green* or a *wrong green* for the purpose of finding out information about how a ball might roll on it. It does not prohibit a player from taking other actions even when done for the purpose of testing or from inadvertently taking the prohibited actions.

An example of an action that is a breach of Rule 13.1e is when:

- A player roughens or scrapes the grass on the *putting green* to determine which way the grain is growing.

Examples of actions that are not a breach of Rule 13.1e are when:

- A player concedes his or her *opponent's* next putt and hits the ball away on the same *line of play* as the player may subsequently use but does not do so deliberately to learn information about the *putting green*.

- A player places the palm of his or her hand on the surface of the *putting green* on his or her *line of play* to determine the wetness of the *putting green*. While the player is doing so to test the *putting green*, this action is not prohibited under Rule 13.1e.

- A player rubs a ball on the *putting green* to clean off mud.

13.1f Relief Must Be Taken from Wrong Green

(1) **Meaning of Interference by Wrong Green**. Interference under this Rule exists when:

- Any part of the player's ball touches a *wrong green* or lies on or in anything (such as a *loose impediment* or an *obstruction*) and is inside the edge of a *wrong green*, or

- A *wrong green* physically interferes with the player's area of intended *stance* or area of intended swing.

(2) **Relief Must Be Taken**. When there is interference by a *wrong green*, a player must not play the ball as it lies.

Instead, the player must take free relief by *dropping* the original ball or another ball in this *relief area* (see Rule 14.3):

- Reference Point: The *nearest point of complete relief* in the same *area of the course* where the original ball came to rest.

- Size of Relief Area Measured from Reference Point: One *club-length*, **but** with these limits:

- Limits on Location of Relief Area:

  » Must be in the same *area of the course* as the reference point,

  » Must not be nearer the *hole* than the reference point, and

  » There must be complete relief from all interference by the *wrong green*.

(3) **No Relief Where Clearly Unreasonable**. There is no relief under Rule 13.1f if interference exists only because the player chooses a club, type of *stance* or swing or direction of play that is clearly unreasonable under the circumstances.

See Committee Procedures, Section 8; Model Local Rule D-3 (the *Committee* may adopt a Local Rule denying relief from a *wrong green* that only interferes with the area of intended *stance*).

DIAGRAM 13.1f: RELIEF FROM WRONG GREEN

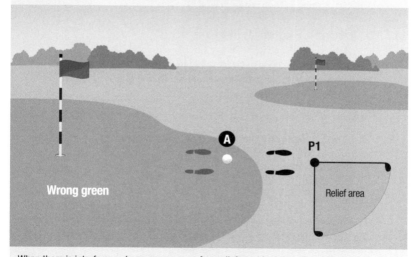

When there is interference by a wrong green, free relief must be taken. The diagram assumes a right-handed player. Ball A lies on the wrong green, and the nearest point of complete relief for Ball A is at P1, which must be on the same area of the course where the original ball came to rest (in this case, the general area). The relief area is one club-length from the reference point, is not nearer to the hole than the reference point and must be in the same area of the course where the original ball came to rest. The player must take complete relief from the wrong green.

Penalty for Playing Incorrectly *Substituted* Ball or Playing Ball from a *Wrong Place* in Breach of Rule 13.1: *General Penalty* Under Rule 6.3b or 14.7a.

If multiple Rule breaches result from a single act or related acts, see Rule 1.3c(4).

13.2   The Flagstick

Purpose of Rule:

This Rule covers the player's choices for dealing with the flagstick. The player may leave the flagstick in the hole or have it removed (which includes having someone attend the flagstick and remove it after the ball is played), but must decide before making a stroke. There is normally no penalty if a ball in motion hits the flagstick.

This Rule applies to a ball played from anywhere on the *course*, whether on or off the *putting green*.

13.2a   Leaving Flagstick in Hole

(1) **Player May Leave Flagstick in Hole.** The player may make a *stroke* with the *flagstick* left in the *hole*, so that it is possible for the ball in motion to hit the *flagstick*.

The player must decide this before making the *stroke*, by either:

- Leaving the *flagstick* where it is in the *hole* or moving it so that it is centred in the *hole* and leaving it there, or

- Having a removed *flagstick* put back in the *hole*.

In either case:

- The player must not try to gain an advantage by deliberately moving the *flagstick* to a position other than centred in the *hole*.

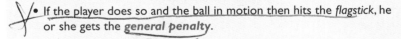

- If the player does so and the ball in motion then hits the *flagstick*, he or she gets the *general penalty*.

Rule 13.2a(1) Interpretations:

13.2a(1)/1 – Player Has the Right to Leave Flagstick in Position Preceding Group Left It

A player is entitled to play the *course* as he or she finds it, which includes the position in which the preceding group left the *flagstick*.

For example, if the preceding group replaced the *flagstick* in a position that is leaning away from the player, the player has the right to play with the *flagstick* in that position should he or she find this advantageous.

If another player or *caddie* centres the *flagstick* in the *hole*, the player may keep it in that position or have the *flagstick* restored to its previous position.

(2) **No Penalty If Ball Hits Flagstick Left in Hole**. If the player makes a *stroke* with the *flagstick* left in the *hole* and the ball in motion then hits the *flagstick*:

- There is no penalty (**except** as provided in (1)), and

- The ball must be played as it lies.

(3) **Limitation on Player Moving or Removing Flagstick in Hole While Ball Is in Motion**. After making a *stroke* with the *flagstick* left in the *hole*:

- The player and his or her *caddie* must not deliberately move or remove the *flagstick* to affect where the player's ball in motion might come to rest (such as to avoid having the ball hit the *flagstick*). If this is done, the player gets the **general penalty**.

- **But** there is no penalty if the player has the *flagstick* in the *hole* moved or removed for any other reason, such as when he or she reasonably believes that the ball in motion will not hit the *flagstick* before coming to rest.

(4) **Limitation on Other Players Moving or Removing Flagstick When Player Has Decided to Leave It in Hole**. When the player has left the *flagstick* in the *hole* and has not authorized anyone to attend the *flagstick* (see Rule 13.2b(1)), another player must not deliberately move or remove the *flagstick* to affect where the player's ball in motion might come to rest.

- If another player or his or her *caddie* does so before or during the *stroke* and the player makes the *stroke* without being aware of this, or does so while the player's ball is in motion after the *stroke*, that other player gets the **general penalty**.

- **But** there is no penalty if the other player or his or her *caddie* moves or removes the *flagstick* for any other reason, such as when he or she:

  » Reasonably believes that the player's ball in motion will not hit the *flagstick* before coming to rest, or

  » Is not aware that the player is about to play or that the player's ball is in motion.

See Rules 22.2 (in *Foursomes*, either *partner* may act for the *side* and action by the *partner* is treated as action of the player); **23.5** (in *Four-Ball*, either *partner* may act for the *side* and action by the *partner* concerning the player's ball or *equipment* is treated as action of the player).

Rule 13.2a(4) Interpretations:

13.2a(4)/1 – Unattended Flagstick Removed Without Player's Authority May Be Replaced

If a player chooses to play with the *flagstick* in the *hole* and another player takes the *flagstick* out of the *hole* without the player's authority, it may be put back in the *hole* while the player's ball is in motion.

However, if the other player's action was a breach of Rule 13.2a(4), he or she does not avoid a penalty by replacing the *flagstick*.

13.2b Removing Flagstick from Hole

(1) **Player May Have Flagstick Removed from Hole.** The player may make a *stroke* with the *flagstick* removed from the *hole*, so that his or her ball in motion will not hit the *flagstick* in the *hole*.

The player must decide this before making the *stroke*, by either:

- Having the *flagstick* removed from the *hole* before playing the ball, or

- Authorizing someone to attend the *flagstick*, which means to remove it by:

  » First holding the *flagstick* in, above or next to the *hole* before and during the *stroke* to show the player where the *hole* is, and

  » Then removing the *flagstick* after the *stroke* is made.

The player is treated as having authorized the *flagstick* to be attended if:

- The player's *caddie* is holding the *flagstick* in, above or next to the *hole* or is standing right next to the *hole* when the *stroke* is made, even if the player is not aware the *caddie* is doing so,

- The player asks any other person to attend the *flagstick* and that person does so, or

- The player sees any other person holding the *flagstick* in, above or next to the *hole* or standing right next to the *hole*, and the player makes the *stroke* without asking that person to move away or to leave the *flagstick* in the *hole*.

Rule 13.2b(1) Interpretations:

13.2b(1)/1 – Flagstick Attendee May Stand Anywhere

A person attending the *flagstick* may stand anywhere when holding the *flagstick* in, above or next to the *hole*.

For example, the attendee may stand directly behind or to either side of the *hole* to avoid standing on another player's *line of play*.

13.2b(1)/2 – Player May Make Stroke While Holding Flagstick

Rule 13.2b(1) allows a player to make a one-handed *stroke* while holding the *flagstick* with the other hand. However, the player may not use the *flagstick* to steady himself or herself while making a *stroke* (Rule 4.3a).

For example, a player may:

- Remove the *flagstick* from the *hole* with one hand before putting and continue to hold it while making a one-handed *stroke* with the other hand.

- Attend his or her own *flagstick* in the *hole* with one hand before and while putting with the other hand. While or after making the one-handed *stroke*, he or she may remove the *flagstick* from the *hole*, but must not deliberately allow the ball in motion to hit the *flagstick*.

(2) **What to Do If Ball Hits Flagstick or Person Attending Flagstick.** If the player's ball in motion hits a *flagstick* that the player had decided to have removed under (1), or hits the person who is attending the *flagstick* (or anything the person is holding), what happens depends on whether this was accidental or deliberate:

Ball Accidentally Hits Flagstick or Person Who Removed or Is Attending It. If the player's ball in motion accidentally hits the *flagstick* or the person who removed or is attending it (or anything the person is holding), there is no penalty and the ball must be played as it lies.

- **Ball Deliberately Deflected or Stopped by Person Attending Flagstick.** If the person who is attending the *flagstick* deliberately deflects or stops the player's ball in motion, Rule 11.2c applies:

  » *Where Ball Is Played from.* The player must not play the ball as it lies and instead must take relief under Rule 11.2c.

  » *When Penalty Applies.* If the person who deliberately deflected or stopped the ball was a player or his or her *caddie*, that player gets the **general penalty** for a breach of Rule 11.2.

For purposes of this Rule, "deliberately deflected or stopped" means the same thing as in Rule 11.2a, and includes when the player's ball in motion hits:

- A removed *flagstick* that was deliberately positioned or left in a particular place on the ground so that it might deflect or stop the ball,

- An attended *flagstick* that the person deliberately failed to remove from the *hole* or to move out of the way of the ball, or

- The person who attended or removed the *flagstick* (or anything the person was holding), when he or she deliberately failed to move out of the way of the ball.

Exception – Restrictions on Deliberately Moving Flagstick to Affect a Ball in Motion (see Rule 11.3).

See Rules 22.2 (in *Foursomes*, either *partner* may act for the *side* and action by the *partner* is treated as action of the player); **23.5** (in *Four-Ball*, either *partner* may act for the *side* and action by the *partner* concerning the player's ball or *equipment* is treated as action of the player).

13.2c Ball Resting against Flagstick in Hole

If a player's ball comes to rest against the *flagstick* left in the *hole*:

- If any part of the ball is in the *hole* below the surface of the *putting green*, the ball is treated as *holed* even if the entire ball is not below the surface.

- If no part of the ball is in the *hole* below the surface of the *putting green*:

  » The ball is not *holed* and must be played as it lies.

» If the *flagstick* is removed and the ball *moves* (whether it falls into the *hole* or *moves* away from the *hole*), there is no penalty and the ball must be *replaced* on the lip of the *hole* (see Rule 14.2).

Penalty for Playing Incorrectly *Substituted* Ball or Playing Ball from a *Wrong Place* in Breach of Rule 13.2c: *General Penalty* Under Rule 6.3b or 14.7a.

If multiple Rule breaches result from a single act or related acts, see Rule 1.3c(4).

In *stroke play*, the player is disqualified if he or she fails to *hole out* as required under Rule 3.3c.

13.3 Ball Overhanging Hole

13.3a Waiting Time to See If Ball Overhanging Hole Will Fall into Hole

If any part of a player's ball overhangs the lip of the *hole*:

* The player is allowed a reasonable time to reach the *hole* and ten more seconds to wait to see whether the ball will fall into the *hole*.

* If the ball falls into the *hole* in this waiting time, the player has *holed out* with the previous *stroke*.

* If the ball does not fall into the *hole* in this waiting time:

  » The ball is treated as being at rest.

  » If the ball then falls into the *hole* before it is played, the player has *holed out* with the previous *stroke*, **but** gets one penalty stroke added to the score for the hole.

Rule 13.3a Interpretations:

13.3a/1 – Meaning of Reasonable Time for Player to Reach Hole

Determining the limits of a reasonable time to reach the *hole* depends on the circumstances of the *stroke* and includes time for a player's natural or spontaneous reaction to the ball not going into the *hole*.

For example, a player may have played the shot from well off the *putting green* and it may take him or her several minutes to reach the *hole* while other players play their shots and all walk to the *putting green*. Or, the player may need to take an indirect route to the *hole* by walking around the *line of play* of another player on the *putting green*.

13.3b What to Do If Ball Overhanging Hole Is Lifted or Moved Before Waiting Time Has Ended

If a ball overhanging the *hole* is lifted or *moved* before the waiting time under Rule 13.3a has ended, the ball is treated as having come to rest:

- The ball must be *replaced* on the lip of the *hole* (see Rule 14.2), and

- The waiting time under Rule 13.3a no longer applies to the ball. (See Rule 9.3 for what to do if the *replaced* ball is then *moved* by natural forces.)

If the *opponent* in *match play* or another player in *stroke play* deliberately lifts or *moves* the player's ball overhanging the *hole* before the waiting time has ended:

- In *match play*, the player's ball is treated as *holed* with the previous *stroke*, and there is no penalty to the *opponent* under Rule 11.2b.

- In *stroke play*, the player who lifted or *moved* the ball gets the general penalty (two penalty strokes). The ball must be *replaced* on its original spot (which if not known must be estimated) (see Rule 14.2).

Rule 13.3b Interpretations:

13.3b/1 – What to Do When Player's Ball Overhanging Hole Moves When Player Removes Flagstick

After the *flagstick* is removed by the player, if the player's ball overhanging the *hole moves*, he or she must proceed as follows:

- If it is *known* or *virtually certain* that the player's removal of the *flagstick* caused the ball to *move*, the ball is *replaced* on the lip of the *hole* and Rule 13.3b applies. The ball is treated as coming to rest and the waiting time under Rule 13.3a no longer applies. There is no penalty to the player since the *flagstick* is a *movable obstruction* (Rule 15.2a(1)).

- If the player's removal of the *flagstick* did not cause the ball to *move*, and the ball falls into the *hole*, Rule 13.3a applies.

- If the player's ball *moved* due to *natural forces* to a new spot not overhanging the *hole* and not because the *flagstick* was removed, there is no penalty and the ball must be played from its new spot (Rule 9.3).

Lifting and Returning
a Ball to Play

Rule 14

RULE 14

Procedures for Ball: Marking, Lifting and Cleaning; Replacing on Spot; Dropping in Relief Area; Playing from Wrong Place

Purpose of Rule:

Rule 14 covers when and how the player may mark the spot of a ball at rest and lift and clean the ball and how to put a ball back into play so that the ball is played from the right place.

- When a lifted or moved ball is to be replaced, the same ball must be set down on its original spot.

- When taking free relief or penalty relief, a substituted ball or the original ball must be dropped in a particular relief area.

A mistake in using these procedures may be corrected without penalty before the ball is played, but the player gets a penalty if he or she plays the ball from the wrong place.

14.1 Marking, Lifting and Cleaning Ball

This Rule applies to the deliberate "lifting" of a player's ball at rest, which includes picking up the ball by hand, rotating it or otherwise deliberately causing it to move from its spot.

14.1a Spot of Ball to Be Lifted and Replaced Must Be Marked

Before lifting a ball under a Rule requiring the ball to be *replaced* on its original spot, the player must *mark* the spot which means to:

- Place a *ball-marker* right behind or right next to the ball, or

- Hold a club on the ground right behind or right next to the ball.

If the spot is *marked* with a *ball-marker*, after *replacing* the ball the player must remove the *ball-marker* before making a *stroke*.

If the player lifts the ball without *marking* its spot, *marks* its spot in a wrong way or makes a *stroke* with a *ball-marker* left in place, the player gets **one penalty stroke**.

If multiple Rule breaches result from a single act or related acts, see Rule 1.3c(4).

When a ball is lifted to take relief under a Rule, the player is not required to *mark* the spot before lifting the ball.

Rule 14.1a Interpretations:

14.1a/1 – Ball May Be Lifted in Any Manner

There are no restrictions on how a ball may be lifted so long as the ball is not lifted in a way that deliberately tests the *putting green* (Rule 13.1e).

For example, after the spot of the ball is *marked* on the *putting green*, the player may lift the ball with the back of the putter or may *move* it to the side with a club.

14.1a/2 – Marking Ball Correctly

Rule 14.1a uses "right behind" and "right next to" to ensure the spot of a lifted ball is *marked* with sufficient accuracy for the player to *replace* it in the right spot.

A ball may be *marked* in any position around the ball so long as it is *marked* right next to it, and this includes placing a *ball-marker* in front of or to the side of the ball.

14.1b Who May Lift Ball

The player's ball may be lifted under the Rules only by:

- The player, or
- Anyone the player authorizes, **but** such authorization must be given each time before the ball is lifted rather than given generally for the *round*.

Exception – Caddie May Lift Player's Ball on Putting Green Without Authorization: When the player's ball is on the *putting green*, his or her *caddie* may lift the ball without the player's authorization.

If the *caddie* lifts the ball without authorization when it is anywhere except on the *putting green*, the player gets **one penalty stroke** (see Rule 9.4).

14.1c Cleaning Lifted Ball

A ball lifted from the *putting green* may always be cleaned (see Rule 13.1b).

A ball lifted from anywhere else may always be cleaned **except** when it is lifted:

- **To See If It Is Cut or Cracked**. Cleaning is not allowed (see Rule 4.2c(1)).

- **To Identify It**. Cleaning is allowed only as needed to identify it (see Rule 7.3).

- **Because It Interferes with Play**. Cleaning is not allowed (see Rule 15.3b(2)).

- **To See If It Lies in Condition Where Relief Is Allowed**. Cleaning is not allowed, unless the player then takes relief under a Rule (see Rule 16.4).

If the player cleans a lifted ball when not allowed, he or she gets **one penalty stroke**.

If multiple Rule breaches result from a single act or related acts, see Rule 1.3c(4).

See Rules 22.2 (in *Foursomes*, either *partner* may act for the *side* and action by the *partner* is treated as action of the player); **23.5** (in *Four-Ball*, either *partner* may act for the *side* and action by the *partner* concerning the player's ball or *equipment* is treated as action of the player).

Rule 14.1c Interpretations:

14.1c/1 – Player Must Be Careful When Lifted Ball May Not Be Cleaned

When a player is applying any of the four Rules mentioned in Rule 14.1c where cleaning is not allowed, there are acts that the player should avoid because, despite there being no intention to clean the ball, the act itself may result in the ball being cleaned.

For example, if a player lifts his or her ball that has grass or other debris sticking to it and throws it to his or her *caddie* who catches it with a towel, it is likely that some of the grass or other debris will be removed, meaning the ball has been cleaned. Similarly, if the player places that ball in his or her pocket or drops it onto the ground, these acts could result in some of the grass or other debris being removed from that ball, meaning that it has been cleaned.

However, if the player takes these actions after lifting a ball that was known to be clean before it was lifted, the player does not get a penalty because the ball was not cleaned.

14.2 Replacing Ball on Spot

This Rule applies whenever a ball is lifted or *moved* and a Rule requires it to be *replaced* on a spot.

14.2a Original Ball Must Be Used

The original ball must be used when *replacing* a ball.

Exception – Another Ball May Be Used When:

- The original ball cannot be recovered with reasonable effort and in a few seconds, so long as the player did not deliberately cause the ball to become unrecoverable,

- The original ball is cut or cracked (see Rule 4.2c),

- Play resumes after it had been stopped (see Rule 5.7d), or

- The original ball was played by another player as a *wrong ball* (see Rule 6.3c(2)).

14.2b Who Must Replace Ball and How It Must Be Replaced

(1) **Who May Replace Ball:** The player's ball must be *replaced* under the Rules only by:

- The player, or

- Any person who lifted the ball or caused it to *move* (even if that person was not allowed to do so under the Rules).

If the player plays a ball that was *replaced* by someone not allowed to do so, the player gets **one penalty stroke**.

(2) **How Ball Must Be Replaced.** The ball must be *replaced* by setting it down on the required spot and letting it go so that it stays on that spot.

If the player plays a ball that was *replaced* in a wrong way but on the required spot, the player gets **one penalty stroke**.

Rule 14.2b(2) Interpretation:

14.2b(2)/1 Player Drops Ball When Ball Is to Be Replaced

When a player *drops* a ball when the Rules require him or her to *replace* the ball, the ball has been *replaced* in a wrong way. If the player *replaces* the ball in a wrong way but on the required spot (this includes if the player *drops* the ball and it comes to rest on the required spot), he or she gets one penalty stroke if the ball is played without correcting the mistake under Rule 14.5 (Correcting Mistake Made in Substituting, Replacing, Dropping or Placing Ball).

But if the player has *dropped* a ball and that ball comes to rest somewhere other than on the required spot, he or she gets the *general penalty* for playing from a *wrong place* if the ball is played without correcting the mistake.

For example:

- In *stroke play*, a player *moves* his or her ball during search and is required to *replace* the ball without penalty. Instead of *replacing* the ball on the original or the estimated spot, the player *drops* the ball on that spot, the ball bounces and comes to rest on another spot, and he or she plays the ball from there. The player has *replaced* the ball in a wrong way and has also played from a *wrong place*.

  Because the player's breaches of the Rules were a combination of a procedural breach (*replacing* the ball in a wrong way under Rule 14.2b(2)) and playing from a *wrong place* in breach of Rule 14.7a, the player gets a total of two penalty strokes under Rule 14.7a (see Rule 1.3c(4) – Applying Penalties to Multiple Breaches of the Rules).

14.2c Spot Where Ball Is Replaced

The ball must be *replaced* on its original spot (which if not known must be estimated), **except** when the ball must be *replaced* on a different spot under Rules 14.2d(2) and 14.2e.

If the ball was at rest on, under or against any *immovable obstruction*, *integral object*, *boundary object* or growing or attached natural object:

- The "spot" of the ball includes its vertical location relative to the ground.
- This means that the ball must be *replaced* on its original spot on, under or against such object.

If any *loose impediments* were removed as a result of the ball being lifted or *moved* or before the ball was *replaced*, they do not need to be *replaced*.

For restrictions on removing *loose impediments* before *replacing* a lifted or *moved* ball see Rule 15.1a, Exception 1.

Rule 14.2c Interpretations:

14.2c/1 – Ball May Be Replaced in Almost Any Orientation

When *replacing* a lifted ball on a spot, the Rules are concerned about only the location. The ball may be aligned in any way when being *replaced* (such as by lining up a trademark) so long as the ball's vertical distance to the ground remains the same.

For example, when using a Rule that does not allow cleaning, the player lifts his or her ball and there is a piece of mud sticking to it. The ball may be aligned in any way when *replacing* it on the original spot (such as by rotating the interfering mud towards the *hole*).

However, the player is not allowed to *replace* the ball in an alignment so the ball rests on the mud unless that was its position before it was lifted. The "spot" of the ball includes its vertical location relative to the ground.

14.2c/2 – Removal of Loose Impediment from Spot Where Ball to Be Replaced

Exception 1 to Rule 15.1a makes clear that, before *replacing* a ball, the player must not remove a *loose impediment* that, if moved when the ball was at rest, would have been likely to cause the ball to *move*. But there are situations where a *loose impediment* may move either when the ball is being lifted or before it is *replaced*, and the player is not required to put the *loose impediment* back before or after *replacing* the ball.

For example:

- A player marks and lifts his or her ball in the *general area* after being requested to do so as it interferes with another player's play. As a result of lifting the ball, a loose twig lying against the ball is moved. The player is not required to put the twig back when the ball is *replaced*.

- A player marks and lifts his or her ball in a *bunker* to see if it is cut. While the ball is lifted, a leaf that had been just behind the *ball-marker* is moved away by the wind. The player is not required to put the leaf back when the ball is *replaced*.

14.2d Where to Replace Ball When Original Lie Altered

If the *lie* of a lifted or *moved* ball that must be *replaced* is altered, the player must *replace* the ball in this way:

(1) **Ball in Sand.** When the ball was in sand, whether in a *bunker* or anywhere else on the *course*:

- In *replacing* the ball on its original spot (which if not known must be estimated) (see Rule 14.2c), the player must re-create the original *lie* as much as possible.

- In re-creating the *lie*, the player may leave a small part of the ball visible if the ball had been covered by sand.

If the player fails to re-create the *lie* in breach of this Rule, the player has played from a *wrong place*.

(2) **Ball Anywhere Except in Sand.** When the ball was anywhere except in sand, the player must *replace* the ball by placing it on the nearest spot with a *lie* most similar to the original *lie* that is:

- Within one *club-length* from its original spot (which if not known must be estimated) (see Rule 14.2c),

- Not nearer the *hole*, and

- In the same *area of the course* as that spot.

If the player knows that the original *lie* was altered but does not know what the *lie* was, the player must estimate the original *lie* and *replace* the ball under (1) or (2).

Exception – For Lies Altered While Play is Stopped and Ball Has Been Lifted, see Rule 5.7d.

Rule 14.2d(2) Interpretations:

14.2d(2)/1 – Altered Lie Might Be "Nearest Spot with Lie Most Similar"

If a player's lie is altered when his or her ball is lifted or *moved* and must be *replaced*, the altered lie might be the nearest spot with a lie most similar to the player's original lie, and the player may be required to play the ball from the altered lie.

For example, a player's ball comes to rest in a divot hole in the fairway. Thinking it is his or her ball, another player plays the ball, making the divot hole a little deeper. If there is no other similar divot hole within one *club-length*, the nearest spot with the lie most similar to the original lie would be a spot in the deepened divot hole.

194

14.2e What to Do If Replaced Ball Does Not Stay on Original Spot

If the player tries to *replace* a ball but it does not stay on its original spot, the player must try a second time.

If the ball again does not stay on that spot, the player must *replace* the ball by placing it on the nearest spot where the ball will stay at rest, but with these limits depending on where the original spot is located:

- The spot must not be nearer the *hole*.
- Original Spot in General Area. The nearest spot must be in the *general area*.
- Original Spot in Bunker or Penalty Area. The nearest spot must be either in the same *bunker* or in the same *penalty area*.
- Original Spot on Putting Green. The nearest spot must be either on the *putting green* or in the *general area*.

Rule 14.2e Interpretations:

14.2e/1 – Player Must Take Penalty Relief When Spot Where Ball Will Remain at Rest Is Nearer Hole

When following Rule 14.2e, there is a possibility that the only spot in the same *area of the course* where the ball will stay at rest when *placed* is nearer the *hole*. In such circumstances, the player must take penalty relief under an allowed Rule.

The player is not allowed to push the ball into the ground to ensure it stays on a spot (see 8.2b/1).

For example, a player's ball comes to rest on the downslope of a *bunker* against a rake and, in removing the rake, the ball *moves*. The player attempts to *replace* the ball as required, but it does not stay. He or she then follows the procedure of Rule 14.2e with no success and finds that there are no other spots to try in that *bunker* that are not nearer the *hole*.

In this case, the player must take unplayable ball relief either by using *stroke and distance* for one penalty stroke (Rule 19.2a) or back-on-the-line relief outside the *bunker* for two penalty strokes (Rule 19.3b).

Penalty for Playing Incorrectly *Substituted* Ball or Playing Ball from a *Wrong Place* in Breach of Rule 14.2: *General Penalty* Under Rule 6.3b or 14.7a.

If multiple Rule breaches result from a single act or related acts, see Rule 1.3c(4).

See Rules 22.2 (in *Foursomes*, either *partner* may act for the side and action by the *partner* is treated as action of the player); 23.5 (in *Four-Ball*, either *partner* may act for the *side* and action by the *partner* concerning the player's ball or *equipment* is treated as action of the player).

Rule 14.2 General Interpretations:

14.2/1 – Ball Does Not Need to Be Replaced on Original Spot When Player Will Play From Another Place

When a player's ball must be *replaced* on its original spot, the player does not need to *replace* the ball if he or she wishes to take relief under a Rule or play the ball from another place.

For example, if a player's ball at rest in a *penalty area* is *moved* by an *outside influence* (Rule 9.6), the player does not need to *replace* the ball before taking relief from the *penalty area*.

He or she may *replace* the ball and then take relief from the *penalty area* or may directly take relief from the *penalty area*.

14.3 Dropping Ball in Relief Area

This Rule applies whenever a player must *drop* a ball in taking relief under a Rule, including when the player must complete taking relief by placing a ball under Rule 14.3c(2).

If the player *improves* the *relief area* before or when *dropping* a ball, see Rule 8.1.

14.3a Original Ball or Another Ball May Be Used

The player may use the original ball or another *ball*.

This means that the player may use any ball each time he or she *drops* or places a ball under this Rule.

14.3b Ball Must Be Dropped in Right Way

The player must *drop* a ball in the right way, which means all three of these things:

(1) **Player Must Drop Ball.** The ball must be *dropped* only by the player. Neither the player's *caddie* nor anyone else may do so.

(2) **Ball Must Be Dropped Straight Down from Knee Height Without Touching Player or Equipment.** The player must let go of the ball from a location at knee height so that the ball:

- Falls straight down, without the player throwing, spinning or rolling it or using any other motion that might affect where the ball will come to rest, and

- Does not touch any part of the player's body or *equipment* before it hits the ground.

"Knee height" means the height of the player's knee when in a standing position.

DIAGRAM 14.3b: DROPPING FROM KNEE HEIGHT

Allowed	Not Allowed

A ball must be dropped straight down from knee height. "Knee height" means the height of a player's knee when in a standing position. But the player does not have to be in a standing position when the ball is dropped.

Rule 14.3b(2) Interpretations:

14.3b(2)/1 – Ball May Fall Only a Short Distance When Dropped from Knee Height

Rule 14.3b(2) and the Definition of "drop" require a player to *drop* a ball from a location at the player's knee height when in a standing position. But, while the ball must fall through the air in order to be *dropped* (rather than placed), the ball will not always fall the distance of the player's knee to the ground.

For example, the player has interference from an *abnormal course condition*, and the player's *relief area* is on a steep slope. If the player is positioned with his or her feet near the bottom of the slope and is facing up the slope to *drop* the ball, it may be that the ball will only fall a short distance when *dropped*, despite being *dropped* from knee height.

(3) **Ball Must Be Dropped in Relief Area.** The ball must be *dropped* in the *relief area*. The player may stand either inside or outside the *relief area* when *dropping* the ball.

If a ball is *dropped* in a wrong way in breach of one or more of these three requirements:

- The player must *drop* a ball again in the right way, and there is no limit to the number of times the player must do so.

- A ball *dropped* in the wrong way does not count as one of the two *drops* required before a ball must be placed under Rule 14.3c(2).

If the player does not *drop* again and instead makes a *stroke* at the ball from where it came to rest after being *dropped* in a wrong way:

- If the ball was played from the *relief area*, the player gets **one penalty stroke** (but has not played from a *wrong place* under Rule 14.7a).

- **But** if the ball was played from outside the *relief area* or after it was placed when required to be *dropped* (no matter where it was played from), the player gets the **general penalty**.

14.3c Ball Dropped in Right Way Must Come to Rest in Relief Area

This Rule applies only when a ball is *dropped* in the right way under Rule 14.3b.

(1) **Player Has Completed Taking Relief When Ball Dropped in Right Way Comes to Rest in Relief Area**. The ball must come to rest in the *relief area*.

It does not matter whether the ball, after hitting the ground, touches any person, *equipment* or other *outside influence* before coming to rest:

- If the ball comes to rest in the *relief area*, the player has completed taking relief and must play the ball as it lies.

- If the ball comes to rest outside the *relief area*, the player must use the procedures in Rule 14.3c(2).

In either case, there is no penalty to any player if a ball *dropped* in the right way accidentally hits any person, *equipment* or other *outside influence* before coming to rest.

Exception – When Ball Dropped in Right Way is Deliberately Deflected or Stopped by Any Person: For what to do when the *dropped* ball is deliberately deflected or stopped by any person before it comes to rest, see Rule 14.3d.

Rule 14.3c(1) Interpretations:

14.3c(1)/1 – What to Do When Dropped Ball Moves After Coming to Rest Against a Player's Foot or Equipment

A player *drops* a ball in the right way, but the ball is accidentally stopped by the player's foot or *equipment* (such as a *tee* that is marking the *relief area*) and comes to rest in the *relief area*. There is no penalty, the player has completed taking relief and must play the ball as it lies.

If the ball then moves when the player moves his foot or the *equipment*, the player must *replace* the ball as required by Rule 9.4 but gets no penalty as the ball's movement was a result of reasonable actions taken in taking relief under a Rule (see Exception 4 to Rule 9.4 – Accidental Movement Anywhere Except on Putting Green While Applying Rule).

(2) **What to Do if Ball Dropped in Right Way Comes to Rest Outside Relief Area**. If the ball comes to rest outside the *relief area*, the player must *drop* a ball in the right way a second time.

If that ball also comes to rest outside the *relief area*, the player must then complete taking relief by placing a ball using the procedures for *replacing* a ball in Rules 14.2b(2) and 14.2e:

- The player must place a ball on the spot where the ball *dropped* the second time first touched the ground.

- If the placed ball does not stay at rest on that spot, the player must place a ball on that spot a second time.

- If the ball placed a second time also does not stay on that spot, the player must place a ball on the nearest spot where the ball will stay at rest, subject to the limits in Rule 14.2e.

DIAGRAM 14.3c: BALL MUST BE DROPPED IN AND COME TO REST IN RELIEF AREA

The ball is dropped in the right way under Rule 14.3b and the ball comes to rest in the relief area, so the relief procedure is complete.	The ball is dropped in the right way under Rule 14.3b, but comes to rest outside the relief area, and so the ball must be dropped the right way a second time.	The ball is dropped in the wrong way as it is dropped outside the relief area, and so the ball must be dropped again in the right way.

Rule 14.3c(2) Interpretations:

14.3c(2)/1 – Ball Dropped in Right Way Twice That Comes to Rest Outside Relief Area Might Be Placed Outside Relief Area

If a player must complete the *dropping* procedure by placing a ball using Rules 14.2b(2) and 14.2e, this might result in the player placing the ball outside the *relief area*.

For example, if the player *drops* the ball for a second time in the right way near the edge of the *relief area* and it comes to rest outside the *relief area*, he or she must place a ball on the spot it first touched the ground after the second *drop*. But, if the placed ball does not stay on that spot after two attempts, the nearest spot not nearer the *hole* where the ball will stay at rest might be inside or outside the *relief area*.

14.3c(2)/2 – Where to Place Ball Dropped in Right Way Twice in Relief Area with a Bush in It

If a player must complete the *dropping* procedure by placing a ball using Rules 14.2b(2) and 14.2e, this might result in the player attempting to place a ball other than on the ground.

For example, if the player is *dropping* into a bush in the *relief area*, and with both *drops* the ball comes to rest outside the *relief area*, Rule 14.3c(2) provides that he or she must place a ball on the spot it first touched the ground after the second *drop*. If the ball first struck the bush when *dropped* for the second time, the "ground" includes the bush, and the player must attempt to place the ball where it first struck the bush. But, if the placed ball does not stay on that spot after two attempts, the player must place the ball on the nearest spot not nearer the *hole* where the ball will stay at rest, subject to the limits in Rule 14.2e.

Rule 14.3c General Interpretations:

14.3c/1 – Relief Area Includes Everything in Relief Area

A player's *relief area* includes tall grass, bushes or other growing things in it. If a player's *dropped* ball comes to rest in a bad lie in the *relief area*, it has still come to rest in the *relief area*.

For example, a player *drops* his or her ball in the right way and it stays in a bush in the *relief area*. The bush is part of the *relief area* and, therefore, the ball is *in play* and the player is not allowed to *drop* again under Rule 14.3c.

14.3c/2 – Ball May Be Dropped in No Play Zone

In *dropping* a ball under a relief Rule, the player may *drop a ball in a no play zone* so long as that *no play zone* is part of the *relief area*. However, the player must then take relief under the Rule that applies.

For example, a player may take relief from a *penalty area* and *drop* a ball in a *no play zone* in an *abnormal course condition*. But, after the *dropped* ball comes to rest in the *relief area* required by Rule 17 (Penalty Area Relief), the player must take relief under Rule 16.1f.

14.3d What to Do if Ball Dropped in Right Way is Deliberately Deflected or Stopped by Person

For purposes of this Rule, a *dropped* ball is "deliberately deflected or stopped" when:

* A person deliberately touches the ball in motion after it hits the ground, or

* The ball in motion hits any *equipment* or other object or any person (such as the player's *caddie*) that a player deliberately positioned or left in a particular location so that the *equipment*, object or person might deflect or stop the ball in motion.

When a ball *dropped* in the right way is deliberately deflected or stopped by any person (whether in the *relief area* or outside the *relief area*) before it comes to rest:

* The player must *drop a ball* again, using the procedures in Rule 14.3b (which means that the ball that was deliberately deflected or stopped does not count as one of the two *drops* required before a ball must be placed under Rule 14.3c(2)).

* If the ball was deliberately deflected or stopped by any player or his or her *caddie*, that player gets the **general penalty**.

Exception – When There Is No Reasonable Chance Ball Will Come to Rest in Relief Area: If a ball *dropped* in the right way is deliberately deflected or stopped (whether in the *relief area* or outside the *relief area*) when there is no reasonable chance it will come to rest in the *relief area*:

* There is no penalty to any player, and

* The *dropped* ball is treated as having come to rest outside the *relief area* and counts as one of the two *drops* required before a ball must be placed under Rule 14.3c(2).

Penalty for Playing Ball from a *Wrong Place* or Playing Ball that was Placed Instead of *Dropped* in Breach of Rule 14.3: *General Penalty* Under Rule 14.7a.

If multiple Rule breaches result from a single act or related acts, see Rule 1.3c(4).

See Rules 22.2 (in *Foursomes*, either *partner* may act for the *side* and action by the *partner* is treated as action of the player); **23.5** (in *Four-Ball*, either *partner* may act for the *side* and action by the *partner* concerning the player's ball or *equipment* is treated as action of the player).

14.4 When Player's Ball is Back in Play after Original Ball Was Out of Play

When a player's ball *in play* is lifted from the *course* or is *lost* or *out of bounds*, the ball is no longer *in play*.

The player has a ball *in play* again only when he or she:

- Plays the original ball or another ball from the *teeing area*, or
- *Replaces*, *drops* or places the original ball or another ball on the *course* with the intent for that ball to be *in play*.

If the player returns a ball to the *course* in any way with the intent for it to be *in play*, the ball is *in play* even if it was:

- *Substituted* for the original ball when not allowed under the Rules, or
- *Replaced*, *dropped* or placed (1) in a *wrong place*, (2) in a wrong way or (3) by using a procedure that did not apply.

A *replaced* ball is *in play* even if the *ball-marker* marking its spot has not been removed.

Rule 14.4 Interpretations:

14.4/1 – Placed Ball Is Not in Play Unless There Was Intent to Put It in Play

When a ball is placed or *replaced* on the ground, it needs to be determined whether it was put down with the intent of putting it *in play*.

For example, the player *marks* the ball on the *putting green* by placing a coin right behind the ball, lifts the ball and gives it to his or her *caddie* to have it cleaned. The *caddie* then places the ball right behind or right next to the coin (not on the ball's original spot) to help the player read the *line of play*

---

from the other side of the hole. The ball is not *in play* as the *caddie* did not place the ball with the intention of putting it *in play*.

In this case, the ball is not *in play* until it is repositioned with the intention of *replacing* the ball as required by Rule 14.2. If the player makes a *stroke* at the ball while it is out of play, the player would be playing a *wrong ball*.

14.4/2 – Test Drops Are Not Allowed

The *dropping* procedure in Rule 14.3 means that there is an element of uncertainty when taking relief under a Rule. It is not in the spirit of the game to test how a *dropped* ball will react.

For example, in taking relief from a cart part (*immovable obstruction*), a player determines his or her *relief area* and realizes that the ball may roll and come to rest in a bush in the *relief area*. Knowing that the *dropped* ball would not be *in play* without intent, the player test *drops* a ball in one side of the *relief area* to see if it rolls into the bush.

Since this act is contrary to the spirit of the game, the *Committee* is justified in disqualifying the player under Rule 1.2a (Serious Misconduct).

14.5 Correcting Mistake Made in Substituting, Replacing, Dropping or Placing Ball

14.5a Player May Lift Ball to Correct Mistake Before Ball Is Played

When a player has *substituted* another ball for the original ball when not allowed under the Rules, or the player's ball *in play* was *replaced*, *dropped* or *placed* (1) in a *wrong place* or came to rest in a *wrong place*, (2) in a wrong way or (3) by using a procedure that did not apply:

- The player may lift the ball without penalty and correct the mistake.
- But this is allowed only before the ball is played.

14.5b When Player May Change to a Different Rule or Relief Option When Correcting Mistake in Taking Relief

When correcting a mistake in taking relief, whether the player must use the same Rule and relief option originally used or may change to a different Rule or relief option depends on the nature of the mistake:

(1) **When Ball Was Put in Play Under Rule That Did Not Apply**.

- In correcting this mistake, the player may use any Rule that applies to his or her situation.

- For example, if the player mistakenly took unplayable ball relief for his or her ball in a *penalty area* (which Rule 19.1 does not allow), the player must correct the mistake by either *replacing* the ball (if it had been lifted) under Rule 9.4, or taking penalty relief under Rule 17 and may use any relief option under that Rule that applies to his or her situation.

(2) When Ball Was Put in Play Under Rule That Applied but Ball Was Dropped or Placed in Wrong Place.

- In correcting this mistake, the player must go on to take relief under the same Rule but may use any relief option under that Rule that applies to his or her situation.

- For example, if when taking relief for an unplayable ball, the player used the lateral relief option Rule (19.2c) and mistakenly *dropped* the ball outside the required *relief area*, in correcting the mistake the player must go on to take relief under Rule 19.2 but may use any of the relief options in Rule 19.2a, b or c.

(3) When Ball Was Put in Play Under Rule That Applied and Was Dropped or Placed in Right Place, but Rule Requires Ball to Be Dropped or Placed Again.

- In correcting this mistake, the player must go on to take relief using the same Rule and the same relief option under that Rule.

- For example, if when taking relief for an unplayable ball, the player used the lateral relief option (Rule 19.2c) and the ball was (1) *dropped* in the right *relief area* but (2) was *dropped* in a wrong way (see Rule 14.3b) or came to rest outside the *relief area* (see Rule 14.3c), in correcting the mistake the player must go on to take relief under Rule 19.2 and must use the same relief option (lateral relief under Rule 19.2c).

Rule 14.5b(3) Interpretations:

14.5b(3)/1 – Player May Change Relief Areas When Dropping Again for Back-On-the-Line Relief

When a player is required to *drop* a ball a second time after using back-on-the-line relief under Rule 16.1c(2) (Abnormal Course Condition Relief), Rule 17.1d(2) (Penalty Area Relief), or Rule 19.2b or Rule 19.3b (Unplayable Ball Relief), he or she is required to *drop* again under the back-on-the-line relief option in the relevant Rule. But, when *dropping* for the second time, the player is allowed to change reference points so that the *relief area* is nearer to or farther from the *hole*.

For example, a player's ball comes to rest in a *penalty area* and he or she chooses to take back-on-the-line relief. The player picks a reference point and *drops* the ball in the right way, but it rolls out of the *relief area*. When the player *drops* again under back-on-the-line relief, he or she may choose a different reference point that is nearer or farther from the *hole*.

14.5b(3)/2 – Player May Change Areas of the Course in the Relief Area When Dropping Again

When a player's *relief area* is located in more than one *area of the course* and he or she is required to *drop* again under that relief option, the player may *drop* in a different *area of the course* within the same *relief area*.

For example, a player chooses to take unplayable ball relief under Rule 19.2c (Lateral Relief) and his or her *relief area* is partially in the *general area* and partially in a *bunker*. The player's *drop* first touches the *bunker* in the *relief area* and comes to rest in the *general area* or outside the entire *relief area*, so the player must *drop* again. When doing so, he or she may *drop* the ball in the *general area* portion of the *relief area*.

14.5c No Penalties for Ball Lifted to Correct Mistake

When a ball is lifted under Rule 14.5a to correct a mistake:

* The player does not count any penalty for actions that were taken relating to that ball after the mistake and before it was lifted, such as for accidentally causing it to *move* (see Rule 9.4b).

* But if those same actions were also in breach of a Rule relating to the ball that was put *in play* to correct the mistake (such as when those actions *improved* the *conditions affecting the stroke* for both the ball now *in play* and the original ball before it was lifted), the penalty applies to the ball now *in play*.

14.6 Making Next Stroke from Where Previous Stroke Made

This Rule applies whenever a player is required or allowed under the Rules to make the next *stroke* from where a previous *stroke* was made (that is, when taking *stroke-and-distance* relief, or playing again after a *stroke* that is cancelled or otherwise does not count).

- How the player must put a ball *in play* depends on the *area of the course* where that previous *stroke* was made.

- In all of these situations, the player may use either the original ball or another ball.

14.6a Previous Stroke Made from Teeing Area

The original ball or another ball must be played from anywhere inside the *teeing area* (and may be teed) under Rule 6.2b.

14.6b Previous Stroke Made from General Area, Penalty Area or Bunker

The original ball or another ball must be *dropped* in this *relief area* (see Rule 14.3):

- Reference Point: The spot where the previous *stroke* was made (which if not known must be estimated).

- Size of Relief Area Measured from Reference Point: One *club-length*, **but** with these limits:

- Limits on Location of Relief Area:

  » Must be in the same *area of the course* as the reference point, and

  » Must not be nearer the *hole* than the reference point.

14.6c Previous Stroke Made from Putting Green

The original ball or another ball must be placed on the spot where the previous *stroke* was made (which if not known must be estimated) (see Rule 14.2), using the procedures for *replacing* a ball under Rules 14.2b(2) and 14.2e.

Penalty for Playing Ball from a *Wrong Place* in Breach of Rule 14.6: *General Penalty* Under Rule 14.7a.

If multiple Rule breaches result from a single act or related acts, see Rule 1.3c(4).

DIAGRAM 14.6: MAKING NEXT STROKE FROM WHERE PREVIOUS STROKE MADE

When a player is required or allowed to make the next stroke from where the previous stroke was made, how the player must put a ball into play depends on the area of the course where that previous stroke was made.

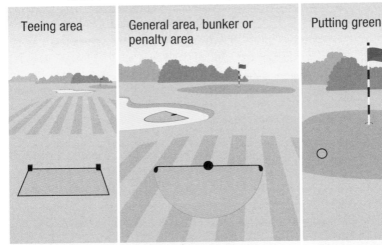

Teeing area	General area, bunker or penalty area	Putting green

The previous stroke was made from the teeing area, so a ball must be played from anywhere inside the teeing area.

The previous stroke was made from the general area, a bunker or a penalty area, so the reference point is the spot where the previous stroke was made. A ball is dropped within one club-length of that reference point, but in the same area of the course as the reference point and not nearer the hole than the reference point.

The previous stroke was made from the putting green, so a ball is placed on the spot where the previous stroke was made.

14.7 Playing from Wrong Place

14.7a Place from Where Ball Must Be Played

After starting a hole:

- A player must make each *stroke* from where his or her ball comes to rest, **except** when the Rules require or allow the player to play a ball from another place (see Rule 9.1).

- A player must not play his or her ball *in play* from a *wrong place*.

Penalty for Playing Ball from a *Wrong Place* in Breach of Rule 14.7a: *General Penalty*.

If multiple Rule breaches result from a single act or related acts, see Rule 1.3c(4).

14.7b How to Complete a Hole after Playing from Wrong Place in Stroke Play

(1) **Player Must Decide Whether to Play Out Hole with Ball Played from Wrong Place or to Correct the Mistake by Playing from Right Place.** What a player does next depends on whether it was a *serious breach* – that is, whether the player could have gained a significant advantage by playing from a *wrong place*:

- **Not a Serious Breach.** The player must play out the hole with the ball played from a *wrong place*, without correcting the mistake.

- **Serious Breach.**

  » The player must correct the mistake by playing out the hole with a ball played from a right place under the Rules.

  » If the player does not correct the mistake before making a *stroke* to begin another hole or, for the final hole of the *round*, before returning his or her *scorecard*, the player is **disqualified**.

- **What to Do If Uncertain Whether Breach Is Serious.** The player should play out the hole with both the ball played from a *wrong place* and a second ball played from a right place under the Rules.

(2) **Player Who Tries to Correct Mistake Must Report to Committee.** If the player tries to correct the mistake under (1) by playing a ball from a right place:

- The player must report the facts to the *Committee* before returning the *scorecard*.

- This applies whether the player played out the hole with only that ball or with two balls (and even if the player scores the same with both balls).

If the player does not report the facts to the *Committee*, he or she is **disqualified**.

(3) **When Player Tried to Correct Mistake, Committee Will Decide Player's Score for Hole.** The player's score for the hole depends on whether the *Committee* decides that there was a *serious breach* in playing the original ball from a *wrong place*:

- **No Serious Breach.**

  » The score with the ball played from a *wrong place* counts, and the player gets the *general penalty* under Rule 14.7a (which means that **two penalty strokes** are added to the score with that ball).

» If a second ball was played, all strokes with that ball (including *strokes* made and any penalty strokes solely from playing that ball) do not count.

• Serious Breach.

» The score with the ball played to correct the mistake of playing from a *wrong place* counts, and the player gets the *general penalty* under Rule 14.7a (which means that **two penalty strokes** are added to the score with that ball).

» The *stroke* made in playing the original ball from a *wrong place* and any more strokes with that ball (including *strokes* made and any penalty strokes solely from playing that ball) do not count.

» If the ball played to correct the mistake was also played from a *wrong place*:

— If the *Committee* decides that this was not a *serious breach*, the player gets the *general penalty* (**two more penalty strokes**) under Rule 14.7a, making a **total of four penalty strokes** that are added to the score with that ball (two for playing the original ball from a *wrong place* and two for playing the other ball from a *wrong place*).

— If the *Committee* decides that this was a *serious breach*, the player is **disqualified**.

Rule 14.7b Interpretations:

14.7b/1 – Player Gets Penalty for Each Stroke Made from Area Where Play Is Not Allowed

When a player's ball comes to rest in an area where play is not allowed, the player must take relief under the appropriate Rule. In *stroke play*, if the player plays the ball from that area (such as a *no play zone* or *wrong green*) the player gets two penalty strokes for each *stroke* made from that area.

For example, a player's ball comes to rest in a *no play zone* within a *penalty area*. The player enters the *no play zone* and makes a *stroke* at the ball, which moves only a few yards and remains in the *no play zone*. The player then makes another *stroke* at the ball and it comes to rest outside the *no play zone*.

Each stroke counts, and the player gets the *general penalty* under Rule 14.7 for playing from a *wrong place* for each *stroke* made from the *no play zone* for a total of four penalty strokes. The player is required to play out the hole with the ball played from the *no play zone*, unless it was a *serious breach*. For a *serious breach*, the player must correct the mistake (see Rule 14.7b).

14.7b/2 – Ball in Wrong Place If Club Strikes Condition Relief Was Taken From

When a player is taking relief from interference by an *abnormal course condition*, he or she is required to take relief from all interference from that condition. If the ball is *dropped* at a spot or comes to rest in a spot where the player has any type of interference from that condition, the ball is in a *wrong place*.

For example, a player's ball comes to rest on a cart path and the player decides to take relief. He or she estimates the *nearest point of complete relief* using the club that would have been used to play the ball from the cart path. Having measured the *relief area* from that point, the player drops a ball that comes to rest in the *relief area* and makes a *stroke*, hitting the cart path during the *stroke*. Because the cart path was in the player's area of intended swing, the player still had interference. Therefore, he or she did not properly determine the *relief area* and gets the *general penalty* for playing from a *wrong place*.

However, if the player had interference from the condition because, for example he or she decided to play in a different direction or his or her feet slipped when making the *stroke* and altered the intended swing, the player would not be considered to have played from a *wrong place*.

Free Relief

Rules 15-16

RULE 15

Relief from Loose Impediments and Movable Obstructions (including Ball or Ball-Marker Helping or Interfering with Play)

Purpose of Rule:

Rule 15 covers when and how the player may take free relief from loose impediments and movable obstructions.

- These movable natural and artificial objects are not treated as part of the challenge of playing the course, and a player is normally allowed to remove them when they interfere with play.

- But the player needs to be careful in moving loose impediments near his or her ball off the putting green, because there will be a penalty if moving them causes the ball to move.

15.1 Loose Impediments

15.1a Removal of Loose Impediment

Without penalty, a player may remove a *loose impediment* anywhere on or off the *course*, and may do so in any way (such as by using a hand or foot or a club or other *equipment*).

But there are two **exceptions:**

Exception 1 – Removing Loose Impediment Where Ball Must Be Replaced: Before *replacing* a ball that was lifted or *moved* from anywhere except the *putting green*:

- A player must not deliberately remove a *loose impediment* that, if moved when the ball was at rest, would have been likely to have caused the ball to *move*.

- If the player does so, he or she gets **one penalty stroke, but** the removed *loose impediment* does not need to be replaced.

This exception applies both during a *round* and while play is stopped under Rule 5.7a. It does not apply to a *loose impediment* that is removed as a result of *marking* the spot of a ball, lifting or *replacing* a ball or causing a ball to *move*.

Exception 2 – Restrictions on Deliberately Removing Loose Impediments to Affect Ball in Motion (see Rule 11.3).

214

Rule 15.1a Interpretations:

15.1a/1 – Removing a Loose Impediment, Including Assistance from Others

Loose impediments come in many shapes and sizes (such as acorns and large rocks), and the means and methods by which they may be removed are not limited, except that removal must not unreasonably delay play (see Rule 5.6a).

For example, a player may use a towel, hand or hat, or may lift or push a *loose impediment* for removal. A player is also allowed to seek help in removing *loose impediments*, such as by asking spectators for assistance in removing a large tree branch.

15.1a/2 – Player Allowed to Break Off Part of Loose Impediment

While Rule 15.1a allows a player to remove a *loose impediment*, he or she may also break off part of a *loose impediment*.

For example, a player's ball comes to rest behind a large branch that has broken off a tree. Rather than seek help from other players to remove the entire tree branch, the player may break off the part that is in his or her way.

15.1a/3 – Removal of Loose Impediment from Relief Area or Spot Where Ball to Be Dropped, Placed or Replaced

Exception 1 to Rule 15.1a makes clear that, before *replacing* a ball, the player must not remove a *loose impediment* that, if moved when the ball was at rest, would have been likely to cause the ball to *move*. This is because when the ball is in its initial location, the player risks the ball *moving* when removing the *loose impediment*.

However, when a ball is to be *dropped* or placed, the ball is not being put back in a specific spot and therefore removing *loose impediments* before *dropping* or placing a ball is allowed.

For example, if a player is applying Rule 14.3b when *dropping* a ball in a *relief area* or Rule 14.3c(2) when a *dropped* ball will not stay in a *relief area* and the player now must place a ball, the player is allowed to remove *loose impediments* from the *relief area* into which a ball will be *dropped* or from on or around the spot on which the player must place a ball.

15.1b Ball Moved When Removing Loose Impediment

If a player's removal of a *loose impediment* causes his or her ball to *move*:

- The ball must be *replaced* on its original spot (which if not known must be estimated) (see Rule 14.2).

- If the *moved* ball had been at rest anywhere **except** on the *putting green* (see Rule 13.1d) or in the *teeing area* (see Rule 6.2b(6)), the player gets **one penalty stroke** under Rule 9.4b, **except** when Rule 7.4 applies (no penalty for ball *moved* during search) or when another exception to Rule 9.4b applies.

Penalty for Playing Incorrectly *Substituted* **Ball or Playing Ball from a** *Wrong Place* **in Breach of Rule 15.1:** *General Penalty* **Under Rule 6.3b or 14.7a.**

If multiple Rule breaches result from a single act or related acts, see Rule 1.3c(4).

15.2 Movable Obstructions

This Rule covers free relief that is allowed from artificial objects that meet the definition of *movable obstruction*.

It does not give relief from *immovable obstructions* (a different type of free relief is allowed under Rule 16.1) or *boundary objects* or *integral objects* (no free relief is allowed).

15.2a Relief from Movable Obstruction

(1) **Removal of Movable Obstruction.** Without penalty, a player may remove a *movable obstruction* anywhere on or off the *course* and may do so in any way.

But there are **two exceptions:**

Exception 1 – Tee Markers Must Not be Moved When Ball Will Be Played from Teeing Area (see Rules 6.2b(4) and 8.1a(1)).

Exception 2 – Restrictions on Deliberately Removing Movable Obstruction to Affect a Ball in Motion (see Rule 11.3).

If a player's ball *moves* while he or she is removing a *movable obstruction*:

- There is no penalty, and

- The ball must be *replaced* on its original spot (which if not known must be estimated) (see Rule 14.2).

(2) **Relief When Ball Is in or on Movable Obstruction Anywhere on Course Except on Putting Green.** The player may take free relief by lifting the ball, removing the *movable obstruction* and *dropping* the original ball or another ball in this *relief area* (see Rule 14.3):

- Reference Point: The estimated point right under where the ball was at rest in or on the *movable obstruction*.

- Size of Relief Area Measured from Reference Point: One *club-length*, **but** with these limits:

- Limits on Location of Relief Area:

  » Must be in the same *area of the course* as the reference point, and

  » Must not be nearer the *hole* than the reference point.

DIAGRAM #1 15.2a: BALL MOVES WHEN MOVABLE OBSTRUCTION REMOVED (EXCEPT WHEN BALL IN OR ON OBSTRUCTION)

Ball moves

Ball must be replaced on its original spot

DIAGRAM #2 15.2a: BALL IN OR ON MOVABLE OBSTRUCTION

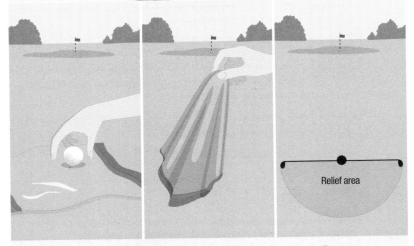

When a ball is in or on a movable obstruction (such as a towel) anywhere on the course, free relief may be taken by lifting the ball, removing the movable obstruction and, except on the putting green, dropping that ball or another ball. The reference point for taking relief is the estimated point right under where the ball was at rest in or on the movable obstruction. The relief area is one club-length from the reference point, is not nearer to the hole than the reference point and must be in the same area of the course as the reference point.

(3) **Relief When Ball Is in or on Movable Obstruction on Putting Green.** The player may take free relief by:

- Lifting the ball and removing the *movable obstruction,* and

- Placing the original ball or another ball on the estimated spot right under where the ball was at rest in or on the *movable obstruction,* using the procedures for *replacing* a ball under Rule 14.2b(2) and 14.2e.

15.2b Relief for Ball Not Found but in or on Movable Obstruction

If a player's ball has not been found and it is *known or virtually certain* that it came to rest in or on a *movable obstruction* on the *course,* the player may use this relief option instead of taking *stroke-and-distance* relief:

- The player may take free relief under Rule 15.2a(2) or 15.2a(3), using the estimated point right under where the ball last crossed the edge of the *movable obstruction* on the *course* as the reference point.

- Once the player puts another ball *in play* to take relief in this way:

» The original ball is no longer *in play* and must not be played.

» This is true even if it is then found on the *course* before the end of the three-minute search time (see Rule 6.3b).

But if it is not *known or virtually certain* that the ball came to rest in or on a *movable obstruction* and the ball is *lost*, the player must take *stroke-and-distance* relief under Rule 18.2.

Penalty for Playing Incorrectly *Substituted* **Ball or Playing Ball from a** *Wrong Place* **in Breach of Rule 15.2:** *General Penalty* **Under Rule 6.3b or 14.7a.**

If multiple Rule breaches result from a single act or related acts, see Rule 1.3c(4).

15.3 Ball or Ball-Marker Helping or Interfering with Play

15.3a Ball on Putting Green Helping Play

Rule 15.3a applies only to a ball at rest on the *putting green*, not anywhere else on the *course*.

If a player reasonably believes that a ball on the *putting green* might help anyone's play (such as by serving as a possible backstop near the *hole*), the player may:

- *Mark* the spot of the ball and lift it under Rule 13.1b if it is his or her own ball, or if the ball belongs to another player, require the other player to *mark* the spot and lift the ball (see Rule 14.1).

- The lifted ball must be *replaced* on its original spot (see Rule 14.2).

In *stroke play* only:

- A player who is required to lift a ball may play first instead, and

- If two or more players agree to leave a ball in place to help any player, and that player then makes a *stroke* with the helping ball left in place, each player who made the agreement gets the *general penalty* (two penalty strokes).

Rule 15.3a Interpretations:

15.3a/1 – Breach of Rule for Leaving Helping Ball in Place Does Not Require Knowledge

In *stroke play*, under Rule 15.3a, if two or more players agree to leave a ball in place on the *putting green* to help any player, and the *stroke* is made with

no knowledge = ~~footgen pen~~
knowledge = DQ

the helping ball left in place, each player who made the agreement gets two penalty strokes. A breach of Rule 15.3a does not depend on whether the players know that such an agreement is not allowed.

For example, in *stroke play*, before playing from just off the *putting green*, a player asks another player to leave his or her ball that is near the *hole*, in order to use it as a backstop. Without knowing this is not allowed, the other player agrees to leave his or her ball by the *hole* to help the other player. Once the *stroke* is made with the ball in place, both players get the penalty under Rule 15.3a.

The same outcome would apply if the player whose ball was near the hole offered to leave the ball *in play* to help the other player, and the other player accepted the offer and then played.

If the players know that they are not allowed to make such an agreement, but still do it, they are both disqualified under Rule 1.3b(1) for deliberately ignoring Rule 15.3a.

15.3a/2 – Players Allowed to Leave Helping Ball in Match Play

In a match, a player may agree to leave his or her ball in place to help the *opponent* since the outcome of any benefit that may come from the agreement affects only their match.

15.3b Ball Anywhere on Course Interfering with Play

(1) Meaning of Interference by Another Player's Ball. Interference under this Rule exists when another player's ball at rest:

- Might interfere with the player's area of intended *stance* or area of intended swing,

- Is on or close to the player's *line of play* such that, given the intended *stroke*, there is a reasonable chance the player's ball in motion could hit that ball, or

- Is close enough to distract the player in making the *stroke*.

(2) When Relief Is Allowed from Interfering Ball. If a player reasonably believes that another player's ball anywhere on the *course* might interfere with the player's own play:

- The player may require the other player to *mark* the spot and lift the ball (see Rule 14.1), and the ball must not be cleaned (**except** when lifted from the *putting green* under Rule 13.1b) and must be *replaced* on its original spot (see Rule 14.2).

- If the other player does not mark the spot before lifting the ball or cleans the lifted ball when not allowed, he or she gets **one penalty stroke**.

- In *stroke play* only, a player required to lift his or her ball under this Rule may play first instead.

A player is not allowed to lift his or her ball under this Rule based only on the player's own belief that the ball might interfere with another player's play.

If the player lifts his or her ball when not required to do so by the other player (**except** when lifting the ball on the *putting green* under Rule 13.1b), the player gets **one penalty stroke**.

15.3c Ball-Marker Helping or Interfering with Play

If a *ball-marker* might help or interfere with play, a player may:

- Move the *ball-marker* out of the way if it is his or her own, or

- If the *ball-marker* belongs to another player, require that player to move the *ball-marker* out of the way, for the same reasons as he or she may require a ball to be lifted under Rules 15.3a and 15.3b.

The *ball-marker* must be moved out of the way to a new spot measured from its original spot, such as by using one or more clubhead-lengths.

Either the lifted ball must be *replaced* on its original spot (see Rule 14.2) or the *ball-marker* must be replaced to *mark* that spot.

Penalty for Breach of Rule 15.3: *General Penalty.*

This penalty also applies if the player:

- Makes a *stroke* without waiting for a helping ball or *ball-marker* to be lifted or moved after becoming aware that another player (1) intended to lift or move it under this Rule or (2) had required someone else to do so, or

- Refuses to lift his or her ball or move his or her *ball-marker* when required to do so and a *stroke* is then made by the other player whose play might have been helped or interfered with.

Penalty for Playing Incorrectly *Substituted* **Ball or Playing Ball from a** *Wrong Place* **in Breach of Rule 15.3:** *General Penalty* **Under Rule 6.3b or 14.7a.**

If multiple Rule breaches result from a single act or related acts, see Rule 1.3c(4).

221

RULE
16

– AGIT

Relief from Abnormal Course Conditions (Including Immovable Obstructions), Dangerous Animal Condition, Embedded Ball

Purpose of Rule:

Rule 16 covers when and how the player may take free relief by playing a ball from a different place, such as when there is interference by an abnormal course condition or a dangerous animal condition.

- These conditions are not treated as part of the challenge of playing the course, and free relief is generally allowed except in a penalty area.

- The player normally takes relief by dropping a ball in a relief area based on the nearest point of complete relief.

This Rule also covers free relief when a player's ball is embedded in its own pitch mark in the general area.

16.1 Abnormal Course Conditions (Including Immovable Obstructions)

This Rule covers free relief that is allowed from interference by _animal holes_, _ground under repair_, _immovable obstructions_ or _temporary water_:

- These are collectively called _abnormal course conditions_, but each has a separate Definition.

- This Rule does not give relief from _movable obstructions_ (a different type of free relief is allowed under Rule 15.2a) or _boundary objects_ or _integral objects_ (no free relief is allowed).

16.1a When Relief Is Allowed

(1) **Meaning of Interference by Abnormal Course Condition**. Interference exists when any one of these is true:

- The player's ball touches or is in or on an _abnormal course condition_,

- An _abnormal course condition_ physically interferes with the player's area of intended _stance_ or area of intended swing, or

- Only when the ball is on the _putting green_, an _abnormal course condition_ on or off the _putting green_ intervenes on the _line of play_.

If the *abnormal course condition* is close enough to distract the player but does not meet any of these requirements, there is no interference under this Rule.

See Committee Procedures, Section 8; Model Local Rule F-23 (the *Committee* may adopt a Local Rule denying relief from an *abnormal course condition* that only interferes with the area of intended *stance*).

DIAGRAM 16.1a: WHEN RELIEF IS ALLOWED FOR ABNORMAL COURSE CONDITION

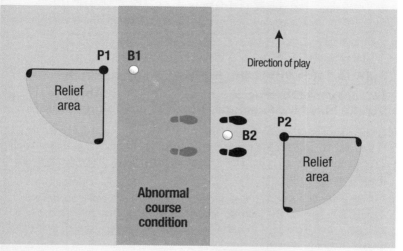

The diagram assumes the player is right-handed. Free relief is allowed for interference by an abnormal course condition (ACC), including an immovable obstruction, when the ball touches or lies in or on the condition (B1), or the condition interferes with the area of intended stance (B2) or swing. The nearest point of complete relief for B1 is P1, and is very close to the condition. For B2, the nearest point of complete relief is P2, and is farther from the condition as the stance has to be clear of the ACC.

(2) **Relief Allowed Anywhere on Course Except When Ball Is in Penalty Area.** Relief from interference by an *abnormal course condition* is allowed under Rule 16.1 only when both:

- The *abnormal course condition* is on the *course* (not *out of bounds*), and

- The ball is anywhere on the *course*, **except** in a *penalty area* (where the player's only relief is under Rule 17).

223

(3) No Relief When Clearly Unreasonable to Play Ball. There is no relief under Rule 16.1:

- When playing the ball as it lies is clearly unreasonable because of something other than an *abnormal course condition* (such as when a player is standing in *temporary water* or on an *immovable obstruction* but is unable to make a *stroke* because of where the ball lies in a bush), or

- When interference exists only because a player chooses a club, type of *stance* or swing or direction of play that is clearly unreasonable under the circumstances.

See Committee Procedures, Section 8; Model Local Rule F-23
(the *Committee* may adopt a Local Rule allowing free relief from interference by temporary immovable obstructions on or off the *course*).

Rule 16.1a(3) Interpretations:

16.1a(3)/1 – Obstruction Interfering with Abnormal Stroke May Not Preclude Player From Taking Relief

In some situations a player may have to adopt an abnormal swing, *stance* or direction of play in playing his or her ball to accommodate a given situation. If the abnormal *stroke* is not clearly unreasonable given the circumstances, the player is permitted to take free relief under Rule 16.1.

For example, in the *general area*, a right-handed player's ball is so close to a *boundary object* on the left side of a hole that he or she must make a left-handed swing to play towards the *hole*. In making the left-handed swing, the player's *stance* is interfered with by an *immovable obstruction*.

The player is allowed relief from the *immovable obstruction* since use of a left-handed swing is not clearly unreasonable in the circumstances.

After the relief procedure for the left-handed swing is complete, the player may then use a normal right-handed swing for the next *stroke*. If the *obstruction* interferes with the right-handed swing, the player may take relief for the right-handed swing under Rule 16.1b or play the ball as it lies.

16.1a(3)/2 – Player May Not Use Clearly Unreasonable Stroke to Get Relief from Condition

A player may not use a clearly unreasonable *stroke* to get relief from an *abnormal course condition*. If the player's *stroke* is clearly unreasonable given the circumstances, relief under Rule 16.1 is not allowed, and he or she must either play the ball as it lies or take unplayable ball relief.

For example, in the *general area*, a right-handed player's ball is in a bad lie. A nearby *immovable obstruction* would not interfere with the player's normal right-handed *stroke*, but would interfere with a left-handed *stroke*. The player states that he or she is going to make the next *stroke* left-handed and believes that, since the *obstruction* would interfere with such a *stroke*, Rule 16.1b allows relief.

However, since the only reason for the player to use a left-handed *stroke* is to escape a bad *lie* by taking relief, use of the left-handed *stroke* is clearly unreasonable and the player is not allowed to take relief under Rule 16.1b (Rule 16.1a(3)).

The same principles would apply to the use of a clearly unreasonable *stance*, direction of play or the choice of a club.

16.1a(3)/3 – Application of Rule 16.1a(3) When Ball Lies Underground in Animal Hole

In deciding whether relief should be denied under Rule 16.1a(3) for a ball lying underground in an *animal hole*, the decision is made based on the *lie* the ball would have at the entrance to the *hole* as opposed to the ball's position underground in the *hole*.

For example, in the *general area*, a player's ball comes to rest underground in a *hole* made by an *animal*. A large bush is immediately next to and overhanging the entrance to the *animal hole*.

The nature of the area at the entrance of the *animal hole* is such that, if the *animal hole* was not there, it would be clearly unreasonable for the player to make a *stroke* at the ball (because of the overhanging bush). In such a situation, the player is not allowed to take relief under Rule 16.1b. The player must play the ball as it lies or proceed under Rule 19 (Ball Unplayable).

If the ball lies in an *animal hole* but is not underground, the spot of the ball is used to determine whether it is clearly unreasonable to play the ball and if Rule 16.1a(3) applies. If Rule 16.1a(3) does not apply, the player is allowed relief without penalty under Rule 16.1b. The same principles would apply to a ball that is underground in an *immovable obstruction*.

16.1b Relief for Ball in General Area

If a player's ball is in the *general area* and there is interference by an *abnormal course condition* on the *course*, the player may take free relief by *dropping* the original ball or another ball in this *relief area* (see Rule 14.3):

- Reference Point: The *nearest point of complete relief* in the *general area*.

- Size of Relief Area Measured from Reference Point: One *club-length*, **but** with these limits:

- Limits on Location of Relief Area:

  » Must be in the *general area*,

  » Must not be nearer the *hole* than the reference point, and

  » There must be complete relief from all interference by the *abnormal course condition*.

DIAGRAM 16.1b: FREE RELIEF FROM ABNORMAL COURSE CONDITION IN GENERAL AREA

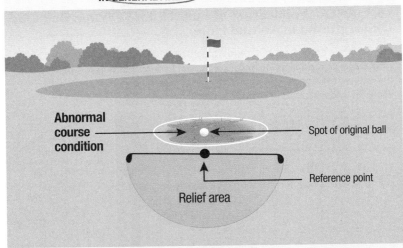

Free relief is allowed when the ball is in the general area and there is interference by an abnormal course condition. The nearest point of complete relief should be identified and a ball must be dropped in and come to rest in the relief area. The relief area is one club-length from the reference point, is not nearer to the hole than the reference point and must be in the general area. When taking relief, the player must take complete relief from all interference by the abnormal course condition.

Rule 16.1b Interpretations:

16.1b/1 – Relief Procedure When Ball Lies in Underground Abnormal Course Condition

When a ball enters an *abnormal course condition* and comes to rest underground (and Rule 16.1a(3) does not apply), the relief procedure that applies depends on whether the ball lies in the *general area* (Rule 16.1b), in a *bunker* (Rule 16.1c), in a *penalty area* (Rule 17.1c) or *out of bounds* (Rule 18.2b).

Examples of whether relief is available and how to take relief are as follows:

- A ball enters an *animal hole* through an entrance that is in a greenside *bunker* and is found at rest underneath the *putting green*. As the ball is not in the *bunker* or on the *putting green*, relief is taken under Rule 16.1b for a ball in the *general area*. The spot where the ball lies in the *animal hole* is used to determine the *nearest point of complete relief* and the *relief area* must be in the *general area*.

- A ball enters an *animal hole* through an entrance that is in a spot that is *out of bounds*. Part of the hole is in bounds and in the *general area*. The ball is found at rest in bounds, underground and in the *general area*. Relief is taken under Rule 16.1b for a ball in the *general area*. The spot where the ball lies in the *animal hole* is used to determine the *nearest point of complete relief* and the *relief area* must be in the *general area*.

- A ball enters an *animal hole* through an entrance that is in the *general area* but only about a foot from a boundary fence. The *animal hole* slopes steeply down below the fence, so that the ball is found at rest beyond the boundary line. Since the ball lies *out of bounds*, the player must take *stroke-and-distance* relief by adding one penalty stroke and play a ball from where the previous *stroke* was made (Rule 18.2b).

- A ball might have entered an *animal hole* through an entrance that is in the *general area* but it is not *known or virtually certain* that the ball that has not been found is in the *abnormal course condition*. In this situation, the ball is *lost* and the player must take *stroke-and-distance* relief by adding one penalty stroke and play a ball from where the previous *stroke* was made (Rule 18.2b).

16.1c Relief for Ball in Bunker

If a player's ball is in a *bunker* and there is interference by an *abnormal course condition* on the *course*, the player may take either free relief under (1) or penalty relief under (2):

(1) **Free Relief: Playing from Bunker.** The player may take free relief under Rule 16.1b, **except** that:

- The *nearest point of complete relief* and the *relief area* must be in the *bunker*.

- If there is no such *nearest point of complete relief* in the *bunker*, the player may still take this relief by using the *point of maximum available relief* in the *bunker* as the reference point.

227

DIAGRAM 16.1c: RELIEF FROM ABNORMAL COURSE CONDITION IN BUNKER

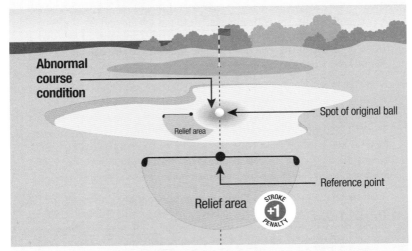

Abnormal course condition

Relief area

Spot of original ball

Reference point

Relief area

STROKE +1 PENALTY

The diagram assumes a right-handed player. When there is interference from an abnormal course condition in a bunker, free relief may be taken in the bunker under Rule 16.1b or relief may be taken outside the bunker for one penalty stroke. Relief outside the bunker is based on a reference line going straight back from the hole through the spot of the original ball in the bunker. The reference point is a point on the course outside the bunker chosen by the player that is on the reference line and is farther from the hole than the original spot (with no limit on how far back on the line). The relief area is one club-length from the reference point, is not nearer to the hole than the reference point, but may be in any area of the course. In choosing this reference point, the player should indicate the point by using an object (such as a tee).

(2) **Penalty Relief: Playing from Outside Bunker (Back-On-the-Line Relief).** For one penalty stroke, the player may *drop* the original ball or another ball (see Rule 14.3) in a *relief area* based on a reference line going straight back from the *hole* through the original spot of the ball:

- Reference Point: A point on the *course* chosen by the player that is on the reference line and is farther from the *hole* than that original spot (with no limit on how far back on the line):

  » In choosing this reference point, the player should indicate the point by using an object (such as a *tee*).

  » If the player *drops* the ball without having chosen this point, the reference point is treated as being the point on the line that is the same distance from the *hole* as where the *dropped* ball first touched the ground.

228

- Size of Relief Area Measured from Reference Point: One *club-length*, **but** with these limits:

- Limits on Location of Relief Area:

  » Must not be nearer the *hole* than the reference point, and

  » May be in any *area of the course*, **but**

  » If more than one *area of the course* is located within one *club-length* of the reference point, the ball must come to rest in the *relief area* in the same *area of the course* that the ball first touched when *dropped* in the *relief area*.

See Interpretation 17.1d(2)/1 – Recommendation That Player Physically Marks Reference Point on Reference Line

Rule 16.1c Interpretations:

16.1c/1 – Player Takes Maximum Available Relief; Then Decides to Take Back-On-the-Line Relief

If the player takes maximum available relief, he or she will still have interference from the *abnormal course condition* and may take further relief by using the back-on-the-line procedure for one penalty stroke. If the player decides to do this, the reference point for back-on-the-line relief is where the ball came to rest after taking maximum available relief.

16.1c/2 – After Lifting Ball Player May Change Relief Options Before Putting a Ball in Play

If a player lifts his or her ball to take relief under Rule 16.1c, he or she is not committed to the intended relief option under Rule 16.1c until the original ball is put *in play* or another ball is *substituted* under that option.

For example, a player elects to take relief from *temporary water* in a *bunker* and lifts the ball with the intention of taking free relief in the *bunker* (Rule 16.1c(1)). The player then realizes that where the Rule requires the ball to be *dropped* in the *bunker* will result in a very difficult shot.

After lifting the ball, but prior to putting a ball *in play*, the player may choose either of the two options of the Rule despite the original intention to take relief under Rule 16.1c(1).

229

16.1d Relief for Ball on Putting Green

If a player's ball is on the *putting green* and there is interference by an *abnormal course condition* on the *course*, the player may take free relief by placing the original ball or another ball on the spot of the *nearest point of complete relief*, using the procedures for *replacing* a ball under Rules 14.2b(2) and 14.2e.

- The *nearest point of complete relief* must be either on the *putting green* or in the *general area*.

- If there is no such *nearest point of complete relief*, the player may still take this free relief by using the *point of maximum available relief* as the reference point, which must be either on the *putting green* or in the *general area*.

DIAGRAM 16.1d: FREE RELIEF FROM ABNORMAL COURSE CONDITION ON PUTTING GREEN

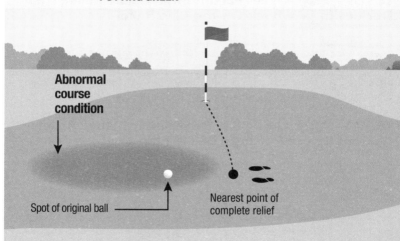

Abnormal course condition

Spot of original ball

Nearest point of complete relief

The diagram assumes the player is left-handed. When a ball is on the putting green and there is interference by an abnormal course condition, free relief may be taken by placing a ball on the spot of the nearest point of complete relief. The nearest point of complete relief must be either on the putting green or in the general area. If there is no such nearest point of complete relief, the player may still take this free relief by using the point of maximum available relief as the reference point, which must be either on the putting green or in the general area.

16.1e Relief for Ball Not Found but in or on Abnormal Course Condition

If a player's ball has not been found and it is *known or virtually certain* that the ball came to rest in or on an *abnormal course condition* on the *course*, the player may use this relief option instead of taking *stroke-and-distance* relief:

- The player may take relief under Rule 16.1b, c or d, using the estimated point where the ball last crossed the edge of the *abnormal course condition* on the *course* as the spot of the ball for purposes of finding the *nearest point of complete relief*.

- Once the player puts another ball *in play* to take relief in this way:

  » The original ball is no longer *in play* and must not be played.

  » This is true even if it is then found on the *course* before the end of the three-minute search time (see Rule 6.3b).

But if it is not *known or virtually certain* that the ball came to rest in or on an *abnormal course condition* and the ball is *lost*, the player must take *stroke-and-distance* relief under Rule 18.2.

16.1f Relief Must Be Taken from Interference by No Play Zone in Abnormal Course Condition

In each of these situations, the ball must not be played as it lies:

(1) **When Ball Is in No Play Zone.** If the player's ball is in a *no play zone* in or on an *abnormal course condition* in the *general area*, in a *bunker* or on the *putting green*:

- **No Play Zone in General Area.** The player must take free relief under Rule 16.1b.

- **No Play Zone in Bunker.** The player must take free relief or penalty relief under Rule 16.1c(1) or (2).

- **No Play Zone on Putting Green.** The player must take free relief under Rule 16.1d.

(2) **When No Play Zone Interferes with Stance or Swing for Ball Anywhere on Course Except Penalty Area.** If a player's ball is outside a *no play zone* and is in the *general area*, in a *bunker* or on the *putting green*, and a *no play zone* (whether in an *abnormal course condition* or in a *penalty area*) interferes with the player's area of intended *stance* or area of intended swing, the player must either:

231

- Take relief if allowed under Rule 16.1b, c or d, depending on whether the ball is in the *general area*, in a *bunker* or on the *putting green*, or

- Take unplayable ball relief under Rule 19.

For what to do when there is interference by a *no play zone* for a ball in a *penalty area*, see Rule 17.1e.

Penalty for Playing Ball from a *Wrong Place* in Breach of Rule 16.1: *General Penalty* Under Rule 14.7a.

Rule 16.1 General Interpretations:

16.1/1 – Relief from Abnormal Course Condition May Result in Better or Worse Conditions

If a player receives a better *lie*, area of intended swing or *line of play* in taking relief under Rule 16.1, this is the player's good fortune. There is nothing in Rule 16.1 that requires him or her to maintain identical *conditions* after relief is taken.

For example, in taking relief from a sprinkler head (*immovable obstruction*) in the rough, the player's *nearest point of complete relief* or *relief area* may be located in the fairway. If this results in the player being able to *drop* a ball in the fairway, this is allowed.

In some situations, the *conditions* may be less advantageous to the player after relief is taken as compared with the *conditions* before relief is taken, such as when the *nearest point of complete relief* or *relief area* is in an area of rocks.

16.1/2 – If Interference by Second Abnormal Course Condition Exists after Complete Relief Taken from First Condition, Further Relief May Be Taken

If a player has interference by a second *abnormal course condition* after taking complete relief from an *abnormal course condition*, the second situation is a new situation and the player may again take relief under Rule 16.1.

For example, in the *general area*, there are two areas of *temporary water* that are close together and the player has interference by one area but not the other. The player takes relief under Rule 16.1 and the ball comes to rest within the *relief area* at a spot where there is no longer interference by the first area of *temporary water*, but there is interference by the second area.

The player may play the ball as it lies or take relief from the second area under Rule 16.1.

The same outcome applies if there is interference by any other *abnormal course condition*.

16.1/3 – Player May Choose to Take Relief from Either Condition When Interference by Two Conditions Exists

There are situations where a player may have interference by two conditions at the same time and, in those situations, the player may choose to take relief from either condition. If, after taking relief from one condition, interference by the second condition exists, the player may then take relief from the second condition.

Some examples of this include when:

- In the *general area*, an *immovable obstruction* interferes with the area of the player's intended swing and the ball lies within an area defined as *ground under repair*.

  The player may first take relief from the *obstruction* under Rule 16.1, *drop* the ball in the *ground under repair* if this is part of the *relief area*, and then have the option of playing the ball as it lies in the *ground under repair* or taking relief under Rule 16.1b.

  Conversely, the player may take relief from the *ground under repair* and, if there is still interference by the *obstruction,* take relief from the *obstruction*.

- A player's ball is *embedded* in the *general area* in *ground under repair*.

  The player has the option of taking relief under Rule 16.1 for interference by the *ground under repair* or under Rule 16.3 for the *embedded ball*.

However, in such situations, the player may not, in a single procedure, concurrently take relief from two conditions by *dropping* a ball in a single *relief area* determined by a combined *nearest point of complete relief* from both conditions, except in the situation where the player has successively taken relief for interference from each condition and is essentially back where the player started.

16.1/4 – How to Take Relief When Ball Lies on Elevated Part of Immovable Obstruction

When a ball lies on an elevated part of an *immovable obstruction*, the *nearest point of complete relief* is on the ground under the *obstruction*. This is to make it easier to establish the *nearest point of complete relief* and to avoid it from being located on the branch of a nearby tree.

For example, a ball comes to rest in the *general area* on the elevated part of an *immovable obstruction*, such as a walkway or bridge over a deep hollow.

If the player elects to take relief in this situation, vertical distance is disregarded, and the *nearest point of complete relief* is the point (Point X) on the ground directly beneath where the ball lies on the *obstruction*, provided that the player does not have interference, as defined in Rule 16.1a, at this point. The player may take relief under Rule 16.1b by *dropping* a ball within the *relief area* determined using Point X as the reference point.

If there is interference from some part of the *obstruction* (such as a supporting column) for a ball located at Point X, the player may then take relief under Rule 16.1b by using Point X as the spot of the ball for purposes of finding the *nearest point of complete relief*.

See Interpretation 16.1/5 for when a ball lies underground and has interference from an *immovable obstruction*.

16.1/5 – How to Measure Nearest Point of Complete Relief When Ball Underground in Abnormal Course Condition

The procedure when a ball lies underground in an *abnormal course condition* (such as a tunnel) is different from when it is elevated. In such a case, determining the *nearest point of complete relief* must account for vertical and horizontal distance. In some cases, the *nearest point of complete relief* could be at the entrance to the tunnel, and in other cases it could be on the ground directly above where the ball lies in the tunnel.

See Interpretation 16.1/4 for when a ball lies on elevated part of an *immovable obstruction*.

16.1/6 – Player May Wait to Determine Nearest Point of Complete Relief When Ball Is Moving in Water

When a ball is *moving* in *temporary water*, whether a player chooses to lift the *moving* ball or *substitute* another ball in taking relief under Rule 16.1, the player is allowed to let the ball *move* to a better spot before determining the *nearest point of complete relief* so long as he or she does not unreasonably delay play (Exception 3 to Rule 10.1d and Rule 5.6a).

For example, a player's ball is *moving* in *temporary water* across the fairway. The player arrives at the ball when it is at Point A and realizes that when it gets to Point B, which is five yards away, his or her *nearest point of complete relief* will be in a much better spot than would be the case if relief is taken from Point A.

So long as the player does not unreasonably delay play (Rule 5.6a), he or she is allowed to delay starting the relief procedure until the ball reaches Point B.

16.2 Dangerous Animal Condition

16.2a When Relief Is Allowed

A "dangerous *animal* condition" exists when a dangerous *animal* (such as poisonous snakes, stinging bees, alligators, fire ants or bears) near a ball could cause serious physical injury to the player if he or she had to play the ball as it lies.

A player may take relief under Rule 16.2b from interference by a dangerous *animal* condition no matter where his or her ball is on the *course*, **except** that relief is not allowed:

- When playing the ball as it lies is clearly unreasonable because of something other than the dangerous *animal* condition (for example, when a player is unable to make a *stroke* because of where the ball lies in a bush) or

- When interference exists only because the player chooses a club, type of *stance* or swing or direction of play that is clearly unreasonable under the circumstances.

Rule 16.2a Interpretations:

16.2a/1 – No Free Relief from Dangerous Course Condition

If a player's ball comes to rest in a spot where the player has interference from a plant or bush that could cause physical harm, such as poison ivy or a cactus, while the player may be faced with challenging circumstances or may be allergic to a given plant, he or she is not entitled to free relief under the Rules.

16.2b Relief For Dangerous Animal Condition

When there is interference by a dangerous *animal* condition:

(1) **When Ball Is Anywhere Except Penalty Area.** The player may take relief under Rule 16.1b, c or d, depending on whether the ball is in the *general area*, in a *bunker* or on the *putting green*.

(2) **When Ball Is in Penalty Area.** The player may take free relief or penalty relief:

- **Free Relief.** Playing from Inside Penalty Area. The player may take free relief under Rule 16.1b, **except** that the *nearest point of complete relief* and the *relief area* must be in the *penalty area*.

235

- Penalty Relief: Playing from Outside Penalty Area.

  » The player may take penalty relief under Rule 17.1d.

  » If there is interference by a dangerous *animal* condition where the ball would be played after taking this penalty relief outside the *penalty area*, the player may take further relief under (1) without additional penalty.

  For purposes of this Rule, the *nearest point of complete relief* means the nearest point (not nearer the *hole*) where the dangerous *animal* condition does not exist.

Penalty for Playing Ball from a *Wrong Place* in Breach of Rule 16.2: *General Penalty* Under Rule 14.7a.

16.3 Embedded Ball

16.3a When Relief Is Allowed

(1) **Ball Must Be Embedded in General Area**. Relief is allowed under Rule 16.3b only when a player's ball is *embedded* in the *general area*.

- There is no relief under this Rule if the ball is *embedded* anywhere except in the *general area*.

- **But** if the ball is *embedded* on the *putting green*, the player may *mark* the spot of the ball and lift and clean the ball, repair the damage caused by the ball's impact, and *replace* the ball on its original spot (see Rule 13.1c(2)).

  Exceptions – When Relief Not Allowed for Ball Embedded in General Area: Relief under Rule 16.3b is not allowed:

- When the ball is *embedded* in sand in a part of the *general area* that is not cut to fairway height or less, or

- When interference by anything other than the ball being *embedded* makes the *stroke* clearly unreasonable (for example, when a player is unable to make a *stroke* because of where the ball lies in a bush).

(2) **Determining Whether Ball Is Embedded**. A player's ball is *embedded* only if:

- It is in its own pitch-mark made as a result of the player's previous *stroke*, and

- Part of the ball is below the level of the ground.

If the player cannot tell for sure whether the ball is in its own pitch-mark or a pitch-mark made by another ball, the player may treat the ball as *embedded* if it is reasonable to conclude from the available information that the ball is in its own pitch-mark.

A ball is not *embedded* if it is below the level of the ground as a result of anything other than the player's previous *stroke*, such as when:

- The ball is pushed into the ground by someone stepping on it,

- The ball is driven straight into the ground without becoming airborne, or

- The ball was *dropped* in taking relief under a Rule.

DIAGRAM 16.3a: WHEN A BALL IS EMBEDDED

Ball is embedded
Part of the ball (embedded in its own pitch-mark) is below the level of the ground.

◄──── **Level of Ground**

Ball is embedded
Despite the fact that the ball is not touching the soil, part of the ball (embedded in its own pitch-mark) is below the level of the ground.

Ball is NOT embedded
Even though the ball is sitting down in the grass, relief is not available because no part of the ball is below the level of the ground.

Rule 16.3a(2) Interpretations:

16.3a(2)/1 – Concluding Whether Ball Is Embedded in Its Own Pitch-mark

It must be reasonable to conclude that the ball is in its own pitch-mark for the player to take relief under Rule 16.3b.

An example of when it is reasonable to conclude that the ball came to rest in its own pitch-mark is when a player's approach shot lands on soft ground just short of the *putting green* in the *general area*. The player sees the ball bounce forward and then spin back. When the player arrives at the ball, he or she sees that it is *embedded* in the only pitch-mark in the area. Since it is

237

reasonable to conclude that the ball spun back into its own pitch-mark, the player may take relief under Rule 16.3b.

However, if a player's tee shot lands in the fairway and the ball bounces over a hill to a position where it could not be seen from the tee but is found in a pitch-mark, it is not reasonable to conclude that the ball is *embedded* in its own pitch-mark and the player is not allowed to take relief under Rule 16.3b.

16.3b Relief for Embedded Ball

When a player's ball is *embedded* in the *general area* and relief is allowed under Rule 16.3a, the player may take free relief by *dropping* the original ball or another ball in this *relief area* (see Rule 14.3):

- Reference Point: The spot right behind where the ball is *embedded*.
- Size of Relief Area Measured from Reference Point: One *club-length*, **but** with these limits:
- Limits on Location of Relief Area:
  - » Must be in the *general area*, and
  - » Must not be nearer the *hole* than the reference point.

See Committee Procedures, Section 8; Model Local Rule F-2 (the *Committee* may adopt a Local Rule allowing relief only for a ball *embedded* in an area cut to fairway height or less).

Penalty for Playing a Ball from a *Wrong Place* in Breach of Rule 16.3: *General Penalty* Under Rule 14.7a.

DIAGRAM 16.3b: FREE RELIEF FOR EMBEDDED BALL

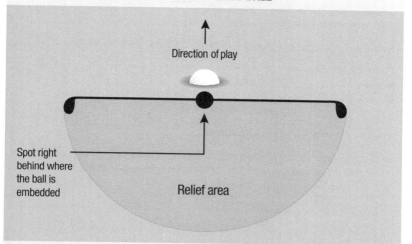

Direction of play

Spot right behind where the ball is embedded

Relief area

When a ball is embedded in the general area, free relief may be taken. The reference point for taking relief is the spot right behind where the ball is embedded. A ball must be dropped in and come to rest in the relief area. The relief area is one club-length from the reference point, is not nearer to the hole than the reference point and must be in the general area.

16.4 Lifting Ball to See If It Lies in Condition Where Relief Allowed

If a player reasonably believes that his or her ball lies in a condition where free relief is allowed under Rule 15.2, 16.1 or 16.3, but cannot decide that without lifting the ball:

- The player may lift the ball to see if relief is allowed, **but:**

- The spot of the ball must first be *marked*, and the lifted ball must not be cleaned (**except** on the *putting green*) (see Rule 14.1).

If the player lifts the ball without having this reasonable belief (**except** on the *putting green* where the player may lift under Rule 13.1b), he or she gets **one penalty stroke**.

If relief is allowed and the player takes relief, there is no penalty even if the player did not *mark* the spot of the ball before lifting it or cleaned the lifted ball.

If relief is not allowed or if the player chooses not to take relief that is allowed:

- The player gets **one penalty stroke** if he or she did not *mark* the spot of the ball before lifting it or cleaned the lifted ball when not allowed, and

- The ball must be *replaced* on its original spot (see Rule 14.2).

Penalty for Playing Incorrectly *Substituted* Ball or Playing Ball from a *Wrong Place* in Breach of Rule 16.4: *General Penalty* Under Rule 6.3b or 14.7a.

If multiple Rule breaches result from a single act or related acts, see Rule 1.3c(4).

Penalty Relief

Rules 17-19

Penalty Areas

Purpose of Rule:

Rule 17 is a specific Rule for penalty areas, which are bodies of water or other areas defined by the Committee where a ball is often lost or unable to be played. For one penalty stroke, players may use specific relief options to play a ball from outside the penalty area.

17.1 Options for Ball in Penalty Area

Penalty areas are defined as either red or yellow. This affects the player's relief options (see Rule 17.1d).

A player may stand in a *penalty area* to play a ball outside the *penalty area*, including after taking relief from the *penalty area*.

17.1a When Ball Is in Penalty Area

A ball is in a *penalty area* when any part of the ball:

- Lies on or touches the ground or anything else (such as any natural or artificial object) inside the edge of the *penalty area*, or
- Is above the edge or any other part of the *penalty area*.

If part of the ball is both in a *penalty area* and in another *area of the course*, see Rule 2.2c.

Rule 17.1a Interpretations:

17.1a/1 – Ball Is in Penalty Area Even if Penalty Area Is Improperly Marked

If stakes defining a body of water as a *penalty area* are improperly located, a player is not allowed to take advantage of such an error by the *Committee*.

For example, a ball is found in an expanse of water that, because of the configuration of the ground, is clearly part of the *penalty area* but is outside the stakes and, thus, technically outside the *penalty area*. The player may not claim that the ball at rest in the water is in *temporary water* since a *penalty area* includes any body of water on the *course*, whether or not marked by the *Committee* (see definition of "penalty area").

17.1a/2 – Ball Lost in Either Penalty Area or Abnormal Course Condition Adjacent to Penalty Area

If a player's ball is not found in an area where there is a *penalty area* and an adjacent *abnormal course condition*, the player must use reasonable judgment (Rule 1.3b(2)) when determining the location of the ball. If, after applying reasonable judgment, it is *known or virtually certain* that the ball has come to rest in one of those areas but both are equally likely, the player must take penalty relief under Rule 17.

17.1b Player May Play Ball as It Lies in Penalty Area or Take Penalty Relief

The player may either:

- Play the ball as it lies without penalty, under the same Rules that apply to a ball in the *general area* (which means there are no specific Rules limiting how a ball may be played from a *penalty area*), or

- Play a ball from outside the *penalty area* by taking penalty relief under Rule 17.1d or 17.2.

Exception – Relief Must Be Taken from Interference by No Play Zone in Penalty Area (see Rule 17.1e).

17.1c Relief for Ball Not Found but in Penalty Area

If a player's ball has not been found and it is *known or virtually certain* that the ball came to rest in a *penalty area*:

- The player may take penalty relief under Rule 17.1d or 17.2.

- Once the player puts another ball *in play* to take relief in this way:

  » The original ball is no longer *in play* and must not be played.

  » This is true even if it is then found on the *course* before the end of the three-minute search time (see Rule 6.3b).

But if it is not *known or virtually certain* that the ball came to rest in a *penalty area* and the ball is *lost*, the player must take *stroke-and-distance* relief under Rule 18.2.

17.1d Relief for Ball in Penalty Area

If a player's ball is in a *penalty area,* including when it is *known or virtually certain* to be in a *penalty area* even though not found, the player has these relief options, each for **one penalty stroke:**

(1) **Stroke-and-Distance Relief**. The player may play the original ball or another ball from where the previous *stroke* was made (see Rule 14.6).

(2) **Back-On-the-Line Relief**. The player may *drop* the original ball or another ball (see Rule 14.3) in a *relief area* that is based on a reference line going straight back from the *hole* through the estimated point where the original ball last crossed the edge of the *penalty area*:

- Reference Point: A point on the *course* chosen by the player that is on the reference line and is farther from the *hole* than the estimated point (with no limit on how far back on the line):

  » In choosing this reference point, the player should indicate the point by using an object (such as a tee).

  » If the player *drops* the ball without having chosen this point, the reference point is treated as being the point on the line that is the same distance from the *hole* as where the *dropped* ball first touched the ground.

- Size of Relief Area Measured from Reference Point: One *club-length*, **but** with these limits:

- Limits on Location of Relief Area:

  » Must not be nearer the *hole* than the reference point, and

  » May be in any *area of the course* except the same *penalty area*, but

  » If more than one *area of the course* is located within one *club-length* of the reference point, the ball must come to rest in the *relief area* in the same *area of the course* that the ball first touched when *dropped* in the *relief area*.

DIAGRAM #1 17.1d: RELIEF FOR BALL IN YELLOW PENALTY AREA

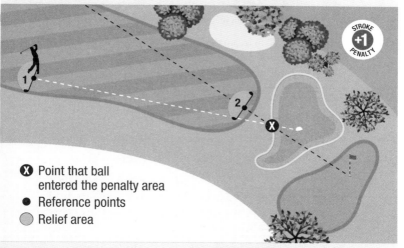

X Point that ball
entered the penalty area

● Reference points

◯ Relief area

When it is known or virtually certain that a ball is in a yellow penalty area and the player wishes to take relief, the player has **two options,** each for one penalty stroke:

(1) The player may take stroke-and-distance relief by playing the original ball or another ball from a relief area based on where the previous stroke was made (see Rule 14.6 and Diagram 14.6).

(2) The player may take back-on-the-line relief by dropping the original ball or another ball in a relief area based on a reference line going straight back from the hole through point X. The reference point is a point on the course chosen by the player that is on the reference line through point X (the point where the ball last crossed the edge of the yellow penalty area). There is no limit on how far back on the line the reference point may be. The relief area is one club-length from the reference point, is not nearer to the hole than the reference point and may be in any area of the course, except the same penalty area. In choosing this reference point, the player should indicate the point by using an object (such as a tee).

Rule 17.1d(2) Interpretations:

17.1d(2)/1 – Recommendation That Player Physically Marks Reference Point on Reference Line

Rule 17.1d allows a player to choose a reference point on the reference line that determines the *relief area* for back-on-the-line relief. Although the player should indicate the point by using an object (such as a tee), he or she may visually select a reference point.

If the player has visually selected a reference point, that point is used to determine the *relief area* and whether a ball must be *dropped* again.

The reason for recommending that the reference point is physically marked is that it assists with the relief procedure and determining whether the ball has been *dropped* in and has come to rest in the *relief area* (Rule 14.3).

(3) **Lateral Relief (Only for Red Penalty Area).** When the ball last crossed the edge of a red *penalty area*, the player may *drop* the original ball or another ball in this lateral *relief area* (see Rule 14.3):

- Reference Point: The estimated point where the original ball last crossed the edge of the red *penalty area*.

- Size of Relief Area Measured from Reference Point: Two *club-lengths*, **but** with these limits:

- Limits on Location of Relief Area:

  » Must not be nearer the *hole* than the reference point, and

  » May be in any area on the *course* except the same *penalty area*, **but**

  » If more than one *area of the course* is located within two *club-lengths* of the reference point, the ball must come to rest in the *relief area* in the same *area of the course* that the ball first touched when *dropped* in the *relief area*.

DIAGRAM #2 17.1d: RELIEF FOR BALL IN RED PENALTY AREA

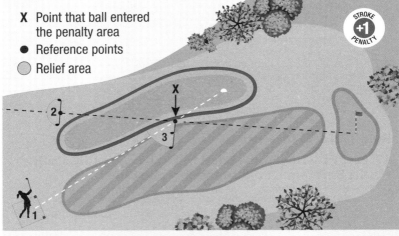

X Point that ball entered the penalty area
● Reference points
◯ Relief area

When it is known or virtually certain that a ball is in a red penalty area and the player wishes to take relief, the player has **three options**, each for one penalty stroke:

(1) The player may take stroke-and-distance relief (see point (1) in Diagram #1 17.1d).

(2) The player may take back-on-the-line relief (see point (2) in Diagram #1 17.1d).

(3) The player may take lateral relief (red penalty area only). The reference point for taking lateral relief is point X, which is the estimated point where the original ball last crossed the edge of the red penalty area. The relief area is two club-lengths from the reference point, is not nearer to the hole than the reference point and may be in any area of the course, except the same penalty area.

See Committee Procedures, Section 8; Model Local Rule B-2 (the *Committee* may adopt a Local Rule allowing lateral relief on the opposite side of a red *penalty area* at an equal distance from the *hole*).

Rule 17.1d(3) Interpretations:

17.1d(3)/1 – Player May Measure Across Penalty Area In Taking Lateral Relief

In taking lateral relief where the ball last crossed the edge of a narrow red *penalty area*, it may be possible for the player to measure the two *club-lengths* from the reference point across the *penalty area* in determining the size of the *relief area*. However, any part of the *penalty area* within the two *club-lengths* as measured from the reference point is not part of the *relief area*.

17.1d(3)/2 – Player Drops Ball Based on Estimate of Where the Ball Last Crossed Edge of Penalty Area That Turns Out to Be the Wrong Point

If the point where a ball last crossed the edge of a *penalty area* is not known, a player must use his or her reasonable judgment to determine the reference point.

Under Rule 1.3b(2), the player's reasonable judgment will be accepted even if that reference point turns out to be wrong. However, there are situations when, before the player has made a *stroke*, it becomes known that the reference point is wrong and this mistake must be corrected.

For example, in *stroke play*, it is *virtually certain* that a player's ball is in a red *penalty area*. The player, having consulted with the other players in the group, estimates where the ball last crossed the edge of the *penalty area*. The player takes lateral relief and *drops* a ball in the *relief area* based on that reference point.

But before making a *stroke* at the *dropped* ball, one of the players in the group finds the player's original ball in the *penalty area* in a position indicating that the ball last crossed the edge of the *penalty area* approximately 20 yards closer to the *hole* than the reference point the player had estimated.

Because this information became known before the player made a *stroke* at the *dropped* ball, he or she must correct the error under Rule 14.5 (Correcting Mistake Made in Substituting, Replacing, Dropping or Placing Ball). In doing so, the player must proceed under Rule 17.1 with respect to the correct reference point and may use any relief option under that Rule (see Rule 14.5b(2)).

17.1e Relief Must Be Taken from Interference by No Play Zone in Penalty Area

In each of these situations, the player must not play the ball as it lies:

(1) **When Ball Is in No Play Zone in Penalty Area**. The player must take penalty relief under Rule 17.1d or 17.2.

(2) **When No Play Zone on Course Interferes with Stance or Swing for Ball in Penalty Area**. If a player's ball is in a *penalty area* and is outside a *no play zone* but a *no play zone* (whether in an *abnormal course condition* or in a *penalty area*) interferes with his or her area of intended *stance* or area of intended *swing*, the player must either:

- Take penalty relief outside the *penalty area* under Rule 17.1d or 17.2, or

- Take free relief by *dropping* the original ball or another ball in this *relief area* (if it exists) in the *penalty area* (see Rule 14.3):

  » Reference Point: The *nearest point of complete relief* from the *no play zone*.

  » Size of Relief Area Measured from Reference Point: One *club-length*, **but** with these limits:

  » Limits on Location of Relief Area:

    — Must be in the same *penalty area* where the ball lies, and

    — Must not be nearer the *hole* than the reference point.

But there is no free relief from interference by the *no play zone* under (2):

- When playing the ball as it lies is clearly unreasonable because of something other than the *no play zone* (for example, when a player is unable to make a *stroke* because of where the ball lies in a bush), or

- When interference exists only because the player chooses a club, type of *stance* or swing, or direction of play that is clearly unreasonable under the circumstances.

For what to do when there is interference by a *no play zone* for a ball anywhere except in a *penalty area*, see Rule 16.1f.

Penalty for Playing Ball from a *Wrong Place* in Breach of Rule 17.1: *General Penalty* Under Rule 14.7a.

17.2 Options After Playing Ball from Penalty Area

17.2a When Ball Played from Penalty Area Comes to Rest in Same or Another Penalty Area

If a ball played from a *penalty area* comes to rest in the same *penalty area* or another *penalty area*, the player may play the ball as it lies (see Rule 17.1b).

Or, for **one penalty stroke**, the player may take relief under any of these options:

(1) **Normal Relief Options.** The player may take *stroke-and-distance* relief under Rule 17.1d(1), back-on-the-line relief under Rule 17.1d(2) or, for a red *penalty area*, lateral relief under Rule 17.1d(3).

Under Rule 17.1d(2) or (3), the estimated point used to determine the *relief area* is where the original ball last crossed the edge of the *penalty area* where the ball now lies.

If the player takes *stroke-and-distance* relief by *dropping* a ball in the *penalty area* (see Rule 14.6) and then decides not to play the *dropped* ball from where it comes to rest:

- The player may take further relief outside the *penalty area* under Rule 17.1d(2) or (3) (for a red *penalty area*) or under Rule 17.2a(2).

- If the player does so, he or she gets **one more penalty stroke**, for a **total of two penalty strokes**: one stroke for taking *stroke-and-distance* relief, and one stroke for taking relief outside the *penalty area*.

(2) **Extra Relief Option: Playing from Where Last Stroke Made Outside a Penalty Area.** Instead of using one of the normal relief options under (1), the player may choose to play the original ball or another ball from where he or she made the last *stroke* from outside a *penalty area* (see Rule 14.6).

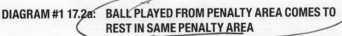

DIAGRAM #1 17.2a: BALL PLAYED FROM PENALTY AREA COMES TO REST IN SAME PENALTY AREA

X Point that ball entered the penalty area

● Reference points

◯ Relief area

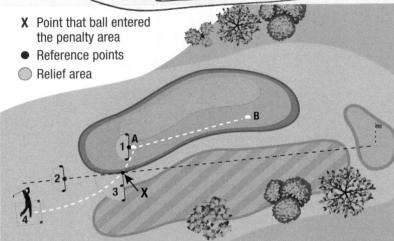

A player plays from the teeing area to point A in the penalty area. The player plays the ball from point A to point B. If the player chooses to take relief, for one penalty stroke there are **four** options. The player may:

(1) Take stroke-and-distance relief by playing the original ball or another ball from a relief area based on where the previous stroke was made at point A (see Rule 14.6 and Diagram 14.6) and is playing his or her 4ᵗʰ shot.

(2) Take back-on-the-line relief by dropping the original ball or another ball in a relief area based on a reference line going straight back from the hole through point X, and is playing his or her 4ᵗʰ shot.

(3) Take lateral relief (red penalty area only). The reference point for taking relief is point X, and the original ball or another ball must be dropped in and played from the two club-length relief area, and the player is playing his or her 4ᵗʰ shot.

(4) Play the original ball or another ball from the teeing area as that was where he or she made the last stroke from outside the penalty area, and is playing his or her 4ᵗʰ shot.

If the player chose option (1) and then decided not to play the dropped ball, the player may take back-on-the-line relief or lateral relief in relation to point X, or play again from the teeing area, adding an additional penalty stroke for a total of two penalty strokes, and would be playing his or her 5ᵗʰ shot.

DIAGRAM #2 17.2a: BALL PLAYED FROM PENALTY AREA COMES TO REST IN SAME PENALTY AREA HAVING EXITED AND RE-ENTERED

X Point that ball entered the penalty area
● Reference points
◯ Relief area

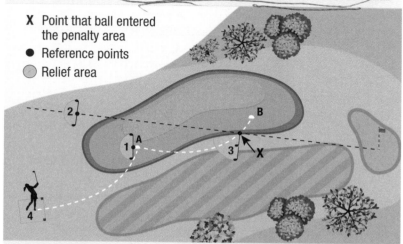

A player plays from the teeing area to point A in the penalty area. The player plays the ball from point A to point B, with the ball exiting the penalty area but crossing back into the penalty area at point X. If the player chooses to take relief, for one penalty stroke there are **four options**. The player may:

(1) Take stroke-and-distance relief by playing the original ball or another ball from a relief area based on where the previous stroke was made at point A (see Rule 14.6 and Diagram 14.6) and is playing his or her 4th shot.

(2) Take back-on-the-line relief by dropping the original ball or another ball in a relief area based on a reference line going straight back from the hole through point X, and is playing his or her 4th shot.

(3) Take lateral relief (red penalty area only). The reference point for taking relief is point X, and the original ball or another ball must be dropped in and played from the two club-length relief area, and the player is playing his or her 4th shot.

(4) Play the original ball or another ball from the teeing area as that was where he or she made the last stroke from outside the penalty area, and is playing his or her 4th shot.

If the player chose option (1) and then decided not to play the dropped ball, the player may take back-on-the-line relief or lateral relief in relation to point X or play again from the teeing area, adding an additional penalty stroke for a total of two penalty strokes, and would be playing his or her 5th shot.

17.2b When Ball Played from Penalty Area Is Lost, Out of Bounds or Unplayable Outside Penalty Area

After playing a ball from a *penalty area*, a player may sometimes be required or choose to take *stroke-and-distance* relief because the original ball is either:

- *Out of bounds* or *lost* outside the *penalty area* (see Rule 18.2), or
- Unplayable outside the *penalty area* (see Rule 19.2a).

If the player takes *stroke-and-distance* relief by *dropping* a ball in the *penalty area* (see Rule 14.6) and then decides not to play the *dropped* ball from where it comes to rest:

- The player may take further relief outside the *penalty area* under Rule 17.1d(2) or (3) (for a red *penalty area*) or under Rule 17.2a(2).
- If the player does so, he or she gets **one more penalty stroke**, for a **total of two penalty strokes**: one stroke for taking *stroke-and-distance* relief, and one stroke for taking relief outside the *penalty area*.

The player may directly take such relief outside the *penalty area* without first *dropping* a ball in the penalty area, **but still gets a total of two penalty strokes**.

Rule 17.2b Interpretations:

17.2b/1 – Examples of Options for Relief Allowed by Rule 17.2b

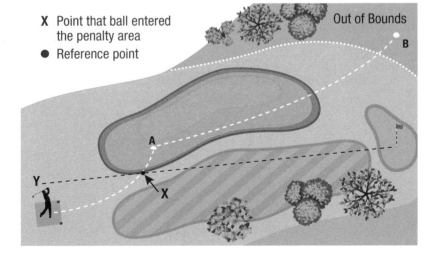

- **X** Point that ball entered the penalty area
- ● Reference point

Out of Bounds

In the diagram, a player plays from the *teeing area* and the ball comes to rest in the red *penalty area* at Point A. The player elects to play from the *penalty area* playing to Point B, which is *out of bounds*.

The player may take *stroke-and-distance* relief under Rule 18.2b by using Point A as the reference point for the *relief area* and will be playing 4.

If the player takes *stroke-and-distance* relief by *dropping* a ball back into the *penalty area* and then decides not to play the *dropped* ball from where it comes to rest:

* The player may take back-on-the-line relief anywhere on dotted line X-Y outside the *penalty area* under Rule 17.1d(2), take lateral relief using point X as the reference point under Rule 17.1d(3) or play another ball from where the last *stroke* was made outside the *penalty area* (in this case the *teeing area*) under Rule 17.2a(2).

* If the player takes any of these three options, he or she gets one more penalty stroke, for a total of two penalty strokes: one stroke for taking *stroke-and-distance* relief plus one stroke for taking any back-on-the-line relief, lateral relief or for playing another ball from where the last *stroke* was made outside the *penalty area* (in this case the *teeing area*). Thus, the player will be playing 5 under any of these options.

The player also has the option to take relief outside the *penalty area* without first *dropping* a ball in the *penalty area*, but will still get a total of two penalty strokes for doing so.

Penalty for Playing Ball from a *Wrong Place* in Breach of Rule 17.2: *General Penalty* Under Rule 14.7a.

17.3 No Relief Under Other Rules for Ball in Penalty Area

When a player's ball is in a *penalty area*, there is no relief for:

* Interference by an *abnormal course condition* (Rule 16.1),

* An *embedded* ball (Rule 16.3), or

* An unplayable ball (Rule 19).

The player's only relief option is to take penalty relief under Rule 17.

But when a dangerous *animal* condition interferes with the play of a ball in a *penalty area*, the player may take either free relief in the *penalty area* or penalty relief outside the *penalty area* (see Rule 16.2b(2)).

RULE 18

Stroke-and-Distance Relief; Ball Lost or Out of Bounds; Provisional Ball

Purpose of Rule:

Rule 18 covers taking relief under penalty of stroke and distance. When a ball is lost outside a penalty area or comes to rest out of bounds, the required progression of playing from the teeing area to the hole is broken; the player must resume that progression by playing again from where the previous stroke was made.

This Rule also covers how and when a provisional ball may be played to save time when the ball in play might have gone out of bounds or be lost outside a penalty area.

18.1 Relief Under Penalty of Stroke and Distance Allowed at Any Time

At any time, a player may take *stroke-and-distance* relief by adding **one penalty stroke** and playing the original ball or another ball from where the previous *stroke* was made (see Rule 14.6).

The player always has this *stroke-and-distance* relief option:

• No matter where the player's ball is on the *course*, and

• Even when a Rule requires the player to take relief in a certain way or to play a ball from a certain place.

Once the player puts another ball *in play* under penalty of *stroke and distance* (see Rule 14.4):

• The original ball is no longer *in play* and must not be played.

• This is true even if the original ball is then found on the *course* before the end of the three-minute search time (see Rule 6.3b).

But this does not apply to a ball to be played from where the previous *stroke* was made when the player:

• Announces that he or she is playing a *provisional ball* (see Rule 18.3b),

• Is playing a second ball in *stroke play* under Rule 14.7b or 20.1c(3).

Rule 18.1 Interpretations:

18.1/1 – Teed Ball May Be Lifted When Original Ball Is Found Within Three-Minute Search Time

When playing again from the *teeing area*, a ball that is placed, *dropped* or teed in the *teeing area* is not *in play* until the player makes a *stroke* at it (definition of "in play" and Rule 6.2).

For example, a player plays from the *teeing area*, searches briefly for his or her ball and then goes back and tees another ball. Before the player plays the teed ball, and within the three-minute search time, the original ball is found. The player may abandon the teed ball and continue with the original ball without penalty, but is also allowed to proceed under *stroke and distance* by playing from the *teeing area*.

However, if the player had played from the *general area* and then *dropped* another ball to take *stroke-and-distance* relief, the outcome would be different in that the player must continue with the *dropped* ball under penalty of *stroke and distance*. If the player continued with the original ball in this case, he or she would be playing a *wrong ball*.

18.1/2 – Penalty Cannot Be Avoided by Playing Under Stroke and Distance

If a player lifts his or her ball when not allowed to do so, the player cannot avoid the one-stroke penalty under Rule 9.4b by then deciding to play under *stroke and distance*.

For example, a player's tee shot comes to rest in a wooded area. The player picks up a ball, believing it is a stray ball, but discovers the ball was the ball *in play*. The player then decides to play under *stroke and distance*.

The player gets one penalty stroke under Rule 9.4b in addition to the *stroke and distance* penalty under Rule 18.1, since at the time the ball was lifted the player was not allowed to lift the ball and had no intention to play under *stroke and distance*. The player's next *stroke* will be his or her fourth.

18.2 Ball Lost or Out of Bounds: Stroke-and-Distance Relief Must Be Taken

18.2a When Ball Is Lost or Out of Bounds

(1) **When Ball Is Lost**. A ball is *lost* if not found in three minutes after the player or his or her *caddie* begins to search for it.

If a ball is found in that time but it is uncertain whether it is the player's ball:

- The player must promptly attempt to identify the ball (see Rule 7.2) and is allowed a reasonable time to do so, even if that happens after the three-minute search time has ended.

- This includes a reasonable time to get to the ball if the player is not where the ball is found.

If the player does not identify his or her ball in that reasonable time, the ball is *lost*.

Rule 18.2a(1) Interpretations:
18.2a(1)/1 – Time Permitted for Search When Search Temporarily Interrupted

A player is allowed three minutes to search for his or her ball before it becomes *lost*. However, there are situations when the "clock stops" and such time does not count towards the player's three minutes.

The following examples illustrate how to account for the time when a search is temporarily interrupted:

- In *stroke play*, a player searches for his or her ball for one minute and finds a ball. The player assumes that ball is his or her ball, takes 30 seconds to decide how to make the *stroke*, choose a club, and plays that ball. The player then discovers that it is a *wrong ball*.

  When the player returns to the area where the original ball was likely to be and resumes search, he or she has two more minutes to search. The time of search stopped when the player found the *wrong ball* and stopped searching.

- A player has been searching for his or her ball for two minutes when play is suspended by the *Committee*. The player continues searching. When three minutes has elapsed from when the player began searching, the ball is *lost* even if the three-minute search time ends while play is suspended.

- A player has been searching for his or her ball for one minute when play is suspended. The player continues to search for one more minute and then stops the search to seek shelter. When the player returns to the *course* to resume play, the player is allowed one more minute to search for the ball even if play has not been resumed.

- A player finds and identifies his or her ball in high rough after a two-minute search. The player leaves the area to get a club. When he or she returns, the ball cannot be found. The player has one minute to search before the ball becomes *lost*. The three-minute search time stopped when the ball was first found.

- A player is searching for his or her ball for two minutes, then steps aside to allow the following group to play through. The search time stops when the search is temporarily stopped, and the player is allowed one more minute to search.

18.2a(1)/2 – Caddie Is Not Required to Start Searching for Player's Ball Before Player

A player may instruct his or her *caddie* not to begin searching for his or her ball.

For example, a player hits a long drive into heavy rough and another player hits a short drive into heavy rough. The player's *caddie* starts walking ahead to the location where the player's ball might be to start searching. Everyone else, including the player, walks towards the location where the other player's ball might be to look for that player's ball.

The player may direct his or her *caddie* to look for the other player's ball and delay search for his or her ball until everyone else can assist.

18.2a(1)/3 – Ball May Become Lost if It is Not Promptly Identified

When a player has the opportunity to identify a ball as his or hers within the three-minute search time but fails to do so, the ball is *lost* when the search time expires.

For example, a player begins to search for his or her ball and after two minutes finds a ball that the player believes to be another player's ball and resumes search for his or her ball.

The three-minute search time elapses and it is then discovered that the ball the player found and believed to be another player's ball was in fact the player's ball. In this case, the player's ball is *lost* because he or she continued the search, failing to identify the found ball promptly.

(2) **When Ball Is Out of Bounds**. A ball at rest is *out of bounds* only when all of it is outside the boundary edge of the *course*.

A ball is in bounds when any part of the ball:

- Lies on or touches the ground or anything else (such as any natural or artificial object) inside the boundary edge, or
- Is above the boundary edge or any other part of the *course*.

A player may stand *out of bounds* to play a ball on the *course*.

DIAGRAM 18.2a: WHEN BALL IS OUT OF BOUNDS

A ball is out of bounds only when all of it is outside the boundary edge of the course.
The diagrams provide examples of when a ball is in bounds and out of bounds.

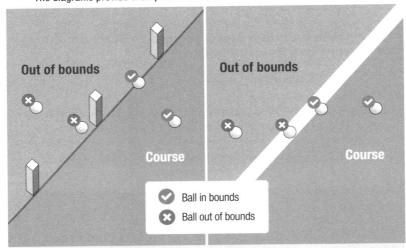

Out of bounds

Course

Out of bounds

Course

✔ Ball in bounds
✘ Ball out of bounds

The boundary edge is defined by the line between the course-side points of the stakes at ground level, and the stakes are out of bounds.

The boundary edge is the course-side edge of the line, and the line itself is out of bounds.

Rule 18.2a(2) Interpretations:

18.2a(2)/1 – Ball Moved Out of Bounds by Flow of Water

If a flow of water (either *temporary water* or *water in a penalty area*) carries a ball *out of bounds*, the player must take *stroke-and-distance* relief (Rule 18.2b). Water is a *natural force*, not an *outside influence*, therefore Rule 9.6 does not apply.

18.2b What to Do When Ball Is Lost or Out of Bounds

If a ball is *lost* or *out of bounds*, the player must take *stroke-and-distance* relief by adding **one penalty stroke** and playing the original ball or another ball from where the previous *stroke* was made (see Rule 14.6).

Exception – Player May Substitute Another Ball Under Other Rule When It Is Known or Virtually Certain What Happened to Ball: Instead of taking *stroke-and-distance* relief, the player may *substitute* another ball as allowed under a Rule that applies when his or her ball has not been found and it is *known or virtually certain* that the ball:

- Came to rest on the *course* and was *moved by an outside influence* (see Rule 9.6) or played as a *wrong ball* by another player (see Rule 6.3c(2)),

- Came to rest on the *course* in or on a *movable obstruction* (see Rule 15.2b) or an *abnormal course condition* (see Rule 16.1e),

- Is in a *penalty area* (see Rule 17.1c), or

- Was deliberately deflected or stopped by any person (see Rule 11.2c).

Penalty for Playing Ball from a *Wrong Place* in Breach of Rule 18.2: *General Penalty* Under Rule 14.7a.

18.3 Provisional Ball

18.3a When Provisional Ball Is Allowed

If a ball might be *lost* outside a *penalty area* or be *out of bounds*, to save time the player may play another ball provisionally under penalty of *stroke and distance* (see Rule 14.6).

For a ball that might be *lost*, this applies:

- When the original ball has not been found and identified and is not yet *lost*, and

- When a ball might be *lost* in a *penalty area* but also might be *lost* somewhere else on the *course*.

But if the player is aware that the only possible place the original ball could be *lost* is in a *penalty area*, a *provisional ball* is not allowed and a ball played from where the previous *stroke* was made becomes the player's ball in play under penalty of *stroke and distance* (see Rule 18.1).

If a *provisional ball* itself might be *lost* outside a *penalty area* or be *out of bounds*:

- The player may play another *provisional ball*.

- That *provisional ball* then has the same relationship to the first *provisional ball* as the first one has to the original ball.

Rule 18.3a Interpretations:

18.3a/1 – When Player May Play Provisional Ball

When a player is deciding whether he or she is allowed to play a *provisional ball*, only the information that is known by the player at that time is considered.

Examples where a *provisional ball* may be played include when:

- The original ball might be in a *penalty area*, but it might also be *lost* outside a *penalty area* or be *out of bounds*.

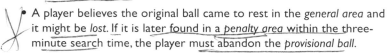

- A player believes the original ball came to rest in the *general area* and it might be *lost*. If it is later found in a *penalty area* within the three-minute search time, the player must abandon the *provisional ball*.

18.3a/2 – Playing Provisional Ball After Search Has Started Is Allowed

A player may play a *provisional ball* for a ball that might be *lost* when the original ball has not been found and identified even if the three-minute search time has not yet ended.

For example, if a player is able to return to the spot of his or her previous *stroke* and play a *provisional ball* before the three-minute search time has ended, the player is allowed to do so.

If the player plays the *provisional ball* and the original ball is then found within the three-minute search time, the player must continue play with the original ball.

18.3a/3 – Each Ball Relates Only to the Previous Ball When It Is Played from That Same Spot

When a player plays multiple balls from the same spot, each ball relates only to the previous ball played.

For example, a player plays a *provisional ball* believing that his or her tee shot might be *lost* or *out of bounds*. The *provisional ball* is struck in the same direction as the original ball and, without any announcement, he or she plays another ball from the tee. This ball comes to rest in the fairway.

If the original ball is not *lost* or *out of bounds*, the player must continue play with the original ball without penalty.

However, if the original ball is *lost* or *out of bounds*, the player must continue play with the third ball played from the tee since it was played without any announcement. Therefore, the third ball was a ball *substituted* for the *provisional ball* under penalty of *stroke and distance* (Rule 18.1), regardless of the *provisional ball's* location. The player has now taken 5 strokes (including penalty strokes) with the third ball played from the tee.

18.3b Announcing Play of Provisional Ball

Before the *stroke* is made, the player must announce that he or she is going to play a *provisional ball*:

- It is not enough for the player only to say that he or she is playing another ball or is playing again.

- The player must use the word "provisional" or otherwise clearly indicate that he or she is playing the ball provisionally under Rule 18.3.

If the player does not announce this (even if he or she intended to play a *provisional ball*) and plays a ball from where the previous *stroke* was made, that ball is the player's ball *in play* under penalty of *stroke and distance* (see Rule 18.1).

Rule 18.3b Interpretations:

18.3b/1 – What Is Considered Announcement of Provisional Ball

Although Rule 18.3b does not specify to whom the announcement of a *provisional ball* must be made, an announcement must be made so that people in the vicinity of the player can hear it.

For example, with other people nearby, if a player states that he or she will be playing a *provisional ball* but does so in a way that only he or she can hear it, this does not satisfy the requirement in Rule 18.3b that the player must "announce" that he or she is going to play a *provisional ball*. Any ball played in these circumstances becomes the player's ball *in play* under penalty of *stroke and distance*.

If there are no other people nearby to hear the player's announcement (such as when a player has returned to the *teeing area* after briefly searching for his or her ball), the player is considered to have correctly announced that he or she has the intent to play a *provisional ball* provided that he or she informs someone of that when it becomes possible to do so.

18.3b/2 – Statements That "Clearly Indicate" That a Provisional Ball Is Being Played

When playing a *provisional ball*, it is best if the player uses the word "provisional" in his or her announcement. However, other statements that make it clear that the player's intent is to play a *provisional ball* are acceptable.

Examples of announcements that clearly indicate the player is playing a *provisional ball* include:

- "I'm playing a ball under Rule 18.3."

- "I'm going to play another just in case."

Examples of announcements that do not clearly indicate the player is playing a *provisional ball* and mean that the player would be putting a ball into play under *stroke and distance* include:

- "I'm going to re-load."
- "I'm going to play another."

18.3c   Playing Provisional Ball Until It Becomes the Ball in Play or Is Abandoned

(1) **Playing Provisional Ball More Than Once.** The player may continue to play the *provisional ball* without it losing its status as a *provisional ball* so long as it is played from a spot that is the same distance or farther from the *hole* than where the original ball is estimated to be.

This is true even if the *provisional ball* is played several times.

But it stops being a *provisional ball* when it becomes the ball *in play* under (2) or is abandoned under (3) and therefore becomes a *wrong ball*.

Rule 18.3c(1) Interpretations:

18.3c(1)/1 – Actions Taken with Provisional Ball Are a Continuation of Provisional Ball

Taking actions other than a *stroke* with a *provisional ball*, such as *dropping*, placing or *substituting* another ball nearer to the *hole* than where the original ball is estimated to be are not "playing" the *provisional ball* and do not cause that ball to lose its status as a *provisional ball*.

For example, a player's tee shot may be *lost* 175 yards from the *hole*, so he or she plays a *provisional ball*. After briefly searching for the original ball, the player goes forward to play the *provisional ball* that is in a bush 150 yards from the *hole*. He or she decides the *provisional ball* is unplayable and *drops* it under Rule 19.2c. Before playing the *dropped* ball, the player's original ball is found by a spectator within three minutes of when the player started the search.

In this case, the original ball remained the ball *in play* because it was found within three minutes of beginning the search and the player had not made a *stroke* at the *provisional ball* from a spot nearer the *hole* than where the original ball was estimated to be.

(2) **When Provisional Ball Becomes Ball in Play**. The *provisional ball* becomes the player's ball *in play* under penalty of *stroke and distance* in either of these two cases:

- When Original Ball Is Lost Anywhere on Course Except in Penalty Area or Is Out of Bounds. The original ball is no longer *in play* (even if it is then found on the *course* after the end of the three-minute search time) and is now a *wrong ball* that must not be played (see Rule 6.3c).

- When Provisional Ball Is Played from Spot Nearer Hole Than Where Original Ball Is Estimated to Be. The original ball is no longer *in play* (even if it is then found on the *course* before the end of the three-minute search time or is found nearer the *hole* than had been estimated) and is now a *wrong ball* that must not be played (see Rule 6.3c).

If the player plays a *provisional ball* into the same general location as the original ball and is unable to identify which ball is which:

- If only one of the balls is found on the *course*, that ball is treated as the *provisional ball* which is now *in play*.

- If both balls are found on the *course*, the player must choose one of the balls to be treated as the *provisional ball* which is now *in play*, and the other ball is treated as *lost* and must not be played.

Exception – Player May Substitute Another Ball Under Other Rule When It Is Known or Virtually Certain What Happened to Ball: The player has an extra option when his or her ball has not been found and it is *known or virtually certain* that the ball:

- Came to rest on the *course* and was moved by an *outside influence* (see Rule 9.6),

- Came to rest on the *course* in or on a *movable obstruction* (see Rule 15.2b) or an *abnormal course condition* (see Rule 16.1e), or

- Was deliberately deflected or stopped by any person (see Rule 11.2c).

When one of those Rules applies, the player may either:

- *Substitute* another ball as allowed under that Rule, or

- Treat the *provisional ball* as the ball *in play* under penalty of *stroke and distance*.

DIAGRAM 18.3c: PROVISIONAL BALL PLAYED FROM SPOT NEARER HOLE THAN WHERE ORIGINAL BALL IS ESTIMATED TO BE

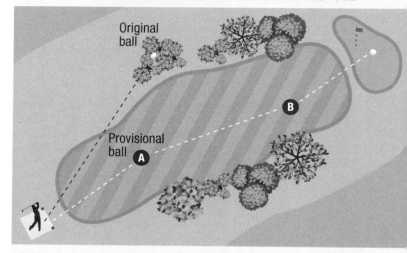

A player's original ball played from the teeing area may be lost in a bush, so the player announces and plays a provisional ball, and it comes to rest at point A. As point A is farther from the hole than where the original ball is estimated to be, the player may play the provisional ball from point A without it losing its status as a provisional ball. The player plays the provisional ball from point A to point B. As point B is nearer the hole than where the original ball is estimated to be, if the player plays the provisional ball from point B, the provisional ball becomes the ball in play under penalty of stroke and distance.

Rule 18.3c(2) Interpretations:

18.3c(2)/1 – Estimated Spot of the Original Ball Is Used to Determine Which Ball Is in Play

Rule 18.3c(2) uses the spot where the player "estimates" his or her original ball to be when determining whether the *provisional ball* has been played from nearer the *hole* than that spot, and whether the original or *provisional ball* is *in play*. The estimated spot is not where the original ball ends up being found. Rather, it is the spot the player reasonably thinks or assumes that ball to be.

Examples of determining which ball is *in play* include:

- A player, believing that his or her original ball might be *lost* or *out of bounds*, plays a *provisional ball* that does not come to rest nearer the *hole* than the estimated spot of the original ball. The player finds a ball and plays it, believing it was the original ball. The player then discovers that the ball that was played was the *provisional ball*.

In this case, the *provisional ball* was not played from a spot nearer the *hole* than the estimated spot of the original ball. Therefore, the player may resume searching for the original ball. If the original ball is found within three minutes of starting the search, it remains the ball *in play* and the player must abandon the *provisional ball*. If the three-minute search time expires before the original ball is found, the *provisional ball* is the ball *in play*.

- A player, believing his or her tee shot might be *lost* or over a road defined as *out of bounds*, plays a *provisional ball*. The player searches for the original ball briefly but does not find it. The player goes forward and plays the *provisional ball* from a spot nearer the *hole* than where the original ball was estimated to be. Then the player goes forward and finds the original ball in bounds. The original ball must have bounced down the road and then come back in bounds, because it was found much farther forward than anticipated.

In this case, the *provisional ball* became the ball *in play* when it was played from a spot nearer the *hole* than where the original ball was estimated to be. The original ball is no longer *in play* and must be abandoned.

18.3c(2)/2 – Player May Ask Others Not to Search for His or Her Original Ball

If a player does not plan to search for his or her original ball because he or she would prefer to continue play with a *provisional ball*, the player may ask others not to search, but there is no obligation for them to comply.

If a ball is found, the player must make all reasonable efforts to identify the ball, provided he or she has not already played the *provisional ball* from nearer the *hole* than where the original ball was estimated to be, in which case it became the player's ball *in play*. If the *provisional ball* has not yet become the ball *in play* when another ball is found, refusal to make a reasonable effort to identify the found ball may be considered serious misconduct contrary to the spirit of the game (Rule 1.2a).

After the other ball is found, if the *provisional ball* is played from nearer the *hole* than where the other ball was found, and it turns out that the other ball was the player's original ball, the *stroke* at the *provisional ball* was actually a *stroke* at a *wrong ball* (Rule 6.3c). The player will get the general penalty and, in *stroke play*, must correct the error by continuing play with the original ball.

18.3c(2)/3 – Opponent or Another Player May Search for Player's Ball Despite the Player's Request

Even if a player prefers to continue play of the hole with a *provisional ball* without searching for the original ball, the *opponent* or another player in *stroke play* may search for the player's original ball so long as it does not unreasonably delay play. If the player's original ball is found while it is still *in play*, the player must abandon the *provisional ball* (Rule 18.3c(3)).

For example, at a par-3 hole, a player's tee shot goes into dense woods, and he or she plays a *provisional ball* that comes to rest near the *hole*. Given this outcome, the player does not wish to find the original ball and walks directly towards the *provisional ball* to continue play with it. The player's *opponent* or another player in *stroke play* believes it would be beneficial to him or her if the original ball was found, so he or she begins searching for it.

If he or she finds the original ball before the player makes another *stroke* with the *provisional ball* the player must abandon the *provisional ball* and continue with the original ball. However, if the player makes another *stroke* with the *provisional ball* before the original ball is found, it becomes the ball *in play* because it was nearer the *hole* than the estimated spot of the original ball (Rule 18.3c(2)).

In *match play*, if the player's *provisional ball* is nearer the *hole* than the *opponent's* ball, the *opponent* may cancel the *stroke* and have the player play in the proper order (Rule 6.4a). However, cancelling the *stroke* would not change the status of the original ball, which is no longer *in play*.

18.3c(2)/4 – When Score with Holed Provisional Ball Becomes the Score for Hole

So long as the original ball has not already been found in bounds, the score with a *provisional ball* that has been *holed* becomes the player's score for the hole when the player lifts the ball from the *hole* since, in this case, lifting the ball from the *hole* is the same as making a *stroke*.

For example, at a short hole, Player A's tee shot might be *lost*, so he or she plays a *provisional ball* that is *holed*. Player A does not wish to look for the original ball, but Player B, Player A's *opponent* or another player in *stroke play*, goes to look for the original ball.

If Player B finds Player A's original ball before Player A lifts the *provisional ball* from the *hole*, Player A must abandon the *provisional ball* and continue with the original ball. If Player A lifts the ball from the *hole* before Player B finds Player A's original ball, Player A's score for the hole is three.

18.3c(2)/5 – Provisional Ball Lifted by Player Subsequently Becomes the Ball in Play

If a player lifts his or her *provisional ball* when not allowed to do so under the Rules and the *provisional ball* subsequently becomes the ball *in play*, the player must add one penalty stroke under Rule 9.4b (Penalty for Lifting or Moving Ball) and must *replace* the ball.

For example, in *stroke play*, believing his or her tee shot might be *lost*, the player plays a *provisional ball*. The player finds a ball that he or she believes is the original ball, makes a *stroke* at it, picks up the *provisional ball*, and then discovers that the ball he or she played was not the original ball, but a *wrong ball*. The player resumes search for the original ball but cannot find it within the three-minute search time.

Since the *provisional ball* became the ball *in play* under penalty of *stroke and distance*, the player is required to *replace* that ball and gets one penalty stroke under Rule 9.4b. The player also gets two penalty strokes for playing a *wrong ball* (Rule 6.3c). The player's next *stroke* is his or her seventh.

(3) **When Provisional Ball Must Be Abandoned.** When a *provisional ball* has not yet become the ball *in play*, it must be abandoned in either of these two cases:

- When Original Ball Is Found on Course Outside Penalty Area Before the End of the Three-Minute Search Time. The player must play the original ball as it lies.

- When Original Ball Is Found in Penalty Area or Is Known or Virtually Certain to Be in Penalty Area. The player must either play the original ball as it lies or take penalty relief under Rule 17.1d.

In either case:

- The player must not make any more *strokes* with the *provisional ball* which is now a *wrong ball* (see Rule 6.3c), and

- All strokes with that *provisional ball* before it was abandoned (including *strokes* made and any penalty strokes solely from playing that ball) do not count.

Rule 18.3c(3) Interpretations:

18.3c(3)/1 – Provisional Ball Cannot Serve as Ball in Play if Original Ball Is Unplayable or in Penalty Area

A player is only allowed to play a *provisional ball* if he or she believes the original ball might be *lost* outside a *penalty area* or might be *out of bounds*. The player may not decide that a second ball he or she is going to play is both a *provisional ball* in case the original ball is *lost* outside a *penalty area* or *out of bounds* and the ball *in play* in case the original ball is unplayable or in a *penalty area*.

If the original ball is found in bounds or is *known or virtually certain* to be in a *penalty area*, the *provisional ball* must be abandoned.

Penalty for Playing Ball from a *Wrong Place* in Breach of Rule 18.3: *General Penalty* Under Rule 14.7a.

RULE
19 Unplayable Ball

Purpose of Rule:

Rule 19 covers the player's several relief options for an unplayable ball. This allows the player to choose which option to use – normally with one penalty stroke – to get out of a difficult situation anywhere on the course (except in a penalty area).

19.1 Player May Decide to Take Unplayable Ball Relief Anywhere Except Penalty Area

A player is the only person who may decide to treat his or her ball as unplayable by taking penalty relief under Rule 19.2 or 19.3.

Unplayable ball relief is allowed anywhere on the *course*, **except** in a *penalty area*.

If a ball is unplayable in a *penalty area*, the player's only relief option is to take penalty relief under Rule 17.

19.2 Relief Options for Unplayable Ball in General Area or on Putting Green

A player may take unplayable ball relief using one of the three options in Rule 19.2a, b or c, in each case adding **one penalty stroke**.

- The player may take *stroke-and-distance relief* under Rule 19.2a even if the original ball has not been found and identified.
- But to take back-on-the-line relief under Rule 19.2b or lateral relief under Rule 19.2c, the player must know the spot of the original ball.

19.2a Stroke-and-Distance Relief

The player may play the original ball or another ball from where the previous *stroke* was made (see Rule 14.6).

Rule 19.2a Interpretations:

19.2a/1 – Player May Take Stroke-and-Distance Relief Even When Spot of Previous Stroke Is Nearer Hole Than Where Unplayable Ball Lies

If a ball comes to rest farther from the *hole* than the spot from which it was played, *stroke-and-distance* relief may still be taken.

Examples where *stroke-and-distance* relief may be nearer the *hole* include when:

- A player's *stroke* from the *teeing area* hits a tree, bounces backwards and comes to rest behind the *teeing area*. The player may play again from the *teeing area* under penalty of one stroke.

- A player has a downhill putt and he or she putts off the *putting green* and the ball rolls off the *green* into a bad lie or into a *penalty area*. The player may play again from the *putting green* under penalty of one stroke.

19.2a/2 – Stroke-and-Distance Relief Is Allowed Only at Spot of the Last Stroke

The option to take *stroke-and-distance* relief for an unplayable ball applies only to where the last *stroke* was made; a player is not allowed to go back to the spot of any earlier *strokes* made before that.

If the *stroke-and-distance* relief option or the back-on-the-line option are not favourable, the only option is to take lateral relief multiple times, taking a penalty each time, until the player can get a ball into a playable location.

19.2b Back-on-the-Line Relief

The player may *drop* the original ball or another ball (see Rule 14.3) in a *relief area* that is based on a reference line going straight back from the *hole* through the spot of the original ball:

- Reference Point: A point on the *course* chosen by the player that is on the reference line and is farther from the *hole* than the spot of the original ball (with no limit on how far back on the line):

» In choosing this point, the player should indicate the point by using an object (such as a tee).

» If the player *drops* the ball without having chosen this point, the reference point is treated as being the point on the line that is the same distance from the *hole* as where the *dropped* ball first touched the ground.

- Size of Relief Area Measured from Reference Point: One *club-length*, **but** with these limits:

- Limits on Location of Relief Area:

  » Must not be nearer the *hole* than the reference point, and

  » May be in any *area of the course*, **but**

  » If more than one *area of the course* is located within one *club-length* of the reference point, the ball must come to rest in the *relief area* in the same *area of the course* that the ball first touched when *dropped* in the *relief area*.

See Interpretation 17.1d(2)/1 – Recommendation That Player Physically Marks Reference Point on Reference Line

19.2c Lateral Relief

The player may *drop* the original ball or another ball in this lateral *relief area* (see Rule 14.3):

- Reference Point: The spot of the original ball.

- Size of Relief Area Measured from Reference Point: Two *club-lengths*, **but** with these limits:

- Limits on Location of Relief Area:

  » Must not be nearer the *hole* than the reference point, and

  » May be in any *area of the course*, **but**

  » If more than one *area of the course* is located within two *club-lengths* of the reference point, the ball must come to rest in the *relief area* in the same *area of the course* that the ball first touched when *dropped* in the *relief area*.

DIAGRAM 19.2: RELIEF OPTIONS FOR BALL UNPLAYABLE IN GENERAL AREA

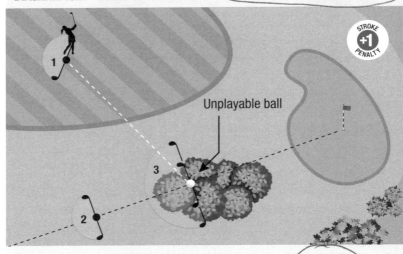

Unplayable ball

A player decides that his or her ball in a bush is unplayable. The player has **three options**, in each case adding one penalty stroke:

(1) The player may take stroke-and-distance relief by playing the original ball or another ball from a relief area based on where the previous stroke was made (see Rule 14.6 and Diagram 14.6).

(2) The player may take back-on-the-line relief by dropping the original ball or another ball in a relief area based on a reference line going straight back from the hole through the spot of the original ball. The reference point is a point on the course chosen by the player that is on the reference line and is farther from the hole than the spot of the original ball. There is no limit on how far back on the line the reference point may be. The relief area is one club-length from the reference point, is not nearer to the hole than the reference point and may be in any area of the course. In choosing this reference point, the player should indicate the point by using an object (such as a tee).

(3) The player may take lateral relief. The reference point is the spot of the original ball. The relief area is two club-lengths from the reference point, is not nearer to the hole than the reference point and may be in any area of the course.

Penalty for Playing Ball from a *Wrong Place* in Breach of Rule 19.2: *General Penalty* Under Rule 14.7a.

Rule 19.2c Interpretations:

19.2c/1 – Reference Point for Lateral Relief When Ball Is Not on the Ground

When a player's ball lies above the ground (such as in a bush or a tree), the player may take lateral relief by using the point on the ground directly below the spot of the ball as his or her reference point:

- The *relief area* is within two *club-lengths* of and no closer to the *hole* than that reference point on the ground (see Rule 19.2c).

- In some cases, this might allow a ball to be *dropped* on a *putting green*.

But, if an unplayable ball lies on the ground, the spot of the original ball itself is always used as the reference point. For example:

- If a player's ball lies at the base of a cliff or a steep slope, the spot of the original ball is the reference point.

- This means that the player may not ignore vertical distance and *drop* a ball at the top of the cliff or slope within two *club-lengths* of a point directly above where the ball lies on the ground at the base of the cliff or slope.

Rule 19.2 General Interpretations:

19.2/1 – No Guarantee Ball Will Be Playable After Taking Unplayable Ball Relief

When taking unplayable ball relief, a player must accept the outcome even if it is unfavourable, such as when a *dropped* ball comes to rest in its original location or in a bad lie in another location in the *relief area*:

- Once the *dropped* ball comes to rest in the *relief area*, the player has a new situation.

- If the player decides that he or she cannot (or does not wish to) play the ball as it now lies, the player may again take unplayable ball relief, for an additional penalty, using any available relief option under Rule 19.

19.2/2 – Ball May be Dropped in Any Area of the Course When Taking Unplayable Ball Relief

A player may take relief by *dropping* a ball into a *relief area in any area of the course* under the unplayable ball relief options. This includes taking relief from the *general area* and *dropping* directly into a *bunker* or *penalty area*, onto a *putting green,* into a *no play zone* or onto a *wrong green*.

However, if the player chooses to *drop* into a *no play zone* or onto a *wrong green*, the player must then continue to take the relief required by the Rules from that *no play zone* or *wrong green*.

Similarly, if the player chooses to *drop* in a *penalty area* and he or she cannot (or does not wish to) play the ball from where it now lies, the only option is to take further relief under penalty of *stroke and distance* by playing from where the previous *stroke* was made because:

- Unplayable ball relief may not be taken again as such relief is not allowed when a ball lies in a *penalty area*.

- Relief from the *penalty area* using the back-on-the-line relief option or the lateral relief option may also not be taken, because the ball did not cross the edge of the *penalty area* before coming to rest and therefore there is no reference point and no way of estimating a reference point for taking such relief.

In taking *stroke-and-distance* relief, the player will get another one-stroke penalty (in addition to the first penalty stroke for taking unplayable ball relief).

19.2/3 – Stroke-and-Distance Reference Point Does Not Change Until Stroke Is Made

The reference point used for taking relief under *stroke-and-distance* does not change until the player makes another *stroke* at his or her ball *in play*, even if the player has *dropped* a ball under a Rule.

For example, a player takes relief for an unplayable ball and *drops* a ball under either the back-on-the-line relief option or lateral relief option. The *dropped* ball stays within the *relief* area but rolls into a place that the player again decides is unplayable.

For one additional penalty stroke the player may again use the back-on-the-line relief option or lateral relief option, or may choose the *stroke-and-distance* relief option using the point where the ball was last played before becoming unplayable the first time as the reference point. This *stroke-and-distance* reference point does not change because the player did not make a *stroke* at the *dropped* ball.

The outcome would be different if the player made a *stroke* at the *dropped* ball, because that spot would become the new *stroke-and-distance* reference point.

19.2/4 – Player May Take Relief Without Penalty if He or She Lifts Ball to Take Unplayable Ball Relief and Discovers Ball Was in Ground Under Repair Before Dropping

If a player lifts his or her ball to take unplayable ball relief and then discovers it was in *ground under repair* or another *abnormal course condition*, the player may still take free relief under Rule 16.1 so long as he or she has not yet put a ball *in play* under Rule 19 to take unplayable ball relief.

19.2/5 – Player Must Find Ball to Use Back-On-the-Line or Lateral Relief Options

The back-on-the-line and lateral relief options under Rule 19.2 and 19.3 may not be used without finding the original ball as both require that ball's original spot as the reference point for relief. If either relief option is used to take unplayable ball relief with reference to a ball that is not the player's ball, the player is treated as taking *stroke-and-distance* relief as that is the only Rule that can be used if the player has not found his or her original ball.

For example, a player finds a stray ball in a bad lie. Mistaking it for his or her ball, the player decides to take lateral relief (Rule 19.2c), *substitutes* a ball and plays it. While walking to play the next *stroke*, the player finds his or her ball. Since the player did not know the spot of the original ball at the time the other ball was *substituted*, he or she is treated as having taken *stroke-and-distance* relief and did so in a *wrong place* (Rule 14.7).

In *match play*, the player loses the hole for playing from a *wrong place*.

In *stroke play*, the player gets one penalty stroke for taking *stroke-and-distance* relief (Rule 18.1) and another two penalty strokes for doing so from a *wrong place*. If the *wrong place* was a *serious breach*, the mistake must be corrected before making a *stroke* to start another hole, or for the final hole of the *round*, before returning his or her *scorecard*.

19.3 Relief Options for Unplayable Ball in Bunker

19.3a Normal Relief Options (One Penalty Stroke)

When a player's ball is in a *bunker*:

- The player may take unplayable ball relief for **one penalty stroke** under any of the options in Rule 19.2, **except** that:

Rule 19

- The ball must be *dropped* in and come to rest in a *relief area* in the *bunker* if the player takes either back-on-the-line relief (see Rule 19.2b) or lateral relief (see Rule 19.2c).

19.3b Extra Relief Option (Two Penalty Strokes)

As an extra relief option when a player's ball is in a *bunker*, for a **total of two penalty strokes**, the player may take back-on-the-line relief outside the *bunker* under Rule 19.2b.

DIAGRAM 19.3:   RELIEF OPTIONS FOR BALL UNPLAYABLE IN BUNKER

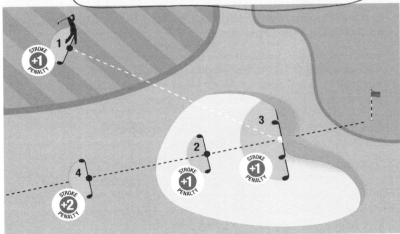

A player decides that his or her ball in a bunker is unplayable. The player has **four options**:

(1) For one penalty stroke, the player may take stroke-and-distance relief.

(2) For one penalty stroke, the player may take back-on-the-line relief in the bunker.

(3) For one penalty stroke, the player may take lateral relief in the bunker.

(4) For a total of two penalty strokes, the player may take back-on-the-line relief outside the bunker based on a reference line going straight back from the hole through the spot of the original ball.

See Interpretation 17.1d(2)/1 – Recommendation That Player Physically Marks Reference Point on Reference Line

Rule 19.3b Interpretations:

19.3b/1 – Taking Unplayable Ball Relief Outside Bunker After First Taking Unplayable Ball Relief in Bunker

If a player's ball lies in a *bunker* and the player takes unplayable ball relief in the *bunker* for one penalty stroke under Rule 19.3a and then decides he or she cannot (or does not wish to) play the *dropped* ball as it now lies, the player is faced with a new situation:

- Unplayable ball relief may again be taken under Rule 19.3a, for one more penalty stroke, for a total of two penalty strokes, by either using *stroke-and-distance* relief and playing again from where the previous *stroke* was made or by using the ball's new spot as the reference point for taking back-on-the-line relief or lateral relief in the *bunker*.

- If the player instead decides to take relief by *dropping* a ball behind the *bunker* using the extra relief option under Rule 19.3b, he or she gets two more penalty strokes in addition to the one-stroke penalty for taking unplayable ball relief the first time, for a total of three penalty strokes.

Penalty for Playing Ball from a *Wrong Place* in Breach of Rule 19.3: *General Penalty* Under Rule 14.7a.

Procedures for Players and Committee When Issues Arise in Applying the Rules

Rule 20

RULE 20

Resolving Rules Issues During Round; Rulings by Referee and Committee

Purpose of Rule:

Rule 20 covers what players should do when they have questions about the Rules during a round, including the procedures (which differ in match play and stroke play) allowing a player to protect the right to get a ruling at a later time.

The Rule also covers the role of referees who are authorized to decide questions of fact and apply the Rules. Rulings from a referee or the Committee are binding on all players.

20.1 Resolving Rules Issues During Round

20.1a Players Must Avoid Unreasonable Delay

Players must not unreasonably delay play when seeking help with the Rules during a *round*:

- If a *referee* or the *Committee* is not available in a reasonable time to help with a Rules issue, the player must decide what to do and play on.

- The player may protect his or her rights by asking for a ruling in *match play* (see Rule 20.1b(2)) or by playing two balls in *stroke play* (see Rule 20.1c(3)).

20.1b Rules Issues in Match Play

(1) **Deciding Issues by Agreement**. During a *round*, the players in a match may agree how to decide a Rules issue:

- The agreed outcome is conclusive even if it turns out to have been wrong under the Rules, so long as the players did not deliberately agree to ignore any Rule or penalty they knew applied (see Rule 1.3b(1)).

- **But** if a *referee* is assigned to the match, the *referee* must rule on any issue that comes to his or her attention in time and the players must follow that ruling.

In the absence of a *referee,* if the players do not agree or have doubt about how the Rules apply, either player may request a ruling under Rule 20.1b(2).

(2) **Ruling Request Made Before Result of Match Is Final.** When a player wants a *referee* or the *Committee* to decide how to apply the Rules to his or her own play or the *opponent's* play, the player may make a request for a ruling.

If a *referee* or the *Committee* is not available in a reasonable time, the player may make the request for a ruling by notifying the *opponent* that a later ruling will be sought when a *referee* or the *Committee* becomes available.

If a player makes a request for a ruling before the result of the match is final:

- A ruling will be given only if the request is made in time, which depends on when the player becomes aware of the facts creating the Rules issue:

  » When Player Becomes Aware of the Facts Before Either Player Starts the Final Hole of the Match. When the player becomes aware of the facts, the ruling request must be made before either player makes a *stroke* to begin another hole.

  » When Player Becomes Aware of the Facts During or After Completion of the Final Hole of the Match. The ruling request must be made before the result of the match is final (see Rule 3.2a(5)).

- If the player does not make the request in this time, a ruling will not be given by a *referee* or the *Committee* and the result of the hole(s) in question will stand even if the Rules were applied in the wrong way.

If the player requests a ruling about an earlier hole, a ruling will be given only if all three of these apply:

- The *opponent* breached Rule 3.2d(1) (giving wrong number of strokes taken) or Rule 3.2d(2) (failing to tell the player about a penalty),

- The request is based on facts the player was not aware of before either player made a *stroke* to begin the hole being played or, if between holes, the hole just completed, and

- After becoming aware of these facts, the player makes a request for a ruling in time (as set out above).

281

Rule 20.1b(2) Interpretations:
20.1b(2)/1 – Request for Ruling Must Be Made in Time

A player is entitled to know the status of his or her match at all times or that a ruling request will be settled later in the match. A request for a ruling must be made in time to prevent a player from trying to apply penalties later in the match. Whether a ruling will be given depends on when the player becomes aware of the facts (not when he or she learned that something was a penalty) and when the request for a ruling was made.

For example, during the first hole of a match without a *referee*, Player A properly lifts his or her ball to check for damage under Rule 4.2c(1), determines that it is cut and *substitutes* a new ball under Rule 4.2c(2). Unknown to Player A, Player B sees the condition of the original ball and privately disagrees with Player A's assessment. However, Player B decides to overlook the possible breach and says nothing to Player A. Both players *hole out* and play from the next *teeing area*.

At the conclusion of the final hole, Player A is the winner of the match, 1 up. Walking off the *putting green*, when the *Committee* is readily available, Player B changes his or her mind and tells Player A that he or she disagrees with the *substitution* that Player A made on the first hole and is making a request to the *Committee* for a ruling.

The *Committee* should determine that the ruling request by Player B was not made in time as Player B was aware of the facts during play of the first hole and, subsequently, a *stroke* was made on the second hole (Rule 20.1b(2)). Therefore, the *Committee* should decide that no ruling will be given.

The match stands as played with Player A as the winner.

20.1b(2)/2 – Ruling Made After Completion of the Final Hole of the Match but Before the Result of the Match Is Final May Result in Players Resuming the Match

If a player becomes aware of a possible breach of the Rules by his or her *opponent* after completing what they thought was the final hole of the match, the player may make a request for a ruling. If the *opponent* was in breach of the Rules, the adjusted match score may require that the players return to the *course* to resume the match.

For example:

- In a match between Player A and Player B, Player B wins by a score of 5 and 4. On the way back to the clubhouse and before the result of the match is final, it is discovered that Player B had 15 clubs in his or her bag. Player A requests a ruling, and the *Committee* determines correctly that the ruling request by Player A was made in time. The players must return to the 15th hole and resume the match. The score in the match is adjusted by deducting two holes from Player B (Rule 4.1b(4)), and Player B is now 3 up with four holes to play.

- In a match between Player A and Player B, Player B wins by a score of 3 and 2. On the way back to the clubhouse, Player A discovers that Player B hit the sand with a practice swing in a *bunker* on the 14th hole. Player B had won the 14th hole. Player A requests a ruling, and the *Committee* determines correctly that the ruling request by Player A was made in time, and that Player B lost the 14th hole for failing to tell Player A about the penalty (Rule 3.2d(2)). The players must return to the 17th hole and resume the match. As the score in the match is adjusted by changing Player B's win of the 14th hole to a loss of hole, Player B is now 1 up with two holes to play.

(3) **Ruling Request Made After Result of Match Is Final.** When a player makes a request for a ruling after the result of the match is final:

- The *Committee* will give the player a ruling only if both of these apply:

  » The request is based on facts the player was not aware of before the result of the match was final, and

  » The *opponent* breached Rule 3.2d(1) (giving wrong number of strokes taken) or Rule 3.2d(2) (failing to tell the player about a penalty) and knew of the breach before the result of the match was final.

- There is no time limit on giving such a ruling.

(4) **No Right to Play Two Balls.** A player who is uncertain about the right procedure in a match is not allowed to play out the hole with two balls. That procedure applies only in *stroke play* (see Rule 20.1c).

Rule 20.1b(4) Interpretations:

20.1b(4)/1 – Playing Out Hole with Two Balls Is Not Allowed in Match Play

The playing of two balls is limited to *stroke play* because, when a match is being played, any incidents in that match concern only the players involved in it and the players in the match can protect their own interests.

However, if a player in a match is uncertain about the right procedure and plays out the hole with two balls, the score with the original ball always counts if the player and *opponent* refer the situation to the *Committee* and the *opponent* has not objected to the player playing the second ball.

However, if the *opponent* objects to the player playing a second ball and makes a ruling request in time (Rule 20.1b(2)), the player loses the hole for playing a *wrong ball* in breach of Rule 6.3c(1).

20.1c Rules Issues in Stroke Play

(1) No Right to Decide Rules Issues by Agreement. If a *referee* or the *Committee* is not available in a reasonable time to help with a Rules issue:

- The players are encouraged to help each other in applying the Rules, **but** they have no right to decide a Rules issue by agreement and any such agreement they may reach is not binding on any player, a *referee* or the *Committee*.

- A player should raise any Rules issues with the *Committee* before returning his or her *scorecard*.

(2) Players Should Protect Other Players in the Competition. To protect the interests of all other players:

- If a player knows or believes that another player has breached or might have breached the Rules and that the other player does not recognize or is ignoring this, the player should tell the other player, the player's *marker*, a *referee* or the *Committee*.

- This should be done promptly after the player becomes aware of the issue, and no later than before the other player returns his or her *scorecard* unless it is not possible to do so.

If the player fails to do so, the *Committee* may disqualify the player under Rule 1.2a if it decides that this was serious misconduct contrary to the spirit of the game.

(3) Playing Two Balls When Uncertain What to Do. A player who is uncertain about the right procedure while playing a hole may complete the hole with two balls without penalty:

- The player must decide to play two balls after the uncertain situation arises and before making a *stroke*.

- The player should choose which ball will count if the Rules allow the procedure used for that ball, by announcing that choice to his or her *marker* or to another player before making a *stroke*.

- If the player does not choose in time, the ball played first is treated as the ball chosen by default.

- The player must report the facts of the situation to the *Committee* before returning the *scorecard*, even if the player scores the same with both balls. The player is **disqualified** if he or she fails to do so.

- If the player made a *stroke* before deciding to play a second ball:

  » This Rule does not apply at all and the score that counts is the score with the ball played before the player decided to play the second ball.

  » **But** the player gets no penalty for playing the second ball.

A second ball played under this Rule is not the same as a *provisional ball* under Rule 18.3.

Rule 20.1c(3) Interpretations:

20.1c(3)/1 – No Penalty for Playing a Ball That Was Not in Play When Two Balls Are Being Played

When a player is uncertain of what to do and decides to play two balls, he or she gets no penalty if one of the balls played was his or her original ball that is no longer *in play*.

For example, a player's ball is not found in a *penalty area* after a three-minute search, so the player properly takes relief from the *penalty area* under Rule 17.1c and plays a *substituted* ball. Then, the original ball is found in the *penalty area*. Not sure what to do, the player decides to play the original ball as a second ball before making any further *strokes*, and chooses to score with the original ball. The player *holes out* with both balls.

The ball played under Rule 17.1c became the ball *in play* and the score with that ball is the player's score for the hole. The score with the original ball could not count because the original ball was no longer *in play*. However, the player gets no penalty for playing the original ball as a second ball.

20.1c(3)/2 – Player Must Decide to Play Two Balls Before Making Another Stroke

Rule 20.1c(3) requires a player to decide to play two balls before making a *stroke* so that his or her decision to play two balls or the choice of which ball to count is not influenced by the result of the ball just played. *Dropping* a ball is not equivalent to making a *stroke*.

Examples of the application of that requirement include:

A player's ball comes to rest on a paved cart path in the *general area*. In taking relief, the player lifts the ball, *drops* it outside the required *relief area* and plays it. The player's *marker* questions the *drop* and advises the player that he or she may have played from a *wrong place*.

Uncertain what to do, the player would like to complete the hole with two balls. However, it is too late to use Rule 20.1c(3) since a *stroke* has already been made and the player must add the *general penalty* for playing from a *wrong place* (Rule 14.7). If the player believes this may be a *serious breach* of playing from a *wrong place*, the player should play a second ball under Rule 14.7 to avoid possible disqualification.

If the player's *marker* questioned the *drop* before the player made a *stroke* at the ball and he or she was uncertain what to do, the player could have completed the hole with two balls under Rule 20.1c(3).

- A player's ball lies in a *penalty area* defined by red stakes. One of the stakes interferes with the player's intended swing and the player is uncertain if he or she is allowed to remove the stake. The player makes his or her next *stroke* without removing a stake.

  At this point, the player decides to play a second ball with the stake removed and get a ruling from the *Committee*. The *Committee* should rule that the score with the original ball is the score that counts since the uncertain situation arose when the ball was in the *penalty area* with interference from the stake, and the player had to make the decision to play two balls before making a *stroke* at the original ball.

20.1c(3)/3 – Player May Lift Original Ball and Drop, Place or Replace It When Playing Two Balls

Rule 20.1c(3) does not require the original ball to be the ball that is played as it lies. Typically, the original ball is played as it lies, and the second ball is put *in play* under whatever Rule is being used. However, putting the original ball *in play* under the Rule is also allowed.

For example, if a player is uncertain whether his or her ball lies in an *abnormal course condition* in the *general area*, the player may decide to play two balls. The player may then take relief under Rule 16.1b (Relief from Abnormal Course Condition) by lifting, *dropping* and playing the original ball and then continuing by placing a second ball where the original ball lay in the questionable area and playing it from there.

In such a case, the player does not need to mark the spot of the original ball before lifting it, although it is recommended that this is done.

20.1c(3)/4 – Order of Playing the Original Ball and Second Ball Is Interchangeable

When a player is uncertain about the right procedure and wants to complete the hole with two balls, the Rules do not require that the original ball be played first, followed by the second ball. The balls may be played in any order the player decides.

For example, uncertain what to do, a player decides to complete the hole with two balls and chooses to score with the second ball. The player may choose to play the second ball before the original ball and may alternate making *strokes* with the original and second ball in completing play of the hole.

20.1c(3)/5 – Player's Obligation to Complete Hole with Second Ball After Announcing Intention to Do So and Choosing Which Ball Should Count

After a player has announced his or her intention to play two balls under Rule 20.1c(3) and has either put a ball in play or made a *stroke* at one of the balls, the player is committed to the procedure in Rule 20.1c(3). If the player does not play, or does not *hole out* with, one of the balls and that ball is the one the *Committee* rules would have counted, the player is disqualified for failing to *hole out* (Rule 3.3c – Failure to Hole Out). However, there is no penalty if the player does not *hole out* a ball that will not count.

For example, a player's ball lies in a rut made by a vehicle. Believing that the area should have been marked as *ground under repair*, the player decides to play two balls and announces that he or she would like the second ball to count. The player then makes a *stroke* at the original ball from the rut. After seeing the results of this *stroke*, the player decides not to play a second ball. Upon completion of the round, the facts are reported to the *Committee*.

If the *Committee* decides that the rut is *ground under repair*, the player is disqualified for failing to *hole out* with the second ball (Rule 3.3c).

However, if the *Committee* decides that the rut is not *ground under repair*, the player's score with the original ball counts and he or she gets no penalty for not playing a second ball.

The result would be the same for a player who made a *stroke* or *strokes* with a second ball but picked it up before completing play of the hole.

20.1c(3)/6 – Provisional Ball Must Be Used as Second Ball When Uncertain

Although Rule 20.1c(3) states that a second ball played under this Rule is not the same as a *provisional ball* under Rule 18.3 (Provisional Ball), the reverse is not true. In deciding to play two balls after playing a *provisional ball* and being uncertain whether the original ball is *out of bounds* or *lost* outside a *penalty area*, the player must treat the *provisional ball* as the second ball.

Examples of using a *provisional ball* as a second ball include when:

- The player is unsure whether his or her original ball is *out of bounds*, so he or she completes the hole with the original ball and the *provisional ball*.

- The player has *knowledge or virtual certainty* that his or her original ball that has not been found is in an *abnormal course condition* and is unsure what to do, so he or she completes the hole with the *provisional ball* and a second ball with relief under Rule 16.1e.

20.1c(3)/7 – Player Allowed to Play One Ball Under Two Different Rules

When a player is uncertain about the right procedure, it is recommended that he or she play two balls under Rule 20.1c(3). However, there is nothing that prevents the player from playing one ball under two different Rules and requesting a ruling before returning his or her *scorecard*.

For example, a player's ball comes to rest in an unplayable spot in an area that he or she believes should be *ground under repair*, but is not marked. Uncertain what to do and willing to accept the one-stroke penalty if it is not *ground under repair*, the player decides to use one ball and drop it in the *relief area* allowed for taking relief from *ground under repair* (Rule 16.1) and simultaneously in part of the *relief area* allowed for taking unplayable ball relief (Rule 19.2) for one penalty stroke.

If the *Committee* decides that the area is *ground under repair*, the player does not get a penalty for taking unplayable ball relief. If the *Committee* decides that the area is not *ground under repair*, the player gets one penalty stroke for taking unplayable ball relief.

If the player used the procedure outlined above and the ball came to rest at a spot where there is interference from the condition (required to drop again for Rule 16.1 but not for Rule 19.2), he or she should get help from the *Committee* or play two balls under Rule 20.1c(3).

(4) **Committee Decision on Score for Hole.** When a player plays two balls under (3), the *Committee* will decide the player's score for the hole in this way:

- The score with the ball chosen (whether by the player or by default) counts if the Rules allow the procedure used for that ball.

- If the Rules do not allow the procedure used for that ball, the score with the other ball played counts if the Rules allow the procedure used for that other ball.

- If the Rules do not allow the procedures used for each of the two balls, the score with the ball chosen (whether by the player or by default) counts unless there was a *serious breach* in playing that ball from a *wrong place*, in which case the score with the other ball counts.

- If there was a *serious breach* in playing each ball from a *wrong place*, the player is **disqualified**.

- All strokes with the ball that does not count (including *strokes* made and any penalty strokes solely from playing that ball) do not count in the player's score for the hole.

"Rules allow the procedure used" means that either: (a) the original ball was played as it lies and play was allowed from there, or (b) the ball that was played was put *in play* under the right procedure, in the right way and in the right place under the Rules.

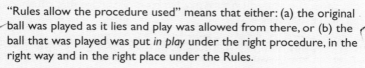

20.2 Rulings on Issues Under the Rules

20.2a Rulings by Referee

A *referee* is an official named by the *Committee* to decide questions of fact and apply the Rules.

A *referee's* ruling on the facts or how the Rules apply must be followed by the player.

- A player has no right to appeal a *referee's* ruling to the *Committee*.

- The *referee* may seek the *Committee's* help before making a ruling or refer a ruling to the *Committee* for review, **but** is not required to do so.

See Committee Procedures, Section 6C (explaining the scope of a *referee's* authority).

20.2b Rulings by Committee

When there is no *referee* to give a ruling or when a *referee* refers a ruling to the *Committee*:

- The ruling will be given by the *Committee*, and

- The *Committee's* ruling is final.

If the *Committee* cannot reach a decision, it may refer the issue to the Rules of Golf Committee of the USGA, whose decision is final.

20.2c Applying "Naked Eye" Standard When Using Video Evidence

When the *Committee* is deciding questions of fact in making a ruling, the use of video evidence is limited by the "naked eye" standard:

- If the facts shown on the video could not reasonably have been seen with the naked eye, that video evidence will be disregarded even if it indicates a breach of the Rules.

- But even where video evidence is disregarded under the "naked eye" standard, a breach of the Rules will still be found if the player was otherwise aware of facts establishing a breach (such as where the player felt the club touch sand in a *bunker* even though that could not be seen by the naked eye).

20.2d When Wrong Rulings Will Be Corrected

If a ruling by a *referee* or the *Committee* is later found to be wrong:

- The ruling will be corrected if possible under the Rules.

- If it is too late to do so, the wrong ruling stands.

If a player takes an action in breach of a Rule based on a reasonable misunderstanding of a *referee's* or *Committee's* instruction during a round or while play is stopped under Rule 5.7a (such as lifting a ball *in play* when not allowed under the Rules), there is no penalty and the instruction is treated like a wrong ruling.

See Committee Procedures, Section 6C (what the *Committee* should do when there has been a wrong ruling).

See Committee Procedures, Section 6C for additional guidance for referees and Committees on handling rules situations.

Rule 20.2d Interpretations:

20.2d/1 – A Wrong Ruling Is Different from an Administrative Mistake

There are limits on when a wrong ruling may be corrected, but there is no time limit for correcting an administrative mistake.

A wrong ruling has occurred when a *referee* or the *Committee* has attempted to apply the Rules to a situation but has done so incorrectly, for example, by:

- Misinterpreting or misunderstanding a Rule,

- Failing to apply a Rule, or

- Applying a Rule that was not applicable or does not exist.

This can be distinguished from an administrative mistake when a *referee* or the *Committee* has made a procedural error in relation to the administration of the competition, for example, by:

- Miscalculating the result of a tie, or

- Applying a player's full handicap strokes in a *stroke-play* competition when only a percentage should be applied.

20.2d/2 – Administrative Errors Should Always Be Corrected

The time frame in Rule 20.2d, which deals with penalties, does not apply to administrative mistakes by the *Committee*. There is no time limit for correcting administrative mistakes.

For example, there is no time limit in correcting:

- A handicap that was miscalculated by the *Committee* causing another player to win the competition.

- A prize that was given to the wrong player after the *Committee* failed to post the winner's score.

20.2e Disqualifying Players After Result of Match or Competition Is Final

(1) **Match Play.** There is no time limit on disqualifying a player under Rule 1.2 (serious misconduct) or Rule 1.3b(1) (deliberately ignoring a known breach or penalty, or agreeing with another player to ignore any Rule or penalty they know applies).

This may be done even after the result of the match is final (see Rule 3.2a(5)).

For when the *Committee* will give a ruling when a request is made after the result of the match is final, see Rule 20.1b(3).

(2) **Stroke Play.** Normally, a penalty must not be added or corrected after a *stroke-play* competition has closed, which is:

- When the result becomes final in the way set by the *Committee* or,

- In *stroke-play* qualifying followed by *match play*, when the player has teed off to start his or her first match.

But a player must be **disqualified** even after the competition is closed if he or she:

- Returned a score for any hole lower than actually taken for any

r   reason other than failing to include one or more penalty strokes
    that, before the competition closed, the player did not know about
    (see Rule 3.3b(3)),

2   - Knew before the competition had closed that the returned *scorecard*
    showed a handicap that was higher than the actual handicap and this
    affected the number of handicap strokes used to adjust the player's
    score (see Rule 3.3b(4)),

3   - Knew before the competition had closed that he or she was in
    breach of any other Rule with a penalty of disqualification, or

4   - Deliberately agreed with another player to ignore any Rule or
    penalty they knew applied (see Rule 1.3b(1)).

5   The *Committee* may also disqualify a player under Rule 1.2 (serious
misconduct) after the competition has closed.

Rule 20.2e Interpretations:

20.2e/1 – Player Found to Be Ineligible During Competition or After Result of Match or Competition Is Final

There is no time limit on correcting the results of a competition when a
player who has competed in the competition is found to be ineligible.

For example, if it is discovered that a player has played in a competition
with a maximum age and the player was over that age, or a player has
played in a competition restricted to amateur golfers when the player was
not an amateur, the player was ineligible.

 In these circumstances, the player is treated as if he or she had not entered
the competition, as opposed to being disqualified from the competition,
and the scores or the results are amended accordingly.

20.3   Situations Not Covered by the Rules

Any situation not covered by the Rules should be decided by the *Committee*:

- Considering all the circumstances, and

- Treating the situation in a way that is reasonable, fair and consistent
with how similar situations are treated under the Rules.

Other Forms of Play

Rules 21–24

RULE 21

Other Forms of Individual Stroke Play and Match Play

Purpose of Rule:

Rule 21 covers four other forms of individual play, including three forms of stroke play where scoring is different than in regular stroke play: Stableford (scoring by points awarded on each hole); Maximum Score (the score for each hole is capped at a maximum); and Par/Bogey (match play scoring used on a hole by hole basis).

21.1 Stableford

21.1a Overview of Stableford

Stableford is a form of *stroke play* where:

- A player's or *side's* score for a hole is based on points awarded by comparing the player's or *side's* number of strokes (including *strokes* made and penalty strokes) on the hole to a fixed target score for the hole set by the *Committee*, and

- The competition is won by the player or *side* who completes all *rounds* with the most points.

The normal Rules for *stroke play* in Rules 1–20 apply, as modified by these specific Rules. Rule 21.1 is written for:

- Scratch competitions, but can be adapted for handicap competitions, and

- Individual play, but can be adapted for competitions involving *partners*, as modified by Rules 22 (*Foursomes*) and 23 (*Four-Ball*), and for team competitions, as modified by Rule 24.

21.1b Scoring in Stableford

(1) **How Points Are Awarded**. Points are awarded to a player for each hole by comparing the player's score to the fixed target score for the hole, which is par unless the *Committee* sets a different fixed target score:

Hole Played In	Points
More than one over fixed target score or no score returned	0
One over fixed target score	1
Fixed target score	2
One under fixed target score	3
Two under fixed target score	4
Three under fixed target score	5
Four under fixed target score	6

A player who does not *hole out* under the Rules for any reason gets zero points for the hole.

To help pace of play, players are encouraged to stop playing a hole when their score will result in zero points.

The hole is completed when the player *holes out*, chooses not to do so or when his or her score will result in zero points.

(2) **Score Entered for Each Hole**. To meet the requirements in Rule 3.3b for entering hole scores on the *scorecard*:

- If Hole Is Completed by Holing Out:

  » When Score Would Result in Points Being Awarded. The *scorecard* must show the actual score.

  » When Score Would Result in Zero Points. The *scorecard* must show either no score or any score that results in zero points being awarded.

- If Hole Is Completed Without Holing Out. If the player does not *hole out* under the Rules, the *scorecard* must show either no score or any score that results in zero points being awarded.

The *Committee* is responsible for calculating how many points the player gets on each hole and, in a handicap competition, for applying handicap strokes to the score entered for each hole before calculating the number of points.

See Committee Procedures, Section 5A(5) (the Terms of the Competition may encourage but not require players to enter the points awarded for each hole on the *scorecard*).

DIAGRAM 21.1b: SCORING IN SCRATCH STABLEFORD

Name: John Smith   Date: 01/03/19

Hole	1	2	3	4	5	6	7	8	9	Out
Yardage	445	186	378	387	181	533	313	412	537	3372
Par	4	3	4	4	3	5	4	4	5	36
J.Smith	3	3	5	4	4	7	5	4	5	40
Points	3	2	1	2	1	0	1	2	2	14

Hole	10	11	12	13	14	15	16	17	18	In	Total
Yardage	206	424	397	202	541	150	593	137	401	3051	6423
Par	3	4	4	3	5	3	5	3	4	34	70
J.Smith	3	4	6	3	4	3	4	5	4	36	76
Points	2	2	0	2	3	2	3	0	2	16	30

Responsibilities
- Committee
- Player
- Player and marker

Marker's Signature:

Player's Signature:

21.1c Penalties in Stableford

(1) **Penalties Other Than Disqualification**. All penalty strokes are added to the player's score for the hole where the breach happened, but there are three **exceptions**:

Exception 1 – Excess, Shared, Added or Replaced Clubs: If a player breaches Rule 4.1b (Limit of 14 Clubs; Sharing, Adding or Replacing Clubs During Round), the *Committee* will deduct **two points** (if the breach applies to only one hole) or **four points** (if the breach applies to two or more holes) under Rule 4.1b from the player's total points for the *round*.

Exception 2 – Time of Starting: If a player breaches Rule 5.3a by (1) arriving late but within five minutes after the starting time or (2) starting early but within five minutes of the starting time (see Rule 5.3 Penalty Statement, Exceptions 1 and 2), the *Committee* will deduct **two points** from the player's total points for the *round*.

Exception 3 – Unreasonable Delay: If a player breaches Rule

5.6a, the *Committee* will deduct **one point** for the first breach and an additional **two points** for the second breach from the player's total points for the *round*. (For a third breach of Rule 5.6a, see Rule 21.1c(2).)

For each exception, the player must report the facts about the breach to the *Committee* before returning the *scorecard* so that the *Committee* may apply the penalty. If the player fails to do so, the player is **disqualified**.

See Committee Procedures, Section 8; Model Local Rule K-3 (how to adopt Pace of Play Policy in *Stableford* with deduction of points used in the penalties for breach).

(2) **Disqualification Penalties**. A player who breaches any of these four Rules is not disqualified but gets **zero points** for the hole where the breach happened:

- Failure to *hole out* under Rule 3.3c,

- Failure to correct mistake of playing from outside *the teeing area* in starting a hole (see Rule 6.1b(2)),

- Failure to correct mistake of playing a *wrong ball* (see Rule 6.3c), or

- Failure to correct mistake of playing from a *wrong place* when there is a *serious breach* (see Rule 14.7b).

If the player breaches any other Rule with a penalty of disqualification, the player is **disqualified**.

21.1d Exception to Rule 11.2 in Stableford

Rule 11.2 does not apply in this situation:

If a player's ball in motion needs to be *holed* to get one point on the hole and any person deliberately deflects or stops the ball at a time when there is no reasonable chance it can be *holed*, there is no penalty to that person and the player gets zero points on the hole.

21.1e When Round Ends in Stableford

A player's *round* ends when the player:

- *Holes out* on his or her final hole (including correction of a mistake, such as under Rule 6.1 or 14.7b), or

- Chooses not to *hole out* on the final hole or already cannot get more than zero points on the hole.

21.2 Maximum Score

21.2a Overview of Maximum Score

Maximum Score is a form of *stroke play* where a player's or *side's* score for a hole is capped at a maximum number of strokes set by the *Committee*, such as two times par, a fixed number or net double bogey.

The normal Rules for *stroke play* in Rules 1–20 apply, as modified by these specific Rules. Rule 21.2 is written for:

- Scratch competitions, but can be adapted for handicap competitions as well, and

- Individual play, but can be adapted for competitions involving *partners*, as modified by Rules 22 (*Foursomes*) and 23 (*Four-Ball*), and for team competitions, as modified by Rule 24.

21.2b Scoring in Maximum Score

(1) **Player's Score on Hole**. A player's score for a hole is based on the player's number of strokes (including *strokes* made and penalty strokes), **except** that the player will get only the maximum score even if the actual score exceeds the maximum.

A player who does not *hole out* under the Rules for any reason gets the maximum score for the hole.

To help pace of play, players are encouraged to stop playing a hole when their score has reached the maximum.

The hole is completed when the player *holes out*, chooses not to do so or when his or her score has reached the maximum.

(2) **Score Entered for Each Hole**. To meet the requirements in Rule 3.3b for entering hole scores on the *scorecard*:

- If Hole Is Completed by Holing Out:

  » When Score Is Lower Than Maximum. The *scorecard* must show the actual score.

  » When Score Is Same as or Higher Than Maximum. The *scorecard* must show either no score or any score at or above the maximum.

- If Hole Is Completed Without Holing Out. If the player does not *hole out* under the Rules, the *scorecard* must show either no score or any score at or above the maximum.

The *Committee* is responsible for adjusting the player's score to the maximum for any hole where the *scorecard* shows either no score or any score above the maximum and, in a handicap competition, for applying handicap strokes to the score entered for each hole.

21.2c Penalties in Maximum Score

All penalties that apply in *stroke play* apply in *Maximum Score*, **except** that a player who breaches any of these four Rules is not disqualified **but** gets the **maximum score** for the hole where the breach happened:

- Failure to *hole out* under Rule 3.3c,

- Failure to correct mistake of playing from outside the *teeing area* in starting a hole (see Rule 6.1b(2)),

- Failure to correct mistake of playing a *wrong ball* (see Rule 6.3c), or

- Failure to correct mistake of playing from a *wrong place* when there is a *serious breach* (see Rule 14.7b).

If the player breaches any other Rule with a penalty of disqualification, the player is **disqualified**.

After applying any penalty strokes, the player's score for a hole cannot exceed the maximum score set by the *Committee*.

21.2d Exception to Rule 11.2 in Maximum Score

Rule 11.2 does not apply in this situation:

If a player's ball in motion needs to be *holed* to score lower than the maximum score on the hole and any person deliberately deflects or stops the ball at a time when there is no reasonable chance it can be *holed*, there is no penalty to that person and the player gets the maximum score on the hole.

21.2e When Round Ends in Maximum Score

A player's *round* ends when the player:

- *Holes out* on his or her final hole (including correction of a mistake, such as under Rule 6.1 or 14.7b), or

- Chooses not to *hole out* on the final hole or already will get the maximum score on the hole.

21.3 Par/Bogey

21.3a Overview of Par/Bogey

Par/Bogey is a form of *stroke play* that uses scoring as in *match play* where:

- A player or *side* wins or loses a hole by completing the hole in fewer strokes or more strokes than a fixed target score for that hole set by the *Committee*, and

- The competition is won by the player or *side* with the highest total of holes won versus holes lost (that is, adding up the holes won and deducting the holes lost).

The normal Rules for *stroke play* in Rules 1–20 apply, as modified by these specific Rules. Rule 21.3 is written for:

- Scratch competitions, but can be adapted for handicap competitions as well, and

- Individual play, but can be adapted for competitions involving *partners*, as modified by Rules 22 (*Foursomes*) and 23 (*Four-Ball*), and for team competitions, as modified by Rule 24.

21.3b Scoring in Par/Bogey

(1) **How Holes Are Won or Lost**. Scoring is done as in *match play*, with holes being won or lost by comparing the player's number of strokes (including *strokes* made and penalty strokes) to the fixed target score (typically par or bogey) set by the *Committee*:

- If the player's score is lower than the fixed score, the player wins the hole.

- If the player's score is the same as the fixed score, the hole is tied (also known as halved).

- If the player's score is higher than the fixed score, or no score is returned, the player loses the hole.

A player who does not *hole out* under the Rules for any reason loses the hole.

To help pace of play, players are encouraged to stop playing a hole when their score exceeds the fixed score (as they have lost the hole).

The hole is completed when the player *holes out*, chooses not to do so or when his or her score exceeds the fixed score.

(2) **Score Entered for Each Hole**. To meet the requirements in Rule 3.3b for entering hole scores on the *scorecard*:

- If Hole Is Completed by Holing Out:
  - » When Score Results in Hole Being Won or Tied. The *scorecard* must show the actual score.
  - » When Score Results in Hole Being Lost. The *scorecard* must show either no score or any score that results in the hole being lost.

- If Hole Is Completed Without Holing Out. If the player does not *hole out* under the Rules, the *scorecard* must show either no score or any score that results in the hole being lost.

The *Committee* is responsible for deciding whether the player won, lost or tied each hole and, in a handicap competition, for applying handicap strokes to the score entered for each hole before deciding the result of the hole.

Exception – No Penalty If No Effect on Result of Hole: If the player returns a *scorecard* with a hole score lower than the actual score but this does not affect whether the hole was won, lost or tied, there is no penalty under Rule 3.3b.

See Committee Procedures, Section 5A(5) (the Terms of the Competition may encourage but not require players to enter the result of the hole on the *scorecard*).

21.3c Penalties in Par/Bogey

(1) Penalties Other Than Disqualification. All penalty strokes are added to the player's score for the hole where the breach happened, **but** there are three **exceptions**:

Exception 1 – Excess, Shared, Added or Replaced Clubs: If a player breaches Rule 4.1b (Limit of 14 Clubs; Sharing, Adding and Replacing Clubs), the *Committee* will deduct **one hole** (if the breach applies to only one hole) or **two holes** (if the breach applies to two or more holes) under Rule 4.1b from the player's total of holes won versus holes lost.

Exception 2 – Time of Starting: If a player breaches Rule 5.3a by (1) arriving late but within five minutes after the starting time or (2) starting early but within five minutes of the starting time (see Rule 5.3 Penalty Statement, Exceptions 1 and 2), the *Committee* will deduct **one hole** from the player's total of holes won versus holes lost.

Exception 3 – Unreasonable Delay: If a player breaches Rule 5.6a:

- Penalty for first breach: The player gets **one penalty stroke** on the hole where the breach occurred.

- Penalty for second breach: The *Committee* will deduct **one hole** from the player's total of holes won versus holes lost.

- For a third breach of Rule 5.6a, see Rule 21.3c(2).

For each exception, the player must report the facts about the breach to the *Committee* before returning the *scorecard* so that the *Committee* may apply the penalty. If the player fails to do so, the player is **disqualified**.

(2) **Disqualification Penalties.** A player who breaches any of these four Rules is not disqualified but **loses the hole** where the breach happened:

- Failure to *hole out* under Rule 3.3c,

- Failure to correct mistake of playing from outside the *teeing area* in starting a hole (see Rule 6.1b(2)),

- Failure to correct mistake of playing a *wrong ball* (see Rule 6.3c), or

- Failure to correct mistake of playing from a *wrong place* when there is a *serious breach* (see Rule 14.7b).

If the player breaches any other Rule with a penalty of disqualification, the player is **disqualified**.

See Committee Procedures, Section 8; Model Local Rule K-4 (how to adopt Pace of Play Policy in *Par/Bogey* with deduction of holes used in the penalties for breach).

21.3d Exception to Rule 11.2 in Par/Bogey

Rule 11.2 does not apply in this situation:

If a player's ball in motion needs to be *holed* to tie the hole and any person deliberately deflects or stops the ball at a time when there is no reasonable chance it can be *holed*, there is no penalty to that person and the player loses the hole.

21.3e When Round Ends in Par/Bogey

A player's *round* ends when the player:

- *Holes out* on his or her final hole (including correction of a mistake, such as under Rule 6.1 or 14.7b), or

- Chooses not to *hole out* on the final hole or has already lost the hole.

21.4 Three-Ball Match Play

21.4a Overview of Three-Ball Match Play

Three-Ball Match Play is a form of *match play* where:

- Each of three players plays an individual match against the other two players at the same time, and

- Each player plays one ball that is used in both of his or her matches.

The normal Rules for *match play* in Rules 1–20 apply to all three individual matches, **except** that these specific Rules apply in two situations where applying the normal Rules in one match might conflict with applying them in another match.

21.4b Playing Out of Turn

If a player plays out of turn in any match, the *opponent* who should have played first may cancel the *stroke* under Rule 6.4a(2):

If the player played out of turn in both matches, each *opponent* may choose whether to cancel the *stroke* in his or her match with the player.

If a player's *stroke* is cancelled only in one match:

- The player must continue play with the original ball in the other match.

- This means the player must complete the hole by playing a separate ball in each match.

21.4c Ball or Ball-Marker Lifted or Moved by One Opponent

If an *opponent* gets **one penalty stroke** for lifting a player's ball or *ball-marker* or causing the ball or *ball-marker* to *move* under Rule 9.5b or 9.7b, that penalty applies only in the match with that player.

The *opponent* gets no penalty in his or her match with the other player.

Rule 21.4 General Interpretations:

21.4/1 – In Three-Ball Match Play Each Player Is Playing Two Distinct Matches

In *Three-Ball match play*, because each player is playing two distinct matches, situations may arise that affect one match but not the other.

For example, Player A concedes the next *stroke*, a hole or the match to Player B. That concession has no effect on the match between Player A and Player C or the match between Player B and Player C.

21.5 Other Forms of Playing Golf

Although only certain forms of play are specifically covered by Rules 3, 21, 22 and 23, golf is also played in many other forms, such as scrambles and greensomes.

The Rules can be adapted to govern play in these and other forms of play.

See Committee Procedures, Section 9 (recommended ways to adapt the Rules for other common forms of play).

Rule 21 General Interpretations:

21/1 – Player May Compete in Multiple Stroke-Play Formats at Same Time

A player may compete simultaneously in multiple forms of *stroke-play* competitions, such as regular *stroke play*, *Stableford*, *Maximum Score*, and *Par/Bogey*.

RULE 22

Foursomes (Also Known as Alternate Shot)

Purpose of Rule:

Rule 22 covers Foursomes (played either in match play or stroke play), where two partners compete together as a side by alternating in making strokes at a single ball. The Rules for this form of play are essentially the same as for individual play, except for requiring the partners to alternate in teeing off to start a hole and to play out each hole with alternate shots.

22.1 Overview of Foursomes

Foursomes (also known as Alternate Shot) is a form of play involving *partners* (in either *match play* or *stroke play*) where two *partners* compete as a *side* by playing one ball in alternating order on each hole.

Rules 1–20 apply to this form of play (with the *side* playing one ball being treated in the same way as the individual player is treated), as modified by these specific Rules.

A variation of this is a form of *match play* known as Threesomes, where an individual player competes against a side of two *partners* who play alternating shots under these specific Rules.

Rule 22.1 Interpretations:

22.1/1 – Individual Handicaps Must Be Recorded on Scorecard

Under Rule 3.3b(4) (Handicap Shown on Scorecard), it is the player's responsibility to make sure that his or her handicap (see 3.3b(4)/1) is correctly shown on the scorecard. In a *Foursomes* competition, this would apply to both the player and his or her *partner*.

If the *side* returns a *scorecard* on which the handicaps are not individually recorded for both the player and the *partner*, such as being combined as a *side* handicap allowance or being omitted, the *side* is disqualified.

22.2 Either Partner May Act for Side

As both *partners* compete as one *side* playing only one ball:

- Either *partner* may take any allowed action for the *side* before the *stroke* is made, such as to *mark* the spot of the ball and lift, *replace*, *drop* and place the ball, no matter which *partner's* turn it is to play next for the *side*.

- A *partner* and his or her *caddie* may help the other *partner* in any way that the other *partner's caddie* is allowed to help (such as to give and be asked for *advice* and take the other actions allowed under Rule 10), **but** must not give any help that the other *partner's caddie* is not allowed to give under the Rules.

- Any action taken or breach of the Rules by either *partner* or either *caddie* applies to the *side*.

In *stroke play*, only one of the *partners* needs to certify the *side's* hole scores on the *scorecard* (see Rule 3.3b).

22.3 Side Must Alternate in Making Strokes

On each hole, the *partners* must make each *stroke* for the *side* in alternating order:

- One *partner* must play first for the *side* from the *teeing area* of all odd numbered holes, while the other *partner* must play first for the *side* from the *teeing area* of all even numbered holes.

- After the *side's* first *stroke* from the *teeing area* of a hole, the *partners* must alternate *strokes* for the rest of the hole.

- If a *stroke* is cancelled or otherwise does not count under any Rule (except when a *stroke* is made in the wrong order in breach of this Rule), the same *partner* who made the *stroke* must make the next *stroke* for the *side*.

- If the *side* decides to play a *provisional ball*, it must be played by the *partner* whose turn it is to play the *side's* next *stroke*.

Any penalty strokes for the *side* do not affect the *partners'* alternating order of play.

Penalty for Making a Stroke in the Wrong Order in Breach of Rule 22.3: *General Penalty*.

In *stroke play*, the *side* must correct the mistake:

- The right *partner* must make a *stroke* from where the *side* made the first *stroke* in the wrong order.

- The *stroke* made in the wrong order and any more strokes before the mistake is corrected (including *strokes* made and any penalty strokes solely from playing that ball) do not count.

- If the *side* does not correct the mistake before making a *stroke* to begin another hole or, for the last hole of the *round*, before returning its *scorecard*, the *side* is **disqualified**.

Rule 22.3 Interpretations:

22.3/1 – When Playing Again from Teeing Area in Mixed Foursomes Ball Must Be Played from Same Teeing Area

In playing mixed *Foursomes* where different *teeing areas* are used by women and men if, for example, a man tees off from the *teeing area* defined by green tee-markers and hits his shot *out of bounds*, the woman must play the next *stroke* from the green *teeing area*.

22.3/2 – Determining Which Ball Is in Play When Both Partners in Foursomes Tee Off from Same Tee

If both the player and his or her *partner* mistakenly tee off from the same *teeing area*, it must be determined whose turn it was to play.

For example, Player A and Player B are *partners* of the *side* A-B. Player A tees off first; then Player B tees off from the same *teeing area*:

- If it was Player A's turn to tee off, Player B's ball would be the *side's* ball *in play* under penalty of *stroke and distance* (Rule 18.1). The *side* has taken 3 strokes (including one penalty stroke) and it is Player A's turn to play next.

- If it was Player B's turn to tee off, the *side* loses the hole in *match play* or gets two penalty strokes in *stroke play* for playing in the wrong order when Player A played first. In *stroke play*, Player B's ball is the *side's* ball *in play*, the *side* has taken 3 strokes (including two penalty strokes) and it is Player A's turn to play next.

22.3/3 – Player May Not Purposely Miss Ball so His or Her Partner Can Play

A player may not change whose turn it is to play by intentionally missing the ball. A "*stroke*" is the forward movement of the club made to strike the ball. Therefore, if a player has intentionally missed the ball, he or she has not made a *stroke* and it is still his or her turn to play.

For example, Player A and Player B are *partners* of the *side* A-B. If Player

A purposely misses the ball so that Player B can hit the shot, Player A has not made a *stroke* as there was no intention of striking the ball. If Player B subsequently plays the ball, side A-B gets the *general penalty* because Player B played in the wrong order as it was still Player A's turn to play.

However, if Player A intends to strike the ball and accidentally misses it, he or she has made a *stroke* and it is Player B's turn to play.

22.3/4 – How to Proceed When Provisional Ball Played by Wrong Partner

If a *side* decides to play a *provisional ball*, it must be played by the *partner* whose turn it is to make the side's next *stroke*.

For example, Player A and Player B are *partners* of the side A-B. Player A plays his or her ball and there is doubt whether the ball is *out of bounds* or *lost* outside a *penalty area*. If the side decides to play a *provisional ball*, Player B must play the *provisional ball*. If, by mistake, Player A plays the *provisional ball*, there is no penalty if the original ball is found and the *provisional ball* does not become the ball *in play*.

However, if the original ball is *lost* and the *provisional ball* becomes the ball *in play*, since Player A played the *provisional ball* in this example, the *side* loses the hole in *match play* or gets a penalty of two strokes in *stroke play* for playing in the wrong order. In *stroke play*, the *provisional ball* must be abandoned and Player B must return to the spot of Player A's last *stroke* at the original ball and put a ball *in play* (Rule 18.2b).

22.4 Starting the Round

22.4a Partner to Play First

The side may choose which *partner* will play from the first *teeing area* in starting the *round*, unless the Terms of the Competition say which *partner* must play first.

The side's *round* starts when that *partner* makes a *stroke* to start the side's first hole.

22.4b Starting Time and Starting Point

Rule 5.3a applies differently to each *partner* based on who will play first for the side:

• The partner who will play first must be ready to play at the starting time and starting point, and must start at (and not before) that time.

- The *partner* who will play second must be present at the starting time either at the starting point or on the hole near where the ball played from the *teeing area* is expected to come to rest.

If either *partner* is not present in this way, the *side* is in breach of Rule 5.3a.

22.5   Partners May Share Clubs

Rule 4.1b(2) is modified to allow *partners* to share clubs, so long as the total number of clubs they have together is not more than 14.

RULE
23 Four-Ball

Purpose of Rule:

Rule 23 covers Four-Ball (played either in match play or stroke play), where partners compete as a side with each playing a separate ball. The side's score for a hole is the lower score of the partners on that hole.

23.1 Overview of Four-Ball

Four-Ball is a form of play (in either *match play* or *stroke play*) involving *partners* where:

- Two *partners* compete together as a *side*, with each player playing his or her own ball, and

- A *side's* score for a hole is the lower score of the two *partners* on that hole.

Rules 1–20 apply to this form of play, as modified by these specific Rules.

A variation of this is a form of *match play* known as Best-Ball, where an individual player competes against a *side* of two or three *partners* and each *partner* plays his or her own ball under the Rules, as modified by these specific Rules. (For Best-Ball with three *partners* on a *side*, each reference to the other *partner* means the other two *partners*).

23.2 Scoring in Four-Ball

23.2a Side's Score for Hole in Match Play and Stroke Play

- When Both Partners Hole Out or Otherwise Complete the Hole Under the Rules. The lower score is the *side's* score for the hole.

- When Only One Partner Holes Out or Otherwise Completes the Hole Under the Rules. That *partner's* score is the *side's* score for the hole. The other *partner* does not need to *hole out*.

- When Neither Partner Holes Out or Otherwise Completes the Hole Under the Rules. The *side* does not have a score for that hole, which means:

» In *match play*, the side **loses the hole**, unless the opposing *side* already had conceded or otherwise lost the hole.

» In *stroke play*, the side is **disqualified** unless the mistake is corrected in time under Rule 3.3c.

Rule 23.2a Interpretations:

23.2a/1 – Result of Hole When No Ball Is Correctly Holed Out

In *Four-Ball match play*, if no player completes a hole, the *side* whose player is last to pick up or be disqualified from the hole wins the hole.

For example, side A-B are playing against *side* C-D in a *Four-Ball* match. On a given hole, by mistake Player A plays Player C's ball and then Player C plays Player A's ball and each *hole out* with that ball. Player B and Player D both play into *penalty areas* and pick up. During play of the next hole, Player A and Player C determine that both of them played a *wrong ball* on the prior hole.

The ruling is that Player A and Player C are disqualified for the prior hole. Therefore, if Player B picked up before Player D, *side* C-D won the hole and if Player D picked up before Player B, *side* A-B won the hole. If it cannot be determined which player picked up first, the *Committee* should rule that the hole was tied.

23.2b Side's Scorecard in Stroke Play

(1) **Side's Responsibility**. The *side's* gross scores for each hole must be entered on a single *scorecard* and, in a handicap competition, each *partner's* handicap must be entered on the *scorecard*.

For each hole:

• The gross score of at least one *partner* must be entered on the *scorecard*.

• There is no penalty for entering more than one *partner's* score on the *scorecard*.

• Each score on the *scorecard* must be clearly identified as the score of the individual *partner* who made it; if this is not done, the *side* is **disqualified**.

• It is not enough to identify a score as the score of the *side* in general.

311

Only one *partner* needs to certify the hole scores on the *side's scorecard* under Rule 3.3b(2).

(2) **Committee's Responsibility.** The *Committee* is responsible for deciding which score counts for the *side* on each hole, including applying any handicaps in a handicap competition:

- If only one score is entered for a hole, that score counts for the *side*.

- If the scores of both *partners* are entered for a hole:

  » If those scores are different, the lowest (gross or net) score for that hole counts for the *side*.

  » If both scores are the same, the *Committee* may count either score. If the score used is found to be wrong for any reason, the *Committee* will count the other score.

If the score that counts for the *side* is not clearly identified as the score of the individual *partner* who made it, or if that *partner* is disqualified relating to the play of the hole, the *side* is **disqualified**.

DIAGRAM 23.2b: SCORING IN SCRATCH FOUR-BALL STROKE PLAY

Names: John Smith and Kate Smith   Date: 10/05/19

Hole	1	2	3	4	5	6	7	8	9	Out
Kate	4		5	4	6	4	3		6	
John	5	3	5		6	4		3	5	
Side Score	4	3	5	4	6	4	3	3	5	37

Hole	10	11	12	13	14	15	16	17	18	In	Total
Kate	5	4	4	4		4	5	3	4		
John	5	3		4	4	4		3	5		
Side Score	5	3	4	4	4	4	5	3	4	36	73

Responsibilities

- Committee
- Player
- Player and marker

Marker's Signature:

Player's Signature:

Rule 23.2b Interpretations:

23.2b/I – Score for Hole Must Be Identified to the Correct Partner

In *Four-Ball* stroke play, *partners* are required to return a *scorecard* with correct hole scores that are identified to the correct *partner*. The following are examples of scoring in *Four-Ball* based on how the *scorecard* is completed and returned by *side* A-B:

- In a handicap competition, Player A and Player B both *holed out* in 4 strokes on a hole where Player B received a handicap stroke and Player A did not. The *marker* recorded a gross score of 4 for Player A, no gross score for Player B, and a net score for the side of 3. The *scorecard* was returned to the *Committee*.

  The ruling is that Player A's score of 4 is the *side's* score for the hole. Only the *Committee* has the responsibility to apply any handicap strokes. The *side's* score is 4 as it is identified to Player A. The *marker's* recording of the net 3 is irrelevant.

- On a hole, Player A picks up and Player B *holes out* in 5 strokes. The *marker* records a score of 6 for Player A and a score of 5 for Player B. The *scorecard* is returned with these scores recorded.

  There is no penalty because the *partner's* score that counts for the *side* on that hole is correctly recorded.

- On a hole, Player A picked up and Player B *holed out* in 4 strokes. By mistake, the *marker* recorded a score of 4 for Player A and no score for Player B. The *scorecard* is returned in this way.

  The ruling is that the *side* is disqualified because the score for the *side* on that hole is identified to Player A, and Player A did not complete play of the hole.

23.2b/2 – Application of Exception to Rule 3.3b(3) for Returning Incorrect Scorecard

The following situations illustrate how Rule 3.3b(3) (Wrong Score for Hole) and Rule 23.2b are to be applied. In all cases, *side* A-B returns a *scorecard* with an incorrect score on a hole and the mistake is discovered after the *scorecard* is returned but before the competition has closed.

- Player A returns a score of 4 and Player B returns a score of 5. Player A touches sand in a *bunker* with a club in making the backswing for a *stroke* and was aware of the penalty for a breach of Rule 12.2b(1) (Restrictions on Touching Sand in Bunker) before returning the *scorecard* but failed to include it in his or her score for the hole.

The Exception to 3.3b(3) does not apply as Player A was aware of the penalty and the *side* is disqualified under Rule 23.2b.

- Player A returns a score of 4 and Player B returns a score of 5. Player A was in breach of Rule 12.2b(1) for touching sand in making a practice swing in a *bunker* but neither *partner* was aware of the penalty before returning the *scorecard*. The Exception to Rule 3.3b(3) applies. As Player A's score was the score to count on the hole, the *Committee* must apply the *general penalty* to Player A's score on that hole for a breach of Rule 12.2b(1).

  Therefore, the *side's* score for the hole is 6. The Rules only allow the side to revert to Player B's score if both *partners'* scores were the same on the hole (Rule 23.2b(2)).

- Player A returns a score of 4 and Player B returns a score of 6. Player A *moved* his or her ball while removing a *loose impediment* in breach of Rule 15.1b. Player A *replaced* the ball but was unaware of the one-stroke penalty. Player B witnessed the entire incident and was aware of the penalty. The *scorecard* is returned with a score of 4 for Player A and 6 for Player B. Player A's score should have been 5 with the one-stroke penalty included.

  The Exception under Rule 3.3b(3) does not apply given Player B's awareness of the incident and the resulting penalty that should have been applied to Player A. The *side* is disqualified under Rule 23.2b.

- Player A and Player B each return scores of 4. Player A lifted his or her ball for identification in the *general area* but the lifting was not reasonably necessary to identify the ball. Neither Player A nor Player B was aware of the penalty for a breach of Rule 7.3 before returning the *scorecard*.

  Since both scores on the *scorecard* are the same, the *Committee* may count either score. If the *Committee* had counted Player A's score that was later found to be wrong, the *Committee* will count Player B's score, which is correct, and there is no penalty to the *side*.

23.2c Exception to Rule 11.2 in Four-Ball

Rule 11.2 does not apply in this situation:

When a player's *partner* has already completed the hole and the player's ball in motion needs to be *holed* to lower the side's score for the hole by one stroke, if any person deliberately deflects or stops the ball at a time when there is no reasonable chance it can be *holed*, there is no penalty to that person and the player's ball does not count for the *side*.

23.3 When Round Starts and Ends; When Hole Is Completed

23.3a When Round Starts

A *side's round* starts when one of the *partners* makes a *stroke* to start his or her first hole.

23.3b When Round Ends

A *side's round* ends:

- In *match play*, when either *side* has won the match (see Rules 3.2a(3) and (4)).

- In *stroke play*, when the *side* completes the final hole, either by both *partners holing out* (including correction of a mistake, such as under Rule 6.1 or 14.7b) or by one *partner holing out* on the final hole and the other *partner* choosing not to do so.

23.3c When Hole Is Completed

(1) **Match Play.** A *side* has completed a hole when both *partners* have *holed out* or had their next *strokes* conceded or either *side* has conceded the hole.

(2) **Stroke Play.** A *side* has completed a hole when one of the *partners* has *holed out* and the other *partner* has either *holed out* or chooses not to do so.

23.4 One or Both Partners May Represent the Side

The *side* may be represented by one *partner* during all or any part of a *round*. It is not necessary for both *partners* to be present or, if present, for both to play on each hole.

If a *partner* is absent and then arrives to play, that *partner* may start play for the *side* only between the play of two holes, which means:

- **Match Play – Before Any Player in Match Starts Hole.** If the *partner* arrives only after any player on either *side* in the match has started play of a hole, that *partner* is not allowed to play for the *side* until the next hole.

- **Stroke Play – Before Other Partner Starts Hole.** If the *partner* arrives only after the other *partner* has started play of a hole, the arriving *partner* is not allowed to play for the *side* until the next hole.

An arriving *partner* who is not allowed to play on a hole may still give *advice* or help to the other *partner* and take other actions for the other *partner* on that hole (see Rules 23.5a and 23.5b).

Penalty for Breach of Rule 23.4: General Penalty.

Rule 23.4 Interpretations:

23.4/1 – Determining Handicap Allowance in Match Play If One Player Unable to Compete

If, in a *Four-Ball* match played under handicap, the player with the lowest handicap is unable to play, the absent player is not disregarded given that he or she may start play for the *side* between the play of two holes, which in *match play* means only before any player on either *side* has started play of a hole.

The handicap strokes are calculated as if all four players are present. If a wrong handicap is declared for the absent player, Rule 3.2c(1) (Declaring Handicaps) applies.

23.5 Player's Actions Affecting Partner's Play

23.5a Player Allowed to Take Any Actions Concerning Partner's Ball That Partner May Take

Although each player on a *side* must play his or her own ball:

- A player may take any action concerning the *partner's* ball that the *partner* is allowed to take before making a *stroke*, such as to *mark* the spot of the ball and lift, *replace*, *drop* and place the ball.

- A player and the player's *caddie* may help the *partner* in any way that the *partner's caddie* is allowed to help (such as to give and be asked for *advice* and take the other actions allowed under Rule 10), **but** must not give any help that the *partner's caddie* is not allowed to give under the Rules.

In *stroke play*, *partners* must not agree with each other to leave a ball in place on the *putting green* to help either of them or any other player (see Rule 15.3a).

Rule 23.5a Interpretations:

23.5a/1 – Actions of Shared Caddie May Result in Penalty for Both Partners

When *partners* in *Four-Ball* share a *caddie* and the *caddie's* breach of a Rule cannot be assigned to one particular *partner*, both *partners* are penalized.

For example, *side* A-B is playing *side* C-D in a *Four-Ball* match. *Partners* A and B share a *caddie* and that *caddie* accidentally *moves* Player C's or Player D's ball other than during search without specific direction from either Player A or Player B. The *caddie* has breached Rule 9.5b (Lifting or Deliberately Touching Ball or Causing It to Move), but there is no way to assign the penalty to one particular *partner* of the *side*. Therefore, both Player A and Player B get one penalty stroke.

23.5b Partner Is Responsible for Player's Actions

Any action taken by the player concerning the *partner's* ball or equipment is treated as having been taken by the *partner*.

If the player's action would breach a Rule if taken by the *partner*:

• The *partner* is in breach of the Rule and gets the resulting penalty (see Rule 23.8a).

• Examples of this are when the player breaches the Rules by:

  » Improving the conditions affecting the stroke to be made by the *partner*,

  » Accidentally causing the *partner's* ball to *move*, or

  » Failing to mark the spot of the *partner's* ball before lifting it.

This also applies to actions by the player's *caddie* concerning the *partner's* ball that would breach a Rule if taken by the *partner* or *partner's caddie*.

If the actions of the player or the player's *caddie* affect the play of both the player's own ball and the *partner's* ball, see Rule 23.8a(2) to find out when there is a penalty for both *partners*.

23.6 Side's Order of Play

Partners may play in the order the *side* considers best.

This means that when it is a player's turn to play under Rule 6.4a (*match play*) or 6.4b (*stroke play*), either the player or his or her *partner* may play next.

Exception – Continuing Play of Hole After Stroke Conceded in Match Play:

- A player must not continue play of a hole after the player's next *stroke* has been conceded if this would help his or her *partner*.

- If the player does so, his or her score for the hole stands without penalty, but the *partner's* score for the hole cannot count for the *side*.

Rule 23.6 Interpretations:

23.6/1 – Abandoning Right to Play in Any Order Side Determines Best

In a *Four-Ball* match, if a *side* states or implies that the player on that *side* whose ball is farthest from the *hole* will not complete the hole, that player has abandoned his or her right to complete the hole, and the side may not change that decision after an *opponent* has played.

For example, *side* A-B is playing *side* C-D in a *Four-Ball* match. All four balls are on the *putting green* with Player A, Player B and Player D lying two while Player C lies four. The balls of Player A and Player C are about 10 feet from the *hole*, Player B's ball is two feet away and Player D's ball is three feet away. Player C picks up. Player A suggests that Player B and Player D should play.

After Player D plays, Player A has abandoned the right to play and his or her score cannot count for the *side* (for example, if Player B missed his or her putt). The outcome would be different if Player B had been farther from the *hole* than Player D. If Player B putts first and misses, Player A would still have the right to complete the hole if he or she does so before Player D plays.

23.6/2 – Partners Must Not Unreasonably Delay Play When Playing in Advantageous Order

Examples of situations where the *partners* of side A-B play in an order they determine is best but may get a penalty under Rule 5.6a for unreasonably delaying play include when:

- Player A's tee shot on a par-3 that is played entirely over a *penalty area* comes to rest in the *penalty area* while Player B's tee shot comes to rest on the *putting green*. The *side* proceeds to the *putting green* without Player A playing a ball under the *penalty area* Rule. Player B takes four putts to complete the hole. Player A then decides to leave the *putting green*, go back to the tee and put another ball *in play*.

- After their tee shots, Player A's ball is 220 yards from the *hole* and Player B's ball is 240 yards from the *hole*. Player A makes his or her second *stroke* before Player B plays. Player A's ball comes to rest 30 yards from the *hole* and the *side* decides to have Player A walk forward and make his or her third *stroke*.

23.6/3 – When Side in Match Play May Have Stroke Cancelled by Opponent

When both players of a *side* play from outside the *teeing area* in a *Four-Ball* match, only the last *stroke* played may be cancelled under Rule 6.1b.

For example, in a *four-ball* match with *side* A-B playing *side* C-D, if Player A and Player B both play from outside the *teeing area* with Player A playing first followed by Player B, *side* C-D may cancel the *stroke* of Player B, but not Player A.

Rule 6.1b requires that cancelling the *stroke* must be done promptly. This also applies if Player A and Player B both played when it was either Player C's turn or Player D's turn to play during play of the hole.

23.7 Partners May Share Clubs

Rule 4.1b(2) is modified to allow *partners* to share clubs, so long as the total number of clubs they have together is not more than 14.

Rule 23.7 Interpretations:

23.7/1 – Partners May Continue to Give Advice and Share Clubs After Concurrent Match Ends

When concurrent *Four-Ball* and single matches are being played, the two players of a *side* are no longer *partners* after the *Four-Ball* match ends. However, the two players that were *partners* are still allowed to give each other *advice* and share clubs for the remainder of both single matches.

For example, *side* A-B is playing *side* C-D in a *Four-Ball* match with concurrent single matches of Player A playing Player C and Player B playing Player D, both matches of 18 holes. Player A and Player B are sharing clubs, all 14 of which Player A brought. If the *Four-Ball* match ends on the 16th hole, but both single matches are tied, Player A and Player B may continue to use the clubs they selected for play (the shared clubs) and give *advice* to each other, despite Player A and Player B no longer being *partners*.

23.8 When Penalty Applies to One Partner Only or Applies to Both Partners

When a player gets a penalty for breach of a Rule, the penalty may apply either to that player alone or to both *partners* (that is, to the *side*). This depends on the penalty and the form of play:

23.8a Penalties Other Than Disqualification

(1) **Penalty Normally Applies Only to Player, Not Partner**.

When a player gets a penalty other than disqualification, that penalty normally applies only to the player and not also to his or her *partner*, **except** in the situations covered by (2).

- Any penalty strokes are added only to the player's score, not to the *partner's* score.

- In *match play*, a player who gets the **general penalty (loss of hole)** has no score that can count for the *side* on that hole, **but** this penalty has no effect on the *partner*, who may continue to play for the *side* on that hole.

(2) **Three Situations Where Player's Penalty Also Applies to Partner**.

- When Player Breaches Rule 4.1b (Limit of 14 Clubs; Shared, Added or Replaced Clubs). In *match play*, the *side* gets the penalty (**adjustment of the match score**); in *stroke play*, the *partner* also gets the **same penalty** as the player.

- When Player's Breach Helps Partner's Play. In either *match play* or *stroke play*, the *partner* also gets the **same penalty** as the player.

- In Match Play When Player's Breach Hurts Opponent's Play. The *partner* also gets the **same penalty** as the player.

Exception – Player Who Makes Stroke at Wrong Ball Is Not Treated as Having Helped Partner's Play or Hurt Opponent's Play:

- Only the player (not the *partner*) gets the **general penalty** for breach of Rule 6.3c.

- This is true whether the ball played as a *wrong ball* belongs to the *partner*, an *opponent* or anyone else.

Rule 23.8a(2) Interpretations:

23.8a(2)/1 – Examples of When Player's Breach Helps Partner's Play

In both *Four-Ball match play* and *stroke play*, when a player's breach of a Rule helps his or her *partner*, the *partner* gets the same penalty.

Examples of when both *partners* of *side* A-B get the same penalty include:

- With *side* A-B playing *side* C-D, Player B's ball is near the *hole* and in a position to help Player A aim his or her putt. Player C requires Player B to mark and lift Player B's ball. Player B declines to lift the ball and Player A putts with Player B's ball helping him or her to aim.

  Player B gets the *general penalty* under Rule 15.3a (Ball on Putting Green Helping Play) for failing to lift the helping ball and, since this helped Player A, Player A also gets the *general penalty*.

- Player B takes a *stance* for a putt and makes the *stroke* while Player A deliberately stands in a location on or close to an extension of the *line of play* behind the ball for any reason. Player B is in breach of Rule 10.2b(4) (Standing Behind Player) for taking a *stance* when Player A is in such a location and will get the *general penalty*.

  Further, when Player A's putt is on the same line as Player B's and Player B makes a *stroke* while Player A is on an extension of Player B's *line of play*, Player B's breach helped Player A so Player A also gets the same penalty as Player B.

- Player A's ball is *out of bounds* and Player A decides not to complete the *hole*. Player B's ball is a similar distance from the *hole*. Player A drops a ball near Player B's ball and plays to the *putting green* and, by doing so, helps Player B.

  As the hole is not complete and the result has yet to be decided, Player A's further play is considered practice in breach of Rule 5.5a (Practice Strokes While Playing Hole). As Player A's practice helped Player B, Player B also gets the *general penalty*.

23.8a(2)/2 – Example of When Player's Breach Hurts Opponent's Play

In *Four-Ball match play*, if a player's breach of a Rule hurts an *opponent's* play, the player's *partner* also gets the same penalty.

For example, *side* A-B are playing *side* C-D in a *Four-Ball* match. Player A provides the wrong number of strokes he or she has taken to either Player C or Player D while all four players are in contention during a *hole*. Side C-D bases its strategy on this information and one of them makes a *stroke*.

Player A gets the *general penalty* under Rule 3.2d(1) (Telling Opponent about Number of Strokes Taken) for not giving the right number of strokes taken. Player B gets the same penalty because the breach hurt an *opponent's* play. *Side* A-B therefore loses the hole.

23.8a(2)/3 – Giving Wrong Number of Strokes Taken or Failing to Tell Opponent about Penalty Is Never Considered to Hurt Opponent When Player Is Out of Contention

When a player in a *Four-Ball* match is out of contention on a hole and he or she either gives the wrong number of strokes taken or fails to notify an *opponent* about a penalty, it is never considered to hurt the *opponent's* play since the player's score on the hole will not be relevant in the match.

For example, *side* A-B is playing *side* C-D in a *Four-Ball* match. Player A has taken 3 *strokes*, Player B 5 *strokes*, Player C 4 *strokes,* and Player D has already picked up. Player B causes his or her ball to *move* and gets one penalty stroke under Rule 9.4. Player B does not tell anyone that he or she got a penalty, *replaces* the ball and makes the *stroke*. Player A and Player C then both *hole out* for scores of 5. Since B failed to tell *side* C-D about the penalty, he or she is disqualified from the hole under Rule 3.2d. But, since Player B's score had no relevance in the outcome of that hole (on the basis that B scored more than 5, C *holed* his or her next *stroke* for a 5 and D had picked up), the breach did not hurt Player C or Player D. Therefore, Player A gets no penalty.

23.8b Disqualification Penalties

(1) **When Breach by One Partner Means Side Is Disqualified.** A *side* is **disqualified** if either *partner* gets a penalty of disqualification under any of these Rules:

- Rule 1.2   Standards of Player Conduct
- Rule 1.3   Playing by the Rules
- Rule 4.1a   Club Allowed in Making a Stroke
- Rule 4.1c   Procedure for Taking Clubs Out of Play
- Rule 4.2a   Balls Allowed In Play of Round
- Rule 4.3   Use of Equipment
- Rule 5.6a   Unreasonable Delay
- Rule 5.7b-c   When Committee Suspends Play and Play Resumes
- Rule 6.2b   Teeing Area Rules

Match Play Only:

- Rule 3.2c   Applying Handicaps in Handicap Match

Stroke Play Only:

- Rule 3.3b(2) Player's Responsibility: Certifying and Returning Scorecard
- Rule 3.3b(3) Wrong Score for Hole
- Rule 3.3b(4) Scoring in a Handicap Competition
- Rule 5.2b   Practising On Course Before or Between Rounds
- Rule 23.2b   Side's Scorecard in Stroke Play

(2) **When Breach by Both Partners Means Side Is Disqualified**.
A *side* is **disqualified** if both *partners* get a penalty of disqualification under any of these Rules:

- Rule 5.3   Starting and Ending Round
- Rule 5.4   Playing in Groups
- Rule 5.7a   When Players May or Must Stop Play

Stroke Play Only:

A *side* is **disqualified** if, at the same hole, both *partners* get penalties of disqualification under any combination of these Rules:

- Rule 3.3c   Failure to Hole Out
- Rule 6.1b   Playing from Outside Teeing Area in Starting Hole
- Rule 6.3c   Wrong Ball
- Rule 14.7   Playing from Wrong Place

(3) **When Breach by One Player Means Only That the Player Has No Valid Score for Hole**. In all other situations where a player breaches a Rule with a penalty of disqualification, the player is not disqualified **but** his or her score on the hole where the breach happened cannot count for the *side*.

In *match play*, if both *partners* breach such a Rule on the same hole, the side loses the hole.

RULE 24 Team Competitions

Purpose of Rule:

Rule 24 covers team competitions (played in either match play or stroke play), where multiple players or sides compete as a team with the results of their rounds or matches combined to produce an overall team score.

24.1 Overview of Team Competitions

- A "team" is a group of players who play as individuals or as *sides* to compete against other teams.

- Their play in the team event may also be part of another competition (such as individual *stroke play*) that takes place at the same time.

Rules 1–23 apply in a team competition, as modified by these specific Rules.

24.2 Terms of Team Competition

The *Committee* decides the form of play, how a team's overall score is to be calculated and other Terms of the Competition, such as:

- In *match play*, the number of points awarded for winning or tying a match.

- In *stroke play*, the number of scores to count in each team's total score.

- Whether the competition may end in a tie and, if not, how the tie will be decided.

Rule 24.2 Interpretations:

24.2/1 – Disqualification May Apply to One or All Rounds in Team Play

If a player is disqualified from a *round* in a team competition in which not all scores count towards the team's total score, the disqualification applies only to that *round* of the competition.

324

However, if a player is disqualified for failing to meet the Code of Conduct standards under Rule 1.2b, it is up to the *Committee* to determine whether that disqualification is for that *round* only or the duration of the competition.

24.3 Team Captain

Each team may name a team captain to lead the team and make decisions for it, such as which players on the team will play in which *rounds* or matches, in what order they will play and who will play together as *partners*.

The team captain may be a player in the competition.

24.4 Advice Allowed in Team Competition

24.4a Person Allowed to Give Advice to Team (Advice Giver)

The *Committee* may adopt a Local Rule allowing each team to name one person (an "advice giver") who may give *advice* and other help as allowed in Rule 10.2b(2) to players on the team during a *round* and who may be asked for *advice* by players on the team:

- The advice giver may be the team captain, a team coach or other person (including a team member playing in the competition).

- The advice giver must be identified to the *Committee* before giving *advice*.

- The *Committee* may allow a team's advice giver to change during a *round* or during the competition.

See Committee Procedures, Section 8; Model Local Rule H-2 (the *Committee* may adopt a Local Rule allowing each team to name two advice givers).

24.4b Restriction on Advice Giver While Playing

If a team's advice giver is a player on the team, he or she is not allowed to act in that role while playing a *round* in the competition.

While playing a *round*, the advice giver is treated like any other playing team member for purposes of the restrictions on *advice* in Rule 10.2a.

24.4c No Advice Between Team Members Other Than Partners

Except when playing together as *partners* on a *side*:

- A player must not ask for *advice* from or give *advice* to a member of his or her team playing on the *course*.
- This applies whether the team member is playing in the *same group as* the player or in another group on the *course*.

See Committee Procedures, Section 8; Model Local Rule H-5 (in a *stroke play* team competition where a player's score for the *round* counts only as part of the team's score, the *Committee* may adopt a Local Rule allowing team members playing in the same group to give each other *advice* even if they are not *partners*).

Penalty for Breach of Rule 24.4: General Penalty.

Rule 24.4 Interpretations:

24.4/1 – Committee May Establish Limits for Team Captains and Advice Givers

The *Committee* may adopt a Local Rule limiting who may serve as a team captain or advice giver and also limit the conduct of a team captain or advice giver.

Examples of limitations include:

- Permitting only an amateur golfer to serve as a team captain and/or advice giver.
- Stating that team captains and/or advice givers are not permitted on *putting greens*.
- That *advice* must be given in person and not via radio, telephone or other electronic means.

Definitions

Abnormal Course Condition

Any of these four defined conditions: A GIT

- *Animal Hole,*

- *Ground Under Repair,*

- *Immovable Obstruction,* or

- *Temporary Water.*

Advice

Any verbal comment or action (such as showing what club was just used to make a *stroke*) that is intended to influence a player in:

- Choosing a club,

- Making a *stroke*, or

- Deciding how to play during a hole or *round*.

But *advice* does not include public information, such as:

- The location of things on the *course* such as the *hole*, the *putting green*, the fairway, *penalty areas, bunkers*, or another player's ball,

- The distance from one point to another, or

- The Rules.

Advice/1 – Verbal Comments or Actions That Are Advice

Examples of when comments or actions are considered *advice* and are not allowed include:

- A player makes a statement regarding club selection that was intended to be overheard by another player who had a similar *stroke*.

- In individual *stroke play*, Player A, who has just *holed out* on the 7th hole, demonstrates to Player B, whose ball was just off the *putting green*, how to make the next *stroke*. Because Player B has not completed the hole, Player A gets the penalty on the 7th hole. But, if

327

both Player A and Player B had completed the 7th hole, Player A gets the penalty on the 8th hole.

- A player's ball is lying badly and the player is deliberating what action to take. Another player comments, "You have no shot at all. If I were you, I would decide to take unplayable ball relief." This comment is *advice* because it could have influenced the player in deciding how to play during a hole.

- While a player is setting up to hit his or her shot over a large *penalty area* filled with water, another player in the group comments, "You know the wind is in your face and it's 250 yards to carry that water?"

Advice/2 – Verbal Comments or Actions That Are Not Advice

Examples of comments or actions that are not *advice* include:

- During play of the 6th hole, a player asks another player what club he or she used on the 4th hole that is a par-3 of similar length.

- A player makes a second *stroke* that lands on the *putting green*. Another player does likewise. The first player then asks the second player what club was used for the second *stroke*.

- After making a *stroke*, a player says, "I should have used a 5-iron" to another player in the group that has yet to play onto the *green*, but not intending to influence his or her play.

- A player looks into another player's bag to determine which club he or she used for the last *stroke* without touching or moving anything.

- While lining up a putt, a player mistakenly seeks *advice* from another player's *caddie*, believing that *caddie* to be the player's *caddie*. The player immediately realizes the mistake and tells the other *caddie* not to answer.

Animal

Any living member of the animal kingdom (other than humans), including mammals, birds, reptiles, amphibians and invertebrates (such as worms, insects, spiders and crustaceans).

Animal Hole

Any hole dug in the ground by an *animal* except for holes dug by *animals* that are also defined as *loose impediments* (such as worms or insects).

The term *animal hole* includes:

- The loose material the *animal* dug out of the hole,

- Any worn-down track or trail leading into the hole, and

- Any area on the ground pushed up or altered as a result of the animal digging the hole underground.

Animal Hole/1 – Isolated Animal Footprint or Hoof Mark Is Not Animal Hole

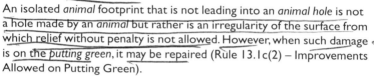

An isolated *animal* footprint that is not leading into an *animal hole* is not a hole made by an *animal* but rather is an irregularity of the surface from which relief without penalty is not allowed. However, when such damage is on the *putting green*, it may be repaired (Rule 13.1c(2) – Improvements Allowed on Putting Green).

Areas of the Course

The five defined areas that make up the *course*:

- The *general area*,

- The *teeing area* the player must play from in starting the hole he or she is playing,

- All *penalty areas*,

- All *bunkers*, and

- The *putting green* of the hole the player is playing.

Ball-Marker

An artificial object when used to *mark* the spot of a ball to be lifted, such as a tee, a coin, an object made to be a *ball-marker* or another small piece of *equipment*.

When a Rule refers to a *ball-marker* being moved, this means a *ball-marker* in place on the *course* to *mark* the spot of a ball that has been lifted and not yet *replaced*.

Boundary Object

Artificial objects defining or showing *out of bounds*, such as walls, fences, stakes and railings, from which free relief is not allowed.

This includes any base and post of a boundary fence, **but** does not include:

329

- Angled supports or guy wires that are attached to a wall or fence, or

- Any steps, bridge or similar construction used for getting over the wall or fence.

Boundary objects are treated as immovable even if they are movable or any part of them is movable (see Rule 8.1a).

Boundary objects are not *obstructions* or *integral objects*.

Boundary Object/1 – Status of Attachments to Boundary Object

Objects that are attached to a *boundary object*, but are not part of that *boundary object*, are *obstructions* and a player may be allowed free relief from them.

If the *Committee* does not wish to provide free relief from an *obstruction* attached to a *boundary object*, it may introduce a Local Rule providing that the *obstruction* is an *integral object*, in which case it loses its status as an *obstruction* and free relief is not allowed.

For example, if angled supports are so close to a boundary fence that leaving the supports as *obstructions* would essentially give players free relief from the *boundary object*, the *Committee* may choose to define the supports to be *integral objects*.

Boundary Object/2 – Status of Gate Attached to Boundary Object

A gate for getting through a boundary wall or fence is not part of the *boundary object*. Such a gate is an *obstruction* unless the *Committee* chooses to define it as an *integral object*.

Boundary Object/3 – Movable Boundary Object or Movable Part of Boundary Object Must Not Be Moved

Boundary objects are treated as immovable, even if part of the object is designed to be movable. To ensure a consistent approach, this applies to all *boundary objects*.

An example of how a movable *boundary object* may come into play during a *round* includes when a boundary stake interferes with a player's *stance* so he or she pulls the stake out of the ground (a breach of Rule 8.1a), but part of it breaks during removal. If the player realizes the mistake before making the next *stroke*, he or she may restore the *improved conditions* by replacing enough of the broken boundary stake to restore the interference to what it was before the stake was removed.

But if the improvement cannot be eliminated (such as when a *boundary object* has been bent or broken in such a way that the improvement cannot be eliminated), the player cannot avoid penalty.

Bunker

A specially prepared area of sand, which is often a hollow from which turf or soil was removed.

These are not part of a *bunker*:

- A lip, wall or face at the edge of a prepared area and consisting of soil, grass, stacked turf or artificial materials,

- Soil or any growing or attached natural object inside the edge of a prepared area (such as grass, bushes or trees),

- Sand that has spilled over or is outside the edge of a prepared area, and

- All other areas of sand on the *course* that are not inside the edge of a prepared area (such as deserts and other natural sand areas or areas sometimes referred to as waste areas).

Bunkers are one of the five defined *areas of the course*.

A *Committee* may define a prepared area of sand as part of the *general area* (which means it is not a *bunker*) or may define a non-prepared area of sand as a *bunker*.

When a *bunker* is being repaired and the *Committee* defines the entire *bunker* as *ground under repair*, it is treated as part of the *general area* (which means it is not a *bunker*).

The word "sand" as used in this Definition and Rule 12 includes any material similar to sand that is used as *bunker* material (such as crushed shells), as well as any soil that is mixed in with the sand.

Caddie

Someone who helps a player during a *round*, including in these ways:

- Carrying, Transporting or Handling Clubs: A person who carries, transports (such as by cart or trolley) or handles a player's clubs during play is the player's *caddie* even if not named as a *caddie* by the player, except when done to move the player's clubs, bag or cart out of the way or as a courtesy (such as getting a club the player left behind).

Definitions

- Giving Advice: A player's *caddie* is the only person (other than a *partner* or *partner's caddie*) a player may ask for *advice*.

A *caddie* may also help the player in other ways allowed by the Rules (see Rule 10.3b).

Club-Length

The length of the longest club of the 14 (or fewer) clubs the player has during the *round* (as allowed by Rule 4.1b(1)), other than a putter.

For example, if the longest club (other than a putter) a player has during a *round* is a 43-inch (109.22 cm) driver, a *club-length* is 43 inches for that player for that *round*.

Club-lengths are used in defining the player's *teeing area* on each hole and in determining the size of the player's *relief area* when taking relief under a Rule.

Club-Length/1 – Meaning of "Club-Length" When Measuring

For the purposes of measuring when determining a *relief area*, the length of the entire club, starting at the toe of the club and ending at the butt end of the grip is used. However, if the club has a headcover on it or has an attachment to the end of the grip, neither is allowed to be used as part of the club when using it to measure.

Club-Length/2 – How to Measure When Longest Club Breaks

If the longest club a player has during a *round* breaks, that broken club continues to be used for determining the size of his or her *relief areas*. However, if the longest club breaks and the player is allowed to replace it with another club (Exception to Rule 4.1b(3)) and he or she does so, the broken club is no longer considered his or her longest club.

If the player starts a *round* with fewer than 14 clubs and decides to add another club that is longer than the clubs he or she started with, the added club is used for measuring so long as it is not a putter.

Committee

The person or group in charge of the competition or the *course*.

See Committee Procedures, Section 1 (explaining the role of the *Committee*).

Conditions Affecting the Stroke   CATS

The *lie* of the player's ball at rest, the area of intended *stance*, the area of intended swing, the *line of play* and the *relief area* where the player will drop or place a ball.

- The "area of intended *stance*" includes both where the player will place his or her feet and the entire area that might reasonably affect how and where the player's body is positioned in preparing for and making the intended *stroke*.

- The "area of intended swing" includes the entire area that might reasonably affect any part of the backswing, the downswing or the completion of the swing for the intended *stroke*.

- Each of the terms "*lie*", "*line of play*" and "*relief area*" has its own Definition.

Course

The entire area of play within the edge of any boundaries set by the *Committee*:

- All areas inside the boundary edge are in bounds and part of the *course*.

- All areas outside the boundary edge are *out of bounds* and not part of the *course*.

- The boundary edge extends both up above the ground and down below the ground.

The *course* is made up of the five defined *areas of the course*.

See Rule 2.2c for when a ball touches two areas of the course.

Drop

To hold the ball and let go of it so that it falls through the air, with the intent for the ball to be *in play*.

If the player lets go of a ball without intending it to be *in play*, the ball has not been *dropped* and is not *in play* (see Rule 14.4).

Each relief Rule identifies a specific *relief area* where the ball must be *dropped* and come to rest.

In taking relief, the player must let go of the ball from a location at knee height so that the ball:

- Falls straight down, without the player throwing, spinning or rolling it or using any other motion that might affect where the ball will come to rest, and

- Does not touch any part of the player's body or *equipment* before it hits the ground (see Rule 14.3b).

Embedded

When a player's ball is in its own pitch-mark made as a result of the player's previous *stroke* and where part of the ball is below the level of the ground.

A ball does not necessarily have to touch soil to be *embedded* (for example, grass and *loose impediments* may be between the ball and the soil).

Equipment

Anything used, worn, held or carried by the player or the player's *caddie*.

Objects used for the care of the *course*, such as rakes, are *equipment* only while they are being held or carried by the player or *caddie*.

Equipment/1 – Status of Items Carried by Someone Else for the Player

Items, other than clubs, that are carried by someone other than a player or his or her *caddie* are *outside influences*, even if they belong to the player. However, they are the player's *equipment* when in the player's or his or her *caddie's* possession.

For example, if a player asks a spectator to carry his or her umbrella, the umbrella is an *outside influence* while in the spectator's possession. However, if the spectator hands the umbrella to the player, it is now his or her *equipment*.

Equipment Rules

The specifications and other regulations for clubs, balls and other *equipment* that players are allowed to use during a *round*. The *Equipment Rules* are found at USGA.org

Flagstick

A movable pole provided by the *Committee* that is placed in the *hole* to show players where the *hole* is. The *flagstick* includes the flag and any other material or objects attached to the pole.

The requirements for a *flagstick* are stated in the *Equipment Rules*.

Flagstick/1 – Objects Are Treated as Flagstick When Used as Flagstick

If an artificial or natural object is being used to mark the position of the *hole*, that object is treated the same as the *flagstick* would be.

For example, if the *flagstick* has been removed and a player wants the position of the *hole* indicated but does not want to waste time getting the *flagstick*, someone else may indicate the position of the *hole* with a club. But, for the purpose of applying the Rules, the club is treated as if it were the *flagstick*.

Four-Ball

A form of play where *sides* of two *partners* compete, with each player playing his or her own ball. A *side*'s score for a hole is the lower score of the two *partners* on that hole.

Four-Ball may be played as a *match-play* competition between one *side* of two *partners* and another *side* of two *partners* or a *stroke-play* competition among multiple *sides* of two *partners*.

Foursomes (also known as "Alternate Shot")

A form of play where two *partners* compete as a *side* by playing one ball in alternating order on each hole.

Foursomes may be played as a *match-play* competition between one *side* of two *partners* and another *side* of two *partners* or a *stroke-play* competition among multiple *sides* of two *partners*.

General Area

The *area of the course* that covers all of the *course* **except** for the other four defined areas: (1) the *teeing area* the player must play from in starting the hole he or she is playing, (2) all *penalty areas*, (3) all *bunkers*, and (4) the *putting green* of the *hole* the player is playing.

The *general area* includes:

- All teeing locations on the *course* other than the *teeing area*, and

- All *wrong greens*.

General Penalty

Loss of hole in *match play* or two penalty strokes in *stroke play*.

Ground Under Repair

Any part of the *course* the Committee defines to be *ground under repair* (whether by marking it or otherwise). Any defined *ground under repair* includes both:

- All ground inside the edge of the defined area, and

- Any grass, bush, tree or other growing or attached natural object rooted in the defined area, including any part of those objects that extends up above the ground outside the edge of the defined area (**but** not when such object is attached to or below the ground outside the edge of the defined area, such as a tree root that is part of a tree rooted inside the edge).

Ground under repair also includes the following things, even if the Committee does not define them as such:

- Any hole made by the Committee or the maintenance staff in:

  » Setting up the *course* (such as a hole where a stake has been removed or the *hole* on a double green being used for the play of another hole), or

  » Maintaining the *course* (such as a hole made in removing turf or a tree stump or laying pipelines, **but** not including aeration holes).

- Grass cuttings, leaves and any other material piled for later removal. **But:**

  » Any natural materials that are piled for removal are also *loose impediments*, and

  » Any materials left on the *course* that are not intended to be removed are not *ground under repair* unless the Committee has defined them as such.

- Any *animal* habitat (such as a bird's nest) that is so near a player's ball that the player's *stroke* or *stance* might damage it (**except** when the habitat has been made by *animals* that are defined as *loose impediments* (such as worms or insects).

The edge of *ground under repair* should be defined by stakes, lines or physical features:

- Stakes: When defined by stakes, the edge of the *ground under repair* is defined by the line between the outside points of the stakes at ground level, and the stakes are inside the *ground under repair*.

- Lines: When defined by a painted line on the ground, the edge of the *ground under repair* is the outside edge of the line, and the line itself is in the *ground under repair*.

- Physical Features: When defined by physical features (such as a flower bed or a turf nursery), the *Committee* should say how the edge of the *ground under repair* is defined.

When the edge of *ground under repair* is defined by lines or physical features, stakes may be used to show where the *ground under repair* is, **but** they have no other meaning.

Ground Under Repair/1 – Damage Caused by Committee or Maintenance Staff Is Not Always Ground Under Repair

A hole made by maintenance staff is *ground under repair* even when not marked as *ground under repair*. However, not all damage caused by maintenance staff is *ground under repair* by default.

Examples of damage that is not *ground under repair* by default include:

- A rut made by a tractor (but the *Committee* is justified in declaring a deep rut to be *ground under repair*).

- An old *hole* plug that is sunk below the *putting green* surface, but see Rule 13.1c (Improvements Allowed on Putting Green).

Ground Under Repair/2 – Ball in Tree Rooted in Ground Under Repair Is in Ground Under Repair

If a tree is rooted in *ground under repair* and a player's ball is in a branch of that tree, the ball is in *ground under repair* even if the branch extends outside the defined area.

If the player decides to take free relief under Rule 16.1 and the spot on the ground directly under where the ball lies in the tree is outside the *ground under repair*, the reference point for determining the *relief area* and taking relief is that spot on the ground.

Ground Under Repair/3 – Fallen Tree or Tree Stump Is Not Always Ground Under Repair

A fallen tree or tree stump that the *Committee* intends to remove, but is not in the process of being removed, is not automatically *ground under repair.* However, if the tree and the tree stump are in the process of being unearthed or cut up for later removal, they are "material piled for later removal" and therefore *ground under repair.*

For example, a tree that has fallen in the *general area* and is still attached to the stump is not *ground under repair.* However, a player could request relief from the *Committee* and the *Committee* would be justified in declaring the area covered by the fallen tree to be *ground under repair.*

Hole

The finishing point on the *putting green* for the hole being played:

- The *hole* must be 4 ¼ inches (108 mm) in diameter and at least 4 inches (101.6 mm) deep.
- If a lining is used, its outer diameter must not exceed 4 ¼ inches (108 mm). The lining must be sunk at least 1 inch (25.4 mm) below the *putting green* surface, unless the nature of the soil requires that it be closer to the surface.

The word "hole" (when not used as a Definition in italics) is used throughout the Rules to mean the part of the *course* associated with a particular *teeing area, putting green* and *hole.* Play of a hole begins from the *teeing area* and ends when the ball is *holed* on the *putting green* (or when the Rules otherwise say the hole is completed).

Holed

When a ball is at rest in the *hole* after a *stroke* and the entire ball is below the surface of the *putting green.*

When the Rules refer to "holing out" or "hole out", it means when the player's ball is *holed.*

For the special case of a ball resting against the *flagstick* in the *hole,* see Rule 13.2c (ball is treated as *holed* if any part of the ball is below the surface of the *putting green*).

Holed/1 – All of the Ball Must Be Below the Surface to Be Holed When Embedded in Side of Hole

When a ball is *embedded* in the side of the *hole,* and all of the ball is not below the surface of the *putting green,* the ball is not *holed.* This is the case even if the ball touches the *flagstick.*

338

Definitions

Holed/2 – Ball Is Considered Holed Even Though It Is Not "At Rest"

The words "at rest" in the definition of *holed* are used to make it clear that if a ball falls into the *hole* and bounces out, it is not *holed*.

However, if a player removes a ball from the *hole* that is still moving (such as circling or bouncing in the bottom of the *hole*), it is considered *holed* despite the ball not having come to rest in the *hole*.

Honour

The right of a player to play first from the *teeing area* (see Rule 6.4).

Immovable Obstruction

Any *obstruction* that:

- Cannot be moved without unreasonable effort or without damaging the *obstruction* or the *course*; and
- Otherwise does not meet the definition of a *movable obstruction*.

The *Committee* may define any *obstruction* to be an *immovable obstruction*, even if it meets the definition of *movable obstruction*.

Immovable Obstruction/1 – Turf Around Obstruction Is Not Part of Obstruction

Any turf that is leading to an *immovable obstruction* or covering an *immovable obstruction*, is not part of the *obstruction*.

For example, a water pipe is partly underground and partly above ground. If the pipe that is underground causes the turf to be raised, the raised turf is not part of the *immovable obstruction*.

Improve

To alter one or more of the *conditions affecting the stroke* or other physical conditions affecting play so that a player gains a potential advantage for a *stroke*.

In Play

The status of a player's ball when it lies on the *course* and is being used in the play of a hole:

339

Definitions

- A ball first becomes *in play* on a hole:

  » When the player makes a *stroke* at it from inside the *teeing area*, or

  » In *match play*, when the player makes a *stroke* at it from outside the *teeing area* and the *opponent* does not cancel the *stroke* under Rule 6.1b.

- That ball remains *in play* until it is *holed*, **except** that it is no longer *in play*:

  » When it is *lifted* from the *course*,

  » When it is *lost* (even if it is at rest on the *course*) or comes to rest out of bounds, or

  » When another ball has been *substituted* for it, even if not allowed by a Rule.

A ball that is not *in play* is a *wrong ball*.

The player cannot have more than one ball *in play* at any time. (See Rule 6.3d for the limited cases when a player may play more than one ball at the same time on a hole.)

When the Rules refer to a ball at rest or in motion, this means a ball that is *in play*.

When a *ball-marker* is in place to *mark* the spot of a ball *in play*:

- If the ball has not been lifted, it is still *in play*, and

- If the ball has been lifted and *replaced*, it is *in play* even if the *ball-marker* has not been removed.

Integral Object

An artificial object defined by the *Committee* as part of the challenge of playing the *course* from which free relief is not allowed.

Integral objects are treated as immovable (see Rule 8.1a). **But** if part of an *integral object* (such as a gate or door or part of an attached cable) meets the definition of *movable obstruction*, that part is treated as a *movable obstruction*.

Artificial objects defined by the *Committee* as *integral objects* are not *obstructions* or *boundary objects*.

Known or Virtually Certain

The standard for deciding what happened to a player's ball – for example, whether the ball came to rest in a *penalty area*, whether it *moved* or what caused it to *move*.

Known or virtually certain means more than just possible or probable. It means that either:

- There is conclusive evidence that the event in question happened to the player's ball, such as when the player or other witnesses saw it happen, or

- Although there is a very small degree of doubt, all reasonably available information shows that it is at least 95% likely that the event in question happened.

"All reasonably available information" includes all information the player knows and all other information he or she can get with reasonable effort and without unreasonable delay.

Known or Virtually Certain/1 – Applying "Known or Virtually Certain" Standard When Ball Moves

When it is not "known" what caused the ball to *move*, all reasonably available information must be considered and the evidence must be evaluated to determine if it is "virtually certain" that the player, *opponent* or *outside influence* caused the ball to *move*.

Depending on the circumstances, reasonably available information may include, but is not limited to:

- The effect of any actions taken near the ball (such as movement of *loose impediments*, practice swings, grounding club and taking a *stance*),

- Time elapsed between such actions and the movement of the ball,

- The *lie* of the ball before it *moved* (such as on a fairway, perched on longer grass, on a surface imperfection or on the *putting green*),

- The conditions of the ground near the ball (such as the degree of slope or presence of surface irregularities, etc), and

- Wind speed and direction, rain and other weather conditions.

Known or Virtually Certain/2 – Virtual Certainty Is Irrelevant if It Comes to Light After Three-Minute Search Expires

Determining whether there is *knowledge or virtual certainty* must be based on evidence known to the player at the time the three-minute search time expires.

Examples of when the player's later findings are irrelevant include when:

- A player's tee shot comes to rest in an area containing heavy rough and a large *animal hole*. After a three-minute search, it is determined that it is not *known or virtually certain* that the ball is in the *animal hole*. As the player returns to the *teeing area*, the ball is found in the *animal hole*.

  Even though the player has not yet put another ball *in play*, the player must take *stroke-and-distance* relief for a *lost* ball (Rule 18.2b – What to Do When Ball is Lost or Out of Bounds) since it was not *known or virtually certain* that the ball was in the *animal hole*, when the search time expired.

- A player cannot find his or her ball and believes it may have been picked up by a spectator (*outside influence*), but there is not enough evidence to be *virtually certain* of this. A short time after the three-minute search time expires, a spectator is found to have the player's ball.

  The player must take *stroke-and-distance* relief for a *lost* ball (Rule 18.2b) since the movement by the *outside influence* only became *known* after the search time expired.

Known or Virtually Certain/3 – Player Unaware Ball Played by Another Player

It must be *known or virtually certain* that a player's ball has been played by another player as a *wrong ball* to treat it as being *moved*.

For example, in *stroke play*, Player A and Player B hit their tee shots into the same general location. Player A finds a ball and plays it. Player B goes forward to look for his or her ball and cannot find it. After three minutes, Player B starts back to the tee to play another ball. On the way, Player B finds Player A's ball and knows then that Player A has played his or her ball in error.

Player A gets the *general penalty* for playing a *wrong ball* and must then play his or her own ball (Rule 6.3c). Player A's ball was not *lost* even though both players searched for more than three minutes because Player A did not start searching for his or her ball; the searching was for Player B's ball. Regarding Player B's ball, Player B's original ball was *lost* and he or she must put another ball *in play* under penalty of *stroke and distance* (Rule 18.2b), because it was not *known or virtually certain* when the three-minute search time expired that the ball had been played by another player.

Lie

GAND HB

The spot on which a ball is at rest and any growing or attached natural object, *immovable obstruction*, *integral object*, or *boundary object* touching the ball or right next to it.

Loose impediments and *movable obstructions* are not part of the *lie* of a ball.

Line of Play

The line where the player intends his or her ball to go after a *stroke*, including the area on that line that is a reasonable distance up above the ground and on either side of that line.

The *line of play* is not necessarily a straight line between two points (for example, it may be a curved line based on where the player intends the ball to go).

Loose Impediment

Any unattached natural object such as:

- Stones, loose grass, leaves, branches and sticks,

- Dead *animals* and *animal* waste,

- Worms, insects and similar *animals* that can be removed easily, and the mounds or webs they build (such as worm casts and ant hills), and

- Clumps of compacted soil (including aeration plugs).

Such natural objects are not loose if they are:

- Attached or growing,

- Solidly embedded in the ground (that is, cannot be picked out easily), or

- Sticking to the ball.

Special cases:

- **Sand and Loose Soil** are not *loose impediments*.

- **Dew, Frost and Water** are not *loose impediments*.

- **Snow and Natural Ice** (other than frost) are either *loose impediments* or, when on the ground, *temporary water*, at the player's option.

- **Spider Webs** are *loose impediments* even though they are attached to another object.

Loose Impediment/1 – Status of Fruit

Fruit that is detached from its tree or bush is a *loose impediment*, even if the fruit is from a bush or tree not found on the *course*.

For example, fruit that has been partially eaten or cut into pieces, and the skin that has been peeled from a piece of fruit are *loose impediments*. But, when being carried by a player, it is his or her *equipment*.

Loose Impediment/2 – When Loose Impediment Becomes Obstruction

Loose impediments may be transformed into *obstructions* through the processes of construction or manufacturing.

For example, a log (*loose impediment*) that has been split and had legs attached has been changed by construction into a bench (*obstruction*).

Loose Impediment/3 – Status of Saliva

Saliva may be treated as either *temporary water* or a *loose impediment*, at the option of the player.

Loose Impediment/4 – Loose Impediments Used to Surface a Road

Gravel is a *loose impediment* and a player may remove *loose impediments* under Rule 15.1a. This right is not affected by the fact that, when a road is covered with gravel, it becomes an artificially surfaced road, making it an *immovable obstruction*. The same principle applies to roads or paths constructed with stone, crushed shell, wood chips or the like.

In such a situation, the player may:

- Play the ball as it lies on the *obstruction* and remove gravel (*loose impediment*) from the road (Rule 15.1a).

- Take relief without penalty from the *abnormal course condition* (*immovable obstruction*) (Rule 16.1b).

The player may also remove some gravel from the road to determine the possibility of playing the ball as it lies before choosing to take free relief.

Loose Impediment/5 – Living Insect Is Never Sticking to a Ball

Although dead insects may be considered to be sticking to a ball, living insects are never considered to be sticking to a ball, whether they are stationary or moving. Therefore, live insects on a ball are *loose impediments*.

Lost

The status of a ball that is not found in three minutes after the player or his or her *caddie* (or the player's *partner* or *partner's caddie*) begins to search for it.

If the search begins and is then temporarily interrupted for a good reason (such as when the player stops searching when play is suspended or needs to stand aside to wait for another player to play) or when the player has mistakenly identified a *wrong ball*:

- The time between the interruption and when the search resumes does not count, and

- The time allowed for search is three minutes in total, counting the search time both before the interruption and after the search resumes.

Lost/1 – Ball May Not Be Declared Lost

A player may not make a ball *lost* by a declaration. A ball is *lost* only when it has not been found within three minutes after the player or his or her *caddie* or *partner* begins to search for it.

For example, a player searches for his or her ball for two minutes, declares it *lost* and walks back to play another ball. Before the player puts another ball *in play*, the original ball is found within the three-minute search time. Since the player may not declare his or her ball *lost*, the original ball remains *in play*.

Lost/2 – Player May Not Delay the Start of Search to Gain an Advantage

The three-minute search time for a ball starts when the player or his or her *caddie* (or the player's *partner* or *partner's caddie*) starts to search for it. The player may not delay the start of the search in order to gain an advantage by allowing other people to search on his or her behalf.

For example, if a player is walking towards his or her ball and spectators are already looking for the ball, the player cannot deliberately delay getting to the area to keep the three-minute search time from starting. In such circumstances, the search time starts when the player would have been in a position to search had he or she not deliberately delayed getting to the area.

345

Lost/3 – Search Time Continues When Player Returns to Play a Provisional Ball

If a player has started to search for his or her ball and is returning to the spot of the previous *stroke* to play a *provisional ball,* the three-minute search time continues whether or not anyone continues to search for the player's ball.

Lost/4 – Search Time When Searching for Two Balls

When a player has played two balls (such as the ball *in play* and a *provisional ball*) and is searching for both, whether the player is allowed two separate three-minute search times depends how close the balls are to each other.

If the balls are in the same area where they can be searched for at the same time, the player is allowed only three minutes to search for both balls. However, if the balls are in different areas (such as opposite sides of the fairway) the player is allowed a three-minute search time for each ball.

Mark

To show the spot where a ball is at rest by either:

• Placing a *ball-marker* right behind or right next to the ball, or

• Holding a club on the ground right behind or right next to the ball.

This is done to show the spot where the ball must be *replaced* after it is lifted.

Marker

In *stroke play*, the person responsible for entering a player's score on the player's *scorecard* and for certifying that *scorecard*. The *marker* may be another player, **but** not a *partner*.

The *Committee* may identify who will be the player's *marker* or tell the players how they may choose a *marker*.

Match Play

A form of play where a player or *side* plays directly against an *opponent* or opposing *side* in a head-to-head match of one or more *rounds*:

• A player or *side* wins a hole in the match by completing the hole in fewer strokes (including *strokes* made and penalty strokes), and

• The match is won when a player or *side* leads the *opponent* or opposing *side* by more holes than remain to be played.

Match play can be played as a singles match (where one player plays directly against one *opponent*), a *Three-Ball* match or a *Foursomes* or *Four-Ball* match between *sides* of two *partners*.

Maximum Score

A form of *stroke play* where a player's or *side's* score for a hole is capped at a maximum number of strokes (including *strokes* made and any penalty strokes) set by the *Committee*, such as two times par, a fixed number or net double bogey.

Movable Obstruction

An *obstruction* that can be moved with reasonable effort and without damaging the *obstruction* or the *course*.

If part of an *immovable obstruction* or *integral object* (such as a gate or door or part of an attached cable) meets these two standards, that part is treated as a *movable obstruction*.

But this does not apply if the movable part of an *immovable obstruction* or *integral object* is not meant to be moved (such as a loose stone that is part of a stone wall).

Even when an *obstruction* is movable, the *Committee* may define it to be an *immovable obstruction*.

Movable Obstruction/1 – Abandoned Ball Is a Movable Obstruction

An abandoned ball is a *movable obstruction*.

Moved

When a ball at rest has left its original spot and come to rest on any other spot, and this can be seen by the naked eye (whether or not anyone actually sees it do so).

This applies whether the ball has gone up, down or horizontally in any direction away from its original spot.

If the ball only wobbles (sometimes referred to as oscillating) and stays on or returns to its original spot, the ball has not *moved*.

Definitions

Moved/1 – When Ball Resting on Object Has Moved

For the purpose of deciding whether a ball must be *replaced* or whether a player gets a penalty, a ball is treated as having *moved* only if it has *moved* in relation to a specific part of the larger condition or object it is resting on, unless the entire object the ball is resting on has moved in relation to the ground.

An example of when a ball has not *moved* includes when:

- A ball is resting in the fork of a tree branch and the tree branch moves, but the ball's spot in the branch does not change.

Examples of when a ball has *moved* include when:

- A ball is resting in a stationary plastic cup and the cup itself moves in relation to the ground because it is being blown by the wind.

- A ball is resting in or on a stationary motorized cart that starts to move.

Moved/2 – Television Evidence Shows Ball at Rest Changed Position but by Amount Not Reasonably Discernible to Naked Eye

When determining whether or not a ball at rest has *moved*, a player must make that judgment based on all the information reasonably available to him or her at the time, so that he or she can determine whether the ball must be *replaced* under the Rules. When the player's ball has left its original position and come to rest in another place by an amount that was not reasonably discernible to the naked eye at the time, a player's determination that the ball has not *moved* is conclusive, even if that determination is later shown to be incorrect through the use of sophisticated technology.

On the other hand, if the *Committee* determines, based on all of the evidence it has available, that the ball changed its position by an amount that was reasonably discernible to the naked eye at the time, the ball will be determined to have *moved* even though no-one actually saw it move.

Natural Forces

The effects of nature such as wind, water or when something happens for no apparent reason because of the effects of gravity.

Nearest Point of Complete Relief

The reference point for taking free relief from an *abnormal course condition* (Rule 16.1), dangerous *animal* condition (Rule 16.2), *wrong green* (Rule 13.1f) or *no play zone* (Rules 16.1f and 17.1e), or in taking relief under certain Local Rules.

It is the estimated point where the ball would lie that is:

• Nearest to the ball's original spot, **but** not nearer the *hole* than that spot,

• In the required *area of the course* and

• Where the condition does not interfere with the *stroke* the player would have made from the original spot if the condition was not there.

Estimating this reference point requires the player to identify the choice of club, *stance*, swing and *line of play* he or she would have used for that *stroke*.

The player does not need to simulate that *stroke* by taking an actual *stance* and swinging with the chosen club (**but** it is recommended that the player normally do this to help in making an accurate estimate).

The *nearest point of complete relief* relates solely to the particular condition from which relief is being taken and may be in a location where there is interference by something else:

• If the player takes relief and then has interference by another condition from which relief is allowed, the player may take relief again by determining a new *nearest point of complete relief* from the new condition.

• Relief must be taken separately for each condition, **except** that the player may take relief from both conditions at the same time (based on determining the *nearest point of complete relief* from both) when, having already taken relief separately from each condition, it becomes reasonable to conclude that continuing to do so will result in continued interference by one or the other.

Nearest Point of Complete Relief/1 – Diagrams Illustrating Nearest Point of Complete Relief

In the diagrams, the term "nearest point of complete relief" in Rule 16.1 (Abnormal Course Conditions) for relief from interference by *ground under repair* is illustrated in the case of both a right-handed and a left-handed player.

The *nearest point of complete relief* must be strictly interpreted. A player is not allowed to choose on which side of the *ground under repair* the ball will be *dropped*, unless there are two equidistant *nearest points of complete relief*. Even if one side of the *ground under repair* is fairway and the other is bushes, if the *nearest point of complete relief* is in the bushes, then that is the player's *nearest point of complete relief*.

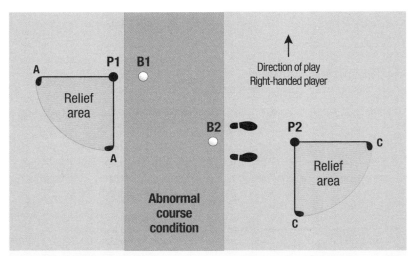

B1 = position of ball in abnormal course condition

P1 = nearest point of complete relief to B1

Relief area P1-A-A = area within which ball is dropped, radius of one club-length from P1

B2 = position of ball in abnormal course condition

Notional stance required to play ball at P2 with club with which the player would expect to make the stroke

P2 = nearest point of complete relief to B2

Relief area P2-C-C = area within which ball is dropped, radius of one club-length from P2

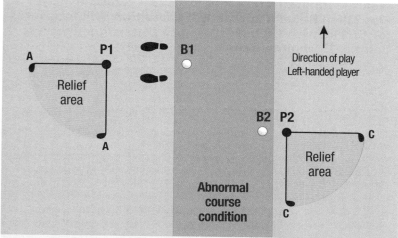

- P1 is the nearest point of complete relief for B1
- ☙ Notional stance to play ball at P1
- Relief area P1-A-A = area within which ball is dropped, radius of one club-length from P1

- P2 is the nearest point of complete relief for B2
- Relief area P2-C-C = area within which ball is dropped, radius of one club-length from P2

Nearest Point of Complete Relief/2 – Player Does Not Follow Recommended Procedure in Determining Nearest Point of Complete Relief

Although there is a recommended procedure for determining the *nearest point of complete relief*, the Rules do not require a player to determine this point when taking relief under a relevant Rule (such as when taking relief from an *abnormal course condition* under Rule 16.1b (Relief for Ball in General Area)). If a player does not determine a *nearest point of complete relief* accurately or identifies an incorrect *nearest point of complete relief*, the player only gets a penalty if this results in him or her *dropping* a ball into a *relief area* that does not satisfy the requirements of the Rule and the ball is then played.

Nearest Point of Complete Relief/3 – Whether Player Has Taken Relief Incorrectly If Condition Still Interferes for Stroke with Club Not Used to Determine Nearest Point of Complete Relief

When a player is taking relief from an *abnormal course condition*, he or she is taking relief only for interference that he or she had with the club, *stance*, swing and *line of play* that would have been used to play the ball from that spot. After the player has taken relief and there is no longer interference for the *stroke* the player would have made, any further interference is a new situation.

For example, the player's ball lies in heavy rough in the *general area* approximately 230 yards from the *green*. The player selects a wedge to make the next *stroke* and finds that his or her *stance* touches a line defining an area of *ground under repair*. The player determines the *nearest point of complete relief* and *drops* a ball in the prescribed *relief area* according to Rule 14.3b(3) (Ball Must Be Dropped in Relief Area) and Rule 16.1 (Relief from Abnormal Course Conditions).

The ball rolls into a good *lie* within the *relief area* from where the player believes that the next *stroke* could be played with a 3-wood. If the player used a wedge for the next *stroke* there would be no interference from the *ground under repair*. However, using the 3-wood, the player again touches the line defining the *ground under repair* with his or her foot. This is a new situation and the player may play the ball as it lies or take relief for the new situation.

Nearest Point of Complete Relief/4 – Player Determines Nearest Point of Complete Relief but Is Physically Unable to Make Intended Stroke

The purpose of determining the *nearest point of complete relief* is to find a reference point in a location that is as near as possible to where the interfering condition no longer interferes. In determining the *nearest point of complete relief*, the player is not guaranteed a good or playable *lie*.

For example, if a player is unable to make a *stroke* from what appears to be the required *relief area* as measured from the *nearest point of complete relief* because either the direction of play is blocked by a tree, or the player is unable to take the backswing for the intended *stroke* due to a bush, this does not change the fact that the identified point is the *nearest point of complete relief*.

After the ball is *in play*, the player must then decide what type of *stroke* he or she will make. This *stroke*, which includes the choice of club, may be different than the one that would have been made from the ball's original spot had the condition not been there.

If it is not physically possible to *drop* the ball in any part of the identified *relief area*, the player is not allowed relief from the condition.

Nearest Point of Complete Relief/5 – Player Physically Unable to Determine Nearest Point of Complete Relief

If a player is physically unable to determine his or her *nearest point of complete relief*, it must be estimated, and the *relief area* is then based on the estimated point.

For example, in taking relief under Rule 16.1, a player is physically unable to determine the *nearest point of complete relief* because that point is within the trunk of a tree or a boundary fence prevents the player from adopting the required *stance*.

The player must estimate the *nearest point of complete relief* and *drop* a ball in the identified *relief area*.

If it is not physically possible to *drop* the ball in the identified *relief area*, the player is not allowed relief under Rule 16.1.

No Play Zone

A part of the *course* where the *Committee* has prohibited play. A *no play zone* must be defined as part of either an *abnormal course condition* or a *penalty area*.

The *Committee* may use *no play zones* for any reason, such as:

- Protecting wildlife, *animal* habitats, and environmentally sensitive areas,

- Preventing damage to young trees, flower beds, turf nurseries, re-turfed areas or other planted areas,

- Protecting players from danger, and

- Preserving sites of historical or cultural interest.

The *Committee* should define the edge of a *no play zone* with a line or stakes, and the line or stakes (or the tops of those stakes) should identify the *no play zone* as different than a regular *abnormal course condition* or *penalty area* that does not contain a *no play zone*.

No Play Zone/1 – Status of Growing Things Overhanging a No Play Zone

The status of growing things that overhang a *no play zone* depends on the type of *no play zone*. This will matter since the growing things may be part of the *no play zone*, in which case the player is required to take relief.

For example, if a *no play zone* has been defined as a *penalty area* (where the edges extend above and below the ground), any part of a growing object that extends beyond the edges of the *no play zone* is not part of the *no play zone*. However, if a *no play zone* has been defined as *ground under repair* (which includes all ground inside the defined area and anything growing that extends above the ground and outside the edges), anything overhanging the edge is part of the *no play zone*.

Obstruction

Any artificial object **except** for *integral objects* and *boundary objects*.

Examples of *obstructions*:

- Artificially surfaced roads and paths, including their artificial borders.

- Buildings and rain shelters.

- Sprinkler heads, drains and irrigation or control boxes.

- Stakes, walls, railings and fences (**but** not when they are *boundary objects* that define or show the boundary edge of the *course*).

- Golf carts, mowers, cars and other vehicles.

- Waste containers, signposts and benches.

- Player *equipment*, *flagsticks* and rakes.

An *obstruction* is either a *movable obstruction* or an *immovable obstruction*. If part of an *immovable obstruction* (such as a gate or door or part of an attached cable) meets the definition of *movable* obstruction, that part is treated as a *movable obstruction*.

See Committee Procedures, Section 8; Model Local Rule F-23 (*Committee* may adopt a Local Rule defining certain *obstructions* as temporary immovable obstructions for which special relief procedures apply).

Obstruction/1 – Status of Paint Dots and Paint Lines

Although artificial objects are *obstructions* so long as they are not *boundary objects* or *integral objects*, paint dots and paint lines are not *obstructions*.

354

Sometimes paint dots and lines are used for purposes other than course marking (such as indicating the front and back of *putting greens*). Such dots and lines are not an *abnormal course condition* unless the *Committee* declares them to be *ground under repair* (see Committee Procedures; Model Local Rule F-21).

Opponent

The person a player competes against in a match. The term *opponent* applies only in *match play*.

Outside Influence

Any of these people or things that can affect what happens to a player's ball or *equipment* or to the *course*:

- Any *person* (including another player), **except** the player or his or her *caddie* or the player's *partner* or *opponent* or any of their *caddies*,

- Any *animal*, and

- Any natural or artificial object or anything else (including another ball in motion), **except** for *natural forces*.

Outside Influence/1 – Status of Air and Water When Artificially Propelled

Although wind and water are *natural forces* and not *outside influences*, artificially propelled air and water are *outside influences*.

Examples include:

- If a ball at rest on the *putting green* has not been lifted and *replaced* and is *moved* by air from a greenside fan, the ball must be *replaced* (Rule 9.6 and Rule 14.2).

- If a ball at rest is *moved* by water coming from an irrigation system, the ball must be *replaced* (Rule 9.6 and Rule 14.2).

Out of Bounds

All areas outside the boundary edge of the *course* as defined by the *Committee*. All areas inside that edge are in bounds.

The boundary edge of the *course* extends both up above the ground and down below the ground:

355

Definitions

- This means that all ground and anything else (such as any natural or artificial object) inside the boundary edge is in bounds, whether on, above or below the surface of the ground.

- If an object is both inside and outside the boundary edge (such as steps attached to a boundary fence, or a tree rooted outside the edge with branches extending inside the edge or vice versa), only the part of the object that is outside the edge is *out of bounds*.

The boundary edge should be defined by *boundary objects* or lines:

- Boundary objects: When defined by stakes or a fence, the boundary edge is defined by the line between the *course*-side points of the stakes or fence posts at ground level (excluding angled supports), and those stakes or fence posts are *out of bounds*.

  When defined by other objects such as a wall or when the *Committee* wishes to treat a boundary fence in a different way, the *Committee* should define the boundary edge.

- Lines: When defined by a painted line on the ground, the boundary edge is the *course*-side edge of the line, and the line itself is *out of bounds*.

  When a line on the ground defines the boundary edge, stakes may be used to show where the boundary edge is, **but** they have no other meaning.

Boundary stakes or lines should be white.

Par/Bogey

A form of *stroke play* that uses scoring as in *match play* where:

- A player or *side* wins or loses a hole by completing the hole in fewer strokes or more strokes (including *strokes* made and any penalty strokes) than a fixed target score for that hole set by the *Committee*, and

- The competition is won by the player or *side* with the highest total of holes won versus holes lost (that is, adding up the holes won and subtracting the holes lost).

Partner

A player who competes together with another player as a *side*, in either *match play* or *stroke play*.

Penalty Area

An area from which relief with a one-stroke penalty is allowed if the player's ball comes to rest there.

A *penalty area* is:

- Any body of water on the *course* (whether or not marked by the *Committee*), including a sea, lake, pond, river, ditch, surface drainage ditch or other open watercourse (even if not containing water), and

- Any other part of the *course* the *Committee* defines as a *penalty area*.

A *penalty area* is one of the five defined *areas of the course*.

There are two different types of *penalty areas*, distinguished by the colour used to mark them:

- Yellow *penalty areas* (marked with yellow lines or yellow stakes) give the player two relief options (Rules 17.1d(1) and (2)).

- Red *penalty areas* (marked with red lines or red stakes) give the player an extra lateral relief option (Rule 17.1d(3)), in addition to the two relief options available for yellow *penalty areas*.

If the colour of a *penalty area* has not been marked or indicated by the *Committee*, it is treated as a red *penalty area*.

The edge of a *penalty area* extends both up above the ground and down below the ground:

- This means that all ground and anything else (such as any natural or artificial object) inside the edge is part of the *penalty area*, whether on, above or below the surface of the ground.

- If an object is both inside and outside the edge (such as a bridge over the *penalty area*, or a tree rooted inside the edge with branches extending outside the edge or vice versa), only the part of the object that is inside the edge is part of the *penalty area*.

The edge of a *penalty area* should be defined by stakes, lines or physical features:

- Stakes: When defined by stakes, the edge of the *penalty area* is defined by the line between the outside points of the stakes at ground level, and the stakes are inside the *penalty area*.

- Lines: When defined by a painted line on the ground, the edge of the *penalty area* is the outside edge of the line, and the line itself is in the *penalty area*.

- Physical Features: When defined by physical features (such as a beach or desert area or a retaining wall), the *Committee* should say how the edge of the *penalty area* is defined.

When the edge of a *penalty area* is defined by lines or by physical features, stakes may be used to show where the *penalty area* is, **but** they have no other meaning.

When the edge of a body of water is not defined by the *Committee*, the edge of that *penalty area* is defined by its natural boundaries (that is, where the ground slopes down to form the depression that can hold the water).

If an open watercourse usually does not contain water (such as a drainage ditch or run-off area that is dry except during a rainy season), the *Committee* may define that area as part of the *general area* (which means it is not a *penalty area*).

Point of Maximum Available Relief

The reference point for taking free relief from an *abnormal course condition* in a *bunker* (Rule 16.1c) or on the *putting green* (Rule 16.1d) when there is no *nearest point of complete relief*.

It is the estimated point where the ball would lie that is:

- Nearest to the ball's original spot, **but** not nearer the *hole* than that spot,

- In the required *area of the course* and

- Where that *abnormal course condition* least interferes with the *stroke* the player would have made from the original spot if the condition was not there.

Estimating this reference point requires the player to identify the choice of club, *stance*, swing and *line of play* the player would have used for that *stroke*.

The player does not need to simulate that *stroke* by taking an actual *stance* and swinging with the chosen club (**but** it is recommended that the player normally do this to help in making an accurate estimate).

The *point of maximum available relief* is found by comparing the relative amount of interference with the *lie* of the ball and the player's area of intended *stance* and swing and, on the *putting green* only, the *line of play*. For example, when taking relief from *temporary water*:

- The *point of maximum available relief* may be where the ball will be in shallower water than where the player will stand (affecting the *stance* more than the *lie* and swing), or where the ball is in deeper water than where the player will stand (affecting the *lie* and swing more than the *stance*).

- On the *putting green*, the *point of maximum available relief* may be based on the *line of play* where the ball will need to go through the shallowest or shortest stretch of *temporary water*.

Provisional Ball

Another ball played in case the ball just played by the player may be:

- *Out of bounds,* or

- *Lost* outside a *penalty area.*

A *provisional ball* is not the player's ball *in play*, unless it becomes the ball *in play* under Rule 18.3c.

Putting Green

The area on the hole the player is playing that:

- Is specially prepared for putting, or

- The *Committee* has defined as the *putting green* (such as when a temporary green is used).

The *putting green* for a hole contains the *hole* into which the player tries to play a ball.

The *putting green* is one of the five defined *areas of the course*. The putting greens for all other holes (which the player is not playing at the time) are *wrong greens* and part of the *general area*.

The edge of a *putting green* is defined by where it can be seen that the specially prepared area starts (such as where the grass has been distinctly cut to show the edge), unless the *Committee* defines the edge in a different way (such as by using a line or dots).

If a double green is used for two different holes:

- The entire prepared area containing both *holes* is treated as the *putting green* when playing each hole.

- But the *Committee* may define an edge that divides the double green into two different *putting greens*, so that when a player is playing one of the holes, the part of the double green for the other hole is a *wrong green*.

Referee

An official named by the *Committee* to decide questions of fact and apply the Rules.

See Committee Procedures, Section 6C (explaining the responsibilities and authority of a *referee*).

Relief Area

The area where a player must *drop* a ball when taking relief under a Rule. Each relief Rule requires the player to use a specific *relief area* whose size and location are based on these three factors:

- **Reference Point:** The point from which the size of *relief area* is measured.

- **Size of Relief Area Measured from Reference Point:** The *relief area* is either one or two *club-lengths* from the reference point, **but** with certain limits:

- **Limits on Location of Relief Area:** The location of the *relief area* may be limited in one or more ways so that, for example:

  » It is only in certain defined *areas of the course*, such as only in the *general area*, or not in a *bunker* or a *penalty area*,

  » It is not nearer the *hole* than the reference point or must be outside a *penalty area* or a *bunker* from which relief is being taken, or

  » It is where there is no interference (as defined in the particular Rule) from the condition from which relief is being taken.

In using *club-lengths* to determine the size of a *relief area*, the player may measure directly across a ditch, hole or similar thing, and directly across or through an object (such as a tree, fence, wall, tunnel, drain or sprinkler head), **but** is not allowed to measure through ground that naturally slopes up and down.

See Committee Procedures, Section 2I (*Committee* may choose to allow or require the player to use a dropping zone as a *relief area* when taking certain relief).

Replace

To place a ball by setting it down and letting it go, with the intent for it to be *in play*.

If the player sets a ball down without intending it to be *in play*, the ball has not been *replaced* and is not *in play* (see Rule 14.4).

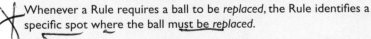

Whenever a Rule requires a ball to be *replaced*, the Rule identifies a specific spot where the ball must be *replaced*.

Replace/1 – Ball May Not Be Replaced with a Club

For a ball to be *replaced* in a right way, it must be set down and let go. This means the player must use his or her hand to put the ball back *in play* on the spot it was lifted or *moved* from.

For example, if a player lifts his or her ball from the *putting green* and sets it aside, the player must not *replace* the ball by rolling it to the required spot with a club. If he or she does so, the ball is not *replaced* in the right way and the player gets one penalty stroke under Rule 14.2b(2) (How Ball Must Be Replaced) if the mistake is not corrected before the *stroke* is made.

Round

18 or fewer holes played in the order set by the *Committee*.

Scorecard

The document where a player's score for each hole is entered in *stroke play*.

The *scorecard* may be in any paper or electronic form approved by the *Committee* that allows:

- The player's score to be entered for each hole,
- The player's handicap to be entered, if it is a handicap competition, and
- The *marker* and the player to certify the scores, and the player to certify his or her handicap in a handicap competition, either by physical signature or by a method of electronic certification approved by the *Committee*.

A *scorecard* is not required in *match play* but may be used by the players to help keep the match score.

Serious Breach

In *stroke play*, when playing from a *wrong place* could give the player a significant advantage compared to the *stroke* to be made from the right place.

In making this comparison to decide if there was a *serious breach*, the factors to be taken into account include:

- The difficulty of the *stroke*,
- The distance of the ball from the *hole*,
- The effect of obstacles on the *line of play*, and
- The *conditions affecting the stroke*.

The concept of a *serious breach* does not apply in *match play*, because a player loses the hole if he or she plays from a *wrong place*.

Side

Two or more *partners* competing as a single unit in a *round* in *match play* or *stroke play*.

Each set of *partners* is a *side*, whether each *partner* plays his or her own ball (*Four-Ball*) or the *partners* play one ball (*Foursomes*).

A *side* is not the same as a team. In a team competition, each team consists of players competing as individuals or as *sides*.

✓ Stableford

A form of *stroke play* where:

- A player's or *side's* score for a hole is based on points awarded by comparing the player's or *side's* number of strokes on the hole (including *strokes* made and any penalty strokes) to a fixed target score for the hole set by the *Committee*, and

- The competition is won by the player or *side* who completes all *rounds* with the most points.

Stance

The position of a player's feet and body in preparing for and making a *stroke*.

✓ Stroke

The forward movement of the club made to strike the ball.

But a *stroke* has not been made if the player:

- Decides during the downswing not to strike the ball and avoids doing so by deliberately stopping the clubhead before it reaches the ball or, if unable to stop, by deliberately missing the ball.

- Accidentally strikes the ball when making a practice swing or while preparing to make a *stroke*.

When the Rules refer to "playing a ball," it means the same as making a *stroke*.

The player's score for a hole or a *round* is described as a number of "strokes" or "strokes taken," which means both all *strokes* made and any penalty strokes (see Rule 3.1c).

Stroke/I – Determining If a Stroke Was Made

If a player starts the downswing with a club intending to strike the ball, his or her action counts as a *stroke* when:

- The clubhead is deflected or stopped by an *outside influence* (such as the branch of a tree) whether or not the ball is struck.

- The clubhead separates from the shaft during the downswing and the player continues the downswing with the shaft alone, whether or not the ball is struck with the shaft.

- The clubhead separates from the shaft during the downswing and the player continues the downswing with the shaft alone, with the clubhead falling and striking the ball.

The player's action does not count as a *stroke* in each of following situations:

- During the downswing, a player's clubhead separates from the shaft. The player stops the downswing short of the ball, but the clubhead falls and strikes and *moves* the ball.

- During the backswing, a player's clubhead separates from the shaft. The player completes the downswing with the shaft but does not strike the ball.

- A ball is lodged in a tree branch beyond the reach of a club. If the player *moves* the ball by striking a lower part of the branch instead of the ball, Rule 9.4 (Ball Lifted or Moved by Player) applies.

Stroke and Distance

The procedure and penalty when a player takes relief under Rules 17, 18 or 19 by playing a ball from where the previous *stroke* was made (see Rule 14.6).

The term *stroke and distance* means that the player both:

- Gets one penalty stroke, and

- Loses the benefit of any gain of distance towards the *hole* from the spot where the previous *stroke* was made.

Stroke Play

A form of play where a player or *side* competes against all other players or *sides* in the competition.

In the regular form of *stroke play* (see Rule 3.3):

- A player's or *side's* score for a *round* is the total number of strokes (including *strokes* made and any penalty strokes) to *hole out* on each hole, and

- The winner is the player or *side* who completes all *rounds* in the fewest total strokes.

Other forms of *stroke play* with different scoring methods are *Stableford*, *Maximum Score* and *Par/Bogey* (see Rule 21).

All forms of *stroke play* can be played either in individual competitions (each player competing on his or her own) or in competitions involving *sides* of *partners* (*Foursomes* or *Four-Ball*).

Substitute

To change the ball the player is using to play a hole by having another ball become the ball *in play*.

The player has *substituted* another ball when he or she puts that ball *in play* in any way (see Rule 14.4) instead of the player's original ball, whether the original ball was:

- *In play*, or

- No longer *in play* because it had been lifted from the *course* or was *lost* or *out of bounds*.

A *substituted* ball is the player's ball *in play* even if:

- It was *replaced, dropped* or placed in a wrong way or *wrong place*, or

- The player was required under the Rules to put the original ball back *in play* rather than to *substitute* another ball.

Tee

An object used to raise a ball above the ground to play it from the *teeing area*. It must be no longer than four inches (101.6 mm) and conform with the *Equipment Rules*.

Teeing Area

The area the player must play from in starting the hole he or she is playing.

The *teeing area* is a rectangle that is two *club-lengths* deep where:

- The front edge is defined by the line between the forward-most points of two tee-markers set by the *Committee*, and

- The side edges are defined by the lines back from the outside points of the tee-markers.

The *teeing area* is one of the five defined *areas of the course*.

All other teeing locations on the *course* (whether on the same hole or any other hole) are part of the *general area*.

Temporary Water

Any temporary accumulation of water on the surface of the ground (such as puddles from rain or irrigation or an overflow from a body of water) that:

- Is not in a *penalty area*, and

- Can be seen before or after the player takes a *stance* (without pressing down excessively with his or her feet).

It is not enough for the ground to be merely wet, muddy or soft or for the water to be momentarily visible as the player steps on the ground; an accumulation of water must remain present either before or after the *stance* is taken.

Special cases:

- **Dew and Frost** are not *temporary water*.

- **Snow and Natural Ice** (other than frost), are either *loose impediments* or, when on the ground, *temporary water*, at the player's option.

- **Manufactured Ice** is an *obstruction*.

Three-Ball

A form of *match play* where:

- Each of three players plays an individual match against the other two players at the same time, and

- Each player plays one ball that is used in both of his or her matches.

Wrong Ball

Any ball other than the player's:

- Ball *in play* (whether the original ball or a *substituted* ball),

- *Provisional ball* (before it is abandoned under Rule 18.3c), or

- Second ball in *stroke play* played under Rules 14.7b or 20.1c.

Examples of a *wrong ball* are:

- Another player's ball *in play*.

- A stray ball.
- The player's own ball that is *out of bounds*, has become *lost* or has been lifted and not yet put back *in play*.

Wrong Ball/1 – Part of Wrong Ball Is Still Wrong Ball

If a player makes a *stroke* at part of a stray ball that he or she mistakenly thought was the *ball in play*, he or she has made a *stroke* at a *wrong ball* and Rule 6.3c applies.

Wrong Green

Any green on the *course* other than the *putting green* for the hole the player is playing. *Wrong greens* include:

- The putting greens for all other holes that the player is not playing at the time,
- The normal putting green for a hole where a temporary green is being used, and
- All practice greens for putting, chipping or pitching, unless the *Committee* excludes them by Local Rule.

Wrong greens are part of the *general area*.

Wrong Place

Any place on the *course* other than where the player is required or allowed to play his or her ball under the Rules.

Examples of playing from a *wrong place* are:

- Playing a ball after *replacing* it on the wrong spot or without *replacing* it when required by the Rules.
- Playing a *dropped* ball from outside the required *relief area*.
- Taking relief under a wrong Rule, so that the ball is *dropped* in and played from a place not allowed under the Rules.
- Playing a ball from a *no play zone* or when a *no play zone* interferes with the player's area of intended *stance* or swing.

Playing a ball from outside the *teeing area* in starting play of a hole or in trying to correct that mistake is not playing from a *wrong place* (see Rule 6.1b).

Committee
Procedures

Contents

Contents

Section 3 Local Rules for General Play 393

Section 4 Additional Considerations for General Play . . 393

III Competitions (Sections 5–7)

Section 5 Before the Competition 396

Contents

Contents

Contents

The Committee

I The Role of the Committee

The Rules of Golf define the Committee as the person or group in charge of a competition or the course. The Committee is essential to the proper playing of the game. Committees have the responsibility of running the course on a day-to-day basis or for a specific competition and they should always act in ways that support the Rules of Golf. This part of the Official Guide to the Rules of Golf provides guidance to Committees in fulfilling this role.

While many of the duties of a Committee are specific to running organized competitions, an important part of the Committee's duties relates to its responsibility for the course during general or every day play.

IA General Play

Even when a competition is not being contested, it is still important for the Committee to ensure that the Rules of Golf can be followed by golfers playing casual rounds or playing their own competitions. This type of play is referred to as general play throughout the Committee Procedures.

During general play, the structure of the Committee is often more informal than in competitions, and in many cases the responsibilities of the Committee will be delegated to or undertaken by one or more course representatives, such as the golf professional, course manager or other employee of the course. The duties of this Committee include:

- Ensuring the course is properly marked (Section 2),

- Establishing any Local Rules for general play (Section 3),

- Establishing and enforcing Pace of Play and Code of Conduct guidelines (Section 4A),

- Considering when to suspend play because of weather or other conditions (Section 4B), and

- Providing Rules support for players when they have a question regarding general play (Section 4C).

IB Competitions

When in charge of a competition, the Committee has responsibilities before, during and after play to ensure the smooth running of the competition under the Rules.

The resources available to a Committee will differ depending on the course or the level of competition being run, and so a Committee may not be able to implement every recommended practice. Where this is the case, the Committee will need to decide its priorities for each competition.

The period before the competition begins is arguably the most important to ensure the smooth running of the competition. The Committee's duties during this period may include:

- Setting the Terms of the Competition (Section 5A),

- Reviewing and adjusting the course marking (Section 5B),

- Reviewing Local Rules and establishing any additional Local Rules (Section 5C),

- Defining if and where players may practise on the course (Section 5D),

- Determining the teeing areas and hole locations to be used (Section 5E),

- Establishing and publishing the draw for match play or groups for stroke play and the starting times (Sections 5F),

- Defining Pace of Play and Code of Conduct policies (Sections 5G and 5H), and

- Preparing materials for players and referees (Section 5I).

Once the competition has started, the Committee is responsible for ensuring that players have the information needed to play under the Rules and to assist them in applying the Rules:

- Providing information to players so they are aware of any Local Rules, Pace of Play or Code of Conduct polices that are in force, as well as other important information such as which teeing areas to use and where holes are located (Section 6A),

- Starting matches and groups on time (Section 6A),

- Ensuring that the course is properly set up, marked and maintained (Section 6B),

- Providing Rules assistance for players (Section 6C),

- Enforcing the Pace of Play policy (Section 6D),

- Suspending play because of weather or other conditions and then determining when play should be resumed (Section 6E),

- Providing an area for players to report the results of a match or return scorecards in stroke play (Section 6F),

- Validating all scores from the round in stroke play (Section 6F), and

- Establishing and publishing any groupings and starting times for players if there are additional rounds that have not been previously published (Section 6G).

The Role of the Committee

Once play has been completed, the Committee's duties include:

- Resolving any ties in stroke play (Section 7A),
- Confirming the final results and closing the competition (Section 7B),
- Awarding any prizes (Section 7C), and
- Dealing with any issues that arise after the competition is closed (Section 7D).

General Play

2 Course Marking for General Play

Marking the course and refreshing those markings as needed is an ongoing task for which the Committee is responsible.

A well-marked course allows a player to play by the Rules and helps to eliminate confusion for players. For example, a player may not know how to proceed if a pond (penalty area) is not marked or if he or she is unable to determine if a ball is in bounds or out of bounds.

2A Out of Bounds

It is important for the Committee to mark the boundaries properly and to maintain the markings so that a player who hits a ball near a boundary can determine if his or her ball is in bounds or out of bounds.

(1) General Guidance for Determining and Marking Boundaries

The Committee can mark the course's boundary in many ways. Stakes or painted lines can be placed in position by the Committee. Existing fences or walls can be used to define boundaries, as can the edge of other permanent structures such as roads or buildings.

In determining the boundaries for the course and marking them, there are a number of items for the Committee to consider:

Properties Bordering the Course

- Where private properties and public roads border the course, it is strongly recommended that the Committee mark these areas as out of bounds. Often these properties will have walls or fences which can be used as the boundaries for the course. When these exist, there is generally no need to move the boundary inside them by placing stakes. But the Committee may wish to move the boundary inwards (for example, by using stakes) to provide some additional protection to the adjacent properties.

- There is no requirement for a course to have boundaries, but it is advisable to prevent play from property that does not belong to the course. But there may be locations where there are large open areas bordering the actual property lines where there would be no objection to players playing. In this case there is no need to place stakes or otherwise define the boundary.

- Where an existing structure such as a wall or fence is used to define the boundary, the entire object will be a boundary object from which free relief is not available.

Use of Stakes

- Boundary stakes should be white, though another colour may be used.

- There may be existing stakes already in place that are a different colour, or the Committee may have a reason for using a different colour to distinguish them from some items on the course. When this is the case, the Committee should notify players on the scorecard, a posting in the clubhouse, a Local Rules sheet or by some other means. The Committee should avoid the use of red or yellow stakes for marking a boundary so as not to cause confusion with penalty areas.

- The distance between stakes may vary, but, ideally, it should be possible to see the base of one stake from the next one to determine if a ball is out of bounds. It is important to check that bushes, trees or the like do not obscure stakes or make it difficult to see from one to the next. In general, stakes should be separated by a distance of no more than 30 paces to allow players to see easily between them.

Use of Paint Lines

- Painted lines used to define the boundary should be white, though another colour may be used. The Committee should avoid the use of red or yellow lines for marking a boundary to avoid confusion with penalty areas.

- When the boundary is defined by a line painted on the ground, the Committee can also place stakes to make the boundary visible from a distance. It should be made clear that the painted line defines the boundary while the stakes are placed to show players that the boundary is there. These stakes do not define the boundary, but they are boundary objects from which free relief is not available unless otherwise specified in the Local Rules (see Model Local Rule A-5).

- There may be times where the Committee may not wish to paint a white line on a road or pavement. In this case, the most unobtrusive way of marking the boundary may be to paint a series of white dots on the ground. When this is done, the Local Rules should be used to advise the players as to how the boundary has been marked (see Model Local Rule A-1).

Other Ways of Marking Out of Bounds

- Where a boundary is defined by a wall, edge of a road or anything other than stakes, fences or lines, the Committee needs to clarify where the edge of the boundary is. For example, when a wall is used to define the boundary, the Committee should specify if the inside edge of the wall defines the boundary or if a ball is only out of bounds when it is beyond the wall (see Model Local Rule A-2).

- A boundary may be defined by a trench, with the ball being out of bounds if it is in or beyond the trench. Stakes may be used to draw attention to the boundary trench. These stakes are boundary objects from which free relief is not available unless otherwise specified in the Local Rules (see Model Local Rule A-5).

Course Marking for General Play

Other Considerations

- Certain features such as maintenance areas, clubhouses and practice grounds, may be marked or defined by Local Rule as out of bounds even though they are on the course's property (see Model Local Rule A-1).

- The Rules do not contemplate an area having more than one status during the play of a hole, and so an area must not be marked as out of bounds for certain strokes, or strokes made from certain areas such as the teeing area.

- The Rules apply to where a ball comes to rest after a stroke and not the area that it crossed when in motion; Committees are not authorized to have a Local Rule saying that a ball played over a certain area is out of bounds even if it does not come to rest in that area.

(2) Marking Internal Boundaries

To maintain the character of a hole or to protect players on adjacent holes, the Committee may establish boundaries between two holes.

If the internal boundary is not connected to other boundaries on the course it is important to mark where the boundary starts and finishes. It is recommended that two stakes be placed side-by-side and at an angle that indicates that the boundary extends indefinitely in the direction desired.

The internal boundary may apply for the play of only one hole or to more than one hole. The hole or holes for which the internal out of bounds applies, and the status of the stakes during the play of holes for which the boundary does not apply, should be clarified through a Local Rule (see Model Local Rule A-4).

2B Teeing Areas

The Committee should always attempt to position the tee-markers far enough forward so that players can use the entire two club-lengths permitted.

There are no restrictions on the width of the teeing area, but it is good practice to place the two tee-markers 5 to 7 paces apart. Placing them further apart than this makes it more difficult for a player to determine if the ball has been teed within the teeing area and can result in divot holes covering a much larger area on par-3 holes.

For guidance on where tee-markers may be located in order for scores to be submitted for handicapping purposes, consult the rules or recommendations contained within the Handicap System operating in the local jurisdiction.

2C Penalty Areas

Penalty areas are areas of the course from which a player is allowed to take relief for one penalty stroke at a spot outside the penalty area that is potentially a significant distance from where his or her ball may have come to rest. As provided in the definition of "penalty area", areas which contain water such as lakes, streams, rivers or ponds are penalty areas and should be marked as such.

The Committee may mark other portions of the course as penalty areas. Among the reasons the Committee may choose to mark other parts or features of the course are:

- To provide an alternative to the stroke-and-distance procedure under Rule 18.1 when the likelihood is that a ball that is in the area will almost always be lost, for example, an area of dense vegetation.

- To provide an alternative to the stroke-and-distance procedure under Rule 19.2 (Unplayable Ball) when the likelihood is that taking relief in relation to the position where the ball lies under the options available in Rules 19.2b and 19.2c will not provide any effective relief, for example, an area of volcanic rock or desert.

(1) Deciding When to Mark Area that Does Not Contain Water as Penalty Area

The Committee should take the following points into consideration before deciding to mark an area that does not contain water as a penalty area:

- The fact that marking a difficult area as a penalty area may improve pace of play does not mean that the Committee should feel compelled to do so. There are many other competing considerations, such as retaining the challenge of the hole, the integrity of the architect's original design intention and providing reasonably consistent outcomes for balls hit into similar types of areas throughout the course. For example, if a jungle borders the fairway on one hole and it has been marked as a penalty area, the Committee should consider treating similar areas the same way on other holes.

- The Committee should consider that a player who loses his or her ball outside a penalty area will have a greater penalty than someone whose ball is lost in the penalty area. If there are areas of thick rough close to the edge of the penalty area where balls could be lost, the Committee may want to consider including such areas in the penalty area.

- The Committee should remember that a player whose ball lies in a penalty area will not be able to use the unplayable ball options in Rule 19. Making the player return to where the ball crossed the edge of the penalty area to take relief rather than having the option of dropping within two club-lengths of where the ball was found may be a significant disadvantage to the player and could negatively impact on pace of play.

- The Committee should not define sandy areas that would normally be bunkers as penalty areas. There may be cases where areas of sand flow naturally into a penalty area such as a beach. In this case the edge of the penalty area and the bunker may be immediately adjacent to each other with a portion of the sand being in the penalty area.

- The Committee should not define properties bordering the course as a penalty area where the properties would normally be marked as out of bounds.

- If a Committee is considering marking an out of bounds area as a penalty area to assist with pace of play, as an alternative the Committee may decide to use the Local Rule giving an alternative to stroke-and-distance relief found in Model Local Rule E-5. While this results in the player getting a two-stroke penalty, it also provides the player the opportunity to move out to the fairway, which might not be an option if the area was marked as a penalty area.

- When penalty areas are added or removed, the Committee should consult the rules or recommendations contained within the Handicap System operating in the local jurisdiction to determine if the change will have an impact on the issued Course Rating.

(2) How to Mark or Define the Edge of a Penalty Area

In taking relief from a penalty area, a player will usually need to know the point where the ball last crossed the edge of the penalty area and whether the penalty area is marked as red or yellow at that point.

- It is recommended that the Committee mark the edges of penalty areas using paint and/or stakes so that there is no doubt for players.

- Where lines are used to define the edge of a penalty area and stakes are used to identify the penalty area, it is at the Committee's discretion whether the stakes should be placed on the line or just outside the edge of the penalty area. Placing stakes just outside the painted line ensures players are entitled to free relief from the hole made by the stake if the stake was to fall out or be removed and the ball came to rest in the hole.

- A Committee may define the edge of a penalty area by clearly describing it in writing but should do so only if there will be little or no doubt where the edge is. For example, where there are large areas of lava or desert that are to be treated as penalty areas, and the border between these areas and the preferred playing areas is well defined, the Committee could define the edge of the penalty area as being the edge of the lava bed or desert.

(3) Determining Where to Mark the Edge of a Penalty Area

Marking the edge of a penalty area clearly is important to allow players to take relief. The Committee should consider the following in determining where to mark the edge of a penalty area:

- Lines and stakes defining the edge of a penalty area should be placed as near as possible along the natural limits of the penalty area, for example, where the ground breaks down to form the depression containing the water. This will ensure that players will not be forced to stand with the ball significantly above or below their feet or in the water after taking relief. Consideration should be given for both right-handed and left-handed players.

- When a penalty area is bordered by parts of the general area where a ball could be lost, it may affect the player's ability to establish if it is known or virtually certain that the ball is in the penalty area and the player would, therefore, not be able to take penalty area relief using Rule 17. For this reason, the Committee may decide to extend the edge of the penalty area outside the normal natural boundaries and include other areas where it may be difficult to find a ball.

- The Committee should consider that a player is not allowed to take free relief from an abnormal course condition when his or her ball lies in a penalty area. For example, if there is an immovable obstruction such as a cart path or sprinkler head close to an area that the Committee is considering marking as a penalty area, the Committee may want to keep the obstruction outside the penalty area in order for a player to be entitled to free relief from it.

(4) Whether to Mark a Penalty Area as Red or Yellow

Most penalty areas should be marked red to give players the additional option of lateral relief (see Rule 17.1d(3)). However, where part of the challenge of the hole is to carry over a penalty area such as a stream that crosses the front of the putting green and there is a good chance that a ball that carries over the stream could fall back into it, the Committee may decide to mark the penalty area as yellow. This ensures that a ball that lands on the far side of the penalty area before rolling back into the penalty area cannot be dropped on the far side under the lateral relief option.

When a penalty area is marked yellow, the Committee should ensure that a player will always be able to drop back-on-the-line under Rule 17.1d(2) or consider adding a dropping zone for the penalty area so that a player would have an option other than stroke and distance.

A Committee does not have to mark any penalty areas yellow. For simplicity, a Committee may decide to mark all penalty areas red so there is no confusion for players as to what relief options are available.

(5) Change in Status of a Penalty Area Between Red and Yellow

The Committee may wish to mark part of a penalty area as red and another part of the same penalty area as yellow. The Committee should determine the best point to make this transition to ensure that wherever a ball enters a yellow penalty area, a player will always be able to drop back-on-the-line under Rule 17.1d(2).

It should be remembered that the player's relief options are based on where the ball last crossed the edge of the penalty area and not where the ball came to rest in it.

At the point where the edge of the penalty area changes, it is recommended that red and yellow stakes be placed right next to each other to make it clear exactly where the status of the penalty area changes.

Status of Penalty Area May Differ Depending on the Teeing Area Used

Where carrying the ball over a penalty area, such as a pond on a par 3, is part of the challenge of a hole from the back tee but not from the forward tee, the Committee may decide to define it with yellow stakes or a yellow line and use a Local Rule to the effect that the area is a red penalty area when played from the forward tee.

Status of Penalty Area May Differ Between Holes

When a penalty area is potentially in play for more than one hole, the Committee may choose to define it as a yellow penalty area during play of one hole and a red penalty area during play of another hole. Where this is the case the penalty area should be marked as yellow and a Local Rule used to clarify that it is to be treated as red when playing the relevant hole (see Model Local Rule B-1).

Status of Edge of Penalty Area Must Not Change During Play of Hole

While a penalty area may be played as yellow for players playing from one teeing area and red from another, a penalty area must not be defined so that one specific portion of the edge of the penalty area is red for a stroke made from one location but is yellow for a stroke made from another location by the same player. For example, it would be inappropriate and confusing to say that the edge of the penalty area on the putting green side of a lake is yellow for a stroke from the fairway side of the penalty area but red for a stroke from the putting green side.

(6) Defining a Penalty Area as a No Play Zone

The Committee may decide to define all or part of a penalty area as a no play zone. See Section 2G for more information on when to mark a penalty area as a no play zone.

(7) Body of Water Adjacent to Course

Where a body of water such as a stream, lake, sea, or ocean, borders the course, it is permissible to mark such an area as a penalty area rather than marking it as out of bounds. The phrase "on the course" in the definition of "penalty area" does not mean on property owned by the course; rather it refers to any area not defined as out of bounds by the Committee.

- When it is possible for a ball to finish on the ground on the opposite side of a body of water, but it is impracticable for the Committee to define the opposite edge, the Committee may adopt a Local Rule stating that when marked on just one side, a penalty area is treated as if it extended to infinity. Accordingly, all ground and water beyond the defined edge of the penalty area is in the penalty area (see Model Local Rule B-1).

- When a penalty area is bounded by out of bounds on one side, such that the edge of the penalty area and the boundary line coincide, the Committee can use a Local Rule to allow the player to take relief on the opposite side of the penalty area to where the ball last crossed the edge (see Model Local Rule B-2) and an additional Local Rule so that there is no need to mark that edge of the penalty area (see Model Local Rule B-1).

2D Bunkers

Normally there is no need to mark the edge of bunkers, but there may be times where the edges of the bunkers are difficult to determine. The Committee should either mark the edges with stakes or painted lines or define the edge through wording in Local Rules (see Model Local Rule C-1).

Position of Rakes

There is not a perfect answer for the position of rakes and it is a matter for each Committee to decide whether it has rakes placed in or out of bunkers.

It may be argued that there is more likelihood of a ball being deflected into or kept out of a bunker if the rake is placed outside the bunker. It could also be argued that if the rake is in the bunker it is most unlikely that the ball will be deflected out of the bunker.

However, in practice, players who leave rakes in bunkers frequently leave them at the side of the bunker which tends to stop a ball rolling into the flat part of the bunker resulting in a much more difficult shot than would otherwise have been the case. When the ball comes to rest on or against a rake in the bunker and the player must proceed under Rule 15.2, it may not be possible to replace the ball on the same spot or find a spot in the bunker which is not nearer the hole.

If rakes are left in the middle of the bunker, the only way to position them is to throw them into the bunker and this causes indentations in the sand. Also, if a rake is in the middle of a large bunker, it is either not used or the player is obliged to rake a large area of the bunker when retrieving the rake, resulting in unnecessary delay.

Therefore, after considering all these aspects, and while recognising that the positioning of rakes is at the Committee's discretion, it is recommended that rakes should be left outside bunkers in areas where they are least likely to affect the movement of the ball.

However, a Committee may decide to position rakes inside bunkers to make it easier for maintenance staff to cut fairways and bunker surrounds.

2E Putting Greens

Normally there is no need to mark the edge of putting greens, but there may be times where it may be difficult to determine the edge of the putting green due to the surrounding areas being cut to a similar height. When this is the case, the Committee may wish to paint small dots to define the edge of the putting green. The status of these dots should be clarified by a Local Rule (see Model Local Rule D-1).

2F Abnormal Course Conditions

While immovable obstructions rarely need to be marked in any way, it is recommended that areas of ground under repair are clearly marked by the Committee.

(1) Deciding What Areas to Mark as Ground Under Repair

In general, when ground conditions are abnormal to the course or it is unreasonable to require a player to play from a specific area, it should be marked as ground under repair.

Before marking any areas as ground under repair, the Committee should review the entire course to assess what types of areas are abnormal to the course in its current condition. Consideration should also be given to the location of any areas which may need to be marked:

- Areas that are in or near a fairway should normally be marked if the Committee considers the damage to the area to be abnormal.
  - » If the fairways of the course are in generally good condition, it might be appropriate to mark a single area of bare ground in the fairway as ground under repair.

» When conditions are such that there are wide spread areas of bare ground, it would make sense not to mark or declare them all to be ground under repair but only mark the areas where a player may have difficulty being able to make a stroke at the ball, such as a heavily damaged or rutted area.

- The farther the area is from the fairway the less appropriate it is that it should be marked as ground under repair. Areas that are well off the fairway or very short of the landing areas should only be marked when the damage is very severe.

- If two or more areas of ground under repair are close together such that a player taking relief from one area may well drop in a position where there would be interference from another one, it would be advisable to mark a single area of ground under repair.

(2) How to Mark or Define the Edge of Ground Under Repair

It is recommended that the Committee identify ground under repair by using paint, stakes or some other clear way of defining it such that there is no doubt as to where the edge of the area is.

- There is no specific colour of stakes or lines to be used for marking areas of ground under repair, but white or blue stakes or lines are commonly used. Yellow and red stakes or lines should not be used to avoid confusion with penalty areas. The way in which ground under repair is marked should be stated in the Local Rules.

- When an area of ground under repair is close to an immovable obstruction, it is a good practice to tie the two areas together to allow relief to be taken from both conditions in one step. This can be done by using paint lines that connect the ground under repair to the immovable obstruction. It should also be clarified by Local Rule that any lined areas connected to an immovable obstruction are one abnormal course condition (see Model Local Rule F-3).

- A Committee can define the edge of ground under repair by describing it, but only if there will be little or no doubt over what constitutes the area or its edges.

» An example where describing the damage is possible and the Committee is justified in declaring any areas as ground under repair without marking them is where there has been significant damage from animal hoof marks (see Model Local Rule F-10).

» At other times it is not appropriate to make a general declaration. For example, for all ruts made by maintenance vehicles to be defined as ground under repair by Local Rule is not appropriate as much of the disturbance is likely to be minor and free relief is not warranted.

Instead, any deep ruts should be marked with painted lines or stakes to avoid any doubt as to when a player is entitled to relief.

2G No Play Zones

The definition of "no play zone" states that it is part of the course where the Committee wishes to prohibit play. No play zones can be either within an abnormal course condition or a penalty area and can encompass the entire area or just a portion of it.

(1) What May Be Marked as a No Play Zone

The Committee can define all or part of an abnormal course condition or a penalty area as a no play zone for any reason. Some common reasons are:

- To protect wildlife, animal habitats, and environmentally sensitive areas.

- To prevent damage to young trees, flower beds, turf nurseries, re-turfed areas or other planted areas.

- To protect players from danger.

- To preserve sites of historical or cultural interest.

When deciding whether to mark a no play zone as an abnormal course condition or a penalty area, the Committee should consider the type of area being marked and whether it would be appropriate for the player to be able to take free relief or penalty relief from the area. For example:

- If the area contains an area of water such as a stream, lake or wetland it should be marked as a penalty area.

- For a small area of rare plants close to a putting green it may be appropriate to mark the area as an abnormal course condition.

- If a large area of sand dunes along the side of a hole is environmentally sensitive, it is too generous to mark the whole area as an abnormal course condition, and so it should be marked as a penalty area.

When a course is next to privately-owned property (such as residential homes or farmlands), the Committee should normally mark those areas that are not part of the course as out of bounds. The Committee should not mark the privately-owned property adjacent to the course as a penalty area and a no play zone because it reduces the penalty for a ball that has come to rest in that area. If it is desired that a player should be prohibited from standing in an area of the course to play a ball that is on the course, the area may be marked as a no play zone (see Model Local Rule E-9).

(2) How to Mark a No Play Zone

The Committee should define the edge of a no play zone with a line or stakes to clarify whether the area is within an abnormal course condition or a penalty area. In addition, the line or stakes (or the tops of those stakes) should also identify that the area is a no play zone.

There is no specific colour of stakes and lines to be used for marking no play zones, but the following are recommended:

- Penalty area no play zone – red or yellow stakes with green tops.

- Abnormal course condition no play zone – white or blue stakes with green tops.

Environmentally sensitive areas may be physically protected to deter players from entering the area (for example, by a fence, warning signs and the like). The Committee could specify in a Code of Conduct a penalty for a player who enters such an area to retrieve a ball or for other reasons.

2H Integral Objects

Integral objects are artificial objects from which free relief is not available. Examples of objects that the Committee can choose to designate as integral objects include:

- Objects that are designed to be part of the challenge of playing the course such as roads or paths from which players have traditionally been expected to play.

- Gates for getting through a boundary wall or fence (see Interpretation "Boundary Object/2").

- Objects that are so close to a boundary or other feature on the course that if free relief is available from the obstruction, it also results in the player being able to drop away from the boundary or other feature when this is not desirable. For example, designating wires that are attached to trees as integral objects ensures that a player does not incidentally get relief from a tree just because he or she has interference from the wire.

- Objects such as artificial walls or pilings that are inside penalty areas or artificial walls or liners of bunkers. For example, when these are close to the edge of the penalty area, a player whose ball is just outside the penalty area could be standing on the wall and get free relief while the player whose ball is just inside the penalty area does not.

The Committee should define these objects as integral objects in the Local Rules (see Model Local Rule F-1).

When only a portion of the obstruction is to be considered an integral object that portion should be distinctively marked and that information communicated to the players. This may be done by marking with distinctively coloured stakes at either end of the portion where free relief is not available or using paint to mark the area.

21 Dropping Zones

(1) When to Use Dropping Zones

A dropping zone is a special form of relief area that may be provided by the Committee. When taking relief in a dropping zone, the player must drop the ball in, and have it come to rest in, the dropping zone. The Committee should add a Local Rule stating under what circumstances the dropping zone may be used (see Model Local Rule E-1).

Dropping zones should be considered when there may be practical problems in requiring players to use the normal relief options under a Rule, such as:

- Rule 13.1f – Wrong Green.

- Rule 16.1 – Abnormal Course Conditions (Including Immovable Obstructions).

- Rule 16.2 – Dangerous Animal Condition.

- Rule 17 – Penalty Area.

- Rule 19 – Unplayable Ball.

- Model Local Rules such as E-5 – Alternative to Stroke and Distance for Lost Ball or Ball Out of Bounds or F-23 – Temporary Immovable Obstructions.

Dropping zones should normally be used to give the player an extra relief option. But the Committee may also require use of a dropping zone as the player's only relief option under a Rule, other than stroke and distance. When the Committee does make the use of a dropping zone mandatory, that replaces any other relief options provided by the relevant Rule and this should be made clear to players.

(2) Where to Position Dropping Zones

The Committee should attempt to place a dropping zone so that the architectural challenge of the hole is maintained, and it is typically not closer to the hole than where the player would be dropping the ball when using one of the options under the relevant Rule. For example, when situating the dropping zone for a penalty area, it should be set in a position where the player would still need to negotiate the penalty area rather than being located on the putting green side of the penalty area.

Dropping zones can be marked in many ways (such as by painted lines on the ground, markers such as tee-markers, or a stake or a sign), and can be any shape, such as a circle or a square. The size of the dropping zone may depend on how often it is likely to be used and where it is located, but the size would normally be expected to have about a one club-length radius or smaller. When marked with paint, a sign or painted marking on the ground should be used to let players know its status.

If a dropping zone is likely to be used frequently, the Committee may wish to consider marking the dropping zone by defining the area in the Local Rules. For example, the dropping zone may be defined as being within one club-length of a physical object such as a sign or a stake. This allows for the object to be moved as needed to ensure the dropping zone remains in good condition.

3   Local Rules for General Play

A Local Rule is a modification of a Rule or an additional Rule that the Committee adopts for general play or a particular competition. The Committee is responsible for deciding whether to adopt any Local Rules and for making sure they are consistent with the principles found in Section 8. The Committee needs to make sure that any Local Rules are available for players to see, whether on the scorecard, a separate handout, a notice board or the course's website.

Local Rules that may be adopted for general play fall into the following general categories:

- Defining Course Boundaries and other Areas of the Course (Sections 8A-8D),

- Defining Special or Required Relief Procedures (Section 8E), and

- Defining Abnormal Course Conditions and Integral Objects (Section 8F).

The Committee should also take note of Section 8L – Unauthorized Local Rules.

A full listing of Model Local Rules can be found at the start of Section 8.

See Section 5C for other types of Local Rules that are more commonly adopted for competitions than for general play.

4   Additional Considerations for General Play

4A Pace of Play and Code of Conduct

To improve the enjoyment of players during general play there are many actions that a Committee can take to improve pace of play and to encourage a good standard of player conduct, such as:

- Reducing group sizes, increasing starting intervals, introducing starter's gaps.

- Considering fundamental changes to course set up such as widening fairways, reducing the thickness or length of rough, or reducing the speed of greens.

- Encouraging players to play from tees that suit their ability.
- Adopting a pace of play policy and a code of conduct.

The following sections give some of the considerations a Committee should take into account when adopting a pace of play policy or a code of conduct.

(1) Pace of Play Policy

- The nature of such a policy will often depend on the available resources of that course.
- For example, a course with limited staff might simply state that each group is expected to keep up with the group in front or that each group is expected to play within a certain amount of time, while another course may be able to have one or more people on the course to monitor the pace of play and, when necessary, speak to groups that are falling behind.
- The enforcement of such a policy is usually best handled through disciplinary measures. Such sanctions are separate from the Rules of Golf and it is a matter for the Committee to write and interpret any such sanctions.

(2) Code of Conduct Policy

- For general play, a Committee might post a notice in the clubhouse area stating what types of behaviour or attire are not acceptable at that course, including in certain areas.
- Enforcement of this policy is usually best handled through disciplinary measures. Such sanctions are separate from the Rules of Golf and it is a matter for the Committee to write and interpret any such sanctions.

4B Suspending Play

Each Committee should consider how it will suspend play if it is determined that weather conditions warrant. A suspension of play can be handled through a variety of methods, depending on the resources available to the course, such as signalling to players through an air horn or by personal notification of the players.

4C Providing Rules Support

Players may have questions on how to resolve Rules issues that have arisen during general play. Each course should identify a person or persons to handle such Rules questions. In many cases that person may be the professional or manager. If that person is unsure of the correct ruling, he or she may refer the question to the appropriate Rules organization for an answer.

Competitions

5 Before the Competition

The resources available to a Committee will differ depending on the course or the level of competition being run and so a Committee may not be able to implement all of the suggested practices. Where this is the case, the Committee will need to decide its priorities for each competition.

The period before the competition begins is arguably the most important in terms of preparation to ensure the smooth running of the competition. The Committee's duties during this period include:

5A Setting the Terms of the Competition

Terms of the Competition determine the structure of each competition including who may enter, how to enter, what the schedule and format of the competition will be and how ties will be decided. It is the responsibility of the Committee to:

- Set clear and concise terms for each competition.

- Make these terms available to players in advance of the competition.

- Interpret the terms should any questions arise.

Other than in exceptional circumstances, the Committee should avoid altering the Terms of the Competition once the competition has started.

It is the responsibility of each player to know and follow the Terms of the Competition.

Sample wording of Terms of the Competition can be found at USGA.org.

(1) Eligibility

The Committee may make Terms of the Competition that restrict who is eligible to play in the competition.

Gender Requirements

A competition may be limited to players of a specific gender.

Age Limits

A competition may be limited to players within a specific age range. If so, it is important to specify the date on which the players must be of age. Some examples are:

- For a junior competition where players must not be older than 18, the Terms of the Competition might state that a player must be 18 or younger on the first day of the year or another date such as the final scheduled day of the competition.

- For a senior competition where players must be 55 or older, the Terms of the Competition might state that a player must have reached his or her 55th birthday on or before the first day of the competition.

Amateur or Professional Status

A competition may be limited to just amateurs, just professionals or allow all players. When a competition is open to anyone, the Committee should ensure that amateurs properly identify themselves and waive their right to any prize money in advance of the competition.

Handicap Limits

The Committee may set restrictions and/or limits on the handicaps eligible for entry or use in a competition. These may include:

- Setting upper or lower limits on handicaps.

- In team formats, such as Foursomes or Four-Ball:

  » Limiting the maximum difference between partners' handicaps. The Committee may also choose to reduce the handicap for the player with the higher handicap to meet the requirement, or

  » Limiting the maximum total handicaps of partners. The Committee may also choose to reduce the handicap for one or both players to meet the requirement.

- For a competition that is played over multiple rounds during which a player's handicap may change, specifying whether each player will play the entire competition with the handicap as at the first day of the competition or if the player will use his or her revised handicap for each round.

Residence and Membership Status

The Committee may limit entry to players who reside in or were born in a specific county, state, country or other geographic area. It may also require that all players are members of a specific club, organization or golf union.

(2) Entry Requirements and Dates

The way to enter the competition and the starting and ending dates for entry should be specified.

Examples include:

- Method of entry, such as completing an online entry form, returning an entry form by mail or entering names on a sheet any time before the player's start time.

- How and when any entry fee is to be paid.

- When entries must be received. The Committee can stop accepting entries on a specific date or allow players to enter up to the day of the event.

- The procedure to be used in determining the field when the competition is oversubscribed, such as accepting entries in the order received, through a qualifier or based on lowest handicaps.

(3) Format, Including Handicap Allowance

The following points in relation to the format of the competition should be specified where required:

- Dates of play or, if it is a match play event over a long period of time, the final date by which each match must be completed.

- Form of play (for example, match play, stroke play or stroke play going into match play).

- Number and order of holes in a round.

- Number of rounds, including whether there will be a cut.

- If there is to be a cut, when it will be made, if ties for the final position will be broken and how many players will continue play in later rounds.

- Which teeing areas are to be used.

- Stroke index allocation, such as the order of holes at which handicap strokes are to be given or received.

- If there will be multiple flights or draws and how they will be organized, see Section 5F(1).

- What prizes will be awarded (including any eligibility restrictions). For competitions involving amateur golfers, the Committee should ensure that prizes for those amateurs are in line with those allowed under the Rules of Amateur Status and that amateurs waive in advance their right to cash prizes or prizes which may exceed the limits.

(4) Terms for Other Forms of Play

Alternative Scoring Methods

When the form of play is Stableford, Maximum Score or Par/Bogey, the Terms of the Competition may need to specify certain aspects in relation to how points will be scored, or the maximum number of strokes that a player can score on each hole.

Stableford

Stableford is a form of stroke play where points are awarded to a player for each hole by comparing the player's score to the fixed target score for the hole. The fixed target score is par unless the Committee sets a different fixed score (see Rule 21.1b).

If the Committee decides to set a different fixed target score, it may set it in the Terms of the Competition as bogey, birdie, or some other fixed score.

Maximum Score

When the form of play is Maximum Score, the Terms of the Competition should specify the maximum number of strokes a player can score on each hole (see Rule 21.2).

The maximum may be set in one of the following ways:

- Relative to par, such as two times par,
- A fixed number, such as 8, 9 or 10, or
- With reference to the player's handicap, for example net double bogey.

When considering what maximum to set for a Maximum Score competition, the Committee should consider the following:

- The maximum par for the holes being played. For example, for a par 3 course it may be appropriate to set the maximum score per hole to be a fixed score of 6; however if there are par 5's on a course then it would not be appropriate to have a fixed score as low as 6.

- The standard of the golfers taking part. For example, for a beginners' competition the maximum score should give the players a reasonable opportunity to complete the holes but be at a level to encourage players to pick up when they have had real difficulty on the hole.

- Whether scores are to be submitted for handicapping purposes. Where the Committee wants a competition to count for handicapping purposes, the maximum hole score should not be set lower than net double bogey.

Par/Bogey

When the form of play is Par/Bogey, the Terms of the Competition should specify the fixed score against which the player's score on a hole is compared to determine whether the player wins or loses a hole. For a Par competition, the fixed score would normally be par, and for a Bogey competition the fixed score would normally be bogey (one over par).

Other Forms of Play

There are many other forms of play such as Scrambles and Greensomes. See Section 9 and/or USGA.org for more information on these and other forms of play.

Team Competitions

When the form of play involves a team competition, the Committee should consider if additional Terms of the Competition are required. Examples include:

- Any restrictions on coaches or advice givers (see Model Local Rule Section 8H).

- In match play:

  » If tied matches will be acceptable or if they must be played until a winner is determined.

  » The number of points awarded for winning or tying a match.

  » If some matches are completed while others cannot be completed on the arranged day due to poor light or weather, the Terms of the Competition should clarify how the completed and incomplete matches will be treated. For example, the Committee could count completed matches to stand as played and incomplete matches to be treated as a tie or replayed on a later date. Or, that all matches are to be replayed, and each team is free to alter its original team.

  » If any remaining matches will be played to a conclusion once a team has won the match or competition.

- In stroke play:

  » The number of scores to count in each team's total score.

  » If the scores to be counted will be based on 18 holes or on a hole-by-hole basis.

- How a tie in the overall competition will be decided, for example by a play-off, a method of matching scores or considering discarded scores.

(5) When Scorecard Has Been Returned

In stroke play, Rule 3.3b holds players responsible for ensuring the accuracy of their hole scores and promptly returning the scorecard to the Committee at the completion of the round.

The Committee should tell players where the scorecards should be returned, have someone available to resolve any potential issues the players might have with the Rules and validate the scores.

When possible, a quiet, private area should be provided for players to use in checking the validity of the scores on their scorecards, speaking with a member of the Committee, if needed, and returning their scorecards.

Specify When Scorecard Is Considered Returned

The Committee should specify when the scorecard is considered returned. Options include:

- Defining the scoring area and allowing a player to make alterations on his or her scorecard up until he or she has left that scoring area. This would mean that, even if the player has handed the scorecard to a referee or recorder, changes could still be made while the player is in the area.

- Providing a box for the player to deposit the scorecard, in which case it is considered returned as soon as the player places it in the box. This approach might not give a player as much protection from returning an incorrect scorecard, but it may be the best method when limited resources are available or many players are finishing at the same time (for example, when there is a shotgun start).

Requesting Players to Provide Other Information on Scorecards

The Committee may request that players assist the Committee by completing scorecard related tasks that are the Committee's responsibility. The Committee must not apply a penalty to a player under the Rules of Golf if he or she fails to comply with these requests or makes a mistake in doing so, but the Committee may provide a disciplinary sanction for a player who fails repeatedly to comply with such a request. For example, the Committee may ask players to:

- Total the scores or, in a Four-Ball competition, determine the score that counts for the side.

- Enter the points scored for each hole on the scorecard in Stableford.

- Enter whether the hole was won, lost or tied in Par/Bogey.

- Enter specific details on the scorecard such as name, date and name of the competition.

Similarly, the Committee may request that players assist the Committee by entering their scores into a computer system at the end of the round, but a player should not be penalized under the Rules of Golf if he or she fails to comply with this request or makes a mistake in doing so. But the Committee may provide a disciplinary sanction, for example in a Code of Conduct, for a player who fails repeatedly to comply with such a request.

(6) How Ties Will Be Decided

In match play and stroke play, the Terms of the Competition can be used to alter the way in which ties are decided.

Match Play

If a match is tied after the final hole, the match is extended one hole at a time until there is a winner (see Rule 3.2a(4)), unless the Terms of the Competition state otherwise.

The Terms of the Competition should specify if the match may end in a tie or if the play-off method will differ from that specified in Rule 3.2a(4). Options include the following:

* The match ends in a tie,

* The match will be extended starting at a specific hole other than the first hole, or

* There will be a play-off over a fixed number of holes (for example, 9 or 18 holes).

In a handicap match, the stroke index allocation as set by the Committee should be used to determine where handicap strokes should be given or received in extra holes unless the Terms of the Competition state otherwise.

A tie in a match should not be decided by a stroke-play play-off.

Stroke Play

The Terms of the Competition should specify whether a competition may end in a tie, or if there will be a play-off or matching of scorecards to determine the winner and other finishing positions.

A tie in stroke play should not be decided by a match.

Play-off in Stroke Play

If there is to be a play-off in stroke play, the Terms of the Competition should set the following:

* When the play-off will be held, for example if it will start at a specific time, as soon as possible after the last group finishes or on a later date.

* Which holes will be used for the play-off.

* The number of holes over which the play-off will be played, for example, if it will be a hole-by-hole play-off or over a longer period such as 2, 4 or 18 holes, and what to do if it there is still a tie after that.

* In the regular form of stroke play, if a play-off for a handicap competition is over fewer than 18 holes, the number of holes played should be used to determine the number of strokes to be deducted. For example, if a play-off is over one hole, one-eighteenth of the handicaps should be deducted from the scores for the play-off hole. Handicap stroke fractions should be applied in accordance with the rules or recommendations contained within the Handicap System operating in the local jurisdiction.

- For play-offs for net competitions where the stroke index allocation is used, such as Four-Ball, Par/Bogey or Stableford competitions, handicap strokes should be applied during the play-off holes as they were assigned for the competition, using the stroke index allocation.

- Players are only required to return a scorecard for the play-off if the Committee issues them to the players.

Matching Scorecards (Also Known as a Scorecard Count-Back)

If a play-off is not feasible or desired, the Terms of the Competition may specify that any ties will be decided by matching scorecards. Even when the winner of a competition is to be decided by a play-off, other positions in the competition may be decided by matching scorecards. The method of matching scorecards should also provide for what will happen if this procedure does not produce a winner.

One method of matching scorecards is to determine the winner based on the best score for the last round. If the tying players have the same score for the last round or if the competition consisted of a single round, determine the winner based on the score for the last nine holes, last six holes, last three holes and finally the 18th hole. If there is still a tie, then the last six holes, three holes and final hole of the first nine holes will be considered in turn. If the round is less than 18 holes, the number of holes used in matching scores may be adjusted.

If this process does not result in a winner, the Committee could consider the competition a tie, or alternatively could decide the winner by chance (such as tossing a coin).

Matching scorecards is also known as a card count-back or a scorecard play-off.

Additional Considerations:

- If this method is used in a competition with a multiple tee start, it is recommended that the "last nine holes, last six holes, etc." are holes 10-18, 13-18, etc.

- For net competitions where the stroke index allocation as set by the Committee is not used, such as individual stroke play, if the last nine, last six, last three holes scenario is used, one-half, one-third, one-sixth, etc. of the handicaps should be deducted from the score for those holes. Handicap stroke fractions should be applied in accordance with the rules or recommendations contained within the Handicap System operating in the local jurisdiction.

- In net competitions where the stroke index allocation as set by the Committee is used, such as Four-Ball stroke play, Par/Bogey or Stableford competitions, handicap strokes should be applied consistently with how they were applied for the competition.

(7) When the Result of the Competition Is Final

It is important for the Committee to clarify in the Terms of the Competition when and how the result of the competition is final as this will affect how the Committee will resolve any Rules issues that occur after play is complete in both match play and stroke play (see Rule 20).

Match Play

Examples of when the Terms of the Competition may state that the result of a match is final include:

- When the result is recorded on an official scoreboard or other identified place, or

- When the result is reported to a person identified by the Committee.

When a match is determined to be final once the result is recorded on an official scoreboard, the Committee may take responsibility for recording the winner's name on the scoreboard or it may pass that responsibility to the players. In some cases the official scoreboard will be a prominent structure and in other cases it might be a sheet of paper in the golf shop or locker room.

In cases where a referee has been assigned by the Committee to accompany a match, any announcement of the result of the match by the referee on the final putting green is not the official announcement unless it was stated as such in the Terms of the Competition.

Stroke Play

Examples of when the Terms of the Competition may state the competition to be closed in stroke play include:

- All results have been posted on the scoreboard or noticeboard,

- The winners have been announced at a prize giving, or

- The trophy has been awarded.

In stroke-play qualifying followed by match play, Rule 20.2e(2) stipulates that the stroke-play portion of the competition is closed when the player has teed off to start his or her first match.

(8) Changing Terms of the Competition After Competition Has Started

The Terms of the Competition set out the structure of the competition and once a competition has started, the terms may be altered only in very exceptional circumstances.

An example of a situation where the Terms of the Competition should not be altered:

- Since players begin a round with the expectation that a certain number of holes will be played and may base their play on that, the number of holes to be played in a round should not be changed once that round has started. For example, if bad weather results in play being suspended after all the players have completed 9 holes of an 18-hole round, the Committee should not announce the results based on only 9 holes.

Examples of situations where there are exceptional circumstances and the Terms of the Competition may be altered:

- If circumstances such as bad weather affect the number of rounds that can be played in the time available, the number of rounds to be played, or number of holes in any rounds not yet started, may be altered to accommodate the circumstances. Similarly, if those circumstances mean the planned format cannot be accommodated in the time available, the format of the competition may be changed.

- The method for deciding ties should not be altered unless there are exceptional circumstances. For example, if the method of deciding a tie for a stroke-play competition was stated to be a hole-by-hole play-off, but bad weather meant such a play-off was not possible, the Committee can change the method of deciding the tie to a scorecard count-back.

(9) Anti-Doping

The Terms of the Competition may require players to comply with an anti-doping policy. It is a matter for the Committee to write and interpret its own anti-doping policy, although guidance in developing such a policy can usually be provided by the national governing body.

5B Marking the Course

When preparing for a competition, the Committee should make sure that the course is properly marked and refresh any markings that might be used for general play, or change them if necessary. While there typically is no one "right" way to mark a course, failing to mark it properly or at all can lead to situations where a player is unable to proceed under the Rules or the Committee will be forced to make decisions while play is ongoing that might result in players being treated differently.

Section 2 provides detailed guidance and recommendations on how to mark the course for general play, but it also applies equally to competitions and should be referenced by the Committee when preparing for competitions.

Where changes are made to the course's marking for a competition, the Committee should ensure these are clearly communicated to any players who regularly play the course so that they are not confused and inadvertently proceed incorrectly.

In addition to the information in Section 2, the Committee may wish to consider the following items:

(1) Out of Bounds

The Committee is responsible for ensuring that all boundaries are marked properly. It is a good practice to paint a small white circle around the base of any white stake or other boundary object that could get moved during play so that it can be returned to its original location. If lines or paint dots are being used to mark a boundary, they should be refreshed so that they can easily be seen. The Local Rules should clarify any boundaries that are defined in any manner other than stakes or fences (see Model Local Rule A-1).

(2) Penalty Areas

Before a competition, the Committee may wish to reassess the marking of some or all penalty areas.

- Penalty areas that contain bodies of water should not be made a part of the general area, but their edges may be adjusted.

- Other penalty areas may be removed or added, or their edges altered to change the difficulty of a hole, such as where it is considered appropriate to provide a more severe penalty for an errant shot. For example, the Committee may decide to mark areas of dense trees and bushes as penalty areas for general play, but not for competitions. Care should be taken in doing this so that it is clearly communicated to any players who regularly play the course so that they are not confused and proceed incorrectly.

- When penalty areas are added or removed, the Committee should consult the rules or recommendations contained within the Handicap System operating in the local jurisdiction to determine if the change will have an impact on the issued Course Rating.

- The colour of some penalty areas may be changed from red to yellow or the reverse. For example, for certain competitions it may be desirable for a penalty area close to a putting green to be marked yellow where the Committee does not want to allow the option of dropping on the putting green side of the penalty area when the ball has fallen back into it. In some cases, it may also make sense to provide a dropping zone as an additional option, for example, for an island green where players have a long carry over water.

- For general play, the Committee may have used a minimal number of stakes to mark penalty areas or they may have been removed, resulting in portions of some penalty areas being outside the marked area. For competitions, all stakes should be inspected and supplemented if necessary to ensure that the penalty areas are properly marked for the competition.

- When possible, it is good practice to paint red or yellow lines around penalty areas rather than just relying on stakes. A line will ensure the proper areas are included or excluded, the edge will not be altered by the removal of a stake and a player will be able easily to determine where to take relief. Typically, when a line has been painted, fewer stakes are required.

(3) Bunkers

For most courses, the Committee should not need to do anything special to prepare bunkers for the competition. They should be freshly raked on the morning of the competition and the rakes placed where the Committee prefers (see Section 2D). If the edge of a bunker is difficult to determine, the Committee should consider whether it could be more clearly defined (either through maintenance practices, marking or a Local Rule) to avoid confusion among players and referees.

(4) Abnormal Course Conditions and Integral Objects

The Committee should review the entire course to ensure that any areas that should be marked as ground under repair are properly marked. It should also clarify the status of any obstructions or integral objects using Local Rules (see Model Local Rule F-1).

Ideally a Committee should mark any areas of ground under repair before the start of a competition. But a Committee can define an area to be ground under repair during the round in match play or stroke play if it is warranted.

Where relief is given from such an unmarked area during the round, the Committee should mark the area as ground under repair as soon as possible to ensure that all other players in the field are aware of the revised status of the area.

(5) No Play Zones

If there are no play zones on the course, the Committee should make sure they are properly identified. The Committee may also consider putting notices in these areas to ensure that players are fully aware that they are not permitted to play from them.

(6) Temporary Obstructions

Temporary structures such as tents or grandstands may be constructed for some competitions. The status of these structures will need to be clarified in the Local Rules as either Immovable Obstructions or Temporary Immovable Obstructions (TIOs). If they are to be treated as TIOs, the Local Rule regarding Temporary Immovable Obstructions should be used (see Model Local Rule F-23). This Local Rule gives a player additional relief if there is interference on the line of sight so that he or she will not be required to play around or over the obstruction.

5C Local Rules (Including Modified Rules of Golf for Players with Disabilities)

The Committee is responsible for deciding whether to adopt any Local Rules and for making sure they are consistent with the principles found in Section 8. A Local Rule is a modification of a Rule or an additional Rule that the Committee adopts for general play or a particular competition. The Committee needs to make sure that any Local Rules are available for players to see, whether on the scorecard, a separate handout, a notice board or the course's website.

When considering adopting a Local Rule, the Committee should keep in mind the following:

- Local Rules have the same status as a Rule of Golf for that competition or course, and

- The use of Local Rules should be limited as much as possible and be used only to deal with the types of situations and policies covered in Section 8

A full list of authorized of Model Local Rules can be found at the start of Section 8.

Local Rules that may be adopted for competitions fall into the following general categories:

- Defining Course Boundaries and other Areas of the Course (Sections 8A-8D),

- Defining Special Relief Procedures (Section 8E),

- Defining Abnormal Course Conditions and Integral Objects (Section 8F)

- Use of Specific Equipment (Section 8G),

- Who May Give Advice to Players (Section 8H),

- When and Where Players May Practise (Section 8I),

- Procedures for Suspension of Play (Section 8J), and

- Pace of Play Policies (Section 8K).

The Committee should also take note of Section 8L – Unauthorized Local Rules.

Modified Rules of Golf for Players with Disabilities

A set of Modified Rules is available for players with disabilities. The Modified Rules only apply if adopted by the Committee and they do not automatically apply to every competition involving players with disabilities.

It is up to each Committee to decide whether to adopt any of the Modified Rules for players with disabilities who are taking part in a competition.

The goal of the Modified Rules is to allow a player with a disability to play fairly with players who have no disabilities, the same disability or different types of disabilities.

See the Modified Rules for players with disabilities for further information and guidance.

5D Defining Practice Areas

Many courses have specific practice areas, such as a practice range and practice greens for putting, bunker play and chipping. Players are permitted to practise in these areas, whether they are inside or outside the boundaries of the course. It is recommended that practice areas that are located on the course be specified in the Local Rules to clarify whether players may practise on those areas before and after their rounds. The Committee may need to define the edges of these areas to limit where players may practise.

The Committee may also change the permissions in relation to when and where practice is allowed as follows:

- A Local Rule may allow practice on limited and defined parts of the course, for example where there is no permanent practice ground. But, where this applies, it is recommended that players not be allowed to practise on any putting greens or from any bunkers on the course.

- A Local Rule may allow practice on the course in general, for example:

  » If the competition starts late in the day and the Committee does not want to restrict players from playing the course earlier in the day, or

>> If there has been a suspension of play and it would be more efficient to allow players to hit a few shots from somewhere on the course as opposed to bringing them back to the practice range.

• Rule 5.2 covers when practice is allowed or prohibited before or between rounds in a competition, but the Committee may adopt a Local Rule to modify those provisions (see Model Local Rule I-1).

• Rule 5.5 gives the Committee the option to adopt a Local Rule to prohibit practice on or around the putting green of the hole just completed (see Model Local Rule I-2).

5E Teeing Areas and Hole Locations

(1) Selecting Teeing Areas

In selecting which teeing areas to use for a competition, the Committee should seek to balance the difficulty of the course with the strength of the field. For example, it would not be advisable and could have a significant effect on pace of play to choose a teeing area that required a forced carry that many of the players in the field are unlikely to be able to make with anything other than their very best stroke.

The Committee may decide to use different teeing areas for competitions than those used for general play. If this is done, the Committee should consult the rules or recommendations contained within the Handicap System operating in the local jurisdiction for guidance on how the issued Course Rating might be impacted. Otherwise, the scores may not be acceptable for submission for handicapping purposes.

The locations of the teeing areas may be changed between rounds, including when more than one round is played on the same day.

It is a good practice to place a small mark, such as a paint dot, behind or under the tee-markers to ensure that if they get moved they can be returned to their original position. When there are multiple rounds, a different number of dots can be used for each round.

If a competition is being played on a course where there are no signs identifying the holes, or where the Committee has decided to play the course in a different order, signs should be installed to identify the holes clearly.

(2) Selecting Hole Locations

The locations of the holes on the putting greens can have a considerable effect on scoring and the pace of play during competitions. Many factors go into the selection of hole locations, with emphasis on the following points:

- In selecting the locations, the ability of the players should be considered so that the locations selected are not so difficult as to slow down play significantly or so easy as not to challenge better players.

- The speed of the greens is a significant factor in choosing the location of the hole. While a hole location may work well for a slower green, it may prove to be too severe when the speed of the greens is increased.

- The Committee should avoid placing a hole on a slope where the ball will not come to rest. When the contours of the green allow, holes should be placed where there is an area of two to three feet around the hole that is relatively level so that putts struck at the proper speed will stop around the hole.

Some additional considerations include:

- Setting holes where there is enough putting green surface between the hole and the front and sides of the putting green to accommodate the approach on that particular hole. For example, placing the hole immediately behind a large bunker when a long approach is required by the majority of the field is usually not recommended.

- Balancing hole locations for the entire course with respect to left, right, centre, front and back locations.

5F Draw, Groups and Starting Times

(1) The Draw

In a match-play competition the draw is used to establish the overall order of matches and which players will make up each first-round match. The draw may be done in a number of ways including:

- Randomly – Players are picked at random and placed in the draw as chosen.

- Qualifying Scores – Players could play one or more qualifying rounds. The players are then placed into the draw based on their scores.

- Handicap – Players could be placed in the draw by handicap so that the player with the lowest handicap plays the one with the highest in the first round, the second lowest against the second highest, and so on.

- Seeding – Certain players, such as a defending champion, could be seeded into the draw in specific locations, while other players are placed either randomly or through qualifying scores.

The draw should be arranged so that the two highest seeded players are on opposite sides of the draw and so on down the line as shown in the following table.

Before the Competition

UPPER HALF	LOWER HALF	UPPER HALF	LOWER HALF
64 QUALIFIERS		**32 QUALIFIERS**	
1 vs. 64	2 vs. 63	1 vs. 32	2 vs. 31
32 vs. 33	31 vs. 34	16 vs. 17	15 vs. 18
16 vs. 49	15 vs. 50	8 vs. 25	7 vs. 26
17 vs. 48	18 vs. 47	9 vs. 24	10 vs. 23
8 vs. 57	7 vs. 58	4 vs. 29	3 vs. 30
25 vs. 40	26 vs. 39	13 vs. 20	14 vs. 19
9 vs. 56	10 vs. 55	5 vs. 28	6 vs. 27
24 vs. 41	23 vs. 42	12 vs. 21	11 vs. 22
4 vs. 61	3 vs. 62	**16 QUALIFIERS**	
29 vs. 36	30 vs. 35	1 vs. 16	2 vs. 15
13 vs. 52	14 vs. 51	8 vs. 9	7 vs. 10
20 vs. 45	19 vs. 46	4 vs. 13	3 vs. 14
5 vs. 60	6 vs. 59	5 vs. 12	6 vs. 11
28 vs. 37	27 vs. 38	**8 QUALIFIERS**	
12 vs. 53	11 vs. 54	1 vs. 8	2 vs. 7
21 vs. 44	22 vs. 43	4 vs. 5	3 vs. 6

For purposes of determining places in the draw, ties in qualifying rounds other than those for the last qualifying place can be decided by:

- The order in which scores are returned, with the first score to be returned receiving the lowest available number and so forth,
- A scorecard play-off, or
- A random draw among the players who are tied at a specific score.

When there is a tie for the final place in the draw, the Committee may choose to have a play-off or add another round of matches to reduce the field to an even number of players. This should be specified in the Terms of the Competition.

In some events, the Committee may choose to seed the defending champion. When this is done, it is typical to seed the champion as either the first or second seed. The Committee should also decide if it will permit the champion to play in the qualifying event and, if so, he or she forfeits the seeding.

Multiple Draws (also known as Flights or Divisions)

While many competitions have all players competing against all the other players, there are times when a Committee can choose to divide the competition into multiple draws (sometimes called flights or divisions). This may be in order to have players of similar abilities compete against each other or in order to have multiple winners.

The makeup of these draws may be determined by handicap, through qualifying or by another method determined by the Committee. The Committee should set out how the draws will be set up in the Terms of the Competition.

While the draws may be set by handicap, there is no requirement that the resulting play within the draw be a handicap competition since all the players should be of relatively equal ability.

In a match-play competition, it is a good idea to make the size of the draws so that it will not be necessary to give players byes and, ideally, a size that means all players will play the same number of matches in a knock-out format, such as 8, 16, 32, 64 or 128. If there are not enough players to fill the final draw, players should be given byes into the second round as needed. There is no requirement that all the draws have the same number of players. For example, the first or championship draw might have 32 players while the other draws might have 16.

(2) Starting Times and Playing Groups

The Committee can set the starting times and groups or allow the players to set their own.

When the Committee allows players to set their own starting time, it has the same status as a starting time set by the Committee (see Rule 5.3a).

There are many considerations in determining the number of players in a group and the interval between groups. When setting starting times and groups, pace of play is an important consideration as well as the amount of time available for play. Groups of two will play faster than groups of three or four. Starting intervals can be closer together for smaller groups. When the Committee chooses to start players on multiple holes (such as holes 1 and 10), it is important to ensure that players will not have an excessive wait if they arrive at the other starting tee before the final group has started.

When a match-play competition will be played over an extended period and players in a match are allowed to agree on when to play during that period, the Committee should:

• Set a date and time by which each match must be completed.

• Specify how the result of the match will be decided should the players fail to complete the match by the specified date, such as disqualifying both players or putting the player named first or second in the draw into the next round.

413

In match play, the Committee sets the draw showing who will play in each match or otherwise specifies how matches are to be determined. When it is possible it is best for each match to have its own starting time, but there may be times when two matches will be started together.

(3) Markers

In stroke play, a player or side always needs to have someone other than the player or a member of the side to mark the scorecard. The Committee may specify or restrict who may act as the marker for each player by specifying that the marker must be a player in the same competition and group, a player with a handicap, or in some other way.

In a format where two or more partners compete together as a side (for example, in a Foursomes or Four-Ball competition), they are not permitted to act as the side's marker. Where the number of sides for a partner format is not even, the Committee may need to find a marker for a side playing on its own or choose to have a group containing three sides.

(4) Starting Areas

The Committee may define a specific area at or near the first teeing area where players must be present and ready to play at the starting time (see Rule 5.3a).

This may be defined by painted lines on the ground, by ropes or in some other way.

5G Pace of Play Policy

The Committee can set its own Pace of Play Policy adopted as a Local Rule (see Rule 5.6b). In practice the nature of such a Policy will be dependent on the number of Committee members available to implement it (see Section 8K).

Pace of Play Policies may contain:

- A maximum time to complete a round, a hole or series of holes or a stroke.
- A definition of when the first group is out of position and when each other group is out of position in relation to the group playing ahead of it.
- When and how a group or individual players may be monitored or timed.
- If and when players may be warned that they are being timed or have had a bad time.
- The penalty structure for breaches of the Policy.

The Committee is responsible for making sure that a competition is played at a prompt pace of play. What is considered a prompt pace can be different based on the course, size of the entry and number of players in each group. To do this:

• The Committee should adopt a Local Rule setting a Pace of Play Policy (see Rule 5.6b).

• Such a Policy should at least set a maximum time for completing the round or parts of the round.

• The Policy should stipulate any penalties for a player's failure to comply with the Policy.

• The Committee should also be aware of other actions that they can take to have a positive impact on pace of play. These include:

  » Management practices such as reducing group sizes, increasing starting intervals and introducing starter's gaps.

  » Considering fundamental changes to course set up such as widening fairways, reducing the thickness or length of rough, or reducing the speed of greens. When changes such as these are made to the course, the Committee should consult the rules or recommendations contained within the Handicap System operating in the local jurisdiction to assess the impact on the issued Course Rating and follow the procedures to make any necessary adjustments.

5H Code of Conduct Policy

The Committee may set its own standards of player conduct in a Code of Conduct adopted as a Local Rule (see Rule 1.2b). If the Committee does not set a Code of Conduct, it is restricted in penalizing players for inappropriate conduct to using Rule 1.2a. The only penalty available for an act that is contrary to the spirit of the game under that Rule is disqualification (see Section 5H(4) for more information).

(1) Setting a Code of Conduct

In setting a Code of Conduct, the Committee should consider the following:

• When setting limits or prohibiting a player's actions through a Code of Conduct, the Committee should consider the different cultures of the players. For example, something that may be considered inappropriate behaviour in one culture may be acceptable under another.

• The penalty structure that will apply for a breach of the Code (see Section 5H(2) for an example).

415

- Who will have the authority to decide penalties and sanctions. For example, it could be the case that only certain Committee members have the authority to apply such penalties or a minimum number of Committee members need to be involved in making such a decision or any member of the Committee has authority to make such a decision.

- Whether there will be an appeals process.

The Committee may include the following within a Code of Conduct:

- A prohibition on players entering all or specified no play zones.

- Specific details of unacceptable behaviour that a player may be penalized for during a round, for example:

  » Failure to care for the course, for example not raking bunkers or not replacing or filling divots.

  » Unacceptable language.

  » Abuse of clubs or the course.

  » Being disrespectful of other players, referees or spectators.

- A dress code.

The Committee may provide in the Code of Conduct that a warning will be given for the first breach of the Code and not a penalty, unless the Committee considers the breach to be sufficiently serious.

A Committee needs to determine whether the Code of Conduct applies to a player's caddie, and whether the player can be penalized under the Code for actions of his or her caddie during the round.

It would not be appropriate to penalize a player under a Code of Conduct for a breach of a spectator code by the player's family or supporters. For example, in a junior competition where family members are not allowed to walk on the fairway, or within a specified distance of the competitors, the player should not be penalized for any breach by a spectator.

(2) Determining Penalties for Breach of Code

When determining the sanctions and penalty structure that will apply, the Committee should consider the following:

- If there will be a warning system before any penalty or other sanction is imposed.

- Whether the sanctions will be of a disciplinary nature or involve penalties under the Rules.

- Whether the penalty for each breach will be set as one penalty stroke, the general penalty, or if penalties will escalate. The Committee should not use any other types of penalties that would apply to a player's score.

- If the Code will allow for disqualification for serious misconduct in failing to meet the Code's standards.

- Whether a penalty will automatically apply whenever a player breaches one of its standards or if such a penalty will be left to the Committee's discretion.

- If different penalties will apply for breaching different aspects of the Code.

- Disciplinary sanctions that a Committee may impose including refusing to allow the player to enter one or more future competitions run by the Committee or requiring the player to play at a particular time of day. Such sanctions are separate from the Rules of Golf and it is a matter for the Committee to write and interpret any such sanctions.

(3) Sample Penalty Structure for a Code of Conduct

The following model penalty structures give an example of how the Committee may choose to penalize breaches of a Code of Conduct in the Local Rule.

The Committee may decide to implement such a penalty structure without a warning or sanction for a first breach, or it may provide different penalties for each item within the Code of Conduct. For example, certain breaches may result in a one-stroke penalty, with other breaches resulting in the general penalty.

Model Penalty Structure

- First breach of the Code of Conduct – warning or Committee sanction

- Second breach – one-stroke penalty

- Third breach – general penalty

- Fourth breach or any serious misconduct – disqualification.

(4) Spirit of the Game and Serious Misconduct

Under Rule 1.2a, a Committee may disqualify a player for serious misconduct for acting contrary to the spirit of the game. This applies whether or not there is a Code of Conduct in place for a competition.

When deciding whether a player is guilty of serious misconduct, the Committee should consider whether the player's action was intentional and whether the act was significant enough to warrant disqualification without first giving a warning and/or applying other penalties when a Code of Conduct is in place.

Examples of actions that could warrant disqualification under Rule 1.2a can be found in Interpretation 1.2a/1.

5I Information for Players and Referees

(1) Local Rules

The Committee should ensure that any Local Rules are posted for players to see, whether on a separate handout on the first tee (sometimes referred to as a "Notice to Players"), the scorecard, a notice board or the course website.

Many organizations that run multiple competitions create a document which contains all the Local Rules they commonly use in all of their competitions. Historically this document has been printed on card stock and is known as a "Hard Card".

If players are required to play balls on the Conforming Ball List (see Model Local Rule G-3) or use clubs on the List of Conforming Driver Heads (see Model Local Rule G-1) or that meet the groove and punch mark specifications (see Model Local Rule G-2), the Committee should consider making the lists available for players to view or provide access to the applicable online databases.

(2) Grouping or Draw Sheets

Sheets that provide the groupings for the round along with their starting times should be produced and posted in locations where players can check them. While players are frequently sent their pairings electronically or can check them on a website, they should also be available at the course so that players can reconfirm their starting time.

(3) Hole Location Sheets

The Committee may wish to provide players with a sheet that shows them the position of the holes on the putting greens. These may be circles with the distance from the front of the green and the nearest side, a piece of paper with just the numbers or a more detailed set of drawings of the green and its surrounds with the location indicated.

(4) Scorecards Including Handicap Stroke Index Allocations

The Committee is responsible for publishing on the scorecard or somewhere else that is visible (for example, near the first tee) the order of holes at which handicap strokes are to be given or received. This allocation will be used for handicap matches and in some forms of net-score stroke play such as Four-Ball, Stableford, Maximum Score (when the maximum score is linked to the player's net score) and Par/Bogey competitions. For guidance on how to determine the order, consult the rules or recommendations contained within the Handicap System operating in the local jurisdiction.

Match Play – In a handicap match, the Committee should clarify the following in the Terms of the Competition:

- If the full difference between handicaps or a percentage of the difference will apply.

- The stroke index allocation to be used to identify the order of holes where players will give or receive handicap strokes.

Where the Committee has authorized a match to begin at a hole other than the 1st, the Committee may alter the stroke index allocation table for such matches.

Stroke Play – In a net-score competition, the Committee should determine the handicap allowances in accordance with the rules or recommendations contained within the Handicap System operating in the local jurisdiction. For example, if full handicap, or a percentage of the handicap, will be applied.

(5) Pace of Play and Code of Conduct Policies

Copies of the Pace of Play and Code of Conduct policies should be available to players before the competition begins. When players are unfamiliar with these policies, the Committee may wish to go over them with the players in advance of the competition.

Referees and others who will be enforcing these policies should be trained and provided with any other additional materials, such as timing sheets or scripts with the specific language they should use to inform players of warnings or possible breaches.

(6) Evacuation Plan

Each Committee should consider how to evacuate players in case of severe weather or another emergency. If it is felt necessary, an evacuation plan may be created and provided to the players. Additional information can be found in Model Local Rule J-1.

6 During the Competition

Once the competition has started, the Committee is responsible for ensuring that players have the information needed to play under the Rules and to assist them in applying the Rules.

6A Starting

Before starting the round, players should be provided with all the information they need to be able to play the course under the Rules.

In stroke play, each player should be given a scorecard and, in net competitions such as Stableford, Maximum Score or Four-Ball, this should include the handicap stroke index allocation as set by the Committee.

When the Committee has prepared additional documents, it should make them available to players before the round, and if possible before players arrive at the first tee so that they have a reasonable amount of time to read them. These could include:

- Local Rules.
- Pace of Play Policy.
- Code of Conduct.
- Evacuation Plan.

Depending on the resources available to them, the Committee may choose to make the documents available in a single location for players to read, for example on a notice board or website. Otherwise they may be provided as hand-outs to players before they start their round.

When resources allow, the Committee should have a starter at the starting tee to ensure the players have all the information they require and that they start on time.

When the time comes for starting the group, the starter should start the first player at the time assigned. If this is not possible due to the location of the group in front (such as when they are delayed by a ball search), the actual time of starting should be noted so that the Committee can use that information when applying a pace of play policy.

The Committee should adopt a consistent method for handling situations when players may be late in arriving at their first tee. This may include having Committee members or others attempt to locate the missing players or having a countdown in front of other players who are present so that it is clear to all when the player is late. It is good practice to have a clock set to the official time close to the tee and for all officials to set their watches to the same time.

6B The Course

(1) Course Maintenance During Round

While it is preferable to have all maintenance on the course completed before the first group reaches each hole to make sure that all players play the course in the same condition, this is sometimes not possible. Where course maintenance, such as cutting of putting greens, fairways or rough, or the raking of bunkers, takes place during a round, the results of the competition stand as played.

While the Committee should attempt to mark all areas that warrant being marked as ground under repair before the competition begins, there will be times when areas are not noticed until play has begun. There will also be times when weather, vehicles, players or spectators may cause additional damage to the course. In these cases, the Committee may decide to mark the areas as ground under repair. The decision to mark an area should be made regardless of whether a player has already played from that area.

(2) Setting Hole Locations and Teeing Areas

In a stroke-play competition, all players should play the course with the tee-markers and holes positioned in the same places. The Committee should avoid moving any tee-markers or holes after groups have played a hole, but there may be situations where this cannot be avoided or where they are moved by someone else in error.

Teeing Area Becomes Unusable After Start of Round

If a teeing area becomes covered in temporary water or for some other reason is not usable after the round has started, the Committee may suspend play or relocate the teeing area if this can be done without giving any player a significant advantage or disadvantage.

Tee-Markers or Hole Moved

If tee-markers or the hole are moved by a member of the course staff, or if tee-markers are moved by a player or anyone else, the Committee should determine if any players have been significantly advantaged or disadvantaged. If so, the round should generally be declared null and void. If the course has not been altered significantly and no player has been given a significant advantage or disadvantage, the Committee may choose to let the round stand.

Moving the Position of the Hole Due to Severity of Position

In stroke play, if it becomes apparent during a round that a hole is positioned such that the ball will not stop near the hole due to the severity of the slope, which has resulted in several players taking an excessive number of putts, the Committee has several options available.

The Committee should consider all factors, including how severe the position is, how many players have completed play of the hole and where the hole is in the round, and take the course of action that it considers to be the fairest to all the players. For example:

- Have play continue with the hole position unchanged on the basis that the conditions are the same for all players in the competition.

- Keep the hole in the same position but take some action to improve the situation such as watering the putting green between groups.

- Declare the round null and void and have all players start the round again with the hole repositioned.

- Suspend play, reposition the hole and have the players who played the hole return at the conclusion of their rounds to replay the hole. The score for the hole for these players is the score achieved after the hole repositioned.

- Have all players disregard their score for the hole in question and play an additional hole (whether on the competition course or elsewhere) for their score for the hole.

The last two options should be taken only in extreme circumstances because they alter the round for some or all players.

In match play, the Committee may move the hole between matches.

Relocating Hole After Ball Already Positioned Nearby on Putting Green

If a ball is on the putting green when the hole has been damaged, the Committee should attempt to repair the hole so that it conforms with the definition of "hole". If this is not possible the players may complete the hole with the hole in its damaged state.

It is not desirable to relocate the hole before all players in the group have completed play of the hole. However, the Committee may relocate the hole in a nearby similar position if doing so is necessary to ensure the proper playing of the game. If this is done before the players in the group have completed the hole, the Committee should require any player whose ball is on the putting green to reposition his or her ball to a position that is comparable to that which the previous stroke had originally given the player. For a ball that lies off the putting green, the Committee should require that ball to be played as it lies.

6C Providing Rules Assistance to Players

A Committee may appoint referees to assist with the administration of a competition. A referee is an official named by the Committee to decide questions of fact and apply the Rules.

(1) Referees in Match Play

In match play, a referee's duties and authority depend on his or her assigned role:

- **When Assigned to One Match for Entire Round.** As the referee is with the match throughout the round, he or she is responsible for acting on any breach of the Rules that he or she sees or is told about (see Rule 20-1b(1) and the definition of "referee").

- **When Assigned to Multiple Matches or to Certain Holes or Sections of the Course.** As the referee is not assigned to accompany the match throughout the round, he or she should avoid becoming involved in a match unless:

  » A player in a match asks for help with the Rules or requests a ruling (see Rule 20.1b(2)). When making a ruling at the request of a player, the referee should always confirm that the request for the ruling was made in time (see Rules 20.1b(2) and 20.1b(3)).

  » A player or players in a match may be in breach of Rule 1.2b (Code of Conduct), Rule 1.3b(1) (Two or More Players Deliberately Agreeing to Ignore any Rule or Penalty they Know Applies), Rule 5.6a (Unreasonable Delay of Play) or Rule 5.6b (Prompt Pace of Play).

  » A player arrives late to his or her first tee (see Rule 5.3).

  » A player's search for a ball reaches three minutes (see Rule 5.6a and definition of "lost").

(2) Referees in Stroke Play

In stroke play:

- A referee is responsible for acting on any breach of the Rules that he or she sees or is told about.

- This applies whether the referee is assigned to one group for the entire round or to monitor multiple groups or certain holes or parts of the course.

(3) Limiting Role of Committee Members and Referees

The Committee is the person or group in charge of the competition or the course, but within that Committee:

- The role of some members may be limited.

- Some decisions may require the agreement of specific members.

- Some responsibilities may be delegated to people outside the Committee.

423

Examples include:

- Specifying that only certain members of the Committee can enforce a Pace of Play Policy by monitoring and timing players or groups, and by deciding when to give warnings or penalties.

- Stating that a minimum of three members of the Committee is required to decide that a player should be disqualified for a serious breach of misconduct under Rule 1.2.

- Giving authority to the professional, manager or other designated person to make rulings on behalf of the Committee.

- Authorizing the head of the maintenance staff to suspend play on behalf of the Committee.

- Preventing a member of the Committee who is competing in a competition from making the decision to suspend play during that competition.

- Limiting which referees have the authority to define an unmarked area to be ground under repair during a competition.

The Committee may limit a referee's duties in stroke play or match play (such as when it believes this will help make rulings consistent for all of the players) by identifying items that may be handled only by the Committee or by a particular set of referees.

Examples of such items are:

- Declaring a part of the course to be ground under repair.

- Enforcing a Pace of Play Policy by monitoring and timing players or groups, and deciding when to give warnings or penalties.

- Disqualifying players for serious misconduct under Rule 1.2.

(4) Referee Authorizes Player to Breach a Rule

A referee's decision is final and therefore if a referee authorizes a player to breach a Rule in error, the player will not be penalized. But see Rule 20.2d and Section 6C(10) or 6C(11) for situations where the error can be corrected.

(5) Referee Warns Player About to Breach Rule

While a referee is not obliged to warn a player who is about to breach a Rule, it is strongly recommended that a referee should do so whenever possible in order to prevent a player from getting a penalty. A referee who acts in accordance with the recommendation by volunteering information on the Rules in order to prevent breaches of the Rules should do so uniformly to all players.

But, in match play where the referee has not been assigned to one match for the entire round, he or she has no authority to intervene. The referee should not warn the player unless asked, and if the player does breach the Rule, the referee should not apply the penalty without the opponent requesting a ruling.

(6) Disagreement with Referee's Decision

If a player disagrees with a referee's decision in match play or stroke play, the player is generally not entitled to a second opinion, whether from another referee or the Committee (see Rule 20.2a), but the referee whose decision is questioned may agree to obtain a second opinion.

The Committee can adopt a policy of always allowing all players a second opinion where they disagree with a referee's decision.

(7) How to Resolve Questions of Fact

Resolving questions of fact is among the most difficult actions required of a referee or the Committee.

- In all situations involving questions of fact, resolution of the doubt should be made in light of all the relevant circumstances and evaluation of the weight of the evidence, including the balance of probabilities where applicable. When the Committee is unable to determine the facts to its satisfaction, it should treat the situation in a way that is reasonable, fair and consistent with how similar situations are treated under the Rules.

- Testimony of the players involved is important and should be given due consideration.

  » In some situations where the facts are not decisive, the doubt should be resolved in favour of the player whose ball is involved.

  » In others, the doubt should be resolved against the player whose ball is involved.

- There is no set process for evaluating the testimony of the players or for assigning the weight to be given to such testimony and each situation should be treated on its own merits. The proper action depends on the circumstances in each case and should be left to the judgment of the referee, or the Committee.

- When a player has been required to determine a spot, point, line, area or location under the Rules, the Committee should determine if the player used reasonable judgment in doing so. If so that decision will be accepted even if, after the stroke is made, the determination is shown to be wrong (see Rule 1.3b(2)).

- Testimony of those who are not a part of the competition, including spectators, should be considered and evaluated. It is also appropriate to use television footage and the like to assist in resolving doubt, although the naked eye standard should be applied when using such evidence (see Rule 20.2c).

- It is important that any questions of fact be resolved in a timely manner such that the competition may proceed in an orderly way. Thus, the referee may be limited to evaluating the evidence available to him or her in a timely manner. Any such ruling may be further reviewed by the referee, or the Committee if additional evidence becomes available after the initial ruling.

If a judgment is made by a referee, the player is entitled to proceed on the basis of that ruling whether it is an interpretation of the Rules of Golf or a resolution of a question of fact. In situations arising in both circumstances, if the ruling is found to be incorrect, the Committee may have the authority to make a correction (see Rule 20.2d and Section 6C(10) or 6C(11)). However, in all circumstances, including both match play and stroke play, the referee or Committee is limited in its ability to make corrections by the guidance contained in Rule 20.2d.

Where there is a question relating to the Rules where it is one player's word against another's and the weight of evidence does not favour either player, the benefit of the doubt should be given to the player who made the stroke or whose score is involved.

(8) True State of the Match Not Determinable

If two players complete their match but do not agree on the result, they should refer the matter to the Committee.

The Committee should gather all available evidence and attempt to ascertain the true state of the match. If, after doing so, it is unable to determine the true state of the match, the Committee should resolve the situation in the fairest way, which could mean ruling that the match should be replayed if possible.

(9) Handling Ruling When Player Proceeds Under Inapplicable Rule

When a player proceeds under a Rule that does not apply to his or her situation and then makes a stroke, the Committee is responsible for determining the Rule to apply in order to give a ruling based on the player's actions.

For example:

- A player took relief away from a boundary object under Rule 16.1b. He or she has proceeded under an inapplicable Rule. As Rule 19.1

(Unplayable Ball) requires the player to have decided to proceed under it before taking relief, the Committee may not apply Rule 19 to the player's actions. As there was no Rule that allowed the player to lift his or her ball in such a situation, the Committee should determine that Rule 9.4 applies and none of the Exceptions save the player from penalty.

- A player decided that his or her ball was unplayable in a penalty area, dropped it according to the procedure of option b or c of Rule 19.2 and played it from within the penalty area. As Rule 17.1 is the only Rule that allows the player to lift his or her ball for relief in a penalty area, the Committee should determine that Rule 17 applies and rule accordingly. As a result, the player is considered to have played from a wrong place (see Rule 14.7) and, in addition, gets the one-stroke penalty under Rule 17.1.

- A player's ball lay in temporary water that he or she mistook for a penalty area. The player dropped and played a ball according to the procedure in Rule 17-1d(2). As Rule 16.1b was the only Rule that allowed the player to lift his or her ball for relief in that situation, the Committee should determine that Rule 16.1b applies and rule accordingly. As a result, assuming that the player did not drop a ball in and play from an area that satisfied Rule 16.1b, the player is considered to have played from a wrong place (see Rule 14.7).

- A player did not know the location of his or her original ball but assumed, without knowledge or virtual certainty, that it was in ground under repair. The player dropped and played another ball under Rules 16.1e and 16.1b. As the player did not know the location of his or her original ball, in these circumstances, Rule 18.1 was the only Rule that the player could have proceeded under. Therefore, the Committee should determine that Rule 18.1 applies and rule accordingly. As a result, the player is considered to have put a ball into play under penalty of stroke and distance and to have played from a wrong place (see Rule 14.7) and, in addition, gets the stroke-and-distance penalty under Rule 18.1.

(10) Handling Wrong Rulings in Match Play

Under Rule 20.2a, a player has no right to appeal a referee's ruling. But, if a ruling by a referee or the Committee is later found to be wrong, the ruling should be corrected if possible under the Rules (see Rule 20.2d). This section clarifies when an incorrect ruling should be corrected in match play.

Correction of Incorrect Ruling by a Referee During Match

- A referee should not correct an incorrect ruling after either player makes another stroke on a hole.

- If no more strokes are made on a hole after a ruling has been made, a referee should not correct an incorrect ruling once either player makes a stroke from the next teeing area.

- Otherwise, an incorrect ruling by a referee should be corrected.

- In a situation where an incorrect ruling can be corrected, if the incorrect ruling has resulted in one or more players lifting his or her ball, the referee is responsible for directing the players to replace their balls and complete the hole, with the correct ruling applied.

- The principles above also apply where a referee fails to penalize a player for a breach of a Rule due to misunderstanding the result of a hole.

  » For example, a referee fails to advise a player of a loss of hole penalty for a breach of the pace of play policy as he or she believed the player had already lost the hole. On the next hole, the referee learns that the player had not lost the hole. If the player or the opponent has made a stroke from the teeing area of that next hole, the referee can no longer correct the error.

Correction of Incorrect Ruling Made on Final Hole of Match Before Result Is Final

Where a referee makes an incorrect ruling on the final hole of a match, it should be corrected at any time up until the result of the match is final, or if the match goes to extra holes, until either player makes a stroke from the next teeing area.

Incorrect Ruling by Referee in Match Results in Player Making Stroke from Wrong Place

If a player in match play proceeds on the basis of a ruling from a referee, which involves dropping a ball and playing from a wrong place and the Committee then learns of the incorrect ruling, the following principles apply:

- Unless a serious breach is involved, or the player has been seriously disadvantaged due to playing from a wrong place, it is too late to correct the ruling once the player has made a stroke from the wrong place. The strokes made after the incorrect ruling stand with no penalty for playing from the wrong place.

- If a serious breach is involved or the player has been seriously disadvantaged due to playing from a wrong place, the Committee should correct the error if the opponent has not yet made his or her next stroke on the hole concerned. Otherwise it is too late to correct the ruling.

- If a serious breach is involved and the opponent does not make a stroke on the hole after the ruling was given, the Committee should correct the ruling if neither player has made a stroke from the next teeing area or, in the case of the final hole of the match, before the result of the match is final. Otherwise it is too late to correct the ruling.

- If a serious breach is involved and it is too late to correct the ruling, the strokes made after the incorrect ruling stand with no penalty.

(11) Handling Wrong Rulings in Stroke Play

A player has no right to appeal a referee's ruling (see Rule 20.2a). But if a ruling by a referee or the Committee is later found to be wrong, the ruling should be corrected if possible under the Rules (see Rule 20.2d). This section clarifies when an incorrect ruling should be corrected in stroke play.

Correction of Incorrect Ruling by Referee in Stroke Play

When possible, a referee should correct an incorrect ruling in stroke play that involves the incorrect application of a penalty or failure to apply a penalty, provided the competition has not closed (see Rule 20.2e).

Player In Stroke Play Incorrectly Advised Stroke Does Not Count

Where a referee in stroke play incorrectly advises a player that his or her stroke does not count and to play again without penalty, the ruling stands and the player's score with the replayed stroke is the player's score for the hole.

Player in Stroke Play Makes Stroke from Wrong Place Due to Incorrect Ruling; Procedure for Player When Error Is Discovered

In stroke play when a player proceeds on the basis of a ruling from a referee, which involves dropping a ball and playing from a wrong place and the Committee then learns of the incorrect ruling by the referee, the following principles apply:

- Unless a serious breach is involved, or the player has been seriously disadvantaged due to playing from a wrong place, it is too late to correct the ruling and the strokes made after the incorrect ruling stand with no penalty for playing from the wrong place.

- If a serious breach is involved or the player has been seriously disadvantaged due to playing from a wrong place, and the player has not made a stroke to begin another hole or, for the final hole of the round, before returning his or her scorecard, the Committee should correct the ruling. The Committee should direct the player to cancel the stroke made from the wrong place and any subsequent strokes and proceed correctly. The player incurs no penalty for playing from a wrong place. If it is too late to correct the ruling, the strokes made after the incorrect ruling stand with no penalty for playing from the wrong place.

Referee Gives Player Incorrect Information; Player Acts on Information in Subsequent Play

Players are expected to recognize when they have breached a Rule and to be honest in applying their own penalties (see Rule 1.3b). But if a referee provides the player with incorrect information on the Rules, the player is entitled to act on such information in his or her subsequent play.

Consequently, the Committee may be required to make a judgment as to both the duration of the player's entitlement and his or her proper score when, as a result of proceeding according to the incorrect information provided, the player is liable to a penalty under the Rules.

In these situations, the Committee should resolve the matter in whatever manner it considers most fair, in light of all the facts and with the objective of ensuring that no player receives an undue advantage or disadvantage. In cases where the incorrect information significantly affects the results of the competition, the Committee may have no option but to cancel the round. The following principles are applicable:

- General guidance on the Rules

    When a member of the Committee or a referee provides incorrect information in the nature of general guidance about the Rules, the player should not be exempt from penalty.

- Specific ruling

    When a referee makes a specific ruling that is contrary to the Rules in that particular situation, the player is exempt from penalty. The Committee should extend this exemption for the duration of the round in circumstances where the player proceeds incorrectly on his or her own in exactly the same manner as advised by a referee earlier in the round. However, that exemption ceases if, in that round, the player becomes aware of the proper procedure or has his or her actions questioned.

    For example, a player asks a referee for help in taking relief from a red penalty area and the referee incorrectly tells the player that he or she must drop again because his or her stance is in the penalty area. If the player drops again for that same reason when taking relief from a red penalty area three holes later the Committee should not penalise the player for playing from a wrong place.

- Guidance on Local Rules or Terms of the Competition

    When a member of the Committee or a referee gives incorrect information on whether a Local Rule or Term of the Competition is in effect, the player should be exempt from penalty for acting on that information. This exemption applies for the duration of the round unless corrected earlier, in which case, the exemption should cease at that point.

For example, if the player is told by a referee that distance-measuring devices that measure effective playing distance are permitted even though the Local Rule prohibiting their use is in effect, that player does not incur a penalty for measuring effective playing distance during the round. However, if the Committee learns of the incorrect ruling, the player should be informed of the mistake as soon as possible.

* Equipment ruling

    When a member of the Committee or a referee rules that a non-conforming club is conforming, the player is exempt from penalty for using the club. This exemption applies for the duration of the competition unless corrected earlier, in which case, the exemption ceases at the completion of the round during which the correction was made.

Player Lifts Ball Without Authority Due to Misunderstanding Referee's Instructions

If a player lifts his or her ball when not permitted to do so as a result of a reasonable misunderstanding of a referee's instructions, there is no penalty, and the ball must be replaced unless the player proceeds under another Rule.

For example, a player's ball comes to rest against a movable obstruction and he or she asks for relief. A referee correctly advises the player that the obstruction may be removed under Rule 15.2 and that the spot of the ball should be marked in case it moves during the removal of the obstruction. The player marks the position of the ball and lifts it before the referee can stop him or her.

The player will normally be penalized one stroke under Rule 9.4 for lifting his or her ball where it is not allowed, but, provided the referee is satisfied that the player misunderstood the instruction, the ball is replaced without penalty.

Player Incorrectly Advised to Continue with Provisional Ball by Referee

A player had reason to play a provisional ball from the teeing area and finds his or her original ball in a penalty area. The player is then incorrectly told by a referee that he or she must continue with the provisional ball and completes the hole with the provisional ball. The player incurs no penalty for playing a wrong ball (the provisional ball, which the player was required to abandon under Rule 18.3c).

If the Committee then becomes aware of the wrong ruling, it should rule that the player's score for the hole consists of the tee shot with the original ball plus the number of strokes the player took to complete the hole with the provisional ball after the incorrect ruling, with the second stroke with the provisional ball being the player's second stroke on the hole. However, if it would have been clearly unreasonable for the player to have played the original ball from the penalty area, he or she must also add one penalty stroke under Rule 17.1 to the score for the hole.

Committee Makes Incorrect Ruling When Player Has Played Two Balls Under Rule 20.1c(3); When Ruling May Be Corrected

In stroke play, a player plays two balls under Rule 20.1c(3), reports the facts to the Committee, and the Committee tells the player to score with the incorrect ball. Such a mistake is an incorrect ruling and not an administrative error. Therefore Rule 20.2d applies and the answer depends on when the Committee learns of its incorrect ruling:

- If the Committee learns of the incorrect ruling before the competition closes, it should correct the ruling by changing the score for the hole in question to that of the correct ball.

- If the Committee learns of the incorrect ruling after the competition has closed, the score with the incorrect ball remains the player's score for the hole in question. Under Rule 20.2d, such a ruling is final once the competition has closed.

Disqualification Penalty Wrongly Applied to Winner of Event; Error Discovered After Two Other Players Play Off for First Place

If, as a result of an incorrect ruling by the Committee, the rightful winner of a competition is disqualified and two other players play-off for first place, the best procedure depends on when the Committee realizes its error. If the Committee learns of its incorrect ruling before the result of the competition is final, the Committee should correct the incorrect ruling by rescinding the disqualification penalty and declaring the player to be the winner. If the Committee learns of the incorrect ruling after the result of the competition is final, the result stands, with the player disqualified.

Application of Disqualification Penalty in Competition in Which Not All Scores Used to Determine Winner

In a scenario such as a multiple round stroke-play team competition when not all the players' scores count towards the team's score for a round, a player's score cannot count for the round when he or she is disqualified but could count for other rounds. For example, when two scores of three team members count, if a player is disqualified in the first of four rounds, the disqualification applies only to the first round and his or her scores for the remaining rounds could still be used.

This applies to all competitions in which not all scores are used to determine the winner (for example, an individual competition in which the player counts his or her three best scores from four rounds).

If a player is disqualified for a breach of Rule 1.3b or the Committee's Code of Conduct, it is up to the Committee to determine whether the disqualification should be for the round or the entire competition.

(12) Combining Match Play and Stroke Play

The combining of match play and stroke play is discouraged as certain Rules are substantially different between the two formats. But there will be times when players either request to combine the two forms of play or, having done so on their own, request a ruling. The Committee should make its best efforts to support players at these times and should use the following guidelines in doing so.

When players request to combine match play and stroke play

If a Committee chooses to allow players to play a match while competing in a stroke-play competition, it is recommended that the players be advised that the Rules for stroke play apply throughout. For example, no concessions are allowed and if one player plays out of turn, the other does not have the option of recalling the stroke.

When players request a ruling having combined match play and stroke play

If the Committee is asked for a ruling when players have combined match play and stroke play, it should apply the Rules of Golf as they would apply to each of match play and stroke play separately. For example, if one player did not complete a hole for whatever reason then he or she is disqualified from the stroke-play competition for a breach of Rule 3.3c. But, for Stableford, Maximum Score and Par/Bogey see Rules 21.1c(2), 21.2c and 21.3c(2) respectively.

6D Enforcing Pace of Play

Where a Pace of Play policy is in place for a competition, it is important the Committee understands and actively enforces the policy to ensure that players adhere to the policy and play proceeds in an orderly manner.

For more information and example polices, see Model Local Rule Section 8K.

6E Suspensions and Resumptions

(1) Immediate and Normal Suspensions of Play

There are two types of suspensions of play that a Committee can order, each with different requirements for when players must stop play (see Rule 5.7b).

- Immediate suspension (such as when there is imminent danger). If the Committee declares an immediate suspension of play, all players must stop play at once and must not make another stroke until the Committee resumes play.

- Normal suspension (such as for darkness or unplayable course). If the Committee suspends play for normal reasons, what happens next depends on whether a group is between two holes or playing a hole.

The Committee should use a way of signalling an immediate suspension that is different than that used for a normal suspension. The signals to be used should be communicated to the players in the Local Rules.

See Model Local Rule J-1 – Methods for Suspending and Resuming Play

When play is suspended, the Committee will need to evaluate if the players should be left in position on the course or brought in to the clubhouse.

Whether a suspension is immediate or normal, the Committee should resume play when it is possible to do so. Players will resume play from where they stopped (see Rule 5.7c).

(2) Deciding When to Suspend and Resume Play

Deciding when play should be suspended and then resumed can be difficult decisions for a Committee. A Committee should take the following guidelines into consideration:

Lightning

The Committee should use whatever means it has available to determine if there is a danger from lightning and take what actions it believes are appropriate. Players may also stop play on their own when they believe there is a danger from lightning (see Rule 5.7a).

When the Committee concludes there is no further danger from lightning and orders play to be resumed, players must resume play. See Interpretation 5.7c/1 for what to do if a player refuses to start because he or she feels there is still a danger from lightning.

Visibility

It is recommended that, if landing areas are no longer visible to players (for example, due to fog or darkness), play should be suspended. Similarly, if players are unable to read the line of play on a putting green due to a lack of visibility, play should be suspended.

Water

If all the area around a hole is covered in temporary water and it cannot be removed, in stroke play the course should be considered unplayable and the Committee should suspend play under Rule 5.7.

In match play, if the water cannot be removed, the Committee may suspend play or relocate the hole.

Wind

Several balls being moved by the wind may be a reason to suspend play, but only one or two balls moving due to the wind on one green would not usually merit the Committee suspending play. On the putting green there are Rules in place to help players avoid getting penalties or for being advantaged if the ball is blown closer to the hole or disadvantaged if the ball is blown farther from the hole (see Rules 9.3 and 13.1).

The Committee should consider suspending play due to wind only if there are several instances of balls moving and players are having problems with replacing the ball on the spot from which it was blown, or at least reasonably close to that spot if the ball will not remain at rest on the original spot.

(3) Resumption of Play

When play is to be resumed following a suspension, players will resume play from where they stopped (see Rule 5.7d).

The Committee should be prepared to consider the following:

- If players were evacuated from the course, whether players should be given time to warm up before resuming play.

- If the practice areas were closed during the suspension, when they should be reopened to give players sufficient time to get ready to play.

- How to get players back to their positions on the course.

- How to ensure that all players are back in position before resuming play. This might include having members of the Committee in position to observe and report when all players have returned.

(4) Whether to Cancel Round

Match Play

A match should not be cancelled once play has begun as both players in a match are playing in the same conditions, without one having an advantage over the other.

If the players stop play by agreement as allowed in Rule 5.7a or the Committee feels that conditions are such that play should be suspended, the match should resume from where it was suspended.

In a team competition, if some matches are completed while others cannot be completed on the arranged day due to poor light or weather, the Terms of the Competition should clarify how the complete and incomplete matches will be treated (see Section 5A(4)). For example:

- The result of completed matches stand as played and incomplete matches are to be continued or replayed on a later date,

- All matches are to be replayed, and each team is free to alter its original team, or

- Any matches that cannot be completed as scheduled are considered to be tied.

Stroke Play

In stroke play there is no set guidance for when a Committee should cancel a round. The proper action depends on the circumstances in each case and is left to the judgment of the Committee.

A round should be cancelled only in a case where it would be very unfair not to cancel it. For example, a small number of players begin a round under extremely bad weather conditions, conditions subsequently worsen and further play that day is impossible, but when play will resume the next day the weather is ideal.

When a round is cancelled, all scores and penalties during that round are cancelled. That would normally include any disqualification penalty, but, if a player is disqualified for a serious misconduct (see Rule 1.2) or for a breach of the Code of Conduct, that disqualification should not be cancelled.

(5) Player Refuses to Start or Picks Up Due to Weather Conditions

If, because of bad weather, a player refuses to start at the time arranged by the Committee or picks up during the round and the Committee later cancels that round, the player gets no penalty as all penalties in a cancelled round are cancelled.

(6) Removal of Temporary Water or Loose Impediments from Putting Green

If temporary water, sand, leaves or other loose impediments accumulate on a putting green during a round, the Committee may do what is necessary to remove the condition, for example by using a squeegee, or by brushing or blowing the putting green. It is not necessary for the Committee to suspend play to take these actions.

In such cases, the Committee may, when necessary, get the help of players to remove the loose impediments or sand. However, a player is in breach of Rule 8.1 if he or she removes temporary water on the line of play without the Committee's permission.

A Committee may adopt a policy that clarifies what actions are considered appropriate for a Committee member, someone designated by the Committee (for example, a member of the maintenance staff), or players, to remove temporary water on the putting green.

See Model Local Rule J-2: Model Local Rule for Allowing Temporary Water on Putting Green to be Removed by a Squeegee.

(7) Match Begun in Ignorance Course Closed

If players begin a match when the course is closed and the Committee then learns of their action, the match should be replayed in its entirety as play on the closed course is considered null and void.

6F Scoring

(1) Match Play

It is usually the players' responsibility to report the result of their match at a location designated by the Committee. If a referee has been assigned to the match, he or she may be assigned this duty instead of the players.

If a player makes a request for a ruling during the match that has not been resolved, the Committee should determine if the request meets the requirements in Rule 20.1b(2) and make its ruling. This may result in the players needing to return to the course to continue the match.

Once the result has been reported, it is considered final and no request for a ruling can be accepted unless it meets the requirements in Rule 20.1b(3).

(2) Stroke Play

In stroke play, players should be given an opportunity to resolve any issues that need to be clarified with the Committee (see Rules 14.7b and 20.1c(4)), check their scorecards and have any mistakes corrected. If there is a mistake on the scorecard, a player may ask the marker or the

Committee to make or ratify a change to his or her scorecard (see Rule 3.3b(2)) up to the time that it is returned.

Once the scorecard has been returned, the Committee should check it to make sure that it has the player's name, handicap (if it is a net competition), the required signatures and correct hole-by-hole scores. The Committee should total the scores and apply the handicap in a net competition.

In other forms of stroke play, such as Stableford or Par/Bogey, or in a Four-Ball competition, the Committee should determine the final result for the player or side. For example, in a Stableford competition, the Committee is responsible for determining the number of points that the player scores for each hole and in total for the round.

6G Making Cuts; Establishing Draws; Creating New Groups

(1) Making Cuts and Creating New Groups

For a competition played over multiple rounds, the Terms of the Competition may state that:

- Players will be regrouped for later rounds based on their total score to that point.

- The size of the field will be reduced for the final round or rounds (often called the "cut").

In both cases, the Committee should generate new groupings and publish them. It is customary for the players with the highest scores to tee off first and the players with the lowest scores to tee off last, although the Committee may choose to alter this.

The Committee can choose how to regroup players who finish with the same total score. For example, the Committee may decide that the first player to return a specific score will receive a later tee time than those who complete the round later with the same score.

If two tees are to be used for later rounds (for example, half the field starts on the first hole and the other half starts on the tenth hole), the Committee may decide to arrange the groups such that the players with the highest scores tee off last on one side (such as from the 10th tee) and the players with the lowest scores tee off last on the other side (such as the 1st tee). This results in the players in the middle of the field being the first to tee off on each tee.

(2) Dealing with Withdrawals and Disqualifications in Match Play

In match play, if a player withdraws or is disqualified from the competition before the start of his or her first match and the Committee has not specified how such a situation is dealt with in the Terms of the Competition, the Committee's options are as follows:

- Declare the player's next opponent the winner by default, or

- If the player withdraws before his or her first-round match:

  » If time permits, produce a new match-play draw, or

  » Replace the player with a player from the list of alternates or reserves, or

  » Where players have qualified through stroke play for the match-play competition, replace the player with the player who is now the final qualifier.

If the player withdraws or is disqualified after his or her first or subsequent match, the Committee could:

  » Declare the player's next opponent the winner by default, or

  » Require all players eliminated by the player in match play to play off for his or her position.

If both finalists in a match-play competition are disqualified, the Committee may decide to conclude the competition without a winner. Alternatively, the Committee could elect to have the defeated semi-finalists play a match to determine the winner of the competition.

If a player in a match-play competition is disqualified, the player should be entitled to any prize he or she won previously in the competition, for example, for winning the stroke-play qualifying competition.

(3) Dealing with Withdrawals and Disqualifications in Stroke Play

If a player withdraws or is disqualified before the first round in a competition (for example, due to failure to start on time), the Committee may replace the player with another player not currently in the field (often called an alternate or reserve) if one is available. Once the player has started his or her first round he or she should not be replaced.

(4) Qualifying for Match Play

When stroke-play qualifying is used to determine the draw(s) for match play, the Committee can choose to break ties for various positions in the draw randomly or by using a scorecard count-back or play-off. This should be specified in the Terms of the Competition.

(5) Misapplication of Handicap Affects Match-Play Draw

In a stroke-play qualifying round for a match-play competition, if the Committee misapplies a player's handicap on a scorecard which results in an incorrect draw, the Committee should deal with the matter in the fairest way possible. The Committee should consider amending the draw and cancelling the matches affected by the error.

If the error is discovered after the second round of the match play starts, it is too late to correct the draw.

7 After the Competition

7A Resolving Ties in Stroke Play

After all the scorecards have been returned in stroke play, the Committee may need to resolve ties for first place or other positions. The Committee should do so by applying the method detailed in the Terms of the Competition (see Section 5A(6)) which should have been specified in advance.

In a qualifier where a fixed number of players will move into match play, or when the competition is a qualifier for a later competition, there may be a play-off or play-offs to decide which players advance, which the Committee should organise.

(1) Disqualification or Concession of Defeat in Stroke-Play Play-Off

In a stroke-play play-off between two players, if one of them is disqualified or concedes defeat, it is not necessary for the other player to complete the play-off hole or holes to be declared the winner.

(2) Some Players Do Not Complete Stroke-Play Play-Off

In a stroke-play play-off between three or more players, if not all of them complete the play-off hole or holes, the order in which the players are disqualified or decide to withdraw determines the result of the play-off if necessary.

7B Finalizing Results

As detailed in Section 5A(7), it is important for the Committee to clarify in the Terms of the Competition when and how the result of the competition is final, as this will affect how the Committee will resolve any Rules issues that occur after play is complete in both match play and stroke play (see Rule 20).

The Committee should ensure that it carries out its responsibilities for finalizing the results of a match or stroke-play competition in line with the Terms of the Competition. For example:

- Where the result of a match will be considered final when the Committee has recorded it on the official scoreboard, the Committee should ensure this is carried out as soon as possible.

- If there are any Rules questions which may impact the result of the stroke-play competition, the Committee should resolve these issues, even if this means delaying the closing of the competition and announcing the winners.

7C Awarding Prizes

If the competition involves amateur golfers, the Committee should make sure it is aware of the regulations concerning prizes that an amateur golfer may accept without breaching the Rules of Amateur Status. Committees should refer to the Rules of Amateur Status and Decisions on the Rules of Amateur Status which are available at USGA.org. Some of the key restrictions are:

- An amateur golfer must not play golf for prize money.

- An amateur golfer must not accept a prize or prize voucher of retail value in excess of the amount permitted by the Governing Body that administers the Rules of Amateur Status in the country where the competition is being played.

- An amateur golfer may accept a symbolic prize of any value. An example of a symbolic prize is one made of gold, silver, ceramic, glass or the like that is permanently and distinctively engraved, such as a trophy, cup, medal or plaque.

- An amateur golfer may accept a prize of any value, including a cash prize, for a hole-in-one made while playing a round of golf.

7D Rules or Scoring Issues Arising After Competition

When an issue regarding the Rules is brought to the attention of the Committee after the competition is closed, the resolution will depend on the nature of the problem. If the issue is one where a player may have proceeded incorrectly under the Rules, the Committee should refer to Rule 20.2e to determine if a penalty of disqualification needs to be applied to the player.

When the issue is due to an administrative error by the Committee, it should correct the error and issue new results. If necessary, the Committee should retrieve any prizes mistakenly presented and award them to the correct players.

Administrative errors include:

- Having allowed ineligible players to enter.

- Miscalculating a player's total score.
- Incorrectly applying a handicap or leaving a player out of the final results.
- Applying the wrong method of deciding ties.

Model Local Rules and Other Forms of Play

Contents

Contents

Contents

Contents

8 Model Local Rules

This Section lists authorized Model Local Rules that may be used by a Committee:

- These can either be adopted in their entirety or can serve as an example of how to write a particular type of Local Rule.

- Local Rules are authorized only if they are consistent with the policies established in this Section.

- A Committee is encouraged to use the recommended text if it fits the local situation to minimize the number of times a player will find different versions of the same Local Rule at different courses or in different competitions.

- The Committee should ensure that the Local Rules are made available to the players whether on the scorecard, through a Notice to Players or in some other way.

- Where a shorthand version of the full text of the Model Local Rule is provided, for example on the back of the scorecard, the Committee should ensure that the full text is available, for example on a noticeboard or on a website.

- Unless otherwise stated the penalty for a breach of a Local Rule should be the general penalty.

Principles for establishing Local Rules:

- Local Rules have the same status as a Rule of Golf for that competition or course.

- Committees are encouraged to use Local Rules only to deal with the types of situations and policies covered in this section and in Section 5.

- If a Local Rule is introduced because of a temporary situation, it should be removed as soon as the situation no longer requires the use of the Local Rule.

- If a Committee changes the wording of a Model Local Rule to fit the particular needs of the course or competition, it needs to ensure that the changes are within the parameters allowed by the Model Local Rule and consistent with the stated purpose.

- In order to ensure that play is conducted in accordance with the Rules of Golf, a Committee must not use a Local Rule to waive or modify the Rules of Golf simply because it might prefer a Rule to be different.

- As a general principle, when a player is playing a round that is to be posted for handicapping purposes, he or she is required to play it under the Rules of Golf. If the Committee authorizes players to play in ways that differ significantly from the Rules of Golf, the player may not be permitted to post the score for handicap purposes. For allowable exceptions, consult the rules or recommendations contained within the Handicap System operating in the local jurisdiction.

If the Committee believes that a Local Rule not covered by these principles may be needed because of local abnormal conditions that interfere with fair play, it should:

- Consult USGA.org to check if any additional Model Local Rule is available to cover such a condition, or

- Consult the USGA directly.

The Model Local Rules in each category are numbered in order – for example, A-1, A-2, etc.

A statement of purpose is given with each Model Local Rule. If a Committee changes the wording of a Model Local Rule to fit the particular needs of the course or competition, it should make sure that such changes are consistent with the stated purpose.

These Model Local Rules are organized in the following categories:

A. Out of Bounds and Course Boundaries

B. Penalty Areas

C. Bunkers

D. Putting Greens

E. Special or Required Relief Procedures

F. Abnormal Course Conditions and Integral Objects

G. Restrictions on Use of Specific Equipment

H. Defining Who May Help or Give Advice to Players

I. Defining When and Where Players May Practise

J. Procedures for Bad Weather and Suspensions of Play

K. Pace of Play Policies

These Model Local Rules cover those situations or issues that arise often enough to justify having a model form. For all other situations where a Local Rule is allowed but model language is not provided, the Committee should write the Local Rule in clear and simple terms. But the Committee is not authorized to write Local Rules which go against the principles in the Rules of Golf. Section 8L gives more information regarding the use of unauthorized Local Rules.

Where a Local Rule is written using the language of the Model Local Rules in this section, the Committee may seek assistance in interpreting the Local Rule from the USGA.

8A Out of Bounds and Course Boundaries

A-1 Defining Boundaries

Purpose. There are many ways in which a Committee may define the boundaries of the course and it is not appropriate or possible to provide a complete list of Model Local Rules that can be used for this purpose.

The key is to be clear and specific when defining boundaries in the Local Rules.

No specific Model Local Rules are included in this section given the variety of options available, but some examples are provided below:

• *Out of bounds* is defined by the line between the *course*-side points at ground level of white stakes and fence posts. *Out of bounds* is also defined by [insert description of other methods of defining *out of bounds*].

• The boundary on [specify hole number] is defined by [insert description of feature].

• The boundary to the left of [specify hole number] is defined by the *course*-side edge of the white paint dots on [specify location, such as the pavement].

• The boundary to the right of [specify hole number] is defined by the *course*-side edge of the white line painted on [name of road].

• The maintenance area between [specify hole numbers] is *out of bounds*. The boundary is defined by the inside edge of the fence posts surrounding the area.

See Sections 2A and 5B(1) for more information on defining out of bounds.

A-2 Clarifying Boundary When Using Wall or Road

Purpose. The definition of "out of bounds" clarifies that when a boundary is defined by objects such as a wall or road, the Committee should define the boundary edge.

Depending on the nature or condition of a wall, there may be good reasons for defining the boundary as being beyond the wall or using the course-side edge of the wall as the boundary.

Model Local Rule A-2.1

"The *course*-side edge of any wall [*course*-side edge of road] defines the boundary of the *course*."

Model Local Rule A-2.2

"A ball is *out of bounds* when it is beyond any wall defining the boundary of the *course*."

A-3 Out of Bounds When Public Road Runs Through Course

<u>Purpose</u>. When a public road runs through a course, it is usually defined as out of bounds. This can make it possible for a ball played from one side of the road to come to rest in bounds on the other side of the road, even though that ball would be out of bounds if it came to rest on the road itself.

If the Committee believes that it is unfair or dangerous to treat those situations differently, it may adopt a Local Rule stating that a ball played from one side of the road that comes to rest on the other side of that road is out of bounds.

If a road crosses a particular hole where the players have to play from one side to the other in the normal course of play, the Committee should specify that this Local Rule does not apply to that road in the play of that hole.

Model Local Rule A-3

"A ball coming to rest on or beyond the road [identify the road or the holes where it comes into play] is *out of bounds*, even if it comes to rest on another part of the *course* that is in bounds for other holes."

A-4 Internal Out of Bounds

<u>Purpose</u>. For course design or safety reasons, a Committee can choose to specify that a particular part of the course is out of bounds during the play of a particular hole.

This is done to stop players who are playing that hole from playing to and from another part of the course. For example, on a dogleg hole, an internal out of bounds may be used to prevent a player from cutting the dogleg by playing a ball to the fairway of another hole.

But a Local Rule stating that a ball is out of bounds if it crosses a boundary even if it re-crosses the boundary and comes to rest on the same part of the course, is not authorized.

Model Local Rule A-4

When the boundary is defined by stakes:

"During play of [specify hole number], the [describe the part of the *course*] on the [specify location or side] of the hole, defined by [specify colour of stakes, for example, white stakes], is *out of bounds*.

These stakes are treated as *boundary objects* during the play of [specify hole number]. For all other holes, they are *immovable obstructions*."

A-5 Stakes Identifying Out of Bounds

Purpose. When out of bounds is defined by a line on the ground, a trench or in another way that might not be visible from a distance, the Committee may place stakes along the boundary to allow players to see where the boundary edge is from a distance.

Boundary objects are not permitted to be moved and free relief is generally not given, but the Committee may provide for relief from these stakes through the following Model Local Rule, which should also clarify the status of these stakes.

It is recommended that such stakes be marked differently than other boundary stakes on the course, for example, white stakes with black tops may be used for this purpose.

Model Local Rule A-5

"Where a boundary is defined by [identify boundary, for example, a white line painted on the ground], white stakes with black tops have been placed for visibility. These stakes [describe any special marking] are [*immovable* | *movable*] *obstructions*."

8B Penalty Areas

B-1 Defining Penalty Areas

Purpose. There are many ways in which a Committee can define penalty areas on the course and so it is not necessary or possible to provide a complete list of Model Local Rules that can be used for this purpose.

The key is to be clear and specific when defining penalty areas in the Local Rules.

No specific Model Local Rules are included in this section given the variety of options available, but some examples are provided below:

• When playing the [specify hole number] the yellow *penalty area* on [specify other hole number] is to be played as a red *penalty area.*

• The red *penalty area* on [specify hole number] extends to and coincides with the *out of bounds* edge.

• The red *penalty area* on [specify hole number] defined on only one side extends to infinity.

While it is a good practice to mark the edges of penalty areas, there are times when the edge of the penalty area can be defined by language on the scorecard or Local Rules sheet. This should only be done when there will be little confusion about where the edge of the penalty area begins, and it can be done in a consistent manner throughout the course. Some examples are:

- All desert areas are red *penalty areas* and the edge of the *penalty area* is where the grass and desert meet.

- All areas of lava are red *penalty areas*.

- Where an artificial wall surrounds the edge of a lake or other body of water, the *penalty area* is defined by the outside edge of the wall.

See Sections 2C and 5B(2) for more information on defining penalty areas.

B-2 Relief on Opposite Side of Red Penalty Area

Purpose. Rule 17.1 gives a player the option to take lateral relief or back-on-the-line relief based on where his or her ball last crossed the edge of a red penalty area. But in some cases (for example, due to the location of the red penalty area right next to a course boundary), those options may leave the player with no reasonable option other than to take stroke-and-distance relief.

A Committee can introduce a Local Rule to allow lateral relief on the opposite side of the red penalty area as an extra relief option under Rule 17.1d.

When considering a Local Rule to allow additional relief:

- The Committee should consider introducing the Local Rule in situations when a player could be seriously disadvantaged if it was not introduced. Two such examples are:

  » Where a boundary coincides with the edge of a penalty area down the side of a hole such that if a ball last crossed into the penalty area on the boundary side, the player would be likely to have no realistic relief option other than to play again under stroke and distance.

  » Where the layout of the penalty area is such that there could be doubt as to where the ball last crossed into the penalty area and the decision on which side of the penalty area the ball last crossed has a considerable impact on where to take relief. This applies if a relatively narrow penalty area is bounded by bushes or thick rough on one side and fairway on the other.

- It is recommended that the Committee specify the location of specific penalty areas that the Local Rule applies to, rather than applying it to all red penalty areas on the course. This Local Rule should not be used to allow a player to use this opposite side relief option to get across a red penalty area to a more favourable location than is available if only normal lateral relief under Rule 17.1d is used and available.

- It may also be desirable to mark the penalty areas where this option is available in a special way such as putting a different coloured top on any stakes where the extra option is available, and this should be stated in the Local Rule.

- Instead of using this Local Rule, the Committee may decide to put one of more dropping zones in place (see Model Local Rule E-1).

Model Local Rule B-2.1

"When a player's ball is in a *penalty area*, including when it is *known or virtually certain* to be in a *penalty area* even though not found, the player may take relief using one of the options under Rule 17.1d.

Or, when the ball last crossed the edge of the red *penalty area* on [specify hole number and location], as an extra relief option adding **one penalty stroke**, the player may *drop* the original ball or another ball on the opposite side of the *penalty area*:

- Reference Point: The estimated point on the opposite edge of the *penalty area* that is the same distance from the *hole* as the estimated point where the original ball last crossed the edge of the red *penalty area*.

- Size of Relief Area Measured from Reference Point: Two *club-lengths*, **but** with these limits:

- Limits on Location of Relief Area:

  » Must not be nearer the *hole* than the reference point, and

  » May be in any *area of the course* except the same *penalty area*, **but**

  » If more than one *area of the course* is located within two *club-lengths* of the reference point, the ball must come to rest in the *relief area* in the same *area of the course* that the ball first touches when *dropped* in the *relief area*.

Penalty for Playing Ball from a Wrong Place in Breach of Local Rule: *General Penalty* **Under Rule 14.7a."**

Model Local Rule B-2.2

Model Local Rule B-2.1 applies but with the following amendment to the first paragraph:

"This Local Rule applies when a player's ball is found in or it is *known or virtually certain* to have come to rest in any red *penalty area* that coincides with a boundary of the *course* and the point where the ball last crossed the edge of the *penalty area* is on the boundary side of that *penalty area*."

MLR B-2.1 AND B-2.2: RELIEF ON OPPOSITE SIDE OF RED PENALTY AREA

- **X** Point that ball entered the penalty area
- **Y** Point on opposite edge the same distance from the hole as X (reference point)
- ⬤ Relief area

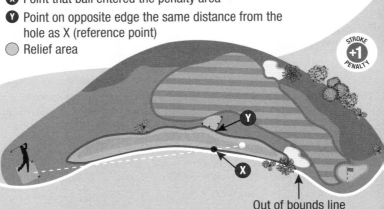

Out of bounds line

If it is known or virtually certain that the player's ball is in a red penalty area, the player may take relief using one of the options under Rule 17.1d or, as an extra relief option when Model Local Rule B-2.1 or B-2.2 is introduced, the player may also take lateral relief on the opposite edge of the penalty area for one penalty stroke.

Reference Point	Size of Relief Area	Limits on Relief Area
The estimated point (point Y) on the opposite edge of the penalty area that is the same distance from the hole as the estimated point (point X) where the original ball last crossed the edge of the red penalty area	Two club-lengths from the reference point	The relief area: • Must not be nearer the hole than the reference point, and • May be in any area of the course except the same penalty area

B-3 Provisional Ball for Ball in a Penalty Area

Purpose. Under Rule 18.3, a player is not allowed to play a ball provisionally if it is known or virtually certain that his or her ball is in a penalty area.

But in unusual cases, the size, shape or location of a penalty area may be such that:

- The player cannot see whether the ball is in the penalty area,
- It would unreasonably delay play if the player had to go forward to look for the ball before returning to play another ball under penalty of stroke and distance, and

- If the original ball is not found, it would be known or virtually certain that the ball is in the penalty area.

For such situations, to save time a Committee may choose to modify Rule 18.3:

- Rule 18.3a is modified to allow the player to play a ball provisionally under Rule 17.1d(1), Rule 17.1d(2) or, for a red penalty area, Rule 17.1d(3).

- Rules 18.3b and 18.3c are modified to state when such a provisional ball must or may be played or abandoned, as stated in the Model Local Rule.

Model Local Rule B-3

"If a player does not know whether his or her ball is in the *penalty area* [identify location], the player may play a *provisional ball* under Rule 18.3, which is modified in this way:

In playing the *provisional ball*, the player may use the *stroke-and-distance* relief option (see Rule 17.1d(1), the back-on-the-line relief option (see Rule 17.1d(2)) or, if it is a red *penalty area*, the lateral relief option (see Rule 17.1d(3)). If a dropping zone (see Model Local Rule E-1) is available for this *penalty area*, the player may also use that relief option.

Once the player has played a *provisional ball* under this Rule, he or she may not use any further options under Rule 17.1 in relation to the original ball.

In deciding when that *provisional ball* becomes the player's ball *in play* or if it must or may be abandoned, Rule 18.3c(2) and 18.3c(3) apply except that:

- When Original Ball Is Found in Penalty Area Within Three-Minute Search Time. The player may choose either to:
  - » Continue to play the original ball as it lies in the *penalty area*, in which case the *provisional ball* must not be played. All strokes with that *provisional ball* before it was abandoned (including *strokes* made and any penalty strokes solely from playing that ball) do not count, or
  - » Continue to play the *provisional ball* in which case the original ball must not be played.

- When Original Ball Is Not Found Within Three-Minute Search Time or Is Known or Virtually Certain to Be in Penalty Area. The *provisional* ball becomes the player's ball *in play*.

Penalty for Breach of Local Rule: *General Penalty*.

B-4 Defining Open Water Course as Part of General Area

Purpose. If an open water course does not usually contain water (such as a drainage ditch or run-off area that is dry except during a rainy season), the Committee can define that area as part of the general area.

The Committee can also choose to mark such an open water course as a penalty area during times of the year when it contains water, or leave it as part of the general area, in which case any water that collects would be treated as temporary water. However, areas that would normally contain water should be marked as penalty areas throughout the year.

See Model Local Rule F-20 for when the open water course may be made part of an abnormal course condition.

Model Local Rule B-4.1

"The [describe specific water course, e.g. ditch] at the [detail where it is located] is to be treated as part of the *general area* and not as a *penalty area*."

Model Local Rule B-4.2

"All [describe specific types of water courses, such as concrete drainage ditches] are to be treated as part of the *general area* and not as a *penalty area*."

B-5 Special Relief When Penalty Area Next to Bunker

Purpose. There may be particular holes where part of the edge of a red penalty area is so close to a bunker that a player taking lateral relief under Rule 17.1d(3) will need to drop a ball in the bunker.

In such a case, a Committee can choose to create an extra relief option allowing the player, for one penalty stroke, to take relief in a dropping zone positioned on the fairway side of the bunker.

Model Local Rule B-5

"This Local Rule allows the use of a dropping zone as an extra relief option when:

- A player's ball is in the red *penalty area* [identify location], including when it is *known or virtually certain* that the ball came to rest in the *penalty area*, and

- The ball last crossed the edge of the red *penalty area* [identify start and end locations such as between two specially marked stakes].

In that case, the player may:

- Take relief under one of the options in Rule 17.1d, adding **one *penalty stroke***, or

- As an extra option, also adding **one penalty stroke**, take relief by *dropping* a ball in and playing it from the nearest dropping zone to the point where the ball last crossed the edge of the red *penalty area* and that is not nearer the *hole* than that point.

Penalty for Playing Ball from a Wrong Place in Breach of Local Rule: *General Penalty* Under Rule 14.7a."

8C Bunkers

C-1 Clarifying Edge of Bunker

<u>Purpose</u>. When it may be difficult to determine the edge of a bunker due to wear or when bunkers blend into areas of sand that are in the general area, the Committee may need to define the edge of the bunker.

No specific Model Local Rules are included in this section given the variety of options available, but some examples are provided below:

- The edge of the *bunker* to the left of [specify hole number] is defined by the outside edge of the [insert colour] stakes. The stakes are *movable obstructions* and are inside the *bunker*.

- The edge of the *bunker* to the right of [specify hole number] is defined by the [identify colour] line painted in the sand,

- Any areas of sand that have been raked are considered to be a part of a *bunker*.

See Sections 2D and 5B(3) for more information on bunkers.

C-2 Changing Status of Areas of Sand

<u>Purpose</u>. The definition of "bunker" specifies that a bunker is a "specially prepared area of sand". However, if a Committee wants to define a prepared area of sand as part of the general area or define a non-prepared area of sand as a bunker, it may do so by Local Rule.

Model Local Rule C-2.1

Defining a prepared area of sand as part of the general area:

"The prepared area[s] of sand [detail holes or locations] are part of the *general area* and not *bunkers*."

Model Local Rule C-2.2

Defining a non-prepared area of sand aš a bunker:

"The area[s] of sand [detail holes or locations] are *bunkers* and not part of the *general area*."

C-3 Clarifying Status of Material Similar to Sand

Purpose. Bunkers on a course sometimes contain materials similar to sand, such as crushed shells or lava dust. Such materials are treated as sand when applying Rule 12. (See the definition of "bunker").

For consistency, the Committee can choose to treat such materials as sand everywhere else on the course as well.

Model Local Rule C-3

"The [identify material such as crushed shell or lava dust] used to fill *bunkers* is treated as sand both when in a *bunker* and everywhere else on the *course*.

This means that these materials are not *loose impediments*. A player must not *improve* the *conditions affecting the stroke* by removing these materials, except when they are on the *putting green* (see Rule 13.1c(1))."

C-4 Declaring Practice Bunkers to Be Part of General Area

Purpose. When a course has bunkers within the boundaries of the course that are used for practising, they do not lose their status as bunkers by default. However, the condition of practice bunkers may be very poor as players frequently do not rake them. If the Committee wishes to provide relief for players, the bunker should be declared to be ground under repair and a part of the general area, which will allow players to take free relief outside the bunker.

Model Local Rule C-4

"The practice *bunker* located [insert details of where the bunker is located] is *ground under repair* and is part of the *general area*. Free relief is available under Rule 16.1b."

8D Putting Greens

D-1 Clarifying Edge of Putting Green

Purpose. At some courses, the areas around putting greens are maintained in such a manner that it may be difficult for a player to determine if his or her ball is on the putting green. In cases like this the Committee can choos to mark the edges of putting greens with painted dots.

Model Local Rule D-1

"The edges of putting greens are defined by [insert colour] dots. The dots are [on][off] the putting green and free relief is not available from them."

D-2 Status of Putting Green When Temporary Putting Green Is Used

Purpose. There may be times when a putting green for a hole cannot be used for some reason, for example due to bad weather, or for reasons related to repair or maintenance. When this is the case, the Committee may wish to prepare a temporary putting green and put a Local Rule in place to define this as the putting green in play for that hole. The putting green that has been replaced by a temporary putting green should be defined as a wrong green so that players are not permitted to play from it.

Model Local Rule D-2

"Temporary _putting greens_ are in play on holes [insert hole numbers] as defined by [insert description, for example, the areas of fairway surrounded by white lines]. Any _putting green_ that has been replaced by a temporary _putting green_ is a _wrong green_ and free relief for interference must be taken under Rule 13.1f.

Penalty for Playing Ball from a Wrong Place in Breach of Local Rule: _General Penalty_ **Under Rule 14.7a.**"

D-3 Prohibiting Relief from Wrong Green When Only Stance Interference Exists

Purpose. There may be situations where a Committee wishes to deny a player relief from a wrong green when the only interference is to the player's stance, for example:

* There is thick rough close to some putting greens and the Committee considers that it would be unfair to require a player to take relief into such areas, or

* One large green is used as the putting green for two separate holes, but the Committee decides to divide the green. It may also chooses not to require a player whose ball is on the putting green for the hole being played to take relief when his or her stance is on the other putting green.

Model Local Rule D-3.1

"Rule 13.1f is modified in this way:

Interference does not exist if a _wrong green_ only interferes with the player's _stance._"

Model Local Rule D-3.2

"Rule 13.1f is modified in this way:

When a player's ball lies on the *putting green* of [specify hole number], interference does not exist for the player's *stance* on the *putting green* of [specify hole number] or the reverse.

Penalty for Playing Ball from a Wrong Place in Breach of Local Rule: *General Penalty* Under Rule 14.7a."

D-4 Prohibiting Play from Fringe of Wrong Green

Purpose. If balls played on a particular hole often come to rest on the green of a nearby hole:

- The nearest point of complete relief when taking relief from that wrong green under Rule 13.1f will usually be on the fairway next to that green, and

- That apron or fringe may become damaged as a result.

To prevent such damage, the Committee can choose to require players to take relief under Rule 13.1f by reference to a modified nearest point of complete relief that avoids interference with both the wrong green and the apron or fringe or by using a dropping zone (see Model Local Rule B-2).

Model Local Rule D-4

"When playing [specify hole number], if the player must take relief under Rule 13.1f because his or her ball came to rest on the *putting green* of [specify hole number] or that *putting green* interferes with his or her *stance* or area of intended swing:

- In finding the *relief area* to be used when taking this relief, the *putting green* of [specify hole number] is defined to include the area of fairway within [specify distance such as two *club-lengths*] from the edge of the *putting green*.

- This means that the *nearest point of complete relief* must avoid interference from this area in addition to the *putting green*.

Penalty for Playing Ball from a Wrong Place in Breach of Local Rule: *General Penalty* Under Rule 14.7a."

D-5 Status of Practice Putting Green or Temporary Putting Green

Purpose. Wrong greens include practice greens for putting or pitching, but the Committee may choose to allow play from them by Local Rule (meaning that a player whose ball lies on such a green must play it from there). A temporary putting green for a hole is typically part of the general area when it is not in use, but the Committee may wish to clarify its status or declare it to be a wrong green. The Committee may also define a practice green or temporary green to be ground under repair which would allow a player to take free relief under Rule 16.1b.

Model Local Rule D-5.1

"The practice green located [insert details of where the green is located] is not a *wrong green* and free relief is not required or permitted under Rule 13.1f."

Model Local Rule D-5.2

"The temporary green located [insert details of where the green is located] is a *wrong green* even when not in use and relief must be taken under Rule 13.1f."

Model Local Rule D-5.3

"The practice green located [insert details of where the green is located] is not a *wrong green* and free relief is not required to be taken under Rule 13.1f, but it is *ground under repair* and a player may take free relief under Rule 16.1b."

D-6 Dividing a Double Green into Two Separate Greens

Purpose. When a course has a green that serves as the putting green for two holes, the Committee may wish to divide the green into two separate greens through a Local Rule. This would require a player who is on the wrong portion of the green to take relief under Rule 13.1f. The method of defining the separation should be specified. This Local Rule may be used in conjunction with Model Local Rule D-3 for cases where the player's ball is on the correct portion of the green but his or her stance is on the other portion of the green.

Model Local Rule D-6

"The green serving holes [specify hole numbers] is considered to be two separate greens divided by [specify method such as coloured stakes]. A player who has interference with the portion of the green for the hole not being played is on a *wrong green* and must take relief under Rule 13.1f.

Penalty for Playing Ball from a Wrong Place in Breach of Local Rule: *General Penalty* **Under Rule 14.7a.**"

8E Special or Required Relief Procedures

E-1 Dropping Zones

Purpose. A dropping zone is a special form of relief area that may be adopted by the Committee. When taking relief in a dropping zone, the player must drop the ball in and have it come to rest in the dropping zone.

Dropping zones should be considered when there may be practical problems in requiring players to use the normal relief options under a Rule such as:

- Rule 13.1f – Wrong Green.

- Rule 16.1 – Abnormal Course Conditions (Including Immovable Obstructions).

- Rule 16.2 – Dangerous Animal Condition.

- Rule 17 – Penalty Areas.

- Rule 19 – Unplayable Ball.

- Model Local Rules E-5 – Alternative to Stroke and Distance for Ball Lost or Ball Out of Bounds or F-23 – Temporary Immovable Obstructions.

The following points apply when dropping a ball in a dropping zone:

- The player does not have to stand in the dropping zone when dropping the ball.

- When a player is using a dropping zone, the relief area is defined by that dropping zone and the ball must be dropped in and come to rest in the dropping zone (see Rule 14.3).

- If the dropping zone is defined by a line on the ground, the line is inside the dropping zone.

See Section 21 for additional information regarding dropping zones.

Model Local Rule E-1.1

This Model Local Rule covers the example of a dropping zone used as an extra option for taking relief from a penalty area, but it may be adapted for any other Rule mentioned above.

"If a ball is in the *penalty area* [identify location], including when it is *known or virtually certain* that a ball that has not been found came to rest in the *penalty area*, the player has these relief options, each for **one penalty stroke**:

- Take relief under Rule 17.1, or

- As an extra option, *drop* the original ball or another ball in the dropping zone [describe how the dropping zone is defined and where located]. The dropping zone is a *relief area* under Rule 14.3.

Penalty for Playing Ball from a Wrong Place in Breach of Local Rule: *General Penalty* **Under Rule 14.7a.**"

Model Local Rule E-1.2

This Model Local Rule covers the example of a dropping zone used as an extra option for taking relief from an abnormal course condition such as a large area of ground under repair, but it may be adapted for any other Rule mentioned above.

"If a ball is in the *ground under repair* [identify location], including when it is *known or virtually certain* that a ball that has not been found came to rest in the *ground under repair*, the player may:

- Take free relief under Rule 16.1, or

- As an extra option, take free relief by *dropping* the original ball or another ball in the dropping zone [describe how the dropping zone is defined and where located]. The dropping zone is a *relief area* under Rule 14.3.

Penalty for Playing Ball from a Wrong Place in Breach of Local Rule: *General Penalty* Under Rule 14.7a.."

Model Local Rule E-1.3

This Model Local Rule covers the example of a dropping zone used as the only relief option available (other than stroke and distance) for taking relief from a penalty area, but it may be adapted for any other Rule mentioned above.

"If a ball is in the *penalty area* [identify location], including when it is *known or virtually certain* that a ball that has not been found came to rest in the *penalty area*, the player may:

- Take stroke-and-distance relief under Rule 17.1d(1), adding **one penalty stroke**, or

- *Drop* the original ball or another ball in the dropping zone [describe how the dropping zone is defined and where located], adding **one penalty stroke**. The dropping zone is a *relief area* under Rule 14.3.

- The player may not take relief under Rules 17.1d(2) or 17.1d(3).

Penalty for Playing Ball from a Wrong Place in Breach of Local Rule: *General Penalty* Under Rule 14.7a."

E-2 Cleaning Ball

Purpose. When conditions such as wet ground conditions throughout parts of the course may cause mud to stick to the ball, the Committee can choose to allow the player to lift, clean and replace the ball in the general area. Such relief should be limited to those portions of the course where needed.

While the Local Rule for Preferred Lies (Model Local Rule E-3) is designed for use only in areas cut to fairway height or less in the general area, this Local Rule can be used throughout the general area or restricted to specific areas. The Committee could choose to use both Local Rules permitting preferred lies in the fairways and cleaning the ball elsewhere in the general area.

It is not advisable to implement this Local Rule once play has begun for a stroke-play round. Doing so would allow players who had more holes to play the advantage of using it for a longer period of time. The Local Rule could be implemented once a match has begun between the play of two holes as opponents have an equal benefit.

For guidance on when and how this Local Rule may be used in order for scores to be submitted for handicapping purposes (for example, if it must be limited to fairway only), consult the rules or recommendations contained within the Handicap System operating in the local jurisdiction.

Model Local Rule E-2

"When a player's ball lies in [identify area, such as the *general area*, at the 6th hole, in the *general area* cut to fairway height or less, etc.], the ball may be lifted cleaned and *replaced* without penalty. The player must *mark* the spot before lifting the ball (see Rule 14.1) and the ball must be *replaced* on its original spot (see Rule 14.2).

Penalty for Playing Ball from a Wrong Place in Breach of Local Rule: *General Penalty* Under Rule 14.7a."

E-3 Preferred Lies

Purpose. When occasional local abnormal conditions might interfere with fair play, the affected parts of the course can be defined as ground under repair. But adverse conditions such as heavy snows, spring thaws, prolonged rains or extreme heat can sometimes damage the course or prevent use of heavy mowing equipment.

When such conditions are widespread on the course, the Committee can choose to adopt a Local Rule for "preferred lies" (also known as "winter rules") to allow fair play or help protect the fairway. Such a Local Rule should be withdrawn as soon as conditions allow.

The use of this Local Rule outside the fairway in the general area is not recommended as it may result in a player receiving free relief from areas where a ball might otherwise be unplayable (such as in areas of bushes or trees).

It is not authorised to implement this Local Rule once play has begun for a stroke-play round. Doing so would allow players who have more holes to play the advantage of using it for a longer period of time. The Local Rule could be implemented once a match has begun between the play of two holes as opponents have an equal benefit.

For guidance on when and how this Local Rule may be used in order for scores to be submitted for handicapping purposes (including the size of the relief area and if it may only be used in the fairway), consult the rules or recommendations contained within the Handicap System operating in the local jurisdiction.

Model Local Rule E-3

"When a player's ball lies in a part of the *general area* cut to fairway height or less [or identify a specific area such as 'on the fairway of the 6th hole'], the player may take free relief once by placing the original ball or another ball in and playing it from this *relief area*:

- Reference Point: Spot of the original ball.

- Size of Relief Area Measured from Reference Point: [Specify size of relief area, such as one *club-length*, one scorecard length or 6 inches] from the reference point, **but** with these limits:

- Limits on Location of Relief Area:

  » Must not be nearer the *hole* than the reference point, and

  » Must be in the *general area*.

In proceeding under this Local Rule, the player must choose a spot to place the ball and use the procedures for *replacing* a ball under Rules 14.2b(2) and 14.2e.

Penalty for Playing Ball from a Wrong Place in Breach of Local Rule: *General Penalty* Under Rule 14.7a."

E-4 Relief from Aeration Holes

Purpose. Aeration holes do not fall within the meaning of holes made by the maintenance staff. Therefore players are not permitted to repair them on the putting green (see Rule 13.1c) or take free relief from them in the general area, but such holes can interfere with the proper playing of the game. If the Committee declares aeration holes to be ground under repair, a player may find it impractical or impossible to obtain complete relief.

Therefore, when recent aeration holes may significantly interfere with the lie of the ball or area of intended swing, the Committee can choose to give relief as it would for ground under repair but exclude relief for interference to the player's stance. This Local Rule should be withdrawn when the aeration holes have healed enough to avoid significant interference.

Model Local Rule E-4

'If a player's ball lies in or touches an aeration hole:

Model Local Rules

(a) <u>Ball in General Area.</u> The player may take relief under Rule 16.1b. If the ball comes to rest in another aeration hole the player may take relief again under this Local Rule.

(b) <u>Ball on Putting Green.</u> The player may take relief under Rule 16.1d.

But interference does not exist if the aeration hole only interferes with the player's stance or, on the *putting green*, on the player's *line of play*.

Penalty for Playing Ball from a Wrong Place in Breach of Local Rule: *General Penalty* **Under Rule 14.7a.**"

E-5 Alternative to Stroke and Distance for Lost Ball or Ball Out of Bounds

Purpose. When a provisional ball has not been played, significant issues with pace of play can result for a player needing to take stroke-and-distance relief for a ball that is out of bounds or cannot be found. The purpose of this Local Rule is to allow a Committee to provide an extra relief option that allows a player to play on without returning to the location of the previous stroke.

The Local Rule is appropriate for general play where golfers are playing casual rounds or playing their own competitions. The Local Rule is not appropriate for competitions limited to highly skilled players (that is, professional competitions and elite amateur competitions). For guidance on when and how this Local Rule may be used in order for scores to be submitted for handicapping purposes, consult the rules or recommendations contained within the Handicap System operating in the local jurisdiction.

Where a Committee has introduced such a Local Rule for general play, and removes it for competitions, it should ensure that all players are aware of this before play begins.

A Committee may introduce such a Local Rule for all play on the course or only for one or two specific holes where it may be especially useful (for example, where players are unable to see the landing area and therefore may not know whether or not to play a provisional ball).

This option allows the player to drop in a large area between the point where the ball is estimated to have come to rest or gone out of bounds and the edge of the fairway of the hole being played that is not nearer the hole.

The player gets two penalty strokes when using this relief option. This means that the relief is comparable to what could have been achieved if the player had taken stroke-and-distance relief.

This Local Rule cannot be used for an unplayable ball, or for a ball that is known or virtually certain to be in a penalty area.

If a provisional ball is played and neither the original ball nor the provisional ball can be found, then the Local Rule may be applied for the provisional ball that cannot be found.

MLR E-5 DIAGRAM 1: BALL NOT FOUND

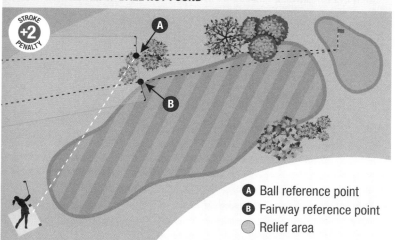

- **A** Ball reference point
- **B** Fairway reference point
- ⬤ Relief area

When a player's ball has not been found, the player may take stroke-and-distance relief, or when Model Local Rule E-5 is introduced, the player has the additional option to drop a ball in and play from the relief area described below for two penalty strokes:

Reference Points	Size of Relief Area	Limits on Relief Area
A. Ball Reference Point: The point where the original ball is estimated to have come to rest on the course (point A) B. Fairway Reference Point: The point of fairway of the hole being played (point B) that is nearest to the ball reference point, but is not nearer the hole than the ball reference point	Anywhere between: • A line from the hole through the ball reference point (point A) (and within two club-lengths to the outside of that line), and • A line from the hole through the fairway reference point (point B) (and within two club-lengths to the fairway side of that line)	The relief area: • Must not be nearer the hole than the ball reference point, and • Must be in the general area

Player Notes:
As the relief area is likely to be very large, the ball could roll a considerable distance from the spot where it first strikes the ground and not need to be dropped again.

469

MLR E-5 DIAGRAM 2: BALL OUT OF BOUNDS

Ⓐ Ball reference point
Ⓑ Fairway reference point
◯ Relief area

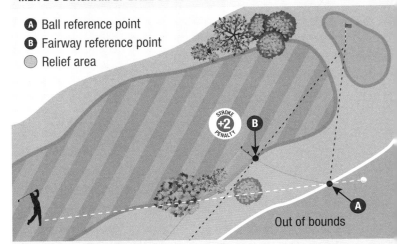

Out of bounds

When a player's ball is known or virtually certain to be out of bounds, the player may take stroke-and-distance relief, or when Model Local Rule E-5 is introduced, the player has the additional option to drop a ball in and play from the relief area described below for two penalty strokes:

Reference Point	Size of Relief Area	Limits on Relief Area
A. Ball Reference Point: The point where the original ball is estimated to have last crossed the edge of the course boundary to go out of bounds (point A) B. Fairway Reference Point: The point of fairway of the hole being played (point B) that is nearest to the ball reference point, but is not nearer the hole than the ball reference point	Anywhere between: • A line from the hole through the ball reference point (point A) (and within two club-lengths to the outside of that line but still on the course), and • A line from the hole through the fairway reference point (point B) (and within two club-lengths to the fairway side of that line)	The relief area: • Must not be nearer the hole than the ball reference point, and • Must be in the general area

Player Notes:
As the relief area is likely to be very large, the ball could roll a considerable distance from the spot where it first strikes the ground and not need to be dropped again.

MLR E-5 DIAGRAM 3: BALL NOT FOUND OR OUT OF BOUNDS
                                    CLOSE TO GREEN

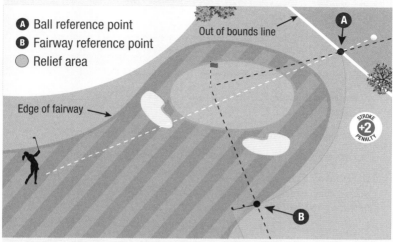

A Ball reference point
B Fairway reference point
○ Relief area

Out of bounds line

Edge of fairway

When a player's ball has not been found or is known or virtually certain to be out of bounds, the player may take stroke-and-distance relief, or when Model Local Rule E-5 is introduced, the player has the additional option to drop a ball in and play from the relief area described below for two penalty strokes:

Reference Points	Size of Relief Area	Limits on Relief Area
A. Ball Reference Point: The point where the original ball is estimated to have come to rest on the course or last crossed the edge of the course boundary to go out of bounds (point A) B. Fairway Reference Point: The point of fairway of the hole being played (point B) that is nearest to the ball reference point, but is not nearer the hole than the ball reference point	Anywhere between: • A line from the hole through the ball reference point (point A) (and within two club-lengths to the outside of that line), and • A line from the hole through the fairway reference point (point B) (and within two club-lengths to the fairway side of that line)	The relief area: • Must not be nearer the hole than the ball reference point, and • Must be in the general area

Player Notes:
As the relief area is likely to be very large, the ball could roll a considerable distance from the spot where it first strikes the ground and not need to be dropped again.

Model Local Rule E-5

"When a player's ball has not been found or is *known or virtually certain* to be *out of bounds*, the player may proceed as follows rather than proceeding under *stroke and distance*.

For **two penalty strokes**, the player may take relief by *dropping* the original ball or another ball in this *relief area* (see Rule 14.3):

Two Estimated Reference Points:

a. Ball Reference Point: The point where the original ball is estimated to have:

- Come to rest on the *course*, or

- Last crossed the edge of the *course* boundary to go *out of bounds*.

b. Fairway Reference Point: The point of fairway of the hole being played that is nearest to the ball reference point, **but** is not nearer the *hole* than the ball reference point.

For purposes of this Local Rule, "fairway" means any area of grass in the *general area* that is cut to fairway height or less.

If a ball is estimated to be *lost* on the *course* or last crossed the edge of the *course* boundary short of the fairway, the fairway reference point may be a grass path or a teeing ground for the hole being played cut to fairway height or less.

Size of Relief Area Based on Reference Points: Anywhere between:

- A line from the *hole* through the ball reference point (and within two *club-lengths* to the outside of that line), and

- A line from the *hole* through the fairway reference point (and within two *club-lengths* to the fairway side of that line).

But with these limits:

Limits on Location of Relief Area:

- Must be in the *general area*, and

- Must not be nearer the *hole* than the ball reference point.

Once the player puts a ball *in play* under this Local Rule:

- The original ball that was *lost* or *out of bounds* is no longer *in play* and must not be played.

- This is true even if the ball is found on the *course* before the end of the three-minute search time (see Rule 6.3b).

But the player may not use this option to take relief for the original ball when:

- That ball is *known or virtually certain* to have come to rest in a *penalty area*, or

- The player has played another ball provisionally under penalty of *stroke and distance* (see Rule 18.3).

A player may use this option to take relief for a provisional ball that has not been found or is known or virtually certain to be out of bounds.

Penalty for Playing Ball from a Wrong Place in Breach of Local Rule: *General Penalty* **Under Rule 14.7a.**"

E-6 Line of Play Relief for Protective Fence

<u>Purpose</u>. A fence (or similar protective screen) is sometimes used to protect players on one hole from shots played at another hole.

If such a fence is close to the playing area for another hole, the Committee can choose to use dropping zones to give a player an extra relief option without penalty when he or she is playing that other hole and the fence is on the line of play.

The player should be entitled to relief only when the ball is nearer the hole than the dropping zone, so that a player whose ball is well away from the fence is not allowed to move forward to the dropping zone. The Committee should take this into consideration when positioning the dropping zone to ensure that this relief will be available only for situations where they believe such free relief is justified.

Model Local Rule E-6

"During play of the [specify hole number], if the protective fence on the [specify hole number] is on a player's *line of play*:

- The player may take free relief by *dropping* a ball in and playing it from the dropping zone (describe location).

- **But** this relief is allowed only if the ball is *in play* nearer the *hole* than where the dropping zone is located (see Rule 14.3).

Penalty for Playing Ball from a Wrong Place in Breach of Local Rule: *General Penalty* **Under Rule 14.7a.**"

E-7 Relief from Electric Boundary Fence

<u>Purpose</u>. Where an electric fence is used as a boundary fence, a Local Rule providing free relief for a ball lying within a certain distance (for example, two club-lengths) of the boundary fence is permitted. In these circumstances, to ensure the safety of the player, the player can measure

the two club-lengths from the fence and has an additional club-length in which to drop the ball no nearer the hole than where the ball originally lay.

It is not otherwise authorized to introduce a Local Rule providing free relief from a boundary fence even if the Committee's reasons for doing so are to protect the fence from any damage.

Model Local Rule E-7

"If a player's ball lies on the *course* and within [specific a distance, such as two *club-lengths*] of the electric boundary fence on hole[s] [specify location(s)], he or she may, without penalty, take relief under Rule 16.1, using as the reference point the point that is [specify distance, such as two *club-lengths*] from the fence and an equal distance from the *hole*.

Penalty for Playing Ball from a Wrong Place in Breach of Local Rule: *General Penalty* Under Rule 14.7a."

E-8 Defining No Play Zones

Purpose. There may be some parts of the course where the Committee wishes to prohibit play, in which case each area must be treated as either within an abnormal course condition or a penalty area.

The Committee can use no play zones for any reason, such as:

- To protect wildlife, animal habitats, and environmentally-sensitive areas.

- To prevent damage to young trees, flower beds, turf nurseries, re-turfed areas or other planted areas.

- To protect players from danger.

- To preserve sites of historical or cultural interest.

See Sections 2G and 5B(5) for more information on No Play Zones and how to mark them distinctively.

Model Local Rule E-8.1

"The area defined by [specify how the area is marked, for example, with green stakes] [specify where it is located, e.g. on the right of the fairway on hole 8] is a *no play zone* that is to be treated as an *abnormal course condition.* Free relief must be taken from interference by the *no play zone* under Rule 16.1f."

Model Local Rule E-8.2

"The area within the [red] [yellow] *penalty area* defined by [specify how the area is marked, for example, with green stakes] [specify where it is located, for example, on the right of the fairway on hole 8] is a *no play zone.* When a ball is in the *no play zone* within the *penalty area*, the ball must not be played as it lies and relief must be taken from interference by the *no play zone* under Rule 17.1e."

E-9 Defining an Area of Out of Bounds as a No Play Zone

Purpose. Although a player may not play a ball from out of bounds, there may be areas that are out of bounds that the Committee may wish to designate as no play zones, for example, to stop players from damaging anything growing in that area when it interferes with the play of a ball on the course. In this case, a player must take free relief if the player's ball is on the course but his or her area of intended stance is in the no play zone which is out of bounds or if his or her swing touches something that is in the no play zone.

Model Local Rule E-9

"The [identify the area *out of bounds* that is to be treated as a *no play* zone] is a *no play zone* and the player must take free relief under Rule 16.1f(2) if his or her ball is on the *course* and anything in the *no play zone* interferes with the player's area of intended *stance* or swing. The player must not play the ball as it lies.

Penalty for Playing Ball from a Wrong Place in Breach of Local Rule: *General Penalty* **Under Rule 14.7a.**"

E-10 Protection of Young Trees

Purpose. To prevent damage to young trees when a player makes a stroke, a Committee can choose to designate them as a no play zone so that:

- If a player has any type of interference as defined in Rule 16.1 from such a tree designated as a no play zone, he or she must take relief under Rule 16.1f.

- If the player's ball lies in a penalty area, he or she must either take free relief under the Local Rule within the penalty area or proceed with penalty under Rule 17.1.

Such trees should be identified by stakes, ribbons or in some other clear way.

When the tree has matured and no longer needs this protection, the Committee should withdraw the Local Rule and/or remove the identifying stake or ribbon from the tree.

Model Local Rule E-10

"The young trees identified by [identify markings] are *no play zones*:

- If a player's ball lies anywhere on the *course* other than in a *penalty area* and it lies on or touches such a tree or such a tree interferes with the player's *stance* or area of intended swing, the player must take relief under Rule 16.1f.

- If the ball lies in a *penalty area*, and interference to the player's *stance* or area of intended swing exists from such a tree, the player must take relief either with penalty under Rule 17.1e or with free relief under Rule 17.1e(2).

Penalty for Playing Ball from a Wrong Place in Breach of Local Rule: *General Penalty* **Under Rule 14.7a.**"

E-11 Ball Deflected by Power Line

Purpose. If a permanent overhead power line may interfere with the reasonable play of a hole, a Committee can require that if a ball hits the power line (and towers, support wires or poles supporting the power line), the stroke does not count and the player must play the stroke again. This Local Rule should not generally be used for power lines that do not interfere with play of a hole or are out of bounds.

A Local Rule that gives a player the option to replay the stroke for a ball that hits a power line should not be implemented.

Model Local Rule E-11

"If it is *known or virtually certain* that a player's ball hit a power line [or tower or a wire or pole supporting a power line] during the play of [specify hole number], the *stroke* does not count. The player must play a ball without penalty from where the previous *stroke* was made (see Rule 14.6 for what to do).

Penalty for Playing Ball from a Wrong Place in Breach of Local Rule: *General Penalty* **Under Rule 14.7a.**"

8F Abnormal Course Conditions and Integral Objects

F-1 Defining Abnormal Course Conditions and Integral Objects

Purpose. There are many ways in which a Committee can define abnormal course conditions and integral objects on the course and so it is not appropriate or possible to provide a complete list of Model Local Rules that can be used for this purpose.

The key is to be clear and specific when defining abnormal course conditions and integral objects in the Local Rules.

The Committee has the scope to adopt Local Rules for the following purposes without the need for them to fit with the Model Local Rules detailed in Section 2:

- Clarifying the status of objects that may be obstructions.

- Declaring any artificial object to be an integral object (and not an obstruction).

- Declaring artificial surfaces and edges of roads to be integral objects.

- Declaring roads and paths that don't have artificial surfaces and edges to be obstructions if they could unfairly affect play.

- Defining temporary obstructions on the course or next to the course as movable, immovable or temporary immovable obstructions.

No specific Model Local Rules are included in this section given the variety of options available, but some examples are provided below:

- *Ground under repair* is defined by any area encircled by a white line [or insert other colour or description as appropriate].

- *Ground under repair* includes exposed rocks in areas cut to fairway height or less [or within a stated distance of the fairway, such as two *club-lengths*].

- Areas in *bunkers* where sand has been removed by the movement of water resulting in deep furrows through the sand are *ground under repair*.

- Mats that are secured and plastic cable ramps that are covering cables are *immovable obstructions*.

- Protective fences around greens are *immovable obstructions*.

- The rails on split rail fences are [*movable* or *immovable*] *obstructions*.

- Retaining artificial walls and pilings when located in *penalty areas* are *integral objects*.

- Wires and other objects [closely] attached to trees are *integral objects*.

- All gates that are for the purpose of getting through boundary walls and fences [or specify the hole(s) on which this applies] are *integral objects*.

See Sections 2F and 5B(4) for more information on abnormal course conditions.

See Sections 2H and 5B(4) for more information on integral objects.

F-2 Limited Relief for Embedded Ball

Purpose. Rule 16.3 normally allows relief whenever a ball is embedded anywhere in the general area (other than in sand in areas that are not cut to fairway height or less).

But a Committee may choose:

- To allow relief only when a ball is embedded in a part of the general area cut to fairway height or less.

- Not to allow free relief for a ball embedded in the wall or lip of a bunker (such as a stacked turf or soil face).

Model Local Rule F-2.1

"Rule 16.3 is modified in this way:

Free relief is allowed only when a ball is *embedded* in part of the *general area* that is cut to fairway height or less.

[Stacked turf faces above *bunkers* are not cut to fairway height or less for the purpose of this Rule.]

Penalty for Playing Ball from a Wrong Place in Breach of Local Rule: *General Penalty* Under Rule 14.7a."

Model Local Rule F-2.2

"Rule 16.3 is modified in this way:

Free relief is not allowed when a ball is *embedded* in [stacked turf faces] [soil faces] above *bunkers*.

Penalty for Playing Ball from a Wrong Place in Breach of Local Rule: *General Penalty* Under Rule 14.7a."

F-3 Ground Under Repair Treated as Part of Nearby Obstruction

Purpose. Ground under repair may be located right next to an immovable obstruction. For example, when a flower bed that the Committee has declared to be ground under repair is surrounded by an artificially-surfaced cart path or when cart traffic causes damage next to a cart path.

This can lead to complicated relief situations. After taking relief from one condition, a player may find that there is now interference by the other condition; and after taking relief from that other condition, the player may find that the first condition once again interferes.

To allow the player to take relief in one step, the Committee can choose to treat both conditions as a single abnormal course condition. When this is done, the areas of ground under repair should either be connected to the immovable obstruction by white lines or should be defined in some other clear way.

This Model Local Rule gives examples of how to address situations of this type:

Model Local Rule F-3.1

When white lines are used to mark the *ground under repair*:

"White-lined areas of *ground under repair* and the [artificially surfaced road or path or other identified *obstruction*] they tie into are treated as a single *abnormal course condition* when taking relief under Rule 16.1."

Model Local Rule F-3.2

When white lines are not used to mark the *ground under repair*:

"Where areas of damaged ground are right next to [artificially surfaced road or path or other identified *obstruction*] they are treated as a single *abnormal course condition* when taking relief under Rule 16.1."

Model Local Rule F-3.3

For decorative planted areas such as flower beds surrounded by an *immovable obstruction* such as a cart path:

"[Describe area, such as decorative planted areas] that are surrounded by an artificially surfaced road or path (including everything growing within that area) and the road or path are treated as a single *abnormal course condition* when taking relief under Rule 16.1."

F-4 Extensive Damage Due to Heavy Rain and Traffic

Purpose. When heavy rain has resulted in many areas of unusual damage to the course (such as deep ruts caused by vehicles or deep footprints caused by spectators), and it is not feasible to define them with stakes or lines, the Committee has the authority to declare such unusual damage to be ground under repair.

Model Local Rule F-4

"*Ground under repair* may include areas of unusual damage, including areas where spectators or other traffic have combined with wet conditions to alter the ground surface materially, but only when so declared by an authorized *referee* or member of the *Committee*.

Penalty for Playing Ball from a Wrong Place in Breach of Local Rule: *General Penalty* Under Rule 14.7a."

F-5 Immovable Obstructions Close to Putting Greens

Purpose. When a ball lies anywhere other than on the putting green, an immovable obstruction on the player's line of play is not, of itself, interference under Rule 16.1. Free relief is normally not allowed.

But if the aprons or fringes of putting greens are cut short enough that putting from off the green is likely to be a common choice of stroke, immovable obstructions that are close to the putting green may interfere with such strokes.

In that case, the Committee can choose to give an extra relief option under Rule 16.1 when a player's ball lies in the general area or on the putting green and an immovable obstruction close to the putting green is on the player's line of play.

The Committee may limit such relief to certain situations, such as only for particular holes or obstructions, or only when the ball and the obstruction are in part of the general area cut to fairway height or less.

Model Local Rule F-5

"Relief from interference by an *immovable obstruction* may be taken under Rule 16.1.

The player also has these extra options to take relief when such *immovable obstructions* are close to the *putting green* and on the *line of play*:

Ball in General Area. The player may take relief under Rule 16.1b if an *immovable obstruction* is:

- On the *line of play*, and is:
  - » Within two *club-lengths* of the *putting green*, and
  - » Within two *club-lengths* of the ball.

Exception – No Relief If Line of Play Clearly Unreasonable. There is no relief under this Local Rule if the player chooses a *line of play* that is clearly unreasonable.

Penalty for Playing Ball from a Wrong Place in Breach of Local Rule: *General Penalty* **Under Rule 14.7a.**"

F-6 Prohibiting Relief from Abnormal Course Condition When Only Stance Interference Exists

Purpose. A Committee may wish to deny relief for interference to the player's stance from some conditions such as animal holes, as interference to the stance does not significantly affect the stroke or if relief for interference to the stance could result in repeatedly taking relief from nearby similar conditions.

Model Local Rule F-6

"Rule 16.1 is modified in this way:

Interference does not exist if [insert condition from which relief is restricted] only interferes with the player's *stance*.

Penalty for Playing Ball from a Wrong Place in Breach of Local Rule: *General Penalty* **Under Rule 14.7a.**"

F-7 Relief from Seams of Cut Turf

Purpose. A portion of the course that has been repaired with cut turf is often marked as ground under repair until it is stable enough for play.

But when the area of turf itself no longer needs to be marked as ground under repair, the Committee may still choose to allow relief when:

- A ball lies in one of the cut turf seams (also known as sod seams).
- A seam interferes with the player's area of intended swing.

When such seams only interfere with the player's stance, there is no need to allow relief.

Model Local Rule F-7

"If a player's ball lies in or touches a seam of cut turf or a seam interferes with the player's area of intended swing:

(a) Ball in General Area. The player may take relief under Rule 16.1b.

(b) Ball on Putting Green. The player may take relief under Rule 16.1d.

But interference does not exist if the seam only interferes with the player's *stance*.

All seams within the area of cut turf are treated as the same seam in taking relief. This means that if a player has interference from any seam after *dropping* the ball, the player must proceed as required under Rule 14.3c(2) even when the ball is still within one club-length of the reference point.

Penalty for Playing Ball from a Wrong Place in Breach of Local Rule: *General Penalty* Under Rule 14.7a."

F-8 Relief from Cracks in Ground

Purpose. In hot and dry conditions, the fairways of a course may suffer due to cracks in the ground. The lie of a ball could be seriously affected if it comes to rest in such a crack, but a player's stance may not be hindered by the condition, in which case a Local Rule that gives relief for the lie of ball and area of intended swing only is recommended.

Model Local Rule F-8

"Cracks in the ground in parts of the *general area* cut to fairway height or less are *ground under repair*. The player may take relief under Rule 16.1b.

[**But** interference does not exist if the crack only interferes with the player's *stance*.]"

Penalty for Playing Ball from a Wrong Place in Breach of Local Rule: *General Penalty* Under Rule 14.7a."

Model Local Rules

F-9 Relief from Tree Roots in Fairway

Purpose. In the unusual situation where exposed tree roots are found in the fairway, it may be unfair not to allow the player to take relief from the roots. The Committee can choose to treat such tree roots in the fairway as ground under repair from which free relief is allowed under Rule 16.1b.

In some circumstances where exposed tree roots are also found in short rough close to the fairway, the Committee can also choose to treat such tree roots within a specified distance from the edge of the fairway, (for example four club-lengths or in the first cut of rough) as ground under repair from which free relief is allowed under Rule 16.1b.

In doing so, the Committee can choose to limit relief to interference with the lie of ball and the area of intended swing.

Model Local Rule F-9.1

"If a player's ball is at rest in a portion of the *general area* cut to fairway height or less and there is interference from exposed tree roots that are in a part of the *general area* cut to fairway height or less, the tree roots are treated as *ground under repair*. The player may take free relief under Rule 16.1b.

[**But** interference does not exist if the tree roots only interfere with the player's *stance*.]

Penalty for Playing Ball from a Wrong Place in Breach of Local Rule: *General Penalty* Under Rule 14.7a.."

Model Local Rule F-9.2

"If a player's ball is in the *general area* and there is interference from exposed tree roots that are in a part of the *general area* cut to fairway height or less [or in the rough within specify number of *club-lengths* of the edge of the ground cut to fairway height or less] [or in the first cut of the rough], the tree roots are treated as *ground under repair*. The player may take free relief under Rule 16.1b.

[**But** interference does not exist if the tree roots only interfere with the player's *stance*.]

Penalty for Playing Ball from a Wrong Place in Breach of Local Rule: *General Penalty* Under Rule 14.7a."

F-10 Damage by Animals

Purpose. There may be times when animals cause damage to the course that is so widespread that it is not practical to mark all the damaged areas as ground under repair. Also, some types of animal damage may not be covered by Rule 16.1.

These Model Local Rules show how the Committee can choose to address these issues.

If animals, including insects, create damage on a course, the Committee can choose to treat such damage as ground under repair from which relief is allowed under Rule 16.1. This is done by defining the areas or the condition rather than attempting to mark all the areas of damage.

A Committee can choose to limit relief only for damage that interferes with the lie of the ball or the area of intended swing.

Model Local Rule F-10

"In the *general area*, areas of damage caused by [type of animal] are treated as *ground under repair* from which relief is allowed under Rule 16.1b.

[**But** interference does not exist if the damage only interferes with the player's *stance*.]

Penalty for Playing Ball from a Wrong Place in Breach of Local Rule: *General Penalty* Under Rule 14.7a."

F-11 Ant Hills

Purpose. Ant hills are loose impediments and may be removed under Rule 15.1. They are not animal holes from which free relief is allowed under Rule 16.1.

But there are situations when ant hills are difficult or impossible to remove (such as when large, hard or conical in shape). In that case, the Committee can adopt a Local Rule giving the player an option to treat such ant hills as ground under repair.

It is not necessary to adopt such a Local Rule for fire ants as fire ants are considered a dangerous animal condition and free relief is available under Rule 16.2.

Model Local Rule F-11

"Large or hard ant hills on the *course* are, at the player's option, *loose impediments* that may be removed under Rule 15.1 or *ground under repair* from which relief is allowed under Rule 16.1.

Penalty for Playing Ball from a Wrong Place in Breach of Local Rule: *General Penalty* Under Rule 14.7a."

F-12 Animal Dung

Purpose. The dung of a bird or other animal is a loose impediment that may be removed under Rule 15.1.

But if there is concern with the effect of dung on fair play, the Committee can give players the option of treating dung as ground under repair from which relief is allowed under Rule 16.1.

If treating the dung as ground under repair will not necessarily give full relief when a ball is on the putting green, a Committee can also allow players to use a greens switch/whip or similar maintenance equipment to remove the dung from the line of play without penalty, even if doing so improves the line of play or other conditions affecting the stroke.

Model Local Rule F-12

"At the player's option, dung from [specify dung from which relief would be given, e.g. goose dung, dog dung] may be treated either as:

- A *loose impediment* that may be removed under Rule 15.1, or

- *Ground under repair* from which relief is allowed under Rule 16.1.

[If dung is found on the *putting green*, the player may also use the greens switch/whip located by the *putting greens* to remove the dung from the *line of play*. If doing so *improves* the *line of play* or other *conditions affecting the stroke*, there is no penalty under Rule 8.1a.]

Penalty for Playing Ball from a Wrong Place in Breach of Local Rule: *General Penalty* Under Rule 14.7a."

F-13 Animal Hoof Damage

Purpose. The hoofs of animals such as deer or elk can cause damage on the course. A Committee may wish to allow players to take relief from this damage as ground under repair without having to mark all such areas.

Since damage caused by animals may be repaired on the putting green the Committee can declare such damage as ground under repair or allow players to repair it.

Model Local Rule F-13

"Damage that is clearly identifiable as having been caused by *animal* hoofs is *ground under repair* from which free relief is allowed under Rule 16.1.

[But on *the putting green*, Rule 16.1 does not apply as such damage may be repaired under Rule 13.1.]

Penalty for Playing Ball from a Wrong Place in Breach of Local Rule: *General Penalty* Under Rule 14.7a."

F-14 Accumulations of Loose Impediments

Purpose. At certain times of the year, piles of loose impediments such as leaves, seeds or acorns may make it difficult for a player to find or play his or her ball. A Committee can choose to treat such piles of loose impediments in the general area or in a bunker as ground under repair from which free relief is allowed under Rule 16.1.

This Local Rule may not be used for penalty areas as relief is not available for abnormal course conditions in penalty areas.

The Local Rule should be limited to the hole(s) where problems are created by such loose impediments and should be withdrawn as soon as conditions allow.

Model Local Rule F-14

"During play of the [specify hole number], any ground with temporary accumulations of [identify types of loose *impediments*] in the *general area* or in a *bunker* is treated as *ground under repair* from which free relief is allowed under Rule 16.1.

Penalty for Playing Ball from a Wrong Place in Breach of Local Rule: *General Penalty* **Under Rule 14.7a.**"

F-15 Mushrooms on Putting Green

Purpose. If mushrooms growing on the putting green may interfere with fair play, the Committee can treat them as ground under repair so that a player may take free relief under Rule 16.1d.

Model Local Rule F-15

"Mushrooms that are attached on the *putting green* are *ground under repair* from which free relief is allowed under Rule 16.1d.

Penalty for Playing Ball from a Wrong Place in Breach of Local Rule: *General Penalty* **Under Rule 14.7a.**"

F-16 Bunker Filled with Temporary Water

Purpose. If a bunker is flooded, free relief under Rule 16.1c may not be sufficient to allow for fair play. A Committee can choose to treat that bunker as ground under repair in the general area from which free relief is allowed outside the bunker.

The Committee should only use this Local Rule on a case-by-case basis and is not authorized to make a Local Rule providing generally that all flooded bunkers are ground under repair.

Model Local Rule F-16

"The flooded *bunker* on [insert location of *bunker*; for example, left of 5th green] is *ground under repair* in the *general area*. It is not treated as a *bunker* during the *round*.

Model Local Rules

If the player's ball lies in or touches this *ground under repair* or the *ground under repair* interferes with the player's *stance* or area of intended swing, the player may take free relief under Rule 16.1b.

All other *bunkers* on the *course*, whether they contain *temporary water* or not, are still *bunkers* for all purposes under the Rules.

Penalty for Playing Ball from a Wrong Place in Breach of Local Rule: *General Penalty* Under Rule 14.7a."

F-17 All Roads and Paths Treated as Obstructions

<u>Purpose</u>. Where roads or paths that are not artificially surfaced may interfere with fair play, the Committee can choose to designate such roads as immovable obstructions from which free relief is allowed under Rule 16.1.

Model Local Rule F-17

"All roads and paths on the *course* [or identify particular types or locations], even if not artificially-surfaced, are treated as *immovable obstructions* from which free relief is allowed under Rule 16.1.

Penalty for Playing Ball from a Wrong Place in Breach of Local Rule: *General Penalty* Under Rule 14.7a."

F-18 Treating Movable Objects to Be Immovable

<u>Purpose</u>. The Committee can choose to treat certain movable objects on the course, such as all stakes (other than boundary stakes), bins and direction poles, to be immovable so as to discourage players from moving them.

The implications of this Local Rule should be fully considered by the Committee in advance as it may result in players breaching Rule 8.1 by moving an obstruction that is treated as immovable.

Model Local Rule F-18

"All stakes [or identify the *movable obstructions* that are to be considered *immovable*] on the *course* are treated as *immovable obstructions* from which free relief is allowed under Rule 16.1. Relief is not allowed to be taken under Rule 15.2.

Penalty for Breach of Local Rule: *General Penalty*."

F-19 Edging Grooves Near Putting Greens

<u>Purpose</u>. Edging grooves are sometimes cut on the apron or fringe of the putting green to keep grasses from creeping onto the putting green. Because it can be difficult to play a ball from such grooves, a Committee

can choose to treat them as ground under repair from which free relief is allowed under Rule 16.1.

Relief should be allowed only for interference with the lie of the ball or the area of intended swing.

Model Local Rule F-19

"The edging grooves around the aprons or fringes of *putting greens* are *ground under repair*. If a player's ball lies in or touches a groove or a groove interferes with the area of intended swing:

(a) <u>Ball in General Area</u>. The player may take free relief under Rule 16.1b.

(b) <u>Ball on the Putting Green</u>. The player may take free relief under Rule 16.1d.

But interference does not exist if the edging groove only interferes with the player's *stance*.

Penalty for Playing Ball from a Wrong Place in Breach of Local Rule: *General Penalty* **Under Rule 14.7a**."

F-20 Concrete Drainage Channels

Purpose. Narrow concrete drainage channels are sometimes found on courses where flooding is common. This can create issues for play because:

- These channels are penalty areas as defined in the Rules.

- But they often run next to cart paths and are more like immovable obstructions than penalty areas.

The Committee can choose to treat these drainage channels as immovable obstructions in the general area rather than as penalty areas.

See Model Local Rule B-4 for when an open water course can be defined to be part of the general area.

Model Local Rule F-20

"Drainage channels that are made of artificial materials and run next to cart paths are treated as *immovable obstructions* in the *general area* and are part of the cart path. A player may take free relief under Rule 16.1b.

Penalty for Playing Ball from a Wrong Place in Breach of Local Rule: *General Penalty* **Under Rule 14.7a**."

F-21 Painted Lines or Dots

Purpose. If the Committee puts paint lines or dots down on the putting green or in a part of the general area cut to fairway height or less (for

Model Local Rules

example, for distance markings), it may treat those areas as abnormal course conditions from which free relief is available under Rule 16.1.

When such paint lines or dots only interfere with the player's stance, there is no need to allow relief.

Alternatively, the Committee can choose to clarify that there is no relief available from such paint lines or dots.

Model Local Rule F-21.1

"Painted lines or dots on the *putting green* or in a part of the *general area* cut to fairway height or less are to be treated as *ground under repair* from which relief is allowed under Rule 16.1.

But interference does not exist if painted lines or dots only interfere with the player's *stance*.

Penalty for Playing Ball from a Wrong Place in Breach of Local Rule: *General Penalty* Under Rule 14.7a."

Model Local Rule F-21.2

"Relief is not allowed from painted lines or dots [describe area, for example, in areas where the grass is not cut to fairway height or less].

Penalty for Playing Ball from a Wrong Place in Breach of Local Rule: *General Penalty* Under Rule 14.7a."

F-22 Temporary Lines and Cables

Purpose. Temporary lines and cables are often placed on the course to provide power and communications for a competition. These cables may be on the surface of the ground or above or below the ground. Such lines and cables are not normally there and are not part of the challenge of playing the course, so the Committee may choose to provide extra relief when they interfere with play.

Model Local Rule F-22

"Temporary lines and cables for power and communications (and mats covering or poles supporting them) are *obstructions*:

1. If they are readily movable, they are *movable obstructions* and a player may remove them without penalty under Rule 15.2.

2. Otherwise they are *immovable obstructions* from which the player may take relief as follows:

(a) Ball in General Area or in Bunker. The player may take relief under Rule 16.1.

(b) <u>Ball in Penalty Area</u>. Rule 16.1b is modified to allow the player the extra option to take free relief from interference by these *immovable obstructions* in a *penalty area* by *dropping* a ball and playing it from this *relief area*:

- <u>Reference Point</u>: The *nearest point of complete relief* in the *penalty area*.

- <u>Size of Relief Area Measured from Reference Point</u>: One *club-length*, **but** with these limits:

- <u>Limits on Location of Relief Area</u>:

    » Must be in the *penalty area* in which the ball came to rest,

    » Must not be nearer the *hole* than the reference point, and

    » There must be complete relief from all interference by the *immovable obstruction*.

3. If a player's ball hits a temporary elevated line or cable, the *stroke* does not count. The player must play a ball without penalty from where the previous *stroke* was made (see Rule 14.6 for what to do).

4. Grass-covered trenches for temporary lines or cables in the *general area* are *ground under repair*, even if not marked. The player may take free relief under Rule 16.1.

But there are two exceptions:

- **Exception 1 – Ball Strikes Elevated Section**: If a ball hits an elevated junction section of cable rising from the ground, the *stroke* counts, and the ball must be played as it lies.

- **Exception 2 – Ball Strikes Wires Supporting Temporary Immovable Obstruction:** Guy wires supporting a temporary *immovable obstruction* (TIO) are part of the TIO and are not covered by this Local Rule, unless the *Committee* states that the guy wires are to be treated as temporary elevated lines or cables under this Local Rule.

Penalty for Playing Ball from a Wrong Place in Breach of Local Rule: *General Penalty* **Under Rule 14.7a.**."

F-23 Temporary Immovable Obstructions

Purpose. When obstructions are temporarily placed on or next to the course, the Committee should specify whether they are movable obstructions (see Rule 15), immovable obstructions (see Rule 16) or temporary immovable obstructions ("TIOs").

TIOs (such as a grandstand or a tent) are not normally present and are not considered to be part of the challenge of playing the course. Because of their temporary nature, this Local Rule provides an additional relief option that is not allowed from immovable obstructions, although the player can still choose to treat the TIO as if it were an immovable obstruction and use the relief procedures available in Rule 16.

The additional relief provided by this Local Rule includes the ability for a player to take relief when the TIO is located on the straight line between his or her ball and the hole (known as "line of sight relief") by moving sideways, keeping the same distance from the hole, so that the TIO is no longer between the player's ball and the hole (also known as moving along the "equidistant arc").

When a player takes relief from a TIO, whether under this Local Rule or the relief procedures in Rule 16, the player is guaranteed complete relief from physical interference. But only when relief is taken using the additional relief option under this Local Rule will the player be guaranteed complete relief from the TIO being on his or her line of sight.

Model Local Rule F-23.

"**Definition of TIO:** A temporary *immovable obstruction* (TIO) is a structure that is temporarily added on or next to the *course*, usually for a particular competition, and is fixed or not readily movable.

Examples of TIOs are temporary tents, scoreboards, grandstands, television towers and toilets.

TIOs include any supporting guy wires connected to them, except when the *Committee* decides the supporting guy wires are to be treated as *immovable obstructions*.

The outermost edge of the TIO is used in determining whether a ball is under the TIO or whether the TIO is on the player's line of sight between the ball and the *hole*.

Lines or stakes may be used to define the edges of a TIO or to connect multiple TIOs into a single, larger TIO.

A TIO is different from an *immovable obstruction* and this Local Rule provides additional relief from interference by a TIO. This means that the player can choose to take relief by using either:

* The procedure for taking relief from an *abnormal course condition* in Rule 16 as if the TIO were an *immovable obstruction* (this relief is also available when the ball lies in a *penalty area* or when the TIO is *out of bounds*), or

* The additional relief option available under this Local Rule.

Model Local Rules

a. When Relief Is Allowed

Relief from a TIO is normally allowed when there is physical interference or line of sight interference from the TIO.

Interference under this Local Rule means that the player has:

- Physical interference,
- Line of sight interference, or
- Both physical and line of sight interference.

(1) Meaning of Physical Interference by Temporary Immovable Obstruction. Physical interference exists when:

- The player's ball touches or lies in or on a TIO, or
- The TIO interferes with the player's area of intended *stance* or area of intended swing.

(2) Meaning of Line of Sight Interference by Temporary Immovable Obstruction. Line of sight interference exists when:

- The player's ball touches or lies in, on or under a TIO, or
- The TIO is on the player's line of sight to the *hole* (that is, the TIO is located on the straight line between the ball and the *hole*), or
- The ball is within one *club-length*, measured on an equidistant arc from the *hole*, of a spot where the TIO would be on the player's direct line of sight to the *hole* (this one *club-length* wide area is commonly referred to as the "corridor").

(3) When No Relief Is Available Despite Having Interference. If the ball touches or is in or on the TIO, relief is always available.

But when the ball neither touches nor is in or on the TIO, there is **no** relief under this Local Rule if any of the following applies:

- From either physical interference or line of sight interference:

  » There is no relief when playing the ball as it lies would clearly be unreasonable because of something other than the TIO (such as when the player is unable to make a *stroke* because of where the ball lies in a bush outside the TIO), and

  » There is no relief when interference exists only because the player chooses a club, type of *stance* or swing or direction of play that is clearly unreasonable under the circumstances; and

- From line of sight interference:

  » There is no relief when it is clearly unreasonable for a player to play the ball far enough that the ball will reach the TIO, and

491

» There is no relief when the player cannot show that there is a *stroke* that he or she could reasonably play that would both (a) have the TIO (including the corridor) on the line of that *stroke*, and (b) result in the ball finishing on a direct line to the *hole*.

b. Relief from Interference for Ball in General Area

If the player's ball is in the *general area* and there is interference by a TIO (including a TIO located *out of bounds*), the player may take free relief by *dropping* the original ball or another ball in and playing it from this *relief area*:

- Reference Point: The *nearest point of complete relief* where both physical and line of sight interference no longer exist.

- Size of Relief Area from Reference Point: The entire area within one *club length* from the reference point, **but** with these limits:

- Limits on Location of Relief Area:

  » Must be in the *general area*,

  » Must not be nearer the *hole* than the reference point, and

  » There must be complete relief from both physical and line of sight interference by the TIO.

If the player has physical interference from the TIO, instead of using this relief procedure he or she may choose to take relief using the procedure for taking relief from an *abnormal course condition* in Rule 16.1b, treating the TIO as if it were an *immovable obstruction*. The relief procedure under Rule 16.1b is also available when the ball lies in a *penalty area* or when the TIO is *out of bounds*. See Clause f of this Local Rule for how to take relief.

c. Relief from Interference for Ball in Bunker or Penalty Area.

If the player's ball is in a *bunker* or a *penalty area* and there is interference by a TIO (including a TIO located *out of bounds*), the player may take either free relief or penalty relief:

(1) Free Relief: Playing from Bunker or Penalty Area. The player may take free relief as provided in Clause b, **except that** the *nearest point of complete relief* where interference no longer exists, and the *relief area* must be in that *bunker* or *penalty area*.

If there is no such point in that *bunker* or *penalty area* where interference no longer exists, the player may still take this relief as provided above by using the *point of maximum available relief* in the *bunker* or the *penalty area* as the reference point.

Model Local Rules

(2) <u>Penalty Relief: Playing from Outside Bunker or Penalty Area.</u> For **one penalty stroke**, the player may *drop* the original ball or another ball in and play it from this *relief area*:

- <u>Reference Point:</u> The *nearest point of complete relief* not nearer the *hole* where both physical and line of sight interference no longer exist that is outside that *bunker* or *penalty area.*

- <u>Size of Relief Area from Reference Point:</u> The entire area one *club-length* from the reference point, **but** with these limits:

- <u>Limits on Location of Relief Area:</u>

  » Any *area of the course* other than in that *bunker* or *penalty* area or on any *putting green*,

  » Must not be nearer the *hole* than the reference point, and

  » There must be complete relief from both physical and line of sight interference by the TIO.

If the player has physical interference from the TIO, instead of using this relief procedure he or she may choose to take relief using the procedure for taking relief from an *abnormal course condition* in Rule 16.1b, treating the TIO as if it were an *immovable obstruction*. The relief procedure under Rule 16.1b is also available when the ball lies in a *penalty area* or when the TIO is *out of bounds*. See Clause f of this Local Rule for how to take relief.

d. Relief When Ball in TIO Not Found

If the player's ball has not been found but is *known or virtually certain* to have come to rest in a TIO:

- The player may take relief under this Local Rule by using the estimated point where the ball last crossed the edge of the TIO on the *course* as the spot of the ball for purposes of finding the *nearest point of complete relief.*

- Once the player puts another ball *in play* to take relief in this way:

  » The original ball is no longer *in play* and must not be played.

  » This is true even if it is then found on the *course* before the end of the three-minute search time (see Rule 6.3b)

But if it is not *known or virtually certain* that the ball came to rest in the TIO, the player must play under penalty of *stroke and distance* (see Rule 18.2).

e. Committee Authority to Modify TIO Relief Procedures

When adopting this Local Rule, the *Committee* may modify the relief procedures in Clauses b and c in either or both of the following ways:

(1) Optional or Mandatory Use of Dropping Zones. The *Committee* may permit or require a player to use a dropping zone as the *relief area* for taking relief under this Local Rule. When doing so, the *Committee* may add the dropping zone for relief from only physical interference or only line of sight interference or it may be used for relief from both types of interference.

(2) "Either Side" Relief Option. The *Committee* may permit the player the option to take relief on the other side of a TIO in addition to the relief options allowed under Clauses b and c of this Local Rule. **But** the *Committee* may provide that either side relief is not allowed if the player is taking relief using the procedures in Rule 16.1.

f. Player May Proceed Under Other Relief Rules

(1) Taking Relief by Using the Procedures in Rule 16.1 or this Local Rule. If a player has physical interference from the TIO as defined in Clause a, the player may either:

- Choose to use the relief procedures in Rule 16.1 or

- Use this Local Rule.

- **But** may not take relief under one of these options and then take relief under the other.

If the player chooses to use the procedure for taking relief from an *abnormal course condition* in Rule 16.1, he or she must treat the TIO as if it an *immovable obstruction* and take relief based on where the ball lies:

- In the *general area* using the procedures in Rule 16.1b.

- In a *bunker* using the procedures in Rule 16.1c.

- In a *penalty area* using the procedures in Rule 16.1c as if the ball lies in a *bunker*.

- On the *putting green* using the procedures in Rule 16.1d.

(2) Taking Relief under Rule 17, 18 or 19. This Local Rule does not prevent the player from taking relief under Rule 17, 18 or 19 rather than taking TIO relief under this Local Rule.

Penalty for Playing Ball from a Wrong Place in Breach of Local Rule: *General Penalty* **Under Rule 14.7a.**"

8G Restrictions on Use of Specific Equipment

G-1 List of Conforming Driver Heads

Purpose. To remove any doubt that drivers being used in a competition are conforming:

- A Committee can choose to require players to use only drivers whose clubheads have been evaluated and approved as conforming under the Equipment Rules.

- A List of Conforming Driver Heads is found at USGA.org.

This Local Rule is recommended for use only in competitions limited to highly skilled players (that is, professional and elite amateur competitions).

Model Local Rule G-1

"Any driver the player uses to make a stroke must have a clubhead, identified by model and loft, which is on the current List of Conforming Driver Heads issued by the USGA.

This list is regularly updated and is found at USGA.org.

Exception – Pre-1999 Driver Heads: A driver with a clubhead that was made before 1999 is exempt from this Local Rule.

Penalty For Making a Stroke with Club in Breach of this Local Rule: Disqualification.

There is no penalty under this Local Rule for carrying but not making a stroke with a driver that is not on the List of Conforming Driver Heads."

G-2 Groove and Punch Mark Specifications

Purpose. Effective 1 January 2010, the Equipment Rules were revised to provide new groove and punch mark specifications for all clubs other than drivers and putters (An exception was made for certain Ping Eye2 irons made before 31 March 1990, as stated below.). Until at least 2024, clubs made before 2010 are not required to meet these specifications.

But a Committee may choose to adopt a Local Rule requiring players to use only clubs that meet all the specifications included in the current Equipment Rules. This is recommended for use only in competitions limited to highly skilled players (that is, professional and elite amateur competitions).

An Equipment Database can be found at USGA.org to assist in finding which clubs may be used.

Model Local Rule G-2

"In making a *stroke*, the player must use clubs that conform to the groove and punch mark specifications in the *Equipment Rules* that took effect on 1 January 2010.

An Equipment Database of fairway woods, hybrids, irons and wedges which have been tested for conformance to the current *Equipment Rules* is found at USGA.org.

Exception – Ping Eye2 Irons Manufactured before 31 March 1990
Ping Eye2 irons manufactured before 31 March 1990 with a groove spacing to groove width ratio of 2.3 to 1 are allowed for play under the Rules of Golf, even when this Local Rule is in effect. In using this Exception, the player is responsible for proving when the club was manufactured. If the player cannot do so, the club must conform to the groove and punch mark specifications that took effect on 1 January 2010.

Penalty For Making a Stroke with Club in Breach of this Local Rule: Disqualification.

There is no penalty under this Local Rule for carrying but not making a *stroke* with a club which does not conform to these groove and punch mark specifications."

G-3 List of Conforming Golf Balls

Purpose. To remove any doubt that the balls being used in a competition are conforming, a Committee may choose to require the player to use only balls which have been evaluated and approved as conforming under the Equipment Rules.

A List of Conforming Golf Balls is found at USGA.org and is updated monthly.

Even if this Local Rule is not in place, any ball used must be a conforming ball.

Model Local Rule G-3

"Any ball used in making a *stroke* must be on the current List of Conforming Golf Balls issued by the USGA.

This list is regularly updated and is found at USGA.org.

Penalty For Making a Stroke with a Ball Not on Current List in Breach of this Local Rule: Disqualification."

G-4 One Ball Rule

Purpose. To prevent a player from using balls with different playing characteristics depending on the nature of the hole or shot to be played during a round, the Committee can choose to require that a player use only a single type of ball that is on the List of Conforming Golf Balls.

Each individual listing on the List of Conforming Golf Balls is considered a different ball. Golf balls of different colours with identical markings are considered different balls.

This Local Rule is recommended for use only in competitions limited to highly skilled players (that is, professional competitions and elite amateur competitions).

Model Local Rule G-4

"During an entire *round*, each ball at which the player makes a *stroke* must be the same brand and model as found in a single entry on the current List of Conforming Balls.

If a different brand and/or model is *dropped*, *replaced* or placed but has not yet been played, the player may correct the mistake by stopping use of that ball, without penalty, under Rule 14.5. The player must *drop*, *replace* or place a ball of the same brand and model as used at the start of the *round*.

When the player discovers he or she has played a ball in breach of this Local Rule, he or she must stop using that ball before playing from the next *teeing area* and complete the *round* with a ball of the same brand and model as used at the start of the *round*; otherwise the player is **disqualified**.

If the discovery is made during the play of a hole, the player may complete play of this hole with the ball played in breach or place a ball of the correct brand and model on the spot where the ball played in breach of this Local Rule was lifted from.

Penalty for Making a Stroke at a Ball in Breach of Local Rule:

The player gets the ***general penalty*** for each hole during which he or she is in breach of this Local Rule."

G-5 Prohibiting Use of Distance-Measuring Devices

Purpose. Although Rule 4.3 allows players to use equipment to measure distance (subject to certain requirements), a Committee can choose to prohibit the use of any electronic distance-measuring devices.

Model Local Rule G-5

"Rule 4.3a(1) is modified in this way:

During a *round*, a player must not obtain distance information by using an electronic distance-measuring device.

Penalty for Breach of Local Rule – see Rule 4.3."

G-6 Prohibiting Use of Motorized Transportation

Purpose. A Committee can choose to prohibit players from using any type of motorized transportation such as a golf cart during a round. This is appropriate when the Committee views walking as an integral part of playing in the competition or when it believes that the use of motorized transportation would be unsafe or might damage the course.

In adopting this Local Rule, the Committee can allow motorized transportation in limited ways, such as to take players from one hole to another when those holes are far apart or allowing members of the Committee to give a player a ride when he or she will play, or has played, again under penalty of stroke and distance.

If a player accepts a ride without the permission of the Committee, the Committee can waive the penalty if it would have authorized the player to ride in that situation had the request been made. For example, if a player who had lost a ball and needed to return to the teeing area accepted a ride from a volunteer when there was no Committee member available, the Committee could waive the penalty if members of the Committee would have given the player the ride if asked.

But, when motorized transportation is not allowed by Local Rule, it is a principle of the Local Rule that players should walk the entire course, so authorization should not be given if a player has been given a ride forward when he or she has not already walked that distance. For example, if a player stops to buy a refreshment after playing his or her tee shot, and then accepts a ride forward to his or her ball from a volunteer, the penalty under the Local Rule should not be waived.

Model Local Rule G-6

"During a *round*, a player or *caddie* must not ride on any form of motorized transportation **except** as authorized or later approved by the *Committee*.

[A player who will play, or has played, under penalty of *stroke and distance* is always authorised to ride on motorized transportation.]

[Players and *caddies* may ride on the shuttle between holes [identify hole] and [identify hole].]

Penalty for Breach of Local Rule: The player gets the **general penalty** for each hole during which there is a breach of this Local Rule. If the breach occurs between the play of two holes, it applies to the next hole."

G-7 Prohibiting Use of Certain Types of Shoes

Purpose. To protect the course from damage, the Committee can prohibit the use of shoes with metal or traditionally designed spikes.

The Committee also may prohibit the use of shoes with other features that may cause undesirable damage.

Model Local Rule G-7

"Rule 4.3a is modified in this way:

During a *round*, a player must not wear shoes with:

* Traditional spikes – that is, spikes having single or multiple points designed to penetrate deeply into the surface of the ground (regardless of whether made of metal, ceramic, plastic or other materials); or

* Spikes of any design that are entirely or partially made of metal, if such metal may come in contact with the *course*.

Penalty for Breach of Local Rule – see Rule 4.3."

G-8 Prohibiting or Restricting Use of Audio and Video Devices

Purpose. Rule 4.3a(4) permits a player to use equipment to listen to audio or watch video of matters unrelated to the competition being played. But the Committee can adopt a Local Rule prohibiting the use of audio and video devices altogether during a round.

Model Local Rule G-8

"Rule 4.3a(4) is modified in this way: During a *round*, a player must not listen to or watch content of any nature on a personal audio or video device.

Penalty for Breach of Local Rule – see Rule 4.3."

8H Defining Who May Help or Give Advice to Players

H-1 Use of Caddie Prohibited or Required; Caddie Restrictions

Purpose. A Committee can choose to modify Rule 10.3 to

* Prohibit the use of caddies,

* Require players to use a caddie, or

* Limit a player's choice of caddie (such as not allowing a caddie to be a professional, a parent or relative, another player in the competition, etc.).

Model Local Rule H-1.1

If caddies are prohibited:

"Rule 10.3a is modified in this way: A player must not have a *caddie* during the *round*.

Penalty for Breach of Local Rule:

* The player gets the ***general penalty*** for each hole during which he or she is helped by a *caddie*.

  If the breach happens or continues between two holes, the player gets the ***general penalty*** for the next hole."

Model Local Rule H-1.2

Or, if there are limits on who the player may have as a caddie:

"Rule 10.3a is modified in this way: A player must not have [identify prohibited type of *caddie* for example, a parent or guardian] as his or her *caddie* during the *round*.

Penalty for Breach of Local Rule:

- The player gets the **general penalty** for each hole during which he or she is helped by such a *caddie*.

- If the breach happens or continues between two holes, the player gets the **general penalty** for the next hole."

Model Local Rule H-1.3

If a player is required to have a caddie:

"Rule 10.3a is modified in this way: A player must have a *caddie* during the *round*.

Penalty for Breach of Local Rule: The player gets the **general penalty** for each hole during which he or she does not have a *caddie*."

H-2 Appointment of Advice Giver in Team Competitions

Purpose. Under Rule 24.4a, in a team competition the Committee can allow each team to name one or two people who may give advice to team members while they are playing on the course:

- Any "advice giver" must be identified to the Committee before giving advice.

- The Committee can limit the types of advice that this person may give (such as not allowing the advice giver to point out the line of play when a ball lies on the putting green).

- The Committee can prohibit an advice giver from walking on certain parts of the course (such as putting greens).

- It is not normal for a Committee to allow two advice givers per team, unless the nature of the competition warrants it, for example in a competition where no caddies are permitted or there is a large number of players on each team.

- The Committee should determine the appropriate penalty for a violation by an advice giver. This may be a penalty to a specific player who was assisted in a prohibited manner or an overall penalty for the team, for example the addition of two strokes to the team's score in a stroke-play event.

Model Local Rule H-2

"Each team may name [one/two] advice giver[s] whom players on the team may ask for *advice* and receive *advice* from during the *round*. The team must identify each advice giver to the *Committee* before any player on the team begins his or her *round*.

[The team may change its advice giver during the *round*, but must tell the *Committee* when it is doing so.]

[The advice giver must not point out a *line of play* [or walk on the *putting green*] when the ball of a team player lies on the *putting green*.]"

H-3 Restricting Who Can Be a Team Captain

Purpose. Under Rule 24.3, in a team competition the Committee can set limits on who may serve as a team captain and on the conduct of the team captain under Rule 24.4a. Where advice givers are allowed (see Model Local Rule H-2), the team captain may also be an advice giver.

Model Local Rule H-3

"A team captain must be [insert eligibility restriction, such as a member of the same club]."

H-4 Treating Advice Giver as Part of the Player's Side

Purpose. The Committee can provide that the advice giver has the same status as a member of the side to ensure the Rules of Golf apply to that person's actions.

Model Local Rule H-4

"The advice giver has the same status as a member of the *side* in relation to each member of his or her team."

H-5 Advice: Team Members in Same Group

Purpose. Under Rule 24.4c, in stroke play where a player's score for the round counts only as part of the team's score, the Committee can adopt a Local Rule allowing team members playing in the same group to give each other advice even if they are not partners.

Model Local Rule H-5

"Rule 10.2 is modified in this way:

Where two players from the same team are playing together in the same group, those players may ask for *advice* and receive *advice* from each other during the *round*."

8I Defining When and Where Players May Practise

I-I Practising Before Rounds

Purpose. Rule 5.2 covers practising on the course before or between rounds during a competition:

- Match Play (Rule 5.2a). Players in a match may practise on the course before or between rounds, as they usually will have an equal chance to do so because they play at the same time.

- Stroke Play (Rule 5.2b). Players must not practise on the course before a round on the day of a competition, as they may not have an equal chance to do so because they usually play in different groups at different times. But they are allowed to practise on a day of the competition after their competition play for the day is complete.

There are many different considerations about whether to allow practice on the course, such as fairness to the players, possible interference with set-up of the course and maintenance activities, the amount of time before or between rounds, or when players are encouraged to play on the course outside the competition.

For these or other reasons, a Committee can choose to adopt a Local Rule that modifies these default provisions by either allowing or prohibiting such practice entirely or by limiting when, where or how such practice may take place.

Model Local Rule I-1.1

"Rule 5.2a is modified in this way:

A player must not practise on the competition course before or between rounds.

[Or, if players are allowed to practise in limited ways: Describe those limits and when, where and how a player may practise on the course.]

Penalty for Breach of this Local Rule:

- Penalty for first breach: *General Penalty* (applied to the player's first hole).

- Penalty for second breach: **Disqualification**."

Model Local Rule I-1.2

"Rule 5.2b is modified in this way:

A player may practise on the competition *course* before or between *rounds*

[Or, if players are allowed to practise in limited ways: Describe those limits and when, where and how a player may practise on the *course*.]

[Or, if players are prohibited from practising on the *course* both before and between *rounds*: "A player must not practise on the competition *course* before or between rounds."]

I-2 Prohibiting Practising on or Near Previous Putting Green

Purpose. Rule 5.5b allows a player, between the play of two holes, to practise putting or chipping on or near the putting green of the hole just completed. But if this may affect pace of play or for other reasons, the Committee can choose to prohibit such practice.

Model Local Rule I-2

"Rule 5.5b is modified in this way:

Between the play of two holes, a player must not:

- Make any practice *stroke* on or near the *putting green* of the hole just completed, or

- Test the surface of that *putting green* by rubbing the *putting green* or rolling a ball.

Penalty for Breach of Local Rule: *General Penalty*."

8J   Procedures for Bad Weather and Suspensions of Play

J-I Methods for Stopping and Resuming Play

Purpose. Rule 5.7b requires players to stop playing immediately if the Committee declares an immediate suspension of play. The Committee should use a distinct method of telling players about an immediate suspension.

The following signals are generally used, and it is recommended that all Committees use these signals where possible:

Immediate Stop:	One prolonged note of the siren.
Normal Stop:	Three consecutive notes of the siren.
Resume Play:	Two short notes of siren.

Model Local Rule J-I

"A suspension of play for a dangerous situation will be signalled by [insert signal to be used]. All other suspensions will be signalled by [insert signal to be used]. In either case, resumption of play will be signalled by [insert signal to be used]. See Rule 5.7b."

J-2 Removal of Temporary Water

Purpose. A Committee may adopt a policy that clarifies what actions are appropriate for a Committee member, someone designated by the

Committee (for example, a member of the maintenance staff), or player, to remove temporary water on the putting green.

Model Local Rule J-2

"If a player's ball lies on the *putting green* and there is interference by *temporary water* on the *putting green*, the player may:

• Take free relief under Rule 16.1d; or

• Have his or her *line of play* squeegeed.

Such squeegeeing should be done across the *line of play* and extend a reasonable distance beyond the *hole* (that is, at least one roller length) and only be carried out by [specify who may carry this out, for example the maintenance staff]."

8K Pace of Play Policies

The following Model Local Rules give some examples of how the Committee can choose to address the issue of Pace of Play. The Committee can adopt other Local Rules to suit the resources available to them and so these are not an exhaustive list.

Other sample policies are available at USGA.org.

K-1 Maximum Time for All or Part of Round

Purpose. In competitions where there are few or no referees on the course, it may be desirable for the Committee to formulate a simple Local Rule that establishes a time limit that it considers adequate for players to complete the round and/or a certain number of holes. These time limits will vary depending on the numbers in groups and the form of play. If a group exceeds the prescribed time limit and is out of position on the course, each player in the group is subject to penalty.

Model Local Rule K-1

"If a group finishes the *round* [or specify number of holes] more than the starting interval behind the group in front and over [specify time, for example, 3 hours 45 minutes] from the time of starting [or specify as required], all players in the group are subject to a penalty of one stroke [or specify as required]."

K-2 Hole-by-Hole and Shot-by-Shot Pace of Play Policy

Purpose. In competitions where there is an adequate number of officials on the course, the Committee can put a Pace of Play policy into effect that allows a set length of time for each hole, and then if players exceed that time, establishes a maximum time to play each stroke.

The Model Local Rule below is an example of a policy for a stroke play competition where players will be individually timed when the group is out of position.

A modified penalty structure which may be used in a pace of play policy is also detailed in Model Local Rule K-5.

Options for Being Out of Position

A group is out of position when it is over the allocated time for the holes that have been played and not in position with the previous group. When defining when a group is out of position the policy should specify when the group is considered out of position by reference to the group in front of them. Some examples are:

- The group is more than the starting interval behind the group in front of them.
- A par 4 or par 5 hole is open before the group reaches the teeing area of that hole.

Time for Making a Stroke

When a group is being timed, each player must make his or her stroke within a specified time limit. The Committee may require all strokes to be made in the same amount of time or it may adopt the optional language shown below to allow an additional period of time for the first player to play from a specific area such as the teeing area or the putting green.

Model Local Rule K-2

"Maximum Allowable Time

The maximum allowable time is the maximum time considered necessary by the *Committee* for a group to complete its *round*. This is expressed in a per-hole and aggregate time format and includes all time associated with playing the game, e.g., for rulings and walking times between holes.

The maximum time allotted for the completion of 18 holes at [insert course name] is [insert maximum time, for example, 4 hours and 05 minutes]. The following procedure applies only if a group is "out of position."

Definition of Out of Position

The first group to start will be considered "out of position" if, at any time during the *round*, the group's cumulative time exceeds the time allowed for the number of holes played. Any following group will be considered out of position if it is [specify when a group is out of position to the group in front of them (see examples above)] and has exceeded the time allowed for the number of holes played.

Model Local Rules

Procedure When Group is Out of Position

1. *Referees* will monitor pace of play and decide whether a group that is "out of position" should be timed. An assessment of whether there are any recent mitigating circumstances, e.g. a lengthy ruling, *lost* ball, unplayable ball, etc. will be made.

   If a decision is made to time the players, each player in the group will be subject to individual timing and a *referee* will advise each player that they are "out of position" and they are being timed.

   In exceptional circumstances, an individual player, or two players within a group of three, may be timed instead of the entire group.

2. The maximum time allocated per *stroke* is [specify a time limit such as 40 seconds].

   [10 extra seconds are allowed for the first player to play: a) a tee shot on a par 3 hole; b) an approach shot to the green; and c) a chip or putt.]

   The timing will start when a player has had sufficient time to reach the ball, it is his or her turn to play and he or she is able to play without interference or distraction. Time taken to determine distance and select a club will count as time taken for the next *stroke*.

   On the *putting green*, timing will start when the player has had a reasonable amount of time to lift, clean and *replace* the ball, repair damage that interferes with the *line of play* and move *loose impediments* on the *line of play*. Time spent looking at the *line of play* from beyond the hole and/or behind the ball will count as part of the time taken for the next *stroke*.

   Timings will be taken from the moment it is decided by the *referee* that it is the player's turn to play and he or she is able to play without interference or distraction.

   Timing ceases when a group is back in position and players will be advised accordingly.

Penalty for Breach of Local Rule:

- Penalty for first breach: One-stroke penalty.
- Penalty for second breach: **General Penalty** applied in addition to the penalty for the first breach.
- Penalty for third breach: **Disqualification**."

Until a player has been advised of a bad time, he or she cannot incur a further bad time.

Procedure When Again Out of Position During Same Round

If a group is "out of position" more than once during a *round*, the above procedure will apply on each occasion. Bad times and the application of penalties in the same *round* will be carried forward until the *round* is completed. A player will not be penalized if he or she has a second bad time before being advised of the earlier bad time."

K-3 Hole-by-Hole and Shot-by-Shot Pace of Play Policy for Stableford

Purpose. For a Stableford competition, the Committee can modify the penalty for a breach of Model Local Rule K-2 to ensure that the penalty will impact the player's score. The Committee may optionally add a verbal warning for the first breach.

Model Local Rule K-3

"The penalty statement to Model Local Rule K-2 is modified in this way:

Penalty for Breach of Local Rule:

* Penalty for first breach: Deduction of **one point** from the total points scored for the *round*.

* Penalty for second breach: Deduction of a further **two points** from the total points scored for the *round*.

* Penalty for third breach: **Disqualification**."

K-4 Hole-by-Hole and Shot-by-Shot Pace of Play Policy for Par/Bogey Competitions

Purpose. For a Par/Bogey competition, the Committee can modify the penalty for a breach of Model Local Rule K-2 to ensure that the penalty will impact the player's score. The Committee may optionally add a verbal warning for the first breach.

Model Local Rule K-4

"The penalty statement to Model Local Rule K-2 is modified in this way:

Penalty for Breach of Local Rule:

* Penalty for first breach: Deduction of **one hole** from the aggregate of holes scored.

* Penalty for second breach: Deduction of a **second hole** from the aggregate of holes scored.

* Penalty for third breach: **Disqualification**."

K-5 Modified Pace of Play Penalty Structure

Purpose. A Committee may modify the penalty for a breach of any Pace of Play policy such that the penalty for a first breach of the policy is a verbal warning from the referee. The example given below is how the penalty statement is modified for a stroke play competition and the penalty statements for match play, Stableford and Par/Bogey competitions could be similarly adjusted.

Model Local Rule K-5

"**Penalty for Breach of Local Rule:**

- Penalty for first breach: Verbal warning from _referee_.

- Penalty for second breach: One-stroke penalty.

- Penalty for third breach: **General Penalty** applied in addition to the penalty for the second breach.

- Penalty for fourth breach: **Disqualification**."

8L Unauthorized Local Rules

While a Committee has significant authority under the Rules of Golf to adopt Local Rules to fit the particular needs of a course or competition, any Local Rules that it chooses to put in place must be consistent with the policies established in Section 8, Model Local Rules.

Rule 1.3c(3) states that the Committee does not have the authority to apply penalties in a different way than stated in the Rules of Golf. Therefore it is inappropriate for a Committee to write an unauthorized Local Rule that waives a penalty or changes a penalty. For example, a Committee cannot change the penalty for using a non-conforming club from disqualification to the general penalty or change the general penalty for failing to replace a ball which was moved to a single stroke. The Committee must not impose penalties when the Rules do not impose them, for example, penalizing a player who failed to total his or her score on the scorecard in stroke play.

In addition, Committees must not write a Local Rule that goes beyond the authorized Local Rules in ways which compromise the basic principles of the Rules of Golf. As examples, allowing players to use preferred lies throughout the general area or giving free relief from divot holes in the fairway compromise the basic principle under Rule 1.1 of playing the ball as it lies.

As a general principle, when a player is playing a round that is to be posted for handicapping purposes, he or she is required to play that round under the Rules of Golf. If the Committee authorizes players to play under Local

Rules that differ significantly from the Rules of Golf, the player may not be permitted to post the score for handicapping purposes. For allowable exceptions, consult the rules or recommendations contained within the Handicap System operating in the local jurisdiction.

If the Committee believes that a Local Rule not covered by the policies established in Section 8 may be needed because of local abnormal conditions that interfere with fair play, it should:

• Consult USGA.org to check if any additional Model Local Rule is available to cover such a condition or situation, or

• Consult the USGA directly.

9   Other Forms of Play

The most established forms of match play, stroke play and partner and team play are detailed in Rules 1–24. This section outlines various alternative forms of play. Detailed modifications to Rules 1–24 that are required for these formats are detailed at USGA.org.

9A Modified Stableford

Modified Stableford is a form of play that gives higher points for good play, but also subtracts points for bad play. For example, four points are awarded for a birdie, two for a par and minus one for a bogey.

9B Greensomes

Greensomes is a variation of Foursomes where both partners play from the teeing area and one of the two tee shots is selected. The partner whose tee shot was not selected then plays the next stroke and each subsequent stroke is made in alternating order until the ball is holed. For example, if the tee shot of player A is selected at the first hole, Player B will play the next stroke, then Player A plays and so on until the ball is holed. Both players then play from the teeing area of the second hole and the process is repeated.

Other variations of Greensomes include:

• Pinehurst Foursomes where both players tee off, then they switch golf balls, meaning Player A plays Player B's ball, and Player B players Player A's ball. After the second shots, they then select which ball they will continue to play, and that ball is then played by alternate-shot until holed.

• Chinese or St Andrews Greensomes where the players decide, before starting the first hole of the round, which player will play the second stroke on all odd-numbered holes and the other player plays the second stroke on all even-numbered holes. This selection of player applies irrespective of whose tee shot is used on that hole. Each subsequent stroke on a hole is made in alternating order.

9C Scramble

A scramble is played with two, three or four-person teams. Each player plays from the teeing area on each hole, one of the tee shots is selected and all the players play their second shots from that spot. One of the second shots is then selected, and all players play their third shots from that spot, and so on until the ball is holed.

There are many variations on the basic scramble format. Some of these include:

- A Texas Scramble is a four-person team scramble, and this normally requires a minimum number of tee shots of each member of the team to be used during the round. Some forms of Texas Scramble require a player to play his or her own ball for the duration of each par 3 hole.

- A Florida Scramble (also known as Dropout Scramble, Step Aside, Stand Aside, Stand Out) provides that the player whose shot is selected does not play the next shot.

- A One-Person Scramble is where each player hits two shots, one ball is selected, two shots are played from that location, one ball is again selected, two shots are played from that location, and so on until the ball is holed.

9D Best Two of Four Scores to Count

This is a four-person team event where scores from only two members of the team count towards the team score on each hole.

The Modified Rules of Golf for Players with Disabilities

Introduction

As part of their governance of the game through writing and interpreting the Rules of Golf, the USGA and The R&A have authorized these Modified Rules for use by players with disabilities.

These Modified Rules only apply if adopted by the *Committee* in charge of a competition. They do not apply automatically to every competition involving players with disabilities.

It is up to each *Committee* to decide whether to adopt any of these Modified Rules for its own competitions.

The goal of these Modified Rules is to allow a player with a disability to play fairly with players who have no disabilities, the same disability or different types of disabilities. The USGA and The R&A have received valuable input from the community of players with disabilities, disability organizations and other sources to identify modifications that are fair and appropriate from all perspectives.

From a practical standpoint, players with certain disabilities often have the same or similar needs. Four such categories of disability have been identified:

- Players who are blind,

- Players who are amputees,

- Players who use assistive mobility devices, and

- Players with intellectual disabilities.

These authorized modifications adapt the Rules of Golf for these categories of disability.

All terms in *italics* are defined in the Rules of Golf, and all Rule number references are to the Rules of Golf.

Modified Rule 1 – For Players Who Are Blind

Purpose:

For a player who is blind, Modified Rule 1 provides recommendations to allow the player to be assisted by both an aide and a caddie at the same time and to give the player a limited exception to the prohibitions on touching sand in a bunker with a club.

The *Committee* may adopt one or more of these modifications for players who are blind:

1.1 Player May Get Help from an Aide

A player who is blind may get help from an aide:

- In taking a *stance*,
- In lining up before the *stroke*, and
- By asking for and getting *advice*.

An aide has the same status under the Rules as a *caddie* (see Rule 10.3), but with the exceptions described in Modified Rule 1.4.

For purposes of Rule 10.2a, a player may ask for and get *advice* from both an aide and a *caddie* at the same time.

1.2 Player May Have Only One Aide at a Time

A player who is blind may have only one aide at a time.

If the player has more than one aide at a time, the player gets the **general penalty** for each hole where that breach happened, in the same way as provided in Rule 10.3a(1).

1.3 Modification of Rule 10.2b(4) (Restriction on Caddie Standing Behind Player)

Rule 10.2b(4) is modified so that there is no penalty if the aide or *caddie* is deliberately positioned on or close to an extension of the *line of play* behind the ball at any time before or during the player's *stroke*, so long as the aide or *caddie* does not help the player in making the *stroke*.

But this does not modify Rule 10.2b(3) (Prohibition on Using Object Placed on Course to Help in Taking Stance).

Modified Rule 1

1.4 Modification of Rule 10.3 (Caddies)

The aide of a player who is blind may also serve as the player's *caddie*, but is not required to do so.

The player may have both an aide and a *caddie* at the same time, in which case:

- That aide must not carry or handle the player's clubs **except** in helping the player in taking a *stance* or lining up before making the *stroke*, or in helping the player as a courtesy as provided in the definition of *caddie*. **But** this does not modify Rule 10.2b(3) (Prohibition on Using Object Placed on Course to Help in Taking Stance).

- If that aide carries or handles the player's clubs in breach of this Rule, the player has two *caddies* at the same time and gets the *general penalty* for each hole where that breach happened (see Rule 10.3a(1)).

1.5 Modification of Rule 12.2b(1) (When Touching Sand Results in Penalty)

Before making a *stroke* at his or her ball in a *bunker*, a player who is blind may, without penalty, touch sand in the *bunker* with his or her club:

- In the area right in front of or right behind the ball, and

- In making the backswing for a *stroke*.

But in doing so, the player must not *improve* the *lie* of the ball more than would result from lightly grounding the club.

The player remains subject to the prohibitions in Rule 12.2b(1) on deliberately touching the sand in the *bunker* to test the condition of the sand or with a club in making a practice swing.

1.6 Modification of Rule 14.1b (Who May Lift Ball)

When a player's ball lies on the *putting green*, Rule 14.1b is modified so that the player's aide, in addition to his or her *caddie*, may lift the ball without the player's authorization.

Modified Rule 2 – For Players Who Are Amputees

Purpose:

For a player who is an amputee, Modified Rule 2 provides for the use of prosthetic devices, making a stroke while anchoring the club and authorization for any other person to drop, place and replace the player's ball.

The *Committee* may adopt one or more of these modifications for players who are amputees (which means both those with limb deficiencies and those who have lost a limb):

2.1 Status of Prosthetic Devices

Use of an artificial arm or leg is not a breach of Rule 4.3a provided the player has a medical reason to use it and the *Committee* decides that its use does not give the player any unfair advantage over other players (see Rule 4.3b). Players in doubt about the use of a device should raise the matter as soon as possible with the *Committee*.

2.2 Modification of Rule 10.1b (Anchoring the Club)

If a *Committee* finds that a player who is an amputee is unable to hold and swing clubs without anchoring because of limb deficiencies or limb loss, the player may make a *stroke* while anchoring the club, without penalty under Rule 10.1b.

2.3 Player Who is an Amputee May Get Help with Dropping, Placing and Replacing Ball

Because physical limitations may make it difficult or impossible for a player who is an amputee to *drop*, place or *replace* his or her own ball, all Rules that require the player to *drop*, place or *replace* a ball are modified so that the player is also allowed, without limitation, to give a general authorization to any other person to *drop*, place and *replace* the player's ball.

Modified Rule 3 – For Players Who Use Assistive Mobility Devices

Purpose:

For a player who uses an assistive mobility device, Modified Rule 3 provides recommendations on how the player may use an assistive mobility device, such as a wheelchair or other wheeled mobility device or a cane or a crutch, to help in taking a stance, making a stroke and otherwise in his or her play.

The *Committee* may adopt one or more of these modifications for players who use assistive mobility devices, such as wheelchairs and other wheeled mobility devices and canes or crutches:

Modified Rules 3.1 to 3.10 apply to all assistive mobility devices, including wheelchairs and other wheeled mobility devices.

Modified Rule 3.11 applies only to wheeled mobility devices.

3.1 Player Using an Assistive Mobility Device May Get Help from an Aide or Any Other Person

A player who uses an assistive mobility device may get help from an aide or any other person, including another player, in these ways:

- Lifting Ball on Putting Green: When the player's ball lies on the *putting green*, Rule 14.1b is modified so that the player's aide, in addition to his or her *caddie*, may lift the ball without the player's authorization.

- Dropping, Placing and Replacing Ball: Because physical limitations may make it difficult or impossible for a player using an assistive mobility device to *drop*, place or *replace* his or her own ball, all Rules that require the player to *drop*, place or *replace* a ball are modified so that the player is also allowed, without limitation, to give a general authorization to any other person to *drop*, place and *replace* the player's ball.

- Positioning Player or Device: Although there is no modification to Rule 10.2b(5), before making a *stroke*, the player may get physical help from any person to help position the player or position or remove the assistive mobility device.

3.2 Player Using an Assistive Mobility Device May Get Advice from an Aide

A player who uses an assistive mobility device may ask for and get *advice* from his or her aide in the same way that a player asks for and gets *advice* from a caddie under Rule 10.2a.

An aide has the same status under the Rules as a *caddie* (see Rule 10.3), but with the exceptions described in Modified Rule 3.9.

For purposes of Rule 10.2a, a player may ask for and get *advice* from both an aide and a *caddie* at the same time.

3.3 Player May Have Only One Aide at a Time

A player who uses an assistive mobility device may have only one aide at a time.

If the player has more than one aide at a time, the player gets the **general penalty** for each hole where that breach happened, in the same way as provided in Rule 10.3a(1).

3.4 Modification of Definition of "Stance"

A player's use of an assistive mobility device may affect his or her *stance* for purposes of various Rules, such as in determining the area of intended *stance* under Rule 8.1a and deciding if there is interference by an *abnormal course condition* under Rule 16.1.

To address this, the definition of *stance* is modified to mean "the position of a player's feet and body, and the position of an assistive mobility device if one is used, in preparing for or making a *stroke*".

3.5 Application of Rule 4.3 (Use of Equipment)

Rule 4.3 applies to the use of assistive mobility devices:

- The player may use assistive mobility devices to help in his or her play if that is allowed under the standards in Rule 4.3b, and

- The player using an assistive mobility device is still subject to the prohibitions in Rule 4.3a against using *equipment* in an abnormal way.

3.6 Modification of Rule 8.1b(5) to Allow Use of an Assistive Mobility Device in Taking a Stance

Under Rule 8.1b(5), there is no penalty if a player *improves* the *conditions affecting the stroke* by firmly placing his or her feet in taking a *stance*, "including a reasonable amount of digging in with the feet in sand".

For a player who uses an assistive mobility device, Rule 8.1b(5) is modified so that a "reasonable amount of digging in with the feet" includes:

• A reasonable amount of digging in with an assistive mobility device, or

• Taking reasonable actions to position an assistive mobility device in taking a *stance* and to try to avoid slipping.

But this modification does not allow the player to go beyond that by building a *stance* so that the assistive mobility device will not slip during the swing, such as by creating a raised mound of soil or sand against which to brace the device.

If the player does so, he or she gets the *general penalty* for altering the surface of the ground to build a *stance* in breach of Rule 8.1a(3).

3.7 Modification of Rule 10.1b (Anchoring the Club)

When a *Committee* finds that a player is unable to hold and swing clubs without anchoring because of the use of an assistive mobility device, the player may make a *stroke* while anchoring the club, without penalty under Rule 10.1b.

3.8 Modification of Rule 10.1c (Making Stroke while Standing Across or on Line of Play)

To cover a player's use of an assistive mobility device in taking a *stance* to play a ball, Rule 10.1c is modified to read:

"c. Making Stroke while Standing Across or on Line of Play

The player must not make a *stroke* from a *stance* with a foot or any part of an assistive mobility device deliberately placed on each side of, or with either foot or any part of an assistive mobility device deliberately touching the *line of play* or an extension of that line behind the ball.

For this Rule only, the *line of play* does not include a reasonable distance on either side.

Exception – If Stance is Taken Accidentally or to Avoid Another Player's Line of Play: There is no penalty."

3.9 Modification of Rule 10.3 (Caddies)

The aide of a player using an assistive mobility device may also serve as the player's *caddie*, but is not required to do so.

The player may have both an aide and a *caddie* at the same time, in which case:

- That aide must not carry or handle the player's clubs **except** in helping the player in taking a *stance* or lining up before making the *stroke*, or in helping the player as a courtesy as provided in the definition of *caddie*. **But** this does not modify Rule 10.2b(3) (Prohibition on Using Object Placed on Course to Help in Taking Stance).

- If that aide carries or handles the player's clubs in breach of this Rule, the player has two *caddies* at the same time and gets the *general penalty* for each hole where that breach happened (see Rule 10.3a(1)).

3.10 Application of Rule 12.2b(1) in Using Assistive Mobility Device to Test Conditions of Sand in Bunker

Under Rule 12.2b(1), a player must not "deliberately touch the sand in the *bunker* with a hand, club, rake or other object to test the condition of the sand to learn information about the next *stroke*".

This applies to using an assistive mobility device to deliberately test the condition of the sand.

But the player may touch the sand with his or her assistive mobility device for any other purpose, without penalty.

3.11 Modification of Lateral Relief Option for Ball in Red Penalty Area and for Unplayable Ball for Player Using a Wheeled Mobility Device

When a player with a wheeled mobility device takes lateral relief for a ball in a red *penalty area* or for an unplayable ball, Rules 17.1d(3) and 19.2c are modified to expand the size of the allowed *relief area* from using two *club-lengths* for measurement to using four *club-lengths* for measurement.

Modified Rule 4 – For Players with Intellectual Disabilities

Purpose:

For a player who has an intellectual disability, Modified Rule 4 provides recommendations to allow the player to be assisted by both an aide and a caddie at the same time and to get advice from that aide.

The *Committee* may adopt one or more of these recommended modifications for players with intellectual disabilities:

4.1 Use of an Aide or Supervisor to Help with Play

The extent of help that players with intellectual disabilities may need will be unique to each individual and will depend on the nature of the disability.

The *Committee* may provide or allow for an on-course aide or supervisor to help players with intellectual disabilities:

- An aide is someone who helps an individual player with an intellectual disability in his or her play and in applying the Rules:

  - » An aide has the same status under the Rules as a *caddie* (see Rule 10.3), but with the exceptions described in Modified Rule 4.3.

  - » For purposes of Rule 10.2a, a player may ask for and get *advice* from both an aide and a *caddie* at the same time.

- A supervisor is someone designated by the *Committee* to help players with intellectual disabilities during the competition:

  - » The supervisor is not assigned to a specific player, but rather is there to help any player as needed.

  - » A supervisor is an *outside influence* for purposes of the Rules.

  - » A player may not ask for or get *advice* from a supervisor.

4.2 Player May Have Only One Aide at a Time

A player with an intellectual disability may have only one aide at a time.

If a player has more than one aide at a time, the player gets the **general penalty** for each hole where that breach happened, in the same way as provided in Rule 10.3a(1).

4.3 Modification of Rule 10.3 (Caddie)

The aide for a player with an intellectual disability may also serve as the player's *caddie*, but is not required to do so.

The player may have both an aide and a *caddie* at the same time, in which case:

- That aide must not carry or handle the player's clubs **except** in helping the player in taking a *stance* or lining up before making the *stroke* (if authorized by the *Committee*), or in helping the player as a courtesy as provided in the definition of *caddie*. **But** this does not modify Rule 10.2b(3) (Prohibition on Using Object Placed on Course to Help in Taking Stance).

- If that aide carries or handles the player's clubs in breach of this Rule, the player has two *caddies* at the same time and gets the *general penalty* for each hole where that breach happened (see Rule 10.3a(1)).

4.4 Modification of Rule 14.1b (Who May Lift Ball)

When a player's ball lies on the *putting green*, Rule 14.1b is modified so that the player's aide, in addition to his or her *caddie,* may lift the ball without the player's authorization.

4.5 Players with Both Intellectual and Physical Disabilities

For players with both intellectual and physical disabilities, it is recommended that the *Committee* use a combination of the Modified Rules so that both types of disabilities are addressed.

All Categories of Disability

Unreasonable Delay

In applying Rule 5.6a's prohibition on unreasonable delay to players with disabilities:

- Each *Committee* should use its discretion and set its own reasonable standards taking into account the difficulty of the *course*, the weather conditions (in view of the impact they could have on the use of assistive mobility devices), the nature of the competition and the extent of the disabilities of the players competing.

- Taking these factors into account, it may be appropriate for *Committees* to use a more relaxed interpretation of what constitutes unreasonable delay.

Players with Other Disabilities

Dropping

In applying Rule 14.3b (Ball Must Be Dropped in Right Way), because physical limitations may make it difficult or impossible for players with certain disabilities to know whether they have *dropped* the ball from knee height, the *Committee* should accept the player's reasonable judgment that he or she has done so. Also, the *Committee* should accept all reasonable efforts to drop the ball from knee height, taking account of the player's physical limitations.

Players with Other Disabilities

These Modified Rules cover the categories of disability and associated challenges that have been identified to date as appropriate for modifying the Rules of Golf to serve the purpose of enabling players with disabilities to play on a fair basis with all other players. As is the case with the Rules of Golf generally, these Modified Rules are regularly reviewed for possible revision on a periodic basis. If *Committees* or players believe that other authorized modifications should be considered, they should contact the USGA.

Many players have physical limitations that may result in some degree of disability and that may affect their ability to play the game. Examples include players who are partially sighted and players who have difficulty gripping a club because of severe arthritis. The above Modified Rules do not specifically apply to such players.

However, any player may ask the *Committee* in charge of a competition for permission to use an artificial device, such as a brace or a gripping aid, to help with a medical condition. Under Rule 4.3b, a player is not in breach of Rule 4.3 for using *equipment* to help with a medical condition if the *Committee* finds that:

- The player has a medical reason for using the *equipment*, and

- The use of that *equipment* would not give the player an unfair advantage over other players.

Alternatively, upon request, the USGA will review and issue a preliminary opinion, on a case-by-case basis, about whether the use of a device for medical reasons is allowed under Rule 4.3. Any player may submit a written request to the USGA for its opinion on a device he or she wishes to use for medical reasons. It remains up to the *Committee* to decide whether the device gives the player any unfair advantage over other players and therefore whether to allow its use or not.